The Collected Poems of DELMORE SCHWARTZ

The Collected Poems of DELMORE SCHWARTZ

Edited by Ben Mazer

FARRAR, STRAUS AND GIROUX

NEW YORK

Farrar, Straus and Giroux
120 Broadway, New York 10271

Grateful acknowledgment is made for permission to reprint poems by Delmore Schwartz from
In Dreams Begin Responsibilities, copyright © 1937 by New Directions Publishing Corp.; *Genesis:
Book One*, copyright © 1943 by Delmore Schwartz; *Vaudeville for a Princess*, copyright © 1950 by
New Directions Publishing Corp., copyright © 1959 by Delmore Schwartz; *Selected Poems: Summer
Knowledge*, copyright © 1959 by Delmore Schwartz; and *A Season in Hell*, copyright © 1939
by Delmore Schwartz. Reprinted by permission of New Directions Publishing Corp.

Library of Congress Cataloging-in-Publication Data
Names: Schwartz, Delmore, 1913–1966, author. | Mazer, Ben, editor.
Title: The collected poems of Delmore Schwartz / edited by Ben Mazer.
Description: First edition. | New York : Farrar, Straus and Giroux, 2024. |
Includes bibliographical references and index. |
Identifiers: LCCN 2023041344 | ISBN 9780374604301 (hardcover)
Subjects: LCGFT: Poetry.
Classification: LCC PS3537 .C79 2024 | DDC 811/.54—dc23/eng/20231108
LC record available at https://lccn.loc.gov/2023041344

Designed by Gretchen Achilles

Our books may be purchased in bulk for promotional, educational,
or business use. Please contact your local bookseller or the Macmillan Corporate
and Premium Sales Department at 1-800-221-7945, extension 5442, or by email at
MacmillanSpecialMarkets@macmillan.com.

www.fsgbooks.com
Follow us on social media at @fsgbooks

1 3 5 7 9 10 8 6 4 2

Contents

A Season in Hell (1939)   105

Genesis: Book One (1943)   129

from *Genesis: Book Two*   313

Vaudeville for a Princess and Other Poems (1950)

from *Summer Knowledge: New and Selected Poems 1938–1958* (1959)

Uncollected Poems

Introduction

This collected edition of the poetry of Delmore Schwartz is a long overdue opportunity for readers to see for the first time the full extent of his poetic works. Delmore (Dwight Macdonald observed that no one ever called him Schwartz) was a controversial poet who could elicit fierce criticism or the highest praise, usually for the same work. The greater bulk of his poetry has been out of print for seventy or eighty years, while an entire two-hundred-page book-length poem that might have been Schwartz's masterpiece has gone unpublished except in brief selections. Many more unpublished poems have been found, too, and at least three of them ("The Error," "The Sad Druggist," and "Immortality") number among Schwartz's most memorable achievements. Yet Delmore's first book of poems, *In Dreams Begin Responsibilities*, when it was issued by New Directions in 1938, received wildly enthusiastic acclaim, and Allen Tate called Delmore the first real innovator "that we've had since Eliot and Pound." He was riding a wave of fame after the publication of his endlessly anthologized short story "In Dreams Begin Responsibilities" in *Partisan Review* in 1937. Soon he was the poetry editor of *Partisan Review*, perhaps the best literary magazine of its time; he was telling James Laughlin at New Directions whom to publish, and how to publicize; and he was teaching writing composition at Harvard, where he would stay until 1947. The last book of his poems published in his lifetime, *Summer Knowledge* (New Directions, 1959), won the prestigious Bollingen Prize from Yale. Schwartz was the youngest poet ever to win it. Yet the poems in his first book have for many decades remained in print only in the revised editions published in *Summer Knowledge*. And his second book of poetry, his translation of Rimbaud's *A Season in Hell* (New Directions, 1939), was attacked by numerous reviewers for incorrect renderings of Rimbaud's French. On the other hand, it was recommended by W. H. Auden in his classes at the University of Michigan, was found to have many good things in it by Eliot, and was the great critic Roger Shattuck's favorite translation of Rimbaud's poem. Delmore's self-proclaimed masterpiece, the book-length poem *Genesis: Book One* (New Directions, 1943), met with mixed reception, and really only incited serious critical response from F. O. Matthiessen and R. P. Blackmur. Yet a newly published letter from John Berryman to James Laughlin had this to say about the poem:

I congratulate you on publishing, or making ready to publish, "Genesis," of which Delmore let me read Book One last week. It will be certainly the first major work you have brought out; if you ever bring out another, you can count yourself immortal twice. My firm and clear opinion, based on Book One, is that 'Genesis' is one of the greatest imaginative works of the century and a work with which, in penetration, range, intelligence, no other American poem of any period can comfortably be compared. Its steadiness and centrality bring to bear, in fact, on all recent poetry and on most of the poetry of the last century, a devastating perspective. For a comparison in English poetry, critics will have to go to the "Prelude," a poem very uneven in inspiration, and to the greatest of the earlier works.

Vaudeville for a Princess (New Directions, 1950) and *Summer Knowledge* met with mixed or tepid reviews; reexamination discloses that there are good things in these books, too. The poems in this late period seem to strive successfully after ideals of clarity, simplicity, meaning, and symbolism. When seen in the light of the previously unpublished poems, there is temptation to see Delmore as having more poetic strength than his compatriots and chief midcentury rivals, Lowell and Berryman. It may be pointed out as well that the origins of the confessionalism of Lowell and Berryman can be found in the confessionalism of Schwartz's *Genesis*.

And what of the enigmatic Schwartz's personality, which has intrigued so many? It is mostly rooted in the bare facts of Schwartz's life, which might be described as the story of a likable underdog who reaches for the stars, all but makes it, and then descends into alcohol and drug addiction, and madness. The facts of Delmore Schwartz's life and career are given most thoroughly in James Atlas's biography, *Delmore Schwartz: The Life of an American Poet* (Farrar, Straus and Giroux, 1977), which reawakened Delmore's fame posthumously. Born in Brooklyn in 1913, Delmore claimed to have developed his passion for poetry while attending George Washington High School upon reading Hart Crane's "The River" in *The American Caravan* for 1927. At George Washington he found rigorous instruction and an admiring fan in one of his teachers, Mary J. Wrinn, who included four of his poems in the anthology *The Poets' Pack of George Washington High School* (W. E. Rudge, 1932). Delmore was eighteen. Published alongside him in the orange clothbound anthology, edited by Ms. Wrinn, was his on-again, off-again high school sweetheart, Gertrude Buckman.

During 1931–32, Delmore was an undergraduate at the University of Wisconsin, where he imbibed early 1930s American bohemianism and, in the school's excellent library, modernism; there, he found all the newest books by Eliot, Pound, Joyce, Auden, and the other leading modern poets. He also found complete runs of *The Criterion*, *The Dial*, *Hound & Horn*, and *transition*, and he studied them devoutly. He wrote long manifesto-like letters to his friend Julian Sawyer back in New York.

In 1932–35, Delmore returned to New York, embarking on the study of philosophy with Sidney Hook and Meyer Schapiro at NYU. From 1935 to 1937, Delmore studied philosophy at the graduate level at Harvard University, where his advisor was Alfred North Whitehead. Suddenly there came a terrific outburst of poems, verse plays, short stories, and criticism, all of which he managed to strategically place in the best literary magazines. Particularly notable was his first publication as a professional in book form. In 1936, his verse play *Choosing Company* appeared in *The New Caravan*, the very anthology in which he had read Crane in 1927. His professors F. O. Matthiessen and David Prall praised the play around Harvard, and the unsigned review in *The New York Times Book Review* singled the play out for praise.

That same year, Delmore won a Bowdoin Prize at Harvard for his essay "Poetry as Imitation." But the big breakthrough came in December 1937 when *Partisan Review* published his story "In Dreams Begin Responsibilities."

He left Harvard without any intention of teaching philosophy, and without a degree. He fully intended to make his career as a professional man of letters, first and foremost, as a poet.

By 1937, he was able to marry his recalcitrant sweetheart Gertrude Buckman, and had managed to involve himself with the fledgling New Directions, writing bold, brazen, conspiratorial, and scheming letters to the publisher James Laughlin.

But then came the critical failures of *A Season in Hell* (1939) and *Genesis: Book One* (1943). Delmore, manic-depressive and always an insomniac, had begun drinking and taking pills, uppers and downers to help him sleep, and had fallen into a deep depression. Gertrude left him. He hung around Harvard for four more years, deteriorating, missing Gertrude and missing New York, lost in the belief that he was a failure. When he returned to New York in 1947, his dissipation seemed to increase, and prolonged abuse of amphetamines was exacerbating his mania, so that he was having psychotic and paranoid episodes.

His 1950 volume *Vaudeville for a Princess*, the last book he would do with New Directions, received a scathing and brutal review from Hugh Kenner in *Poetry*. When he went to make his selected poems in 1959, Delmore reprinted only three poems from *Vaudeville*.

The doomed marriage to the novelist Elizabeth Pollet. The stint with

Saul Bellow at Princeton, sitting in for R. P. Blackmur. The two books of fiction. The book of critical essays that was not published in his lifetime. The book-length critical study of T. S. Eliot that was never published. *Genesis: Book Two* was written at the same time as *Genesis: Book One*, in the 1930s and 1940s. When asked at a party in the 1940s when the entirety of *Genesis* would be published, Delmore answered, "Posthumously." By the late fifties friends had found him a position teaching at Syracuse, where he mentored the young Lou Reed. Then he left Syracuse, drifted back to Manhattan and from boardinghouse to boardinghouse, carrying his manuscripts with him, leaving some of them behind on the way. Finally, in 1966, he suffered a heart attack alone, his body unclaimed for two days. But it is the poems that count now. And it is the glory of the poems that survives here, awaiting new life.

from

In Dreams Begin
Responsibilities

(1938)

II

Coriolanus and His Mother: The Dream of One Performance

(A Narrative Poem)

He that is incapable of living in a society is a god
or beast.

—ARISTOTLE

To be radical is to get to the root of things. The root of
the individual, however, is the individual himself.

—MARX

"There is differency between a grub and a butterfly;
yet your butterfly was a grub."

—MENENIUS

For James Laughlin

One: "O Me! Make You a Sword of Me!"

Theatre, the place to stare, rustle of programs,
Many have come, are being seated. The house
Is full, the audience is distinguished,
And in a box-seat sit five ghosts, and one,
A boy with guttural voice full of emotion.
The lights dim, half-darkness now accents
The footlights' glitter before the curtain. The curtain
Rises on the heart of man,
                            Rome, Rome,
The history-ridden arena shown by
A temple painted on a canvas backdrop;
On fluted columns, fat and white, there rests
The pediment wherein a writhing frieze
Of armed men strain to kill the other team
World without end, word without end of hatred.

The rumor of a crowd comes near. Many
Come crowding on the stage, bunched in their anger,
Holding aloft their clubs, their staves, their torches,
Knowing a mob's emotion.
                            Hunger, debts,
Poverty bring this demonstration. One,
Brutus, articulate, using their interest,
Mounts near the temple, tells them what they mean:

"Two years ago, you poor people one day   *North's*
Gathered together; one encouraging another,   *Plutarch*
You all forsook the city, stood upon
A height beside the Tiber, made no show
Of actual rebellion, except to cry,
As you marched up and down the meager height:
'The rich men drive us from the city. The rich men
'Leave us no air, no water, nor even ground
'To bury our dead. To live in Rome, to live
'In this great city is to be used and slain
'In the murderous war warred to increase

'The rich man's riches.'
                    So! So!
You cried then, you poor people, so you were given
What?
The usual concessions which, as usual,
Made you forget the reason for your pain.
But hunger you cannot forget! Awake!
Seize your enemy, O, grasp his throat,
Demand your right to live, your right to eat,
Have you no right to eat? He who denies it
Murders you! Deny the rich! Deny
Your murderers! Shout in their perfumed ears
That you refuse to die while they are rich!"

Their roar responds. He pants, the actor's pause,
To show the large emotion on his face,

—And now, shuffling, diverting gaze,
Toga'd Menenius, canny patrician, comes,
Fat and untidy, dragging his robe along,
Good-humored extravert, rosy and robust,
And not too finicky:
                    "Listen!" he says,
Contemptuous yet soothing, knowing their will
And their necessity; divided from them
And so against them; requiring them
And therefore politic; consoling them
With the old Platonic metaphor in which
The state, that knot of common weakness,
Consistent need, poor fear, and aching will,
Becomes an animal or organism
Wherein each organ must deny itself
That the great corpse may be well-fed.
"How metaphors may serve the ruling class,
Hypostasis itself shall soothe the poor!"
Sighs one great ghost beside me, as I stare,
Knowing not where I am but everywhere,
Lavish of mind and in attention such
Each whisper thunders in the crowded air,

THE COLLECTED POEMS OF DELMORE SCHWARTZ

Striking the heart where all the meanings touch,
All pieties, all choices, every care!

"Listen," Menenius says, "Be sensible,
We do our best to handle everything,
Be patient, boys, and in the end, you know,
Everyone will be satisfied."
                                    But now
Marcius comes striding through the burly crowd,
O like an obelisk his obvious posture,
His look as Caesar's face strict on a coin,
Barbarous strength and beauty there:

"You stink!" he cries, "You scum!" he shouts, shocked by
Their protest, offended by their being,
Nursing in mind, older than any thought,
A hatred of all who issue sweat, urine,
Or excrement, the child's profound distaste
Once for all smitten, never, alas! outworn.

"So you assume our rôle, faeces of man!
The garrulity of your idleness
Swelling your vast conceit, you arrogant
Presumptuous intolerable apes!
If the nobility would merely once
Abate their maudlin rule, I, all alone,
I, I, I,
Would thrash a hundred thousand of your kind!"
Bullying empty extravagance, his tongue
Betrays a pathic source beneath the eye,
The wound and rage not of a ruling class
(Whose prudent tact Menenius displayed,
Joking and friendly) but himself alone
Is represented in his gross excess,
Himself alone prepossessed long ago
By an antipathy un-understood,
A tenderness moving the mind unknown.

"O don't mind us, we only work here and
And, hunger breaks stone walls, and, dogs must eat,
And, meat is made for mouths. Does God provide
Grain for the rich men only?"
                                So Brutus stammered,
Stricken and awed by his loud prejudice:
"O now you are their tongue!" Marcius replied,
"I must consult your heart before I blink,
"You, paid official, who, on their discontent
Erect your dignity—"
                        A sudden cry,
A newsboy loudly shouting "War!
War is declared! The Volscians are in arms!"
Quickly the meeting is transformed,
Marcius forgets his enemy,
The bitter broken poor forget their need,
And all adjourn, each one to find his rôle,
In the lightning's dramatic thrust and sequent moan.

"So by death's poverty is poverty escaped,
Negation negated in the chess of death,"
Says the great ghost beside me in the box,
While murmurs move the darkened audience,
"War being the state's good health, the state, alas!
Being, as knock-kneed Hegel said,
Organized pain, a formal agony:
In war's magnified ache, brilliantly blared,
The poor mistake their grandeur and their grief;
Adding their weakness, they affirm the state,
The stranger's grain, the stranger's wealth is seized!
The ruling class in intuition know
That thus the state persists, and thus,
By the extension of their perpetual need
Unto another's property, they are maintained,
And by the'expense of anger on the stranger,
The poor are fed."
                        So, as the curtain falls
Upon the risen interest of all,
Marx bites his nails, resumes his revery,

THE COLLECTED POEMS OF DELMORE SCHWARTZ

Ghosts being possessed by consciousness,
Consumed by memory, and powerless.

A new scene. On a side street. Twilight
Blackens the roof-tops. Brutus and his fellow,
The voices of the poor, confer in whispers,
Hold in analysis the soul of Marcius,
Surd irreducible, a glittering diamond,
Unpurchased by their tactic or their smile,
Occult to them.
               "Listen! Speak quietly.
Was ever man so proud as is this Marcius?"
"No man so proud,
              he has no equal, none."
"When we were made their voices did you see
How his lip formed a sneer direct at me?"
"He mocks the moon, he holds in his contempt
The shadow which he treads at noon."
                     "And God himself
Is mocked, I think, in this man's singular heart."
"He is insane, alone in his fantasy,
Gazing at his sole image in a glass
Where no light shines but arbitrary pride."
"We are not safe until he's cast aside."

Another scene: it is the sitting room
Where wife and mother of the hero sew
To beguile attention while their hearts await
News of the war, the distant thunder's boom.

"Sing merrily, enjoy this strong today,"
So says the Roman mother, the widowed one,
Moved by her own obsession,
                    "Daughter, sing,
Were he my husband as he is my son,
This would delight me O much more than when
In the ecstasy of the darkness I conceived,
Moved by the thrusting self-delighting spoon
Which made my son, my spear."

                    So she exults
That there is war and that her son makes war,
And with an urgent dogma she insists
That the meek girl, his wife, shall also feel   *Virgilia*
Her own harsh appetite,
                    while Sigmund Freud
Mutters beside me in the haunted night,
"This is the origin, this, this is the place,
Mother in love with son and son with her,
And his aloneness in the womb began,
Always unhappy apart from that tight cache:
O womb and egg, nervous environment,
How you have marred and marked this childhood's man!
Unconscionable bag which none evade,
How your great warmth commits him to the shade."

"O no!" The black-browed ghost in haste replies,
As the curtain falls, and furniture is moved,
And the orchestra tunes up, the hidden musician
Tightening and pricking his violin in the pit,
"But as a drowning man must cherish land,
And as in hunger bread must be soft gold,
So, in a society which lives by war,
The soldier boy is best. As the assassin
Admires the knife, as the mariner
Considers the sea, as the tailor
Respects the wish to dress, O as
The leaning doctor listens for the heart,
Man murders, travels, sews and bends in fear
To get the good which the means of life make dear!
Man lives and dies to buy the dears of life,
Every man dies for that which gives him life!
Not that poor widow, but society
Nursed him to being, taught him what to be:
She is the actual mother, only for her
Has he become the narrow murderer!"

At which the curtain rises, silencing him:

Distant, we see Corioli's great fort,
We hear the shocking guns, the thud and flash;
A team in miniature is running forth
In loose array, as if involved in games,
And as two football teams in scrimmage there
Men mix and wrestle, grunt, leap forward, fall,
The rush, the furor, pop! bang! whoa!
All shows in little to our frigid gaze.
The cry, the anger, the chaos, and the gong
Are far too distant to be serious.
The trumpet's imagination and éclat
Are much too large for each one striving there,
Aware of running men and puffs of smoke
And prickly sweat and nothing else but fear.
The while, to our perspective, nothing near
The moving pins lack actuality,
Until a messenger comes breathlessly,
Speaks through a megaphone the victory:

"Marcius! Marcius defeats the defensive host,
Marcius alone! While we hung back, afraid,
And angered him until he called us swine,
Timid cows, geese, not men, he walked ahead
Unto the Volscians' ranks, who, being amazed,
Retreat, enter their gates, begin to run,
Marcius upon them,
                          while we keep safely back,
An obvious danger there, he follows them
Into the gates, which they raise up! And thus
He's trapped! Alone within the gates! Himself
Alone to answer all the city!
                          "Slain!
Slain doubtless," says our general,   *Lartius*
While all, knowing him, know his iron and rage,
Bow heads and feel, though namelessly, in awe
That there, his enemies on every side,
Occurs his apotheosis before he dies,
His marrow satisfaction,
                          until he runs

Phenomenal! miraculous! Upon our epitaphs
Out from the gates, waving his glossy sword,
Having somehow beaten all men from him,
Opened the gates and issued thence
                                        to cry
"Again! And more! Renew the attack once more!"
(Although the subtle blood streams from his limbs)
And curses us as pusillanimous,
Naming us wooden things, things dull, clogged,
Inanimate,
                and cries, obsessed, "Once more!
Attack once more!" As if, with pathic hate,
Misanthropos with sensuous emotion,
Hating all men, he was fulfilled in war.

Lartius our general demurs and then permits
Marcius to'attack once more, with volunteers,
Who, when with famous bravado he calls on them,
Painting with fustian voice the life-in-death,
Offer their wills to him, shout, cheering him,
Take him upon their shoulders, at which he cries,
Narcissus baritone in brittle armor:
"O me alone! Make you a sword of me!"

Elsewhere Cominius, a normal one,
Admits retreat, calls foolish further war,
Considers true and Roman a pause *pro tem,*
Knowing not Marcius' walking dream,
                                        who now
Leads the attack, seeks out of all men, one,
His utmost foe, Aufidius, (for hate,
Love, and desire concentrate their blaze.)
Their bravest man, known to him long before.

And the attack succeeds, the Volscians flee,
Aufidius is met, but in the vicious strife,
Then, striking each other with his being's whip,
Each grasping his self as individual,
Aufidius is rescued by his men,

Even as the fortress falls,
                    Marcius the winner,
Marcius victorious, Caius Marcius hero!
His obsessed radical spirit ruling the day.

The megaphone'd one retires. Now we see
All met to formalize the victory:

Cominius wishes to render him
The glittering glory of the circumstance
And in ovation rounds such speech for him
As must delight all sensible of fame,
Fame the huge face confronting every man
Who walks amid his fellows, finding in them
The'audience of his play and satisfaction.
"—No man may live alone, but with his mother
Having lived once, he's brutally bereft
By every absence, every solitude—"
So interrupts a great ghost by my side,   *Aristotle*
Private of all for whom truth is a bride!
But Marcius is dismayed, shy as young men,
Or prudery of those whose intense sex
Denies itself.
                    His secret vice thus published
Amid the torchlight scene, the dress parade,
Enormously gratified and therefore shamed,
(As two tugging their love become aware
That a whole public laugh, enjoy and stare)
Blushes, feigns modesty.
                    And then, when Lartius
Gives him ten times his proper share of all
Won on the field, he must refuse at once,
Money's not relevant unto his measure,
And the refusal may dress his nakedness,
His sheer delight, his shame to be delighted,
—*His* sort of heart to depend on another one!

The rank and file misunderstand him. This,
They think, is courtesy to them.

FROM IN DREAMS BEGIN RESPONSIBILITIES   [13]

They cheer as if
Marcius bequeathed them immortality!

But their applause strikes instantly
Hemorrhage of anger from him. That *he*, Marcius,
Should seek their plaudits, look to them!
—Flies from his tongue the phlegm and spit of rage:
No one may touch him, none; no one reward him,
Pay him. His self must be self-fed. He is
His own, not theirs.
                    Cominius suggests
That this excess is sentimental,
(The rest stand by, perplexed) but chooses then
(Of subtle intuition *le mot juste*)
The one garland this shaven virgin will wear,
A name, a name additional and new,
(Not to exclude his own but fatten it),
New word, new syllable, new tone for his
Intense selfhood to breathe and whisper:
CAIUS MARCIUS CORIOLANUS,
                         Marcius,
Blushing and moved, consents and turns away.
"His autograph, his signature, his own,
As in Napoleon, Alcibiades,
Jacob whose name was Israel, and Saul,
Translated at Damascus, Caesar, Czar,
Kaiser, and Charlemagne, George Eliot,
Stella, Vanessa, Aloysius, Jones,
Between the anonymous and nomenclature
Both vaudeville and history resume
The continuum of fame and mockery
In which all wince and which is poetry!"
—Thus mocks one ghost who gazes there beside me.

The curtain falls. The orchestra begins,
Bomb! Bomb! Bomb! Beethoven sobs.   *Overture to*
He too beside me in the crowded box,   *Coriolanus*
And slumped in his cliché, chin to his breast:
Bomb! Bomb! Bomb! What awe and care!

Then sweetly, thinly, fluted the melody
Of the soul in private pitying itself,
Tenderly touching every grouch and sore.

—And then the music ceases. The bright lights flood
Theatre, audience, our straining gaze, and now,
Amazed as never before, myself I see
Enter between the curtain's folds, appear
As many titter and some clap hands in glee,
A sad young clown in gown of domino,
X-ray, cartoon, Picasso's freak in blue,
From the box-seat I see myself on show.

Between the Acts

PLEASURE

I come, I said, to be useful and to entertain. What else can one do? Between the acts something must be done to occupy our minds or we become too aware of our great emptiness. It is true, we might converse with one another. But then we would learn again how little all of us have to say to each other. Love is not American. Neither is conversation, but that is not exactly what I mean.

One ought to be amusing, but unfortunately I know very few witty sayings, entertaining stories. I find that my idea of the comical is not, as they say, objective. I have tried for some time to invent a good story for this occasion, but the best I could do is this new wrinkle, entitled "Turning The Tables": ABC says to DEF: "Who was that lady I saw you with last night? Some fun, hey boy!" DEF, offended by the lightness with which his passion is regarded, replies: "That was no lady, that was *your* wife." A good story too, at least to me, is Stendhal's remark on first eating ice-cream: "What a pity it is not a sin!" Becoming more serious in order to approach nearer to my true subject, I recall the fact that Fichte drank champagne for the first time when his infant boy said "I" for the first time. Let me continue with two more quotations bearing on this Laokoön-like process and presentation which we are here to see. "I can hire half the working-class to fight the other half." So said Jay

Gould at about the same time that Engels, intimate friend of a member of the audience, was observing with the most perfect justice that the most appalling evil produced by class conflict was its corruption and degradation of the *ruling-class*—barbarism, inexorable cynicism, contempt for all values on the part of those who enjoy the greatest benefits of society. Sophocles observes that man is the most admirable of beings. It is true. The most disgusting also, one ought to add. It is dialectical. The possibility of the one means the possibility of the other.

Now take this world's champion of men, Coriolanus, whose life we passively suffer to step over our faces (as we sit here, in the prepared darkness). All things are tied together, though sometimes loosely. Hence, more and more facts are dragged on the stage, as this moving individual passes before the footlights. Who knows if there will, indeed, be sufficient room? No doubt that I am an intruder, but try to eject me. The sky cannot be excluded. It is the greatest natural object. The state cannot be omitted. It is the greatest artificial object. The individual requires our focussed gaze. He is the greatest subject, natural and artificial. Then there is his mother, his wife, his child, all his fathers, all his children. What an enormous crowd it may become! And the audience is already so complex, so full of foreigners.

Besides, there are questions of emphasis. "The individual is the only verifiable actuality, the individual, his experience from moment to moment." So said one in French at about the same time as Lev Davidovitch, better known as Trotzky, justly remarked that "The individual—is an abstraction!" He is right and yet you know and so do I as we sit here in this theatre—the essential stareotorium, one might say—we both know that we cannot regard the warm identity beneath our faces as being no more than an abstraction. Man is always *in* the world, yes! inconceivable apart from being surrounded by a greater whole than himself. And yet he is at the same time himself and in and by himself and by travelling here and there may separate himself from any particular interior in which he finds himself. There is a thought which will take a considerable amount of chewing and then you will only have to spit it out again. As I said, all this bears upon what is taking place here. Also on Coriolanus the individual. Food, for example, improves the spirit, coffee consoles the soul. Most men, to quote again, lead lives of quiet desperation, the victims, all of them, of innumerable intentions. Hence the enormous *spiritual* and emotional quality of food and drink. There is also tobacco and alcohol, although wine too is not American.

Why be desperate, even quietly? Thus one might ask. Because one end merely leads to another one, one activity to another one, one activity to another in an inexhaustible *endlessnessness* which is exasperating, metaphysically speaking, although such speech is not the fashion. Do not, however, be disconsolate nor given over to unutterable despair. Consider the nature of pleasure. It is a maligned word, meaning merely the innocence and intrinsicality of being, each thing and each state taken as final and for itself. A cup of coffee destroys your sadness. To be born, we are told, is the greatest of all pains—all else a dilution and weakening which offends the masochist. Though this be but a gynecologist's truth, yet let us remember it. Pleasure is what it is as is the rose. It justifies itself. To have pleasure, to be pleased, to enjoy oneself, that is sufficient, and only the Philistine asks: What for? Although there is a question of the permanent, the intermittent, the conflicting, and the exclusive, but let us not discuss this now.

Pleasure has a hundred thousand obvious forms, plentiful variety for the most fickle spirit. Pleasure of convalescence (how voluptuous weakness can be); pleasure of need (a dry crust of bread); pleasure of the first time and the last time; pleasure of mere looking (as the sunlight delights itself upon the tumbling fountain, as the small morning makes the metropolis unreal); pleasure of being a child (mixture of curiosity, wantonness, and the gradual stages); pleasure of having a child (O my son Absalom, graduating from high school!); pleasure of discovery and pleasure of memory, freshness and nostalgic sweetness, surprise and return. Pleasure of arising, the keenness of breakfast; pleasure of sleeping (there one is Caesar); the pleasure of the old, a stronger tobacco, to possess the time that is past; the pleasure of the young, who are not yet tired; the pleasure of marriage—the mystery of being called Mrs. for the first time; the pleasure, do not deny it, of the funeral (that, after all, the conclusion should have a certain sublimity and repose); pleasure of the grandchild (a difficult pleasure, needing so much strength to last that long and so many refusals, year after year); the pleasure of ritual, the gloves drawn on precisely; the pleasure of spontaneity, kissed by the overjoyed, the wave's foaming white head, touched at the lips.

Delight in the silver, delight in the rock, delight in the soft silk, delight in the stubble, delight in the thimble, delight in the mountain, happiness of the virgin, the satisfaction of custom, joy in denial (the firmness of the soldier, the rigor of the surgeon, the formal athlete, the painstaking scholar), and the sweetness of saying yes.

Eating too is a fine thing, though it makes difficulties (do not laugh; economy and original sin may in fact be inseparable) and there is the pleasure at the conclusion of effort, the best of all delights, as the swimmer returned to the sunlight, his being glowing in the warmth responsive to the shocking chill of the waters (surrounded by them, he understood his body). Or the pleasure of the idle who, prone, full-length made almost unknowingly a few exact perceptions, especially of those who hurry. And the satisfaction of the guilty (thus to have an identity not dissipated by their weakness); the delight of the famous, their self-regard coming from the outside; the joy of narration, thus to invent and, inventing, understand; the sweetness of the musician, from thunder and whisper tone's moving constellations; and also the pleasure of small pains, the sweetness of anger, as Homer observes; the delight of the game (from out of the scrimmage came the tall and plunging figure and ran to a touchdown!), the pleasure of the task, the pleasure of the opus (the span, the parts, the detail, the conclusion), the delight, clear as fresh water, of theory and knowing (O lucid mathematics!). To each age and each stage a special quality of satisfaction, enough for everyone, and enough for all time, no need to compete. States of being suffice. Let the handsome be familiar with the looking-glass, and let the ugly be gourmets (since so many cannot be beautiful, let eating be socially superior to portraits). Let this unwarranted sadness come to an end, sound and fury signify a multitude of enjoyments, the pleasure of pain, the pleasure indeed of pleasure. Pleasure believes in friends, pleasure creates communities, pleasure crumbles faces into smiles, pleasure links hand in hand, pleasure restores, pain is the most selfish thing. And yet, I know, all this is nothing, nothing consoles one, and our problem and pain are still before us.

Let us continue to gaze upon it. Let us, I say, make a few sharp clear definite observations before we die. Let us judge all things according to the measure of our hearts (otherwise we cannot live). Let us require of ourselves the strength and power to view our selves and the heart of man *with* disgust.

Two: "His Soaring Insolence, the Common Muck."

Absurd and precarious my presence there,
Looped by the spotlight in assured discourse,

Harangue, imperative, prayer and wish,
True story and confession, who knows what?
Double, absorbed, monstrous, amazed, ashamed,
With much relief myself I see retire
And as the curtain rises on ACT TWO
Regain my sense of place, sharpened anew.

Triumphal march, the formidable Arch,
Thick crowds, harassed police, the brilliant sunlight.
—Bearing the truck of all his honors, wearing
The hat of his new name,
                              puffed by the herald,
Hailed by the populace, Marcius returns,
Aquiline profile, statuesque in the car.

Some who await him stand in attitudes
Equivocal; for perspectivity
Possesses infinite degrees,
Every nuance of love and hate therein,
As if all were a metaphor of place, profound,
Elliptic, solid, flat, far, thin and round!

The ruling class, as in Menenius,
Take simple pride in their validity
Displayed in him. The tribunes fear in him   *"Death in's*
Pure tyranny. His mother   *nervy arm . . ."*
Hopes he has many wounds, exults, exults,
Mouths of the death which he bestows as if
She would have all restored to the dark womb.
Cannons burst! Sirens scream! The crowd
Enjoys its own excitement. The occasion
Engenders its own increase, applause
Engenders applause, whirling confetti,
Roses and laurel fall,
                              all gaze, stare, cheer,
Murmur of him. Nurse holds up baby boy
As gaze may be infectious, cook is dressed
In Sunday's clothes, the old, the strange, the ill
Who stay in private rooms the whole year long,

Press against rich and poor, packed at the curb,
Passionate to see him, hardly aware
Of the tumult, the brass, the flashing heat,
Their congregated act,
                    while Marcius stands
Hiding his strange emotion amid the roar,
Secretly pleased despite himself, ashamed
To take of their plaudits so much flushing pleasure,
Guilty to think he gets his joy from them,
And half-aware of their powerful entity.

"*Noli me tangere!* How large they shout,   *"He loves your people.*
Each would partake of my world's championship,   *But tie him not to be*
Each thinks himself myself and I am fucked   *their bedfellow."*
By every craven knight vicarious there.
—Yet what a sweetness is that roaring kiss
Spreading in waves throughout the whorish air."

Arrived to the station where his mother waits,
Also his wife, his child, his friends,
Rapt self-absorption fades or rather descends
Unto that great primordial circumstance
Which holds him yet,   *Plutarch: "He did all to*
                        please his mother. The
               "O Mother, Mother," kneeling,   *only thing that made*
Thus he descends to her, "All that I did   *him love honor was the*
I did for you."   *joy he saw his mother*
          The snub-nosed Freud exclaims,   *did take of him."*
Seated beside me in the heavy box,
"This is the place! Early historians
Call this Volumnia his wife. Avon alone
Grasps the identity of mother and bride,
The infant's choice, whatever man decide!"

His wife waits silently, ungreeted by him,
Wholly unseen,
              till mother remind the boy
His son's meek mother waits to be recognized,
Speaks with slight irony of his new name,
Strictly retains the womb's authority.

       THE COLLECTED POEMS OF DELMORE SCHWARTZ

Quick change: the Capitol: the Senate's chamber,
The ruling class resolved to raise him up
Highest in office and complete in power,
All public hope fulfilled.
                    Cominius
Addresses the Senate, recites his life *in toto*.
—He's interrupted as our squeamish virgin
Arises, tortured, will not stay, he says,
To hear his nothings monstered, he a monster
Thus to respond, monstrously delicate,
And make his exit like a puking girl
Upset by joy.
                    Cominius continues,
Utters the public face which all can see,
The abstract terms of all biography,
Hiding desire and shame, the personal one
Known to himself in the bedroom all alone.
And yet the bragged *données* contain his soul,
His self *pur sang*, if but their rule be seen
—Marcius, at sixteen, a mere boy still,
The most precocious soldier! Again and again
War after war, the champion in each,
Until before Corioli his war alone,
Sole, single, absolute, *per se*, alone
(Aseity such as is God's alone)
Against the enemy despite his wounds
Until their vast defeat.
                    Cominius
Proposes him consul as his meager due—

"Why," says the ghost next to the unknown one,
(The small anonymous filth whose face is hidden
By a white mask un-understood by all,
And who calls up in me an unknown fear)
"Why does his lauding advocate omit
His irreparable childhood, infancy
And foetusdom, the animal
Delighted by the breast, the boy denied
A rôle in the running game, the boy's amaze

When he walked home alone from school,
                                  enjoyed
His revery, found solitude most sweet,
Prided himself thereon, and felt contempt
For all not self-contained as he,
                        the boy,
He who would skate alone on the hard lake
Under the faëry moon, Diana's day,
The child, the foetus too, the widow's son,
Her only son, who fed him, praised him, warned
Her dainty son to keep from common boys,
Showed herself gratified in him alone:
The past is always present, present as past,
It grasps us like Athena by the hair!"

"By six," the father of Nicomachus
Murmurs to me, "By six, the man is made,
Habitus, virtue, and his lasting shade."
"Before his birth" the later ghost replies,
"His greatest mother chose his greatest prize!"
"The past is always present, present as past,
It grasps us like Athena by the hair,
The hair above the mind whose thick coils knot
Until the soul arises from the body's rot,"
So said the saddest ghost beside me there.

The whole Senate consents, unhesitant,
Calls Marcius back, confirms him Consul if,
A mere formality, the poor people give
Their votes to him, when, as the custom is,
He stands before them dressed in ashen gown,
Showing his wounds to them.
                            Marcius, nauseous once more,
Asks the omission of this ritual,
Asks that the right be taken from the people,
Maintains the bad smell of the people's breath,
Calls this a braggart nakedness and shame.
—But the tribunes insist.
                       Outside, the people

Discuss their Marcius, laugh, admire him,
Holding themselves in humorous contempt,
Feigning each other's stupidity, till one,
Amid their serious, mock-serious
Discussion of their power and his virtue
And his contempt of them and yet his due,
States that all this is well and good, but he
Must take a leak.

                "Little the people wish,"
Says one great ghost in that distinguished box,
"Little they get. Being nor good nor evil,
Except as driven, they desire merely
A bit of salt for cucumbers in May,
A movie once a week, a game to play,
A visit to the zoo, two weeks in June,
Someone with whom to speak, something
To read while eating, someone to touch
Wholly and privately, both hard and soft,
A little self-respect, a place to sleep,
Stories of immortality.

                  Their whole wish is
Modest and not too urgent till the strict
Inevitable mathematic come to reduce
Little to nothing, almost nothing, a crust,
That some may get still more and more,
                        they must!"
Shuddering as a young girl does
Examined by doctors with mustachios,
Our Marcius, standing in a little box,
Appears before the people.

                 Crouching rabbits
Regard the square-jawed lion, who is dressed
In his own nakedness and in
Humility's gray gown. He asks their votes
Precisely as he would and as he must,
The bluster voice which always hides the shy
Betraying his self-infatuated I:

"My own desert requires no less!" Keep clean
Your teeth and wash your faces! Voices!
I sweated for your voices, for your voices
I tore my heart in fury!
                              O I never
Desired to trouble the poor by begging from them!"

"You never loved the common people,"
                                        one
Meekly and hopefully asserts,
—"Honor me then, dear Sirs, my virtue is
Not to be common in my love. Your voices!
Your voices, Gentlemen!"
                              His irony
Tortures himself and merely, so it seems,
Perplexes the mild and generous poor people
Passing before him in his little box.
—Gladly they recognize his wounds, his virtues,
Freely they choose him, grant him their full voices,
Strive with his mocking words, mean well, depart
Aware of something wrong somewhat somewhere,
With him, with them, with both, who knows, who knows?
Indeed who knows?
                         Cupid, a nearby fountain,
Pisses his puddle on the Square, chipped boy
Piercing our hero's to-fro heart.
                                   Beside me
Stagira murmurs approval of the scene,
—"Avon, a mother's son, knew what men mean,
A pencil of all hearts."
                         The later ghost
Marvels to see one man detest the host,
Speaks of the secret and gigantic mother
Which makes each man a sister and a brother.
The orchestra tunes up: a spreading moan
—Ludwig van Beethoven, Marcius in tone,
Rumors in woodwinds all that is to come,
Massing crescendo of the poor king numb.

Meanwhile we see the tribunes huddle,
Winking, conspiratorial, malicious,
Come to the people with their facile tongues
And in contempt of them much more confirmed,
Equipped and cynical than Marcius is,
Quickly persuade the people to reverse
The'election, take away his crown, reject him,
Till with their cheap ken they transform the people
Into an ignorant passionate crowd,
Willed to the hurt of our undrowned Narcissus,
Our self-regardant lion, his raided heart.

"Who is the fifth ghost in this heavy box?
Who is the small masked one who says no word?
Tell me his name!"
                        But no one answers me.
"O tell me, tell me, O Immanuel Kant,"
I said when they were silent, frenzied then,
"You who diminished knowledge, inverted hope,
Divided day from night, assigned the night
The avid dreams of the practical heart."

Between the Acts

JUSTICE

What! The same voluble fellow again—such is your speech with yourself, I
suppose, upon seeing me again, though this time in a dress suit with a top hat
(as if to appeal to the snob and fop in every man, or at least to the upper-class
sentiments in all of the lower and middle class). Yes! What a button-holing
mariner! What a jack-in-the-box I am, but truly with a decent motive—to
entertain, to be useful,—and also to arrive at a point. What point? I do not
actually know, except that there must be a point and when I get there I will
recognize it, though I scarcely expect to get there very soon, and one who
did would equal all the seven wonders of nature of the ancients—the camel,
the rainbow, the echo, the cuckoo, the negro, the volcano, and the sirocco.

I have been thinking about justice. Naturally: look at what surrounds us. Justice: a fine word and immediately suggesting how beautiful a thing the fact must be, if there is such a fact, either possible or actual. A round, complete, self-contained datum, like an enormous globe radiating a dazzling light which illuminates every corner, subterfuge, and mystery *between* human beings, not creating, as the sun does (being like all natural things involved in the dialectic of nature) so many morbid shadows, and the black broom of night at once with the bright bloom of day.

What could I think of, desiring to amuse as well as instruct, also to be pleased and to learn myself—of what but the ancient short story made known to me in childhood by my crippled father, a brief history which has prepossessed me to this day, even with the archness in which my poor father attempted to hide the essential viciousness and despair of the narrative.

"Once upon a time," said my father, seated in his wheelchair, and summoning unknowingly in that traditional opening the continuous present necessary to the interest of any story, "Once upon a time," he repeated, "an old farmer named Schrecklichkeitunendlich" (a name chosen to tickle me) "and his young son Hans, aged ten, went to town taking with them their brown pony named Ego." "Ego, Father?" I asked, "That is a strange name for a pony or anyone else." "No, no," said my bitter father, "It is a well known name." "I have never heard of anyone with that name," I said stubbornly. "Please," said my father, angered, "If you continue to interrupt me, I will never finish the story, which you begged me to tell you. Father, son and pony," my father continued, "started for the marketplace, and Hans rode the pony. It was a beautiful blue-and-gold day in the month of June, and all three were pleased with all things, the father because he was going to sell the pony and with the proceeds buy a gun with which to kill deer, the son because he had been promised a pair of boxing gloves by the father, and the pony merely glad because he was exercising himself and the weather was fine.

"The three travelers had gone but a mile—the town being four miles distant—when a man with a whip came along from the opposite direction, and seeing them, said indignantly: 'O pitiless boy! You who are young and strong ride the pony, while your father, the weak old man, walks beside you and by such exertion shortens his days. Get down from the pony, let your father ride, honor your father, remember his weakness.' Intimidated by this,

THE COLLECTED POEMS OF DELMORE SCHWARTZ

father and son said nothing, the traveler went on his way absentmindedly, Hans dismounted, and his father mounted the pony."

"But they should have had two ponies," I said to my father. "They had only one," my father replied, "The number of ponies is not infinite. Many people have only one pony, and as for us, as you know, we have none," said my father in his embittered voice and continued.

"They went forward another mile and another stranger approached, holding a gun in his hand, stopped them, took the pony by the halter, standing there as if he were an official authority: 'Evil old man,' he said, 'Selfish father! The young boy must walk while the father rides, as if he were a king and would like to live forever.'"

"A king, Father?" I inquired, "kings do not live forever. No one does." "By king, I meant an important person," he said, annoyed and impatient. "Do not, please, interrupt me so often.

"The stranger stood there so threateningly that the father dismounted. Satisfied, the stranger passed on, leaving father and son completely perplexed, not knowing at all what to do. Suddenly, Hans was inspired: 'Father, Father!' he said, 'We will both ride the pony.' The father saw how intelligent this idea was and said with pride: 'Hans, you are a smart boy,' and soon both were mounted on the pony and jogging toward town. The pony's pace slowed up a bit, but not otherwise did he show himself troubled by the additional weight.

"But soon a third stranger came along, saw them and stopped them. This one brandished a sword and said, in a tone of the greatest moral indignation and self-righteousness: 'O heartless humans! Both of you riding one weak and young pony! What ruthless cruelty toward the dumb and inoffensive beast! Dismount before you kill him, or I will report you to both the civil and sacred authorities!' Both father and son dismounted hurriedly, and clumsily (for it is difficult for two to dismount from a horse at the same time). 'Something is always wrong,' said the father aloud, as he dismounted and the stranger, satisfied, departed.

"'Hans,' said the father, 'We will both walk and the pony will walk beside us. Then perhaps all will be content.' No sooner had he said this, than a fourth stranger appeared. Hans drew back and wished to hide in the wood until the stranger passed, especially since the newcomer carried a whip, *and* a gun, *and* a sword. But the father decided against hiding. 'What is wrong with you?' said the stranger in a voice whose kindliness stunned them with surprise, 'Why don't you ride the pony? Why are you so stupid? What is a pony for, if not to ride?' Then the stranger passed on, before they could tell him of the difficulties involved in riding the pony.

"Desperate by this time, the farmer said: 'Son, only one choice remains. If either of us ride the pony, we will remain at the mercy of these denunciations of the first, second, and third class. We must carry the pony, then perhaps all sides will be satisfied.' 'The pony may not like it, Father.' 'He is silent. If he says anything, we will whip him.' And so they lifted the pony on their backs, although it was a difficult and clumsy thing to do."

"Father," I said at this point, in disbelief, "You are inventing this story. You ought not to tell me falsehoods. No one carries a pony upon his back. That is ridiculous." My father was greatly angered and slapped me savagely, making me howl with pain. "Don't ever call your father a liar," he said, "It's enough that your mother does so."

"Finish the story, Father, please," I said meekly, weeping.

"After a slow and painful effort, the farmer and Hans managed to reach the marketplace, carrying the pony upon their backs and looking very strange. In the marketplace, idlers were congregated, who, when they saw this sight, began to laugh and their laughter increased in intensity and volume. 'What are you good-for-nothings laughing about?' said the father, challenging them, while Hans in shame hid his head in his father's sleeve. The leader, the biggest wiseacre of all, answered: 'Why, you damned fool! Whoever heard of carrying a pony? A pony is supposed to carry you.' Their laughter increased still more at this sally, and the farmer felt completely helpless—at the end of his rope—and besides he could not stand being laughed at, being very sensitive. So he took out his revolver, which he had had in his pocket all the while, and—bang! bang! bang!—shot the pony, shot his son, and, shrugging his shoulders, and brushing the hair back from his forehead, shot himself."

My mother entered at this moment and began to argue with my father for telling the child such a story, and soon all the hate between them made each bring up past wrongs on each other's part, and in their heat they forgot my presence and spoke shamelessly and brutally, while I wept loudly, watching them, weeping because of the sad end of the story, because they were denouncing each other and because I had been slapped for calling my father a liar.

Three: "There Is a World Elsewhere"

—Over the soft pudding of my face
I passed my hand to'assure myself of where
My place was, where my gaze and gazing mind:
The warm bath of awareness mounts again.
His story was my story, he was I,
Myself divided in identity,
Dressed in a dress-suit, seated secretly
Where all my studied ghosts surrounded me.

Now has the hero come to get his prize
—The Senate's gift and office.
                            Waiting there,
(The while the well-coached crowd approaches him,
As yet unheard),
                    Marcius makes inquiries
About Aufidius, his perfect foe,
Necessitous to him.
                        The day, the joy,
The glory and circumstance of honor
Hardly concern him (all taken for granted,
Being achieved)
                    but with what interest
Hears how Aufidius bears him full hate,
Wishes a cause to seek him out once more,
Strive with him once for all
                            and kill him!
—Affirms the dogma of his being thus.

The tribunes come, pretend to warn him,
                                    he
Perceives their plot, denounces them,
                                    asserts
That all concessions only
Increase class conflict and unite the poor,
Raising their appetite:
                    "He's right," says Marx,
Absorbed beside me.
                    Brutus and Velutus
Provoke him more, knowing their man full well,
Mention a scandal long forgot, scratch hard
All of his paining skin,
                    until his choler,
Indulged like a thirst, mouthed with bulging eyes,
Alienates everyone on every side.

—O apoplectic then, he speaks as if
For his own class, but they, patricians there,
Standing beside hm, censure him, regret
His utterance, perceive his drunkenness,
And seek to soothe all partisans.
                                    He howls
A theory of the state, he calls the people
Hydra, a monster, he requires the Senate
To end the tribunes' power,
                            he insists
That they take on his spirit and his humor
—While they, not fed as he, stand coldly by,
Outside his passion, moved to pure distaste,
Trying to quiet him, take him away.

At which he blazes! All not with him
Are against him!
                    "Enough, enough!"
Menenius says;
                    "Traitor!" the tribunes cry,
"O not enough! Take more!" Narcissus howls,
"That many-headed monster must be strapped,

THE COLLECTED POEMS OF DELMORE SCHWARTZ

His tongues plucked out and every loud inch whipped.
Erect! O noblemen, be not debased,
They are the Senators, you are displaced!"
But no response. But he is quite alone,
Foreign, alien, estranged.
               The crowd arrives,
Whipped on by Brutus,
               "Arrest him now,"
Brutus demands, "The city is the people,"
("The city is the people," the people echo,)
"And he their enemy, let him be killed,
Borne to the rock Tarpeian and cast down!"
Thus the deliberate tribune asks his death,
"Tarpeian death, hurled from the naked rock,
Forth from the falling sky to rising ruin."
And the poor people, whipped on by the tribunes,
Echo their voices, move to seize the hero.

—Whereat he draws his sword, himself unsheathed,
And still defies them.
             "Down with that sword,"
Menenius cries. "Lay hands on him,"
Brutus demands.
           The Senate's guard arrives,
Briefly the crowd is beaten back,
Marcius is hurried elsewhere by his friends.

The orchestra resumes. Beethoven blows
The raw emotion through the passive air
As through the body's darkness. Well he knows
(And well the violins are sworded there)
Responsive anger savage in the head,
Hammered and stammered till its fist is fed.

"This man," murmurs the Stagirite to me,
"Breaks down the categories. Every man
Divided by them, yet a surd remains,
Himself and not his genus, species, class,
And not his time, his place, his quantity:

Something remains,
                        each man a quality,
As is the color, blue, the taste of, sweet,
Indivisible, individual, alone,
But of all personal animals
Marcius is most extreme, most radical,
Discolors with his teeth each element,
Which gave him being, cooks it, pukes it up,
So by transforming all, himself to be,
Though vomiting be all activity,
Till in the vomit's tint and smell he sees
His unique essence living as disease."

"O as disease indeed!" Marx intervenes,
"See what a fracture such uniqueness means!
He who would rend himself from his own class
Shall feel his self ragged as broken glass."

"His mother's breast," intrudes the Viennese,
"Delighted him too much, fixed his disease.
The child misunderstood, blind animal:
Dark Id rules all, and though impersonal,
Fixed to the womb this individual:
'O Mutter, Mutter, it is cold outside:'
So speaks his wish to die, such is his pride."

"O no!" Karl Marx insists, "You do not see
His veritable mother, the genuine She
From whom he sucked his pieties, his mind,
His sword, his words, his war, his unchewed rind,
His anger, his desires. She is here
Near to him as his hands and feet are near!"

The house of Marcius now. The living room.
—Nobles convened to meet their class's woe.
All members of the ruling class,
They speak as such, adjudge his character
And find him wanting too, or rather too
Abnormal, alien, foreign, strange, a freak,

Not of their kind, though they admire him
As one admires the sun, shading his eyes.

"He is too noble for the world," says one,
"He is a god or beast, he is the one
Whom Aristotle in his *Politics*
Refers to as apart from any city,
Not one to live in a community,
Superior or inferior to the state,
Disdains the shadow which he treads at noon,
And would not flatter God for what is His,
No, would not recognize the Deity,
—The only one perfect and all alone."

Enter Cominius with word that now
The wound can still be bandaged, the people
Pacified
      (forgiving, forgetful, relative)
The people will pardon him,
                if he but
Affirm the people's rights, the tribune's office
And show such courtesy as strangers get
To those who will be dogs if they are pets,
—Who merely wish to sit down and be friends.

His friends plead with him, kindly, carefully,
Call on his loyalty, ask that but once,
That he but once not make his mouth his heart,
Or civil war and the class war will burn,
Or he will die.
          And thus they touch him not,
Or rather butter the obelisk, his callous height,
For he invites Tarpeian death, insists
That ten times worse will never alter him,
Nor height a million times as high as is
The rock Tarpeian change his attitude
And make him politic.
            O in New York
His swollen heart would find true properties!

We have such pyramids as financiers
Descend when their arithmetic's full sum
Betrays a debt the smashing pavement pays.

One puny qualm he has: "I muse my mother
Does not approve me further."
       So he says
As she appears, appeals to her at once,
His only audience:
      "Am I not true,
Mutter, am I not true to my own nature?"
In baby lisp requesting flattery.

But she, annoyed and firm, and not as he,
Calls him too foolish, yes, a very child,
Once who would eat his cake before he has it,
And show his private parts in company.

"I am as you," she says, though she is not,
As proud, contemptuous, intransigent,
But with an adult mind and not a child's,
Prudent, reasonable,
      "O go," she says,
"Repent to the tribunes."
        "No," he says.
"You are too absolute," she cries, "Beg, kneel,
Tell them you have a soldier's violent tongue."
"No, no," he says, although already moved,
"I cannot change my face."—such is his claim—
"Revise my heart, no, not for God himself,
How then for them?
      The unwashed stinking horde!"
"I beg you," says Volumnia, "*I* do,
Sweet son!"
    "O well!" thus he consents, consents
And calls himself a whore, describes consent
With such disgust that he offends himself,
Reneges again, refuses, stricken by
His grimace in the glass of his own voice.

Her anger mounts. "You are an absolute,
You recognize not mother, wife, nor child,
Nor any relative. You are alone."
—Never before so harsh!
                              Denies her still,
Though in the streets the crowds are packed, and wait,
Till she tugs wholly at the silver cord.
—First for the city and his own friends' sake,
The ground on which he stands, from which he rose;
Then, knowing, intuitive, she says she is
The senators, the city, his son, his wife,
(Freud bursts to speak beside me,) she unites
All in one picture, She, enormous mother,
All stimuli, all bells, and every cue.

—Still he denies, although with weakening face,
Still she pursues, cries out in rage that she
Pays for the insane pride sucked from her breast,
Pays for the ego which her womb fed well,
Which now preempts all things, thinks all is his.

"Chide me no more!" Marcius, consenting, hurt,
Obedient to the womb's authority:
"I'll be a mountebank, an easy whore
Who sleeps with every sex and every lie,
Perjure myself, juggle their jogging hearts
With my sweet temper, kiss each pimpled face,
Answer their perjury with my own honor,
And come back consul—perfectly forgiven!"
"O what an *anima*!" says Aristotle;
"How torn by contradictions!" says Karl Marx,
"O as a girl finds heavy in her self
And bigger day by day, more obvious,
That joy's commission which shall be her shame,
So does the ton of evil in this man
Move to dénouement, issue, tragedy.
As a society contains within itself
The child which shall destroy it, so does he
Nurse in his breast the striving love and hate

Which shall annul him!"
                          "O he yields," says Freud,
"To childhood's queen, that is, his very mother!"
"Not to Volumnia," Karl Marx replies,
"But to the mother obsessing all men's eyes!
Volumnia was refused until she pressed
His biggest mother toward his much-used breast!
Fame is her face, economy her bone,
No man departs from her and lives alone!"
"A man may go away," says Plato's son,
"Travel beneath the moon until he has won
Virtue, knowledge, the good. Wherever he goes
One mother shadows him and shows
Prior to him in actuality,
—As his mind's words, his warm identity!"

Now at the Forum. Brutus and Velutus
Coach the poor people, prompt their will, dictate
Their act, prepare to provoke their Marcius,
Knowing him well, to self-destroying anger,
Any pretext or wound.
                          He comes before them,
A staring audience which shows as if
The city painted its own image there.
The tribunes question him and he replies
Adequately, gravely, quietly,
Acknowledges the people's rights.
                          His friends
Chime in, apologize, call this enough,
The meeting verges on its happy end
—Yet he cannot suppress a single query,
Why he's been crowned and then crudely uncrowned
Within an hour?
                 Seizing their chance, the tribunes
Accuse him,
            call him traitor!
                          charge his will
Of tyranny and kingship!
                          False and true,

His rage explodes immediately! He
Defies them, frenzied, his tongue hysterical,
Defies a million deaths from them.
                                    The people,
Prompted, pulled by a string or button, roar.
"Exile or death?" the tribunes quickly ask.
"Exile!" the people roar,
While Marcius foams, spitting every curse:
"I exile you!" he cries, "Your breath I hate!
I banish you. There is a world elsewhere."
Thus does the king, falsely accused, enact
His empty kingship, striking his own heart,
While the poor people praise their worthy voices,
Wishing a little good and to be friends.

·

Between the Acts

THERE WAS A CITY

Here I am once more, dressed in a toga to suit the occasion. I am sure you
will agree that this performance is nothing, if not engrossing. Surely the
consequences will provide that fine thing, *katharsis*, concerning which one
member of the audience has long been an expert; *katharsis* equal and even
superior to that of the sexual act, which begins everything and ends noth-
ing, and often, as everyone knows, produces as aftermath the most unutter-
able sadness, even in those so self-delighting that they are intoxicated by the
comeliness of their own shadows.

I do not doubt that my appearance here is questionable. Why, you may ask,
does this voluble intruder come upon the stage and interrupt the occasion
with what he seems to regard as of interest to us? Let me confess, in reply,
that I am not very sure of what I am saying, but that I have a grave need of
speech which I can justify to myself. My reason, my justification is the fact
that I am here. Since I am here, it would be well for you to hear what I have to
say. If I remained silent, you might be deceived as to what you are seeing. Let
the observer be observed by all observers in the act of observing what there

is to observe. May I confess, however, that I am not sure of this justification itself. It is very difficult to be sure of anything. Let us, however, rather risk foolishness than permit any fact to remain obscure.

To continue with my memoirs, there was a city. That city occupied a place near the sea. Historians disagree as to the reason for choosing this place. Some say that an old father committed incest with his daughter and came here, seeking a certain strangeness for his new family. Some, however, insist that men came from across the sea seeking precious metals on this coast and remained here because they were tired. Thirdly, it is said that this community was founded because the sea provided a means of commerce with other nations from whom desirable commodities could be obtained. Lastly, there are some who speak with certainty of their belief that an indolent pleasure-seeking man chose this place because he was pleased by views of the sea and also admired the countryside and enjoyed the climate. All agree, however, that the decision which brought the first one to this place to begin the city was his own desire; whatever that desire may have been, he was seeking its satisfaction.

The time soon came when the beginning was obscure and unconsidered, apart from the fact of desire. The owners of ships were the most important men in this community. This was because ships carried from other nations the commodities deemed to be necessary or desirable. As a result, the building of ships was very important. Such matters occupied both the educational system and the games of the children. In order to make the ships, it was necessary above all to cut down forests for wood. The neighboring countryside was abundantly forested. Equally important was the craft of making a ship, and great honor was paid to the shipbuilder. The commodities brought from other nations were paid for, in general, either by a shipment of lumber or by completely made ships. This led to numerous conflicts. The shipowners protested against the sale of ships to other nations in too great a quantity because it deprived them of their commercial advantage. The owners of the ships and the owners of the forests attempted to profit by the needs of each other. After a time, a crisis arose as a result of the fact that the neighboring forests were depleted. Consequently, many became aware of the relationship of the city to Nature. Another region of forests was acquired further inland, but after a time this too was completely cut down, and it became necessary to make war upon a distant city to obtain additional forests. The result of each crisis was that first the making and the owning of ships was seized by one group of owners, and later shipbuilding, shipping,

THE COLLECTED POEMS OF DELMORE SCHWARTZ

and the ownership of forests all became the ownership of one group, the group which at first had merely owned ships.

In this city there was a boy who lived a personal life in which at every given opportunity he judged, that is to say, evaluated the kind of being and the ways of life which surrounded him. Such judging was natural to him, made him lonely, sprang from his desire to know what he might enact, possess, and attain when he was permitted to choose, if he were permitted to do so. Such judging was as much a matter of his body's intuitive responses as of a conscious effort to decide what various objects and processes were worth to him. He strolled by the seaside, regarded the sea, the ships in the harbor, the sailors washing the decks. He walked on the great avenue where stood the big houses of the rich merchants, the owners of ships. He gazed with no little curiosity into their windows, striving to see if life had a different quality there. He looked long into the display windows of the shopkeepers, where were shown all the goods which had been obtained from many nations. He studied the diamonds in the jeweller's window, and observed that a thing of intrinsic goodness had a certain toughness. He sat in the waiting-room of a doctor and saw that many were ill for a long time and he stood where tickets were bought for journeys and knew that many wish to go away and many return. He cracked the nuts given him by a grocer, ate the meat contained in them, decided that it would be foolish to consider eating a major satisfaction. He made the acquaintance of a druggist who permitted him to try his salves and ointments. He found them delicate. When, however, the druggist used his own cosmetics and simpered toward him, he fled, astonished by the arbitrary nature of taste. From a close vantage-point, he gazed upon the sailors with their whores in the bushes near the driveway, and he knew that the body desires to penetrate and exhaust and make fat the body of another. A dentist told him that teeth were near the ego. He met metaphysicians who discussed the sea and painters who painted ships, but he was not as yet impressed. He met a theologian who told him that since all men must die, he would be foolish to concern himself with the practical arrangements of life, but wise to prepare himself with a decent character for the event of immortality. He spoke with an undertaker who told him that one must make a living and that in time one became used to everything. He observed children and saw how cruel they were in their games and knew that only later among a few adults who had escaped from childhood could one expect kindness, charity, an exact awareness of the torture and the tenderness of the ego. He saw how those who had authority were corrupted by the mere formality of their offices. During this prolonged examination he was by himself, had no friends, was regarded by his family as worse than useless. So great was his interest, however, that nothing deterred him, no one offended him by contempt, not even his father, who helped to build ships.

Boys who were clever or ambitious in this city were told to become builders of ships. If one were fortunate, courteous, hard-working, and extremely intelligent, one might attain to the privilege of sleeping with the daughters of the great merchants, the owners of ships. Boys were told that life was very sweet in their great houses as their sons-in-law. Then, by natural succession, one might hope to become oneself an owner of ships and forests, and a lord among the men of the city, walking in the assurance of all who possess themselves and inspire meekness, strict attention, admiring glances.

But he rejected these brilliant promises. They were not enough and they were already exemplified by young men of thinning hair and slight paunch who seemed to be endeavoring to remember what they had desired. He rejected the notion of hierarchy or stair implicit in this scheme. The rich did not seem to him to be at the top of the stair and the poor striving to climb at least one more flight. When he had reached this conclusion, however, he met an old sailor who argued that the people in the city were detained in a prison, the prison of the way in which each made his living and all secured the goods deemed necessary or desirable. The old sailor said that the objects of attention were dictated by this fact; conscious life was preoccupied and not free; the attitudes toward Nature were determined by the operation of instruments in the fields and on the water; the relationship between a man and his brother was determined by each one's function and no man's heart. Yet, said the old sailor, this is what at the beginning was desired, although no more. The honorable, the justifiable, the notable, the beautiful were dictated by a center of feeling which was itself merely a narrow response to the manifold forms of the way in which each good in general was made, secured, kept, taken, and given.

The boy was shocked to hear this, and disturbed by the old sailor's advice, namely, to go to sea and to seek among the rocking scenes of indeterminacy a certain freedom of feeling, also freedom from the ways of the city. This seemed to him merely the counsel of evasion and escape. A pause occurred in which his decisive response prepared itself. It would be like no other man's since no one had lived the days which he had lived. He had seen

THE COLLECTED POEMS OF DELMORE SCHWARTZ

many desires and satisfactions and been somewhat impressed by all of them. No one of them failed to enter into the new and unique center of feeling which prepared itself in his heart; just as the muscles of the runner have been minutely determined by his daily rounds about the track, so that even the cinders and the airs of early morning have affected them and entered into their very being.

This boy was at the moment of falling in love and all the love he had seen was present in him, though differently. All men are in love, the forms of love are many: such was the knowledge present in him. As his first enactment of the long fate of love, he went to sea and in this act was contained the potentialities of the future of the city. For he discovered a new land of forests and thus from his original longing transformed the shipbuilding of the city and thus in the end its way of life. Or he discovered a new means of moving ships and transformed the commerce of the city. His new center of feeling, though derived from the city, made it necessary for him to murder the captain of the ship in order that he might proceed in the ways of his own origination. Let us depart from him, even as he departs from the city on his voyage toward himself and the future. See him! He stands at the prow, observing the glittering possibilities of the waters as the ship moves forward in time. He is in love. I am in love with him!

Four: "Like to a Lonely Dragon"

I

Lifting his silly nightgown up,
My twin retires once more; I am once more
Beside myself. I feel myself
Behind my face, quiet as moonlight is,
Pale guilt within the night.
                         His utterance,
Jejeune and lyrical, is mine, my own.
He tells my secrecy, my private mind,
My very heart in accents crude and broad,
And I am gratified to have it known

(Let it be known, I think, that is my pleasure,
Let it be fully known, if it is true,
Of every mind with technique mine alone
Sleeps such a dream, endures this brutal night),
But shamed by his voluble nakedness.

The parting scene comes now. Now at the gate
Marcius commences exile, separates
From mother, wife, and son, from friends and Rome,
(A few patricians, the imitative young,
Entranced by him, are also there)
Dismisses tears and their extended arms,
Limp attitudes of farewell and of grief
—And though Cominius would go with him
For a full month until he's once more rooted
("But what are men," says Plutarch, "plants, to stay
Fixed in one place? The mind's a traveler,
The wandering mind which makes us moving souls,"
So says one ghost by me, equivocal,)
Marcius refuses. He would go alone
Like to a lonely dragon, so he says,
Telling them that they soon will hear of him
And what they hear will be but as before,
The future like the past as one stone like
Another stone in hardness.
                              The city is a beast,
A many-headed beast which butts him hence,
Or so he says, wholly unmodified.
"A beast, indeed! His mother is a beast,
Great womb, great height, great strength," says one late ghost.

"Mother, my letters will be regular.
I am sufficient, I will be myself."
Though he to the audience seems precarious,
Sinking in quicksand or the soft of water
Or trembling on a perilous height, in fact,
("All men are sometime acrobats,
Or tight-rope walkers, teetering their strut.")

He to himself is strong, the tough Narcissus
Rather takes pleasure in this exile's wound,
And thinks it shows him perfect once again,
Reaches again for that sweet solitude
When he walked home alone from school, when he
Was the whole world in his mother's womb.

"The navel-cord is cut!" the Marxian cries,
"The belly-button bleeds! The hero dies!
Thus will he pay the dialectical price;
Each virtue when too swollen is a vice!
O with what blindness he departs from Rome!"

Beethoven's tears accompany the poem.

II

CHOOSE

No introduction, no idle remarks, I am tired as you of too much discussion and come now merely to bring the story forward.

Marcius, having departed from Rome went from place to place. He spoke to no one, he knew no one, he had no place to go, he ate and slept alone, and he had only his sense of hatred and of appalling injury, the savage anger which obsessed his revery, only this passion, to occupy the lucid day of many objects and the vague night when nothing exists. No purpose, no desire, except the vindictive appetite, nothing of which to think but his past victories and his uncontrollable longing to smash certain faces, which made him clench his fists merely, as he proceeded on his journey to no end.

At first he was gratified in his unceasing walk because he was alone with his towering shadow, which compared itself with nothing, either in the sterile desert or the cool forest. And at first he was gratified by the strange bedrooms in which he was alone with his own smell, the only one which did not offend him. Soon he was less pleased and a blister on his foot made him feel an incomparable pity for himself. Later he was annoyed because he had no one to speak to, except the one whom he asked for something to eat and a place to sleep. Meanwhile he still considered himself completely independent and was under the impression that he was proving his self-sufficiency. One night, however, he dreamed that he had returned to Rome, recanted, unsaid his pride, and begged their forgiveness, asked to be killed or permitted to remain, the least of citizens in Rome. He awoke then, wholly disgusted and angered by his own weakness, determined to go further and further from Rome, travelling a greater number of miles each day in order to deny the dream and convince himself that what occurred in the prone passivity of sleep had nothing to do with himself awake. Stiff-necked, hardening his heart, hating the need which sleep disclosed, he came at last, after the worst despair, to a lake ringed by pines after a long journey in a barren and flat terrain. It was a perfect day in the middle of September. The lake sparkled a million times and the soft wind crossed the shuffled, shuffling waters. The night before he had dreamed the identical dream of returning and begging forgiveness. He has come to despise his sleep and to be afraid of not remaining awake. Desolate, desolate. Even his mother against him, even his sleep betraying him, even his hatred become ambiguous; Narcissus, Brutus, Judas, knowing no place to go, having no desire, attained to the emptiness for which he had striven, sick at heart more than ever before, he kneels by the water, bends over it, and then, staring at the water, kneeled above it, he sees his own face there, folded over and over, distorted under the ripple, undulating, and he coughs! amazed to hear the sound of his body in the silence, sneezes! in a sudden chill, in his body's weakness and disbelief. He sees his face, his thick lips, curly hair, flaring nostrils, broad forehead. His haunted eyes regard themselves, round lakes full of a kind of sweat. They still get pleasure from their own unmoved look. He is somewhat aware of the rippling water, and of the sky, the eternal gem, reflected therein, a curious hat or backdrop for his head.

It is the moment of vision and decision. Staring upon that face which is his own, he sees his own life, and the lives rejected and the choices chosen, and the immediacy of anger and pleasure, and the abstracted stare of memory, and the strangeness, to himself, of his own face, the most peculiar of flowers.

And then his mother's face replaces his own and blooms until it has become an enormous image, quivering or trembling in the water or in the sky. She looks at him as if she were waiting for him to speak to her and he gazes back, afraid and yet unable to turn away, trying to believe what he sees before him, whether in the water or the sky. And then, as if decided that he will not speak to her, she says to him:

"You cannot depart from me. You are nothing apart from me, you do not exist without me. I will be with you no matter where you go. Your lips are mine, your globe-like head and your deep body, your swinging arms, your strength, system, and urge, habit, complexion, and dress. I fed you. I gave you each part of your being, or you took that part from me. The word of your tongue is mine. Your effort to depart from me is your pain, your evil. I am your mother or Rome. I am Volumnia or Rome.

"But I am yours. You are your own; lips, face, hair, look, your own, your property. This is your freedom. You are free, self-choosing, a king. Your words are yours, although they are mine. Although you have taken yourself from me, nevertheless your speech is your choice, your life is your making, your being is your own. Nothing compels you, no imperative dictates to you, the actuality of your choice is what it is for you, your individuality grasps the uniqueness of each moment. This surpasses me. This is your freedom. Choose!"

III

"A GOODLY HOUSE, THE FEAST SMELLS WELL"

Inveterate, gratuitous, too much,
Ambiguous, I tire even myself.

—The curtain rises on a night in which
All's indeterminate except the moon,
Marcius in white, and two enormous signs,
Painted in phosphorus at right and left
As if alternatives were parts of place
And choice a bird which whirls upon the air
And comes to rest
              only to rise once more.
To ANTIUM, at left, as advertised;
To ROME, at right, and Marcius in between
Outstretched upon the ground.
                Night over all

Except the rounding moon which dreams of snow,
Unnatural as both signs.
                         "Don't," he says,
Prone there upon the ground as if in bed
In possibility, "Won't, cannot, must not,
Deny the coercive heart.
                         Friendship is green,
The hearth is glowing. Man cannot live alone,
That world is colorless, an infinite gray,
Nothing to do, nothing to wish and act,
Dance in a vacuum to no audience,
And no applause,
                         But they hurt me, hit me,
Whispered behind my back and shut the door,
Nobles as well as poor. And no one said,
'O no, he is our friend, shall stay with us,
Eat at our table and play games with us,
Till the mob stone our children and our house.'
No one in Rome said this—
                              bone, stone, unknown,
Thrown and alone—
                         I'll go to Antium,
Seek out Aufidius, my worst enemy;
He and his friends be my good company,
My heart's my own!
                         I choose myself, I'll die
Crying to Rome its fate, that I am I!"

"This is the turning-point," said Aristotle,
"This the peripety, he now has done
All that a man can do, committed his will
Once and for all, purchased his only fate.
He's helpless now, as one who, stepping, falls,
The rest is his great chute, descent, career."
"Every act is a boomerang," says Freud,
"A ricochet, a knife which cuts the butcher."
"This man still eats his heart," Beethoven said,
"It is a pretty dish and he will starve:

Chords spread upon the air their synthesis
Of all that is involved within the kiss,
Her lips the curved soft fruit of blood, her breath
Excitement's rhythm, quite aware of death.
How many actualities pass by unnamed,
Music anonymous shall witness this,
Music essentially vague shall wholly tell
With what variety man goes to hell!"

Now Jew is silent and the Greek is still,
Bent over the fate of that sad animal.
While I, I am afraid of that fifth ghost
Who is unknown, who has not said one word.

A scene that's quickly done. Marcius before
The house of Aufidius in Antium.
In mean apparel, muffled and disguised,
Regards the sour twilight and the city,
A handsome city to his exiled gaze,
One which has suffered many a widow from him,
Hearsed many an heir too soon.
                                    He asks the street
Where great Aufidius stays, wholly aware
How times have changed, how dialectical
His straight heart turns the curving world.
He vows his love to Antium, his hate to Rome.

A hall in the house of great Aufidius.
Music within blooms with its order and love,
Radiant, resolving all voices in its own.
He enters hesitant and wholly muffled;
The sound of banqueting
                         strikes at his heart,
Music and food, mutual being, three
Baskets or contexts by which man's heart is kept
From falling through nothingness.
                              Where Marcius stands
An angle of the dining room is seen

And three men's faces show at the long table,
Eating and laughing, caught unknowingly
In two dual aims, to eat and yet guffaw.

"The feast smells well. But I am not a guest."
Marcius instructs himself,
                              he hears the clink
Of glasses met, the brittle tap of fork
Against the plate;
                    sudden, an active hush
While one would tell a story of their fellow,
Until at the sweet crux, all roar,
                                      even
The silly fool whose foolishness is told
Glad to be famous there and then and thus.

—Wishes himself that fool, himself unfed,
As a servant enters crying, "Wine! Wine!"
Wine that the warm glow of company
May be sustained, renewed, increased to blaze.

The servant sees him, the servant as the snob
Sees his mean dress, asks with impudence
Just what he wants.
                    "Aufidius," he replies,
Telling himself that he deserves no welcome
Other than this.
                  A second servant joins;
Both being a little drunk and hi-de-ho,
Refuse to call Aufidius, abuse him.
"Get out before I throw you out," says one;
"Sure, you're a pretty guest," the other says.
"Where do you live?" they ask.
                                Marcius replies,
"Under the sky, under the canopy!
With crows, with eagles, with vultures, and with God!"
"Get out! This is no place for you!" they cry,
Pushing him roughly,
                      bringing his choler

Until he jaws at them with old contempt
And the row brings in Aufidius.
                              His name
(Not recognizing him in his mean dress)
Aufidius requires. He
With a slight pun of hesitation
Calls himself *Caius Marcius*, then, wholly,
Coriolanus, bursts out his whole history—
All pride, rancor, rage against Rome,
The cruelty and envy of the people
And how the bastard nobles all forsook him—
Offers himself unto Aufidius,
As victim, or as friend to knock down Rome.

"Most absolute sir!" just as his mother did,
Aufidius welcomes him. "Come in, come in!"
He jubilates, joy overbrims. "Come in!
This is a second wedding night for me;
Shake hands with all and eat and drink with us,
Welcome a million times! For your own sake
Will we tear Rome to pieces! Marcius, come in!"

The servants too rejoice that war is come,
While the hubbub rises from the dining room,
For war, says one, in fact unites all men,
While peace makes cuckolds, peace makes idleness,
Boredom and quietness.
                              "When peace rules us
Men have no need of friendship, therefore sleep,
Quarrel, grow old, insensible and stupid."

A public place in Rome. The tribunes speak
Of Marcius' absence and the city's peace.
Rome fattens, rid of its poor absolute;
All's well, the people sing at work,
Or so the tribunes say.
                              Even Menenius
Admits the happiness, regrets that Marcius
Could never temporize, reports that none,

Nor mother, wife, nor he, knows where he is,
Has heard from him.
                          Citizens pass, profess
Their grateful ease and thank the useful tribunes
Who now judge Marcius once again, repeat
That though brave soldier, he was arrogant,
Proud, ambitious past imagination,
Self-loving, harsh, wished to be king of Rome.

And as they speak, amid their sleek content,
News shakes them, shocks them:
                                    Coriolanus!
Coriolanus leads the Volscian host!
Ravishes colonies and comes toward Rome!
Terror rises. Panic
Seizes the populace. The patricians
Hurry to meet
                    and fear convulses all!

And now the Volscian camp. As he shakes Rome,
He gnaws Aufidius with every tooth,
Unknowingly, though vowed to show, in all,
Humility, and move with modesty,
And loyalty.
                    But the true surd
Is irreducible. The individual
Is uncontrollable. To him, to him
The soldiers draw, forget Aufidius,
Render him virtual kingship.

Aufidius is deathly jealous. "He is,
He is," he says, "by nature but one thing,
Cannot be otherwise, cannot deny
His nature more than a triangle can.
For this was he banished, and for this
—So virtue lies in circumstance alone,
And every time interprets us—
                          becomes
The idol of all hearts, the man I kill!"

"So our virtues lie in the
interpretation of time."
—IV, 7, 50.

THE COLLECTED POEMS OF DELMORE SCHWARTZ

The orchestra begins. Bomb! Bomb! Bomb!
Rome and her strangest child in double harm!
Evil is complex. Though man walk alone
He steps upon the whole world
                                    and is thrown!

Between the Acts

HE IS A PERSON

Ladies and Gentlemen, here I am for the last time, dressed as a knight in armor in order to recall the days when our fathers thought they understood good and evil and old Nobodaddy (concerning whom I intend to remain silent). I would venture to say that this performance was near its conclusion. Conclusion, however, is a fiction, in fact, for we know neither beginning nor end, only the report of them. For we are always in the middle of everything, and our lives are, need I say, infinitely divisible; like Achilles and the tortoise, we shall never get home, and I, a veritable Coleridge, must buttonhole you once more, the most belated Shakespearean fool.

Here I am finally to provide you with an abstract picture postcard of the wounded nudity about which all things whirl, that is to say, the soul. In the Shakespearean night, the souls of the poor fool and the brave hero and the gentle lady shiver and huddle in a nakedness which no dress covers. In the precise center of this oblong postcard a human being is shown, possessing hair, eyes, hands, feet, arms, belly, genitals, and the other parts which make possible thought, movement, and love. This human being might be mistaken for Joseph, who had a many-colored coat; Moses, for whom God burned; David, who threw stones so well; Ulysses, who wished to go home; Orestes, who was hunted; Oedipus, who destroyed his own eyesight (perhaps secretly desiring the vision of Tiresias); Peter, betrayed by the cock; Dante, the greatest traveller; or the remorseless Morning Star, John Milton, who seduced our first mother. He might be mistaken for any one of these famous gentlemen. For look you! he undergoes that pain of all vertebrates, the labor of standing up. He endures the loneliness of all conscious beings. He ties his shoelaces in his own style, which merely shows that like those famous heroes, he is betrayed by his body, his feet hurt him and he must blow his nose. In his own style, he ties his shoelaces, and enacts the other motions which distinguish his identity amid the infinite host. He adjusts his hat and his tie before the oval mirror in the hallway in his own inimitable idiom. His uniqueness is obvious, though he resembles other members of his family. His voice has a certain intonation which has never been heard from another man. His step on the stairs and his key in the lock can be recognized as his. No one, not the most precise counterfeiter, can duplicate his handwriting, for no one writes with precisely such curls. His handwriting is, however, merely a symptom of his nervous system. He is original.

Now, as he stands there and moves toward himself, a breathing animal, almost divine, let us ask once more the question which we do not evade. Who is he? Let us begin again as we always begin again in order that we may continue. What is he? He is his father and his mother, neither of whom are represented on the postcard. He is his childhood, which is also absent. He is his adolescence, which is each one's *vaterland*. He is his young manhood. Let us begin again. He is his fatherland, which is his adolescence, and he is his mother, which is his childhood. None of this can be represented upon the postcard, and you, when you look at any man, remember that you do not truly see him. For he is his past and his past is unseen, although it is one of the greatest of powers. His past holds him and he must move forward in time, dragging every fear and every beauty of every year with him. They will never release him! He carries his habits, which are his childhood, strapped to him like his wristwatch, beating.

And he moves, because he must, and thus he is betrayed to the unending agony of conscious being. Thus he moves forward to what he has not yet been. Here his pain awaits him and here he is as yet nothing. The repetition of yesterday and the day before will never suffice, but he must create again and again from what has been the unheard-of future. The future of time which is nothing cannot be grasped by the repetition of what has been. It is not enough. He must create what has never existed. The necessity of the future intrudes and he must choose, although as most often he merely choose what has already existed. Such is the nothingness which faces him. He is the future. He is a person!

See him, in admiration and fear. Remark the original face which is unrecognizable, never before having been. Regard his face and suppose the unknown

THE COLLECTED POEMS OF DELMORE SCHWARTZ

heart and the secret head, which create the nature of what is to come. The past is transformed in him. The world begins again. All is torn in him and altered in the richest exchanges. Passionate nonesuch, his heart consumes the world. His freedom breaks his heart. His freedom creates the future. He is the mystery, irreducible. His freedom is his mystery. With his freedom he does it, his unknown creative act. With that mystery, his own identity, he who will never have sufficient names, invents the future! O my beauty! See him, sharply and exactly. Coriolanus, Caius Marcius Coriolanus, Coriolanus, the individual.

Five: "As if a Man Were Author of Himself"

That twin goes back: too much and not enough,
Led by the ecstasy of his tongue,
Hiding what wish and hope I do not know,
And by ideas possessed and tricked
By his imagination like an heir
Straining in mind unto a vast access
Upon a change as radical as death—
And I, by now accustomed to be twice,
And by their wits' tuition tossed side to side,
Hunger for what necessity has supplied.

The curtain rises on the heart of man
As always in America and Asia
But now on Rome in crisis.
                    Fear and dread
Tighten all people. As love makes one, so fear
Makes one; all have one will, one hope,
That Marcius, spewed out like a pit or rind,
Be sucked back by some intimate appeal,
His anger turned from them.
                    Cominius
Has been ambassador to him, returned,
And now reports the hapless interview:

—That Marcius would not answer; when he did,
Refused his name and called himself a nothing
Until a fire was his name,
                              Rome burning down!
"I kneeled before him," says Cominius,
"I called on every piety of his,
But like a metal his impervious face
—Then, faintly, he dismissed me, as if he spoke
Distant from me a thousand miles away!
—Only his mother might penetrate his hate."
Menenius, though demurring, is the next
Sent as ambassador—
                          to beg, solicit, plead,
All that auld lang syne may, in kneeling suit.
"—O," says Menenius, "I'll come to him
When he has had his dinner and fed well."
O plum, O filet mignon, charlotte russe,
Thus we depend on our immediacies,
Or so the old boy says.
                          The next scene shows
The Volscian host advanced, their general's tent,
Menenius arrived upon his mission,
Confronted by the soldier boy on guard:
"No visitors from Rome. *He* says *no one*;
None of his hometown boys can see him. You,
You treated him like dirt."
                              "Listen, I was,"
The old boy urges, "his best friend. We ate
And slept together!
                      Tell me, has my old chum
Had dinner yet? For I would speak to him
After he's had his coffee and dessert."
—As Marcius enters with Aufidius,
To cry *Away* to *O my son! my son!*
And the ludicrous tears of fat Menenius:
"I have no wife, no mother and no child,
And if I knew you once, that is long past,
And now a nothingness is in between."
—Gives him, however, a letter of reprieve,

THE COLLECTED POEMS OF DELMORE SCHWARTZ

To save his person,
                                turns away, and asks
Aufidius to mark him obdurate,
Loyal and unattached by any string,
Chain, wire, or bond to Rome.
                                        The soldiers watch
And call him noble, call their general
A rock perturbed by nothing in the world.
"Response! A man responds," says Sigmund Freud,
"Leaps back from that which strikes him, or falls down,
Departs, achieves a callous, or soars up,
Or goes to Africa or goes to wine,
A bird, a beast, a boxer, or he dies,
A fugitive,
                a sailor, tailor, jailer,
Barber or surgeon,
                        all faces or replies
To the world's repeated fist, so various
And inescapable,
                        questions or blows,
And a man responds, inventing every choice,
Adjusts, I say, with much imagination,
Seeks salves or runs away, gets bandages
And goes to sleep, makes speeches or denies
That that which is is what it is or seems,
Seems and is not,
                        so this much-struck man now tries
A harder face each blow, a stranger answer,
A greater void, the womb, the wish to die—"

As mother, wife, and child in mourning clothes
Enter the tent of Coriolanus,
Muster all pathos, show very sad and meek,
Raise hands for his heart to take him down to them,
And stand in silence as our Marcius cries,
"Let me not be a father, husband, son!
Corrupt and rot, all warmth, affection, love!
Let nature die in me and instinct starve,
Their kneeling bodies be unmeaning blur!

O I will stand as stiff and staunch as stone,
As if a man were author of himself,
I will be author of myself alone!"

"It is the moment, Love," the Marxian cries,
"This man cuts every vine and so he dies!"
"Each would be God," exclaims the Stagirite,
"Desire has no top, is infinite!"

But, saying this, Coriolanus yields,
Yields slightly, kisses wife, and kneels
Before his kneeling mother, calls her best,
Best mother, his Olympus, his great height,
And is appalled to see his mother kneel,
The womb to drop down so.
                     Success's sweets,
It is the scene of Joseph satisfied,
The exile welcomed home on his own terms,
All lives within his will and whim.
                     Respond,
Respond, his mother means, showing to him
His only child, who is, she says, himself,
Will be as he, a needle of the sword,
And thus she rings all gongs to call him home.

"We sue for peace," Volumnia says,
Thinking the moment ripe and soft,
—At which he freezes quite, begs them no plea,
Summons Aufidius and other Volscians
To see him still untouched.
                     Volumnia pleads.
"Again, again, we must see this again,"
So speaks the Viennese, "Mother and son,
The two exhausting their relationship,
A well-known fact of all communities
—Where's Hamlet and his Gertrude, Oedipus,
That ignorant man,
             and Baudelaire?"
Volumnia speaks: "Rome is our nurse,

She suckles all of us. When you ruin Rome,
You tread your mother's womb, which made you real!"

"You tread my womb, which made a son for you,"
So speaks his wife.
                    And little Marcius cries,
"You will not tread on me. I'll run away
And fight when I get big!"
                        Amusing all
By this sheer mimicry of Marcius,
Rifting the serious a moment which
Gives Marcius difficulty with his face.

"All, all depends on him, on his sole heart.
He is contingency, it is his will.
He is the future of time, it is his choice.
Rome lives or dies by him; his heart,
His complex heart, decides the day or night!"
So speaks in ecstasy the Stagirite.
"It is his freedom, there rests all to come;
It is his self-creating will which rules,
But what he chooses—look! his mother's hand
Gave it him, look! look! he chooses her!"

For now the scene becomes hysterical
—"O now," the Marxian cries, "She would profess
That she is Rome, she would prevail by painting
Rome as her own face,
                        and one cannot
Discriminate Volumnia and Rome
In any sentence."
                    "O Marcius, Marcius,
Reconcile communities; be famous for
Your pity and your ruth,"
                            her foreign words
("She is convinced, she knows," Karl Marx affirms.)
But he not yet convicted,
                            though she cries out,
"I am the hen that clucked you to the war,

I made you what you are, and no man, none,
Owes mother what you owe me."
                                        Again they kneel,
Commanded by Volumnia.
                                  He will not yield,
Although excruciated.
                              He will not yield,
He turns his face away,
Until she says, despairing, "Come,
Come wife, come child, this stranger's mother
Must be a Volscian. Come, he is no Roman,
He is no son, no husband and no father."

His knees slip under him, his weakness shows.
He cries out loudly, "Mother, Mother, Mother!
You win! God turns his face from us, appalled!
You win Rome's victory today,
                                        but for your son,
You bring all danger on him, if not death,
You succor Rome but not your only son."

Soon he dismisses them with promised peace.
He will not go with them, no, he will stay,
An immigrant at Antium.
                              He asks
Aufidius, if he, Aufidius,
Could answer differently a mother
Or grant her less than he.
                                  Aufidius
Pretends content,
                        aside vows Marcius' death,
Grateful for this excuse, new turncoat shift.

While Marcius courteously escorts
Mother and wife and child to carriages
To bring them back to Rome with happiness,
Congratulates them on their victory,
And turns to find how he must show himself
In the fresh disorder which his heart has made.

THE COLLECTED POEMS OF DELMORE SCHWARTZ

The scene in Rome. No hope or little hope
Abides.
      "Displace," Menenius cites, "displace
The capital with your little finger, then
Your hope is justified."
          Displaced!
A newsboy means, the capital has been
Displaced! Volumnia's little finger did it!
She has prevailed with him and Rome is saved!
Joy is insane!
      Volumnia returns
And she is named the breathing life of Rome.

"She is, she is!" announces Sigmund Freud,
"All issue from the womb and must return;
The dandled, wiped and powdered babe
Cannot forget and cannot understand."

"Nature is no machine," says Aristotle,
"But like a whore she spreads herself, and man
Can do there what he wishes, all extremes."

"Who is that silent one?" I asked in fear,
"Who is that ghost who has not said one word?
Will he speak out before this play is done,
Take off his mask and show? He gives me dread,
You are my friends, you tell me all you know,
—Though my stupidity distort it all—
Tell me his name now,
              free me from my fear!"
None answer, all intent, *katharsis* near!

For now the last scene shows: in Antium
Aufidius conspires. The Volscians are
Indeterminate as to the blunted war,
But hardly holding him at fault in it.
The city's lords convene. Marcius presents
All possible apology to them,
Points to the prizes won by him, Rome's shame,

The prosperous treaty made—
                              "Traitor! Traitor!"
Aufidius calls out. The murderers
Close in on Marcius,
                        who, merely amazed,
Is not yet angered,
                        "Marcius! Traitor!
Maudlin and pusillanimous!"
Aufidius reiterates,
                        Marcius explodes!
The insult lights his wrath.
                              "You lie!" he answers,
"You boy!" Aufidius calls back, "You boy!"
Though some would temporize, be moderate,
Marcius by this is overwhelmed:
                              "A boy!
A boy!" he howls, appalled, "Marcius!
Coriolanus in Corioli,
That is the name I took with my own hands."
(All tact is overthrown)
                           "I cut my name
Into your soldiers' hearts. I, I, I,
Alone I did it! Boy!"
                        Aufidius
Grasps his permission here,
                              though one lord calls
For mercy to the boy,
                        Aufidius
Summons his fellows,
                        Marcius draws his sword,
They leap at him. *Kill! Kill! Kill!*
His heart is pierced.
                        Aufidius stands on him,
And thus the'exhausted hero is struck down,
"And thus the'exhausted hero is struck down,"
Says Aristotle, as the curtain falls,
"Even in the affirmation of himself."
"Acting the part which brought him to this pass,"
Marx chimes, with pity in his angry voice,

THE COLLECTED POEMS OF DELMORE SCHWARTZ

"True to himself amid so many truths."
"His choice, his wish, his heart, such is his fate,
All, all depends on the self-squeezing heart,"
Thus Aristotle adds, "Man's will is free,
This man became the man he chose to be!"

My face is covered by my hands to hide
Intolerable emotion, distorted look.

"Who is that man with you, O who is he?"
I questioned them as they began to fade,
"Who is the white masked one who said no word?"

"He is the one who saw what you did not!
He is the one who heard what you did not,"
So called the Stagirite, faint and unclear,
"He is the one you do not know, my dear."

III

Poems of Experiment and Imitation

The Repetitive Heart

Eleven Poems in Imitation of the Fugue Form

I

All of us always turning away for solace

From the lonely room where the self must be honest,
All of us turning from being alone (at best
Boring) because what we want most is to be
Interested,
          play billiards, poking a ball
On the table, play baseball, batting a ball
On the diamond, play football, kicking a ball
On the gridiron,
             70,000 applauding.

This amuses, this indeed is our solace:
Follow the bouncing ball! O, fellow, follow,
See what is here and clear, one thing repeated,
Bounding, evasive, caught and uncaught, fumbled,
—Follow the bouncing ball; and thus you follow,
Fingering closely your breast on the left side,

The bouncing ball you turned from for solace.

II

    "mentrechè il vento, come fa, si tace"

Will you perhaps consent to be
Now that a little while is still
(Ruth of sweet wind) now that a little while
My mind's continuing and unreleasing wind

Touches this single of your flowers, this one only,
Will you perhaps consent to be
My many-branchéd, small and dearest tree?

My mind's continuing and unreleasing wind
—The wind which is wild and restless, tired and asleep,
The wind which is tired, wild and still continuing,
The wind which is chill, and warm, wet, soft, in every influence,
Lusts for Paris, Crete and Pergamus,
Is suddenly off for Paris and Chicago,
Judaea, San Francisco, the Midi,
—May I perhaps return to you
Wet with an Attic dust and chill from Norway
My dear, so-many-branchéd smallest tree?

Would you perhaps consent to be
The very rack and crucifix of winter, winter's wild
Knife-edged, continuing and unreleasing,
Intent and stripping, ice-caressing wind?
My dear, most dear, so-many-branchéd tree
My mind's continuing and unreleasing wind
Touches this single of your flowers, faith in me,
Wide as the—sky!—accepting as the (air)!
—Consent, consent, consent to be
My many-branchéd, small and dearest tree.

III

All clowns are masked and all *personae*
Flow from choices; sad and gay, wise,
Moody and humorous are chosen faces,
And yet not so! For all are circumstances,
Given, like a tendency
To colds or like blond hair and wealth,
Or war and peace or gifts for mathematics,
Fall from the sky, rise from the ground, stick to us
In time, surround us: Socrates is mortal.

THE COLLECTED POEMS OF DELMORE SCHWARTZ

Gifts and choices! All men are masked,
And we are clowns who think to choose our faces
And we are taught in time of circumstances
And we have colds, blond hair and mathematics,
For we have gifts which interrupt our choices,
And all our choices grasp in Blind Man's Buff:
"My wife was very different, after marriage,"
"I practice law, but botany's my pleasure,"
Save postage stamps or photographs,
But save your soul! Only the past is immortal.

Decide to take a trip, read books of travel,
Go quickly! Even Socrates is mortal,
Mention the name of happiness: it is
Atlantis, Ultima Thule, or the limelight,
Cathay or Heaven. But go quickly
And remember: there are circumstances,
And he who chooses chooses what is given,
He who chooses is ignorant of Choice,
—Chooses love, for love is full of children,
Full of choices, children choosing
Botany, mathematics, law and love,
So full of choices! So full of children!
And the past is immortal, the future is inexhaustible!

IV

for Rhoda

Calmly we walk through this April's day,
Metropolitan poetry here and there,
In the park sit pauper and *rentier*,
The screaming children, the motor car
Fugitive about us, running away,
Between the worker and the millionaire
Number provides all distances,
It is Nineteen Thirty-Seven now,
Many great dears are taken away,
What will become of you and me

(This is the school in which we learn . . .)
Besides the photo and the memory?
(. . . that time is the fire in which we burn.)

(This is the school in which we learn . . .)
What is the self amid this blaze?
What am I now that I was then
Which I shall suffer and act again,
The theodicy I wrote in my high school days
Restored all life from infancy,
The children shouting are bright as they run
(This is the school in which they learn . . .)
Ravished entirely in their passing play!
(. . . that time is the fire in which they burn.)

Avid its rush, that reeling blaze!
Where is my father and Eleanor?
Not where are they now, dead seven years,
But what they were then?
                 No more? No more?
From Nineteen-Fourteen to the present day,
Bert Spira and Rhoda consume, consume
Not where they are now (where are they now?)
But what they were then, both beautiful;
Each minute bursts in the burning room,
The great globe reels in the solar fire,
Spinning the trivial and unique away.
(How all things flash! How all things flare!)
What am I now that I was then?
May memory restore again and again
The smallest color of the smallest day:
Time is the school in which we learn,
Time is the fire in which we burn.

V

Dogs are Shakespearean, children are strangers.
Let Freud and Wordsworth discuss the child,

Angels and Platonists shall judge the dog,
The running dog, who paused, distending nostrils,
Then barked and wailed; the boy who pinched his sister,
The little girl who sang the song from *Twelfth Night*,
As if she understood the wind and rain,
The dog who moaned, hearing the violins in concert.
—O I am sad when I see dogs or children!
For they are strangers, they are Shakespearean.

Tell us, Freud, can it be that lovely children
Have merely ugly dreams of natural functions?
And you, too, Wordsworth, are children truly
Clouded with glory, learnéd in dark Nature?
The dog in humble inquiry along the ground,
The child who credits dreams and fears the dark,
Know more and less than you: they know full well
Nor dream nor childhood answer questions well:
You too are strangers, children are Shakespearean.

Regard the child, regard the animal,
Welcome strangers, but study daily things,
Knowing that heaven and hell surround us,
But this, this which we say before we're sorry,
This which we live behind our unseen faces,
Is neither dream, nor childhood, neither
Myth, nor landscape, final, nor finished,
For we are incomplete and know no future,
And we are howling or dancing out our souls
In beating syllables before the curtain:
We are Shakespearean, we are strangers.

VI

"As in water face answereth to face, so the heart of man to man."

Do they whisper behind my back? Do they speak
Of my clumsiness? Do they laugh at me,
Mimicking my gestures, retailing my shame?

I'll whirl about, denounce them, saying
That they are shameless, they are treacherous,
No more my friends, nor will I once again
Never, amid a thousand meetings in the street,
Recognize their faces, take their hands,
Not for our common love or old times' sake:
They whispered behind my back, they mimicked me.

I know the reason why, I too have done this,
Cruel for wit's sake, behind my dear friend's back,
And to amuse betrayed his private love,
His nervous shame, her habit, and their weaknesses;
I have mimicked them, I have been treacherous,
For wit's sake, to amuse, because their being weighed
Too grossly for a time, to be superior,
To flatter the listeners by this, the intimate,
Betraying the intimate, but for the intimate,
To free myself of friendship's necessity,
Fearing from time to time that they would hear,
Denounce me and reject me, say once for all
That they would never meet me, take my hands,
Speaking for old times' sake and our common love.

What an unheard-of thing it is, in fine,
To love another and equally be loved!
What sadness and what joy! How cruel it is
That pride and wit distort the heart of man,
How vain, how sad, what cruelty, what need,
For this is true and sad, that I need them
And they need me. What can we do? We need
Each other's clumsiness, each other's wit,
Each other's company and our own pride. I need
My face unshamed, I need my wit, I cannot
Denounce them once for all, they cannot
Turn away. We know our clumsiness,
Our weakness, our necessities, we cannot
Forget our pride, our faces, our common love.

THE COLLECTED POEMS OF DELMORE SCHWARTZ

VII

I am to my own heart merely a serf
And follow humbly as it glides with autos
And come attentive when it is too sick,
In the bad cold of sorrow much too weak,
To drink some coffee, light a cigarette
And think of summer beaches, blue and gay.
I climb the sides of buildings just to get
Merely a gob of gum, all that is left
Of its infatuation of last year.
Being the servant of incredible assumption,
Being to my own heart merely a serf.

I have been sick of its cruel rule, as sick
As one is sick of chewing gum all day;
Only inside of sleep did all my anger
Spend itself, restore me to my rôle,
Comfort me, bring me to the morning
Willing and smiling, ready to be of service,
To box its shadows, lead its brutish dogs,
Knowing its vanity the vanity of waves.

But when sleep too is crowded, when sleep too
Is full of chores impossible and heavy,
The looking for white doors whose numbers are
Different and equal, that is, infinite,
The carriage of my father on my back,
Last summer, 1910, and my own people,
The government of love's great polity,
The choice of taxes, the production
Of clocks, of lights and horses, the location
Of monuments, of hotels and of rhyme,
Then, then, in final anger, I wake up!
Merely wake up once more,
                                          once more to resume
The unfed hope, the unfed animal,
Being the servant of incredible assumption,
Being to my own heart merely a serf.

VIII

Abraham and Orpheus, be with me now:
You saw your love's face abstract, the weak-kneed stilts,
You saw and knew, and knew how near "no more,"
(As one who scrutinizes mystery, the air,)
How poised on nothing, weighted on the air,
The touched, seen substance, the substance of care:
Surround me, be round me, be with me like the air,
Abraham and Orpheus, be with me now.

Love love exhausts and time goes round and round,
Time circles in its idiot defeat,
And that which circles falls, falls endlessly,
Falls endlessly, no music shapes the air
Which did, can, shall restore the end of care,
For love exhausts itself and time goes round,
I shudder in the traffic, buildings stand,
Will fall and night will fall, the electric light be snapped
To spread its yellow genius on the floor,
And you knew too who knew and knew "no more"
That love exhausts itself and falls and time goes round.

Abraham and Orpheus, be with me now:
No longer the grandstand, nor the balcony,
Nor the formal window gives me cool perspective:
Love sucked me to the moving street below,
I see the price of care, turning to keep,
I am a price, I turn to keep, I care,
But time which circles dissipates all care,
As you knew too, who lifted up the knife,
And you, musician in the after-life,
Drowning in the shadow all love always bears,
As every solid thing must shadow in the light:
I ask your learnéd presence, I care and fear,
Abraham and Orpheus, be near, be near.

IX

"the withness of the body"
—WHITEHEAD

The heavy bear who goes with me,
A manifold honey to smear his face,
Clumsy and lumbering here and there,
The central ton of every place,
The hungry beating brutish one
In love with candy, anger, and sleep,
Crazy factotum, dishevelling all,
Climbs the building, kicks the football,
Boxes his brother in the hate-ridden city.

Breathing at my side, that heavy animal,
That heavy bear who sleeps with me,
Howls in his sleep for a world of sugar,
A sweetness intimate as the water's clasp,
Howls in his sleep because the tight-rope
Trembles and shows the darkness beneath.
—The strutting show-off is terrified,
Dressed in his dress-suit, bulging his pants,
Trembles to think that his quivering meat
Must finally wince to nothing at all.

That inescapable animal walks with me,
Has followed me since the black womb held,
Moves where I move, distorting my gesture,
A caricature, a swollen shadow,
A stupid clown of the spirit's motive,
Perplexes and affronts with his own darkness,
The secret life of belly and bone,
Opaque, too near, my private, yet unknown,
Stretches to embrace the very dear
With whom I would walk without him near,
Touches her grossly, although a word
Would bare my heart and make me clear,

Stumbles, flounders, and strives to be fed
Dragging me with him in his mouthing care,
Amid the hundred million of his kind,
The scrimmage of appetite everywhere.

X

A dog named Ego, the snowflakes as kisses
Fluttered, ran, came with me in December,
Snuffing the chill air, changing, and halting,
There where I walked toward seven o'clock,
Sniffed at some interests hidden and open,
Whirled, descending, and stood still, attentive,
Seeking their peace, the stranger, unknown,
With me, near me, kissed me, touched my wound,
My simple face, obsessed and pleasure bound.

"Not free, no liberty, rock that you carry,"
So spoke Ego in his cracked and harsh voice,
While snowflakes kissed me and satisfied minutes,
Falling from some place half believed and unknown,
"You will not be free, nor ever alone,"
So spoke Ego, "Mine is the kingdom,
Dynasty's bone: you will not be free,
Go, choose, run, you will not be alone."

"Come, come, come," sang the whirling snowflakes,
Evading the dog who barked at their smallness,
"Come!" sang the snowflakes, "Come here! and here!"
How soon at the sidewalk, melted, and done,
One kissed me, two kissed me! So many died!
While Ego barked at them, swallowed their touch,
Ran this way! And that way! While they slipped to the ground,
Leading him further and farther away,
While night collapsed amid the falling,
And left me no recourse, far from my home,
And left me no recourse, far from my home.

XI

My heart beating, my blood running,
The light brimming,
My mind moving, the ground turning,
My eyes blinking, the air flowing,
The clock's quick-ticking,
Time moving, time dying,
Time perpetually perishing!
Time is farewell! Time is farewell!

Abide with me: do not go away,
But not as the dead who do not walk,
And not as the statue in the park,
And not as the rock which meets the wave,
But quit the dance from which is flowing
Wishes and turns, gestures and voices,
Angry desire and fallen tomorrow,
Quit the dance from which is flowing
Your blood and beauty: stand still with me.

We cannot stand still: time is dying,
We are dying: Time is farewell!

Stay, then, stay! Wait now for me,
Deliberately, with care and circumspection,
Deliberately
Stop.
When we are in step, running together,
Our pace equal, our motion one,
Then we will be well, parallel and equal,
Running together down the macadam road,
Walking together,
Controlling our pace before we get old,
Walking together on the receding road,
Like Chaplin and his orphan sister,
Moving together through time to all good.

Twenty-four Poems

Prothalamion

"little soul, little flirting,
  little perverse one
    where are you off to now?
  little wan one, firm one
    little exposed one . . .
      and never make fun of me again."

Now I must betray myself.
The feast of bondage and unity is near,
And none engaged in that great piety
When each bows to the other, kneels, and takes
Hand and hand, glance and glance, care and care,
None may wear masks or enigmatic clothes,
For weakness blinds the wounded face enough.
In this sense, see my shocking nakedness.

I gave a girl an apple when five years old,
Saying, Will you be sorry when I am gone?
Ravenous for such courtesies, my name
Is fed like a raving fire, insatiate still.
But do not be afraid.
For I forget myself. I do indeed
Before each genuine beauty, and I will
Forget myself before your unknown heart.

I will forget the speech my mother made
In a restaurant, trapping my father there
At dinner with his whore. Her spoken rage
Struck down the child of seven years
With shame for all three, with pity for
The helpless harried waiter, with anger for
The diners gazing, avid, and contempt,

And great disgust for every human being.
I will remember this. My mother's rhetoric
Has charmed my various tongue, but now I know
Love's metric seeks a rhyme more pure and sure.

For thus it is that I betray myself,
Passing the terror of childhood at second hand
Through nervous, learnéd fingertips.
At thirteen when a little girl died,
I walked for three weeks neither alive nor dead,
And could not understand and still cannot
The adult blind to the nearness of the dead,
Or carefully ignorant of their own death.
—This sense could shadow all time's curving fruits,
But we will taste of them the whole night long,
Forgetting no twelfth night, no fête of June,
But in the daylight knowing our nothingness.

Let Freud and Marx be wedding guests indeed!
Let them mark out the masks that face us there,
For of all anguish, weakness, loss and failure,
No form is cruel as self-deception, none
Shows day-by-day a bad dream long lived
And unbroken like the lies
We tell each other because we'are rich or poor.
Though from the general guilt not free
We can keep honor by being poor.

The waste, the evil, the abomination
Is interrupted. The perfect stars persist
Small in the guilty night,
                        and Mozart shows
The irreducible incorruptible good
Risen past birth and death, though he is dead.
Hope, like a face reflected on the windowpane,
Remote and dim, fosters a myth or dream,
And in that dream, I speak, I summon all
Who are our friends somehow and thus I say:

"Bid the jewellers come with monocles,
Exclaiming, Pure! Intrinsic! Final!
Summon the children eating ice cream
To speak the chill thrill of immediacy.
Call for the acrobats who tumble
The ecstasy of the somersault.
Bid the self-sufficient stars be piercing
In the sublime and inexhaustible blue.

"Bring a mathematician, there is much to count,
The unending continuum of my attention:
Infinity will hurry his multiplied voice!
Bring the poised impeccable diver,
Summon the skater, precise in figure,
He knows the peril of circumstance,
The risk of movement and the hard ground.
Summon the florist! And the tobacconist!
All who have known a plant-like beauty:
Summon the charming bird for ignorant song.

"You, Athena, with your tired beauty,
Will you give me away? For you must come
In a bathing suit with that white owl
Whom, as I walk, will hold in my hand.
You too, Crusoe, to utter the emotion
Of finding Friday, no longer alone;
You too, Chaplin, muse of the curbstone,
Mummer of hope, you understand!"

But this is fantastic and pitiful,
And no one comes, none will, we are alone,
And what is possible is my own voice,
Speaking its wish, despite its lasting fear;
Speaking its hope, its promise and its fear
The voice drunk with itself and rapt in fear,
Exaggeration, braggadocio,
Rhetoric and hope, and always fear:

"For fifty-six or for a thousand years,
I will live with you and be your friend,
And what your body and what your spirit bears
I will like my own body cure and tend.
But you are heavy and my body's weight
Is great and heavy: when I carry you
I lift upon my back time like a fate
Near as my heart, dark when I marry you.

"The voice's promise is easy, and hope
Is drunk, and wanton, and unwilled;
In time's quicksilver, where our desires grope,
The dream is warped or monstrously fulfilled.
In this sense, listen, listen, and draw near:
Love is inexhaustible and full of fear."

This life is endless and my eyes are tired,
So that, again and again, I touch a chair,
Or go to the window, press my face
Against it, hoping with substantial touch,
Colorful sight, or turning things to gain once more
The look of actuality, the certainty
Of those who run down stairs and drive a car.
Then let us be each other's truth, let us
Affirm the other's self, and be
The other's audience, the other's state,
Each to the other his sonorous fame.

Now you will be afraid, when, waking up,
Before familiar morning, by my mute side
Wan and abandoned then, when, waking up,
You see the lion or lamb upon my face
Or see the daemon breathing heavily
His sense of ignorance, his wish to die,
For I am nothing because my circus self
Divides its love a million times.

I am the octopus in love with God,
For thus is my desire inconclusible,

Until my mind, deranged in swimming tubes,
Issues its own darkness, clutching seas,
—O God of my perfect ignorance,
Bring the New Year to my only sister soon,
Take from me strength and power to bless her head,
Give her the magnitude of secular trust,
Until she turns to me in her troubled sleep,
Seeing me in my wish, free from self-wrongs.

Father and Son

> "From a certain point onward there is no longer any turning back. That is the
> point that must be reached."
> —FRANZ KAFKA

Father:
On these occasions, the feelings surprise,
Spontaneous as rain, and they compel
Explicitness, embarrassed eyes—

Son:
Father, you're not Polonius, you're reticent,
But sure. I can already tell
The unction and falsetto of the sentiment
Which gratifies the facile mouth, but springs
From no felt, had, and wholly known things.

Father:
You must let me tell you what you fear
When you wake up from sleep, still drunk with sleep:
You are afraid of time and its slow drip,
Like melting ice, like smoke upon the air
In February's glittering sunny day.
Your guilt is nameless, because its name is time,
Because its name is death. But you can stop
Time as it dribbles from you, drop by drop.

Son:
But I thought time was full of promises,
Even as now, the emotion of going away—

Father:
That is the first of all its menaces,
The lure of a future different from today;
All of us always are turning away
To the cinema and Asia. All of us go
To one indeterminate nothing.

Son:

                    Must it be so?
I question the sentiment you give to me,
As premature, not to be given, learned alone
When experience shrinks upon the chilling bone.
I would be sudden now and rash in joy,
As if I lived forever, the future my toy.
Time is a dancing fire at twenty-one,
Singing and shouting and drinking to the sun,
Powerful at the wheel of a motor-car,
Not thinking of death which is foreign and far.

Father:
If time flowed from your will and were a feast
I would be wrong to question your zest.
But each age betrays the same weak shape.
Each moment is dying. You will try to escape
From melting time and your dissipating soul
By hiding your head in a warm and dark hole.
See the evasions which so many don,
To flee the guilt of time they become one,
That is, the one number among masses,
The one anonymous in the audience,
The one expressionless in the subway,
In the subway evening among so many faces,
The one who reads the daily newspaper,

Separate from actor and act, a member
Of public opinion, never involved.
Integrated in the revery of a fine cigar,
Fleeing to childhood at the symphony concert,
Buying sleep at the drugstore, grandeur
At the band concert, Hawaii
On the screen, and everywhere a specious splendor:
One, when he is sad, has something to eat,
An ice cream soda, a toasted sandwich,
Or has his teeth fixed, but can always retreat
From the actual pain, and dream of the rich.
This is what one does, what one becomes
Because one is afraid to be alone,
Each with his own death in the lonely room.
But there is a stay. You can stop
Time as it dribbles from you, drop by drop.

Son:
Now I am afraid. What is there to be known?

Father:
Guilt, guilt of time, nameless guilt.
Grasp firmly your fear, thus grasping your self,
Your actual will. Stand in mastery,
Keeping time in you, its terrifying mystery.
Face yourself, constantly go back
To what you were, your own history.
You are always in debt. Do not forget
The dream postponed which would not quickly get
Pleasure immediate as drink, but takes
The travail of building, patience with means.
See the wart on your face and on your friend's face,
On your friend's face and indeed on your own face.
The loveliest woman sweats, the animal stains
The ideal which is with us like the sky . . .

Son:
Because of that, some laugh, and others cry.

Father:
Do not look past and turn away your face.
You cannot depart and take another name,
Nor go to sleep with lies. Always the same,
Always the same self from the ashes of sleep
Returns with its memories, always, always,
The phoenix with eight hundred thousand memories!

Son:
What must I do that is most difficult?

Father:
You must meet your death face to face,
You must, like one in an old play,
Decide, once for all, your heart's place.
Love, power, and fame stand on an absolute
Under the formless night and the brilliant day,
The searching violin, the piercing flute.
Absolute! Venus and Caesar fade at that edge,
Hanging from the fiftieth story ledge,
Or diminished in bed when the nurse presses
Her sickening unguents and her cold compresses.
When the news is certain, surpassing fear,
You touch the wound, the priceless, the most dear.
There in death's shadow, you comprehend
The irreducible wish, world without end.

Son:
I begin to understand the reason for evasion,
I cannot partake of your difficult vision.

Father:
Begin to understand the first decision.
Hamlet is the example; only dying
Did he take up his manhood, the dead's burden,
Done with evasion, done with sighing,
Done with revery.
                        Decide that you are dying

Because time is in you, ineluctable
As shadow, named by no syllable.
Act in that shadow, as if death were now:
Your own self acts then, then you know.

Son:
My father has taught me to be serious.

Father:
Be guilty of yourself in the full looking-glass.

The Ballad of the Children of the Czar

I

The children of the Czar
Played with a bouncing ball

In the May morning, in the Czar's garden,
Tossing it back and forth.

It fell among the flowerbeds
Or fled to the north gate.

A daylight moon hung up
In the Western sky, bald white.

Like Papa's face, said Sister,
Hurling the white ball forth.

II

While I ate a baked potato
Six thousand miles apart,

In Brooklyn, in 1916,
Aged two, irrational.

When Franklin D. Roosevelt
Was an Arrow Collar Ad.

O Nicholas! Alas! Alas!
My grandfather coughed in your army,

Hid in a wine-stinking barrel,
For three days in Bucharest

Then left for America
To become a king himself.

III

I am my father's father,
You are your children's guilt.

In history's pity and terror
The child is Aeneas again;

Troy is in the nursery,
The rocking horse is on fire.

Child labor! The child must carry
His fathers on his back.

But seeing that so much is past
And that history has no ruth

For the individual,
Who drinks tea, who catches cold,

Let anger be general:
I hate an abstract thing.

IV

Brother and sister bounced
The bounding, unbroken ball,

The shattering sun fell down
Like swords upon their play,

Moving eastward among the stars
Toward February and October.

But the Maywind brushed their cheeks
Like a mother watching sleep,

And if for a moment they fight
Over the bouncing ball

And sister pinches brother
And brother kicks her shins,

Well! The heart of a man is known:
It is a cactus bloom.

V

The ground on which the ball bounces
Is another bouncing ball.

The wheeling, whirling world
Makes no will glad.

Spinning in its spotlight darkness,
It is too big for their hands.

O pitiless, purposeless Thing,
Arbitrary and unspent,

Made for no play, for no children,
But chasing only itself.

The innocent are overtaken,
They are not innocent.

They are their father's fathers,
The past is inevitable.

VI

Now, in another October
Of this tragic star,

I see my second year,
I eat my baked potato.

It is my buttered world,
But, poked by my unlearned hand,

It falls from the high chair down
And I begin to howl.

And I see the ball roll under
The iron gate which is locked.

Sister is screaming, brother is howling,
The ball has evaded their will.

Even a bouncing ball
Is uncontrollable,

And is under the garden wall.
I am overtaken by terror

Thinking of my father's fathers,
And of my own will.

Far Rockaway

"the cure of souls."
—HENRY JAMES

The radiant soda of the seashore fashions
Fun, foam, and freedom. The sea laves
The shaven sand. And the light sways forward
On the self-destroying waves.

The rigor of the weekday is cast aside with shoes,
With business suits and the traffic's motion;
The lolling man lies with the passionate sun,
Or is drunken in the ocean.

A socialist health takes hold of the adult,
He is stripped of his class in the bathing suit,
He returns to the children digging at summer,
A melon-like fruit.

O glittering and rocking and bursting and blue,
—Eternities of sea and sky shadow no pleasure:
Time unheard moves and the heart of man is eaten
Consummately at leisure.

The novelist tangential on the boardwalk overhead
Seeks his cure of souls in his own anxious gaze.
"Here," he says, "With whom?" he asks, "This?" he questions,
"What tedium, what blaze?"

"What satisfaction, fruit? What transit, heaven?
Criminal? justified? arrived at what June?"
That nervous conscience amid the concessions
Is a haunting, haunted moon.

Socrates' Ghost Must Haunt Me Now

Socrates' ghost must haunt me now,
Notorious death has let him go,
He comes to me with a clumsy bow,
Saying in his disuséd voice,
That I do not know I do not know,
The mechanical whims of appetite
Are all that I have of conscious choice,
The butterfly caged in electric light
Is my only day in the world's great night,
Love is not love, it is a child
Sucking his thumb and biting his lip,
But grasp it all, there may be more!
From the topless sky to the bottomless floor
With the heavy head and the fingertip:
All is not blind, obscene, and poor.
Socrates stands by me stock-still,
Teaching hope to my flickering will,
Pointing to the sky's inexorable blue
—Old Noumenon, come true, come true!

For the One Who Would Not Take His Life in His Hands

Athlete, virtuoso,
Training for happiness,
Bend arm and knee, and seek
The body's sharp distress,
For pain is pleasure's cost,
Denial is the route
To speech before the millions
Or personal with the flute.

The ape and great Achilles,
Heavy with their fate,

Batter doors down, strike
Small children at the gate,
Driven by love to this,
As knock-kneed Hegel said,
To seek with a sword their peace,
That the child may be taken away
From the hurly-burly and fed.

Ladies and Gentlemen, said
The curious Socrates,
I have asked, What is this life
But a childermass,
As Abraham recognized,
A working with the knife
At animal, maid and stone
Until we have cut down
All but the soul alone:
Through hate we guard our love,
And its distinction's known.

For the One Who Would Take Man's Life in His Hands

Tiger Christ unsheathed his sword,
Threw it down, became a lamb.
Swift spat upon the species, but
Took two women to his heart.
Samson who was strong as death
Paid his strength to kiss a slut.
Othello that stiff warrior
Was broken by a woman's heart.
Troy burned for a sea-tax, also for
Possession of a charming whore.
What do all examples show?
What must the finished murder know?

You cannot sit on bayonets,
Nor can you eat among the dead.
When all are killed, you are alone,
A vacuum comes where hate has fed.
Murder's fruit is silent stone,
The gun increases poverty.
With what do these examples shine?
The soldier turned to girls and wine.
Love is the tact of every good,
The only warmth, the only peace.

"What have I said?" asked Socrates,
"Affirmed extremes, cried yes or no,
Taken all parts, denied myself,
Praised the caress, extolled the blow,
Soldier and lover quite deranged
Until their motions are exchanged.
—What do all examples show?
What can any actor know?
The contradiction in every act,
The infinite task of the human heart."

Saint, Revolutionist

Saint, revolutionist,
God and sage know well,
That there is a place
Where that much-rung bell,
The well-beloved body,
And its sensitive face
Must be sacrificed.

There is, it seems, in this
A something meaningless,
Hanging without support

And yet too dear to touch,
That life should seek its end
Where no will can descend,
Facing a gun to see
Long actuality.

What is this that is
The good of nothingness,
The death of Socrates
And that strange man on the cross
Seeking out all loss?
For men love life until
It shames both face and will.

Neither in hell nor heaven
Is the answer given,
Both are a servant's pay:
But they wish to know
How far the will can go,
Lest their infinite play
And their desires be
Shadow and mockery.

O Love, Sweet Animal

O Love, sweet animal,
With your strangeness go
Like any freak or clown,
Bemuse the child in her
Because she is alone,
Many years ago
Frightened by a look.
Brush your heavy fur
Against her, long and slow,
Stare at her like a book,

Her interests being such
No one can look too much.
Tell her that you know
Everything is given
As soon as it is taken,
For you is time forgiven:
Informed by hell and heaven,
You are not mistaken.

By Circumstances Fed

By circumstances fed
Which divide attention
Among so many dead,
Even in the blooming sun,
For this is not ended,
Never having begun,
And this is attended
By a fire-like power,
Converting every feature
Into its own nature,
As, once in the drugstore,
Between the salves and ointments
I suddenly saw, so strange there,
Amid the sand and soda,
Rich in all appointments,
My own face in the mirror.

What Is to Be Given

What is to be given,
Is spirit, yet animal,

Colored, like heaven,
Blue, yellow, beautiful.

The blood is checkered by
So many stains and wishes,
Between it and the sky
You could not choose, for riches.

Yet let me now be careful
Not to give too much
To one so shy and fearful
For like a gun is touch.

A Young Child and His Pregnant Mother

At four years Nature is mountainous,
Mysterious, and submarine. Even

A city child known this, hearing the subway's
Rumor underground. Between the grate,

Dropping his penny, he learned out all loss,
The irretrievable cent of fate,

And now this newest of the mysteries,
Confronts his honest and his studious eyes—

His mother much too fat and absentminded,
Gazing far past his face, careless of him,

His fume, his charm, his bedtime, and warm milk,
As soon the night will be too dark, the spring

Too late, desire strange, and time too fast,
This first estrangement is a gradual thing,

(His mother once so svelte, so often sick!
Towering father did this: what a trick!)

Explained too cautiously, containing fear,
Another being's being, becoming dear:

All men are enemies: thus even brothers
Can separate each other from their mothers!

No better example than this unborn brother
Shall teach him of his exile from his mother,

Measured by his distance from the sky,
Spoken in two vowels,
                              I am I.

Concerning the Synthetic Unity of Apperception

"Trash, trash!" the king my uncle said,
"The spirit's smoke and weak as smoke ascends.

"Sit in the sun and not among the dead,
"Eat oranges! Pish tosh! The car attends.

"All ghosts come back. They do not like it there,
"No silky water and no big brown bear,

"No bear and no siestas up above."
"Uncle," I said, "I'm lonely. What is love?"

This drove him quite insane. Now he must knit
Time with apperception, bit by tiny bit.

Faust in Old Age

"Poet and veteran of childhood, look!
See in me the obscene, for you have love,

For you have hatred, you, you must be judge,
Deliver judgment, Delmore Schwartz.

Well-known wishes have been to war.
The vicious mouth has chewed the vine.

The patient crab beneath the shirt
Has churned such interests as Indies meant.

For I have walked within and seen each sea,
The fish that flies, the broken burning bird,

Born again, beginning again, my breast!
Purple with persons like a tragic play.

For I have flown the cloud and fallen down,
Fucked Venus, sneering at her moan.

I took the train that takes away remorse;
I cast down every king like Socrates.

I knocked each nut to find the meat;
A worm was there and not a mint.

Metaphysicians could have told me this,
But each learns for himself, as in the kiss.

Polonius I poked, not him
To whom aspires spire and hymn,

Who succors children and the very poor;
I pierced the pompous Premier, not Jesus Christ,

I pricked Polonius, and Moby Dick,
The ego bloomed into an octopus.

Now come I to the exhausted West at last;
I know my vanity, my nothingness,

Now I float will-less in despair's dead sea,
Every man my enemy.

Spontaneous, I have too much to say,
And what I say will no one not old see:

"If we could love one another, it would be well.
But as it is, I am sorry for the whole world, myself
apart. My heart is full of memory and desire, and
in its last nervousness, there is pity for those I
have touched, but only hatred and contempt for
myself."

At This Moment of Time

Some who are uncertain compel me. They fear
The Ace of Spades. They fear
Love offered suddenly, turning from the mantelpiece,
Sweet with decision. And they distrust
The fireworks by the lakeside, first the spuft,
Then the colored lights, rising.
Tentative, hesitant, doubtful, they consume
Greedily Caesar at the prow returning,
Locked in the stone of his act and office.
While the brass band brightly bursts over the water
They stand in the crowd lining the shore
Aware of the water beneath Him. They know it. Their eyes
Are haunted by water.

Disturb me, compel me. It is not true
That "no man is happy," but that is not
The sense which guides you. If we are
Unfinished (we are, unless hope is a bad dream),
You are exact. You tug my sleeve
Before I speak, with a shadow's friendship,
And I remember that we who move
Are moved by clouds that darken midnight.

The Sin of Hamlet

The horns in the harbor booming, vaguely,
Fog, forgotten, yesterday, conclusion,
Nostalgic, noising dim sorrow, calling
To sleep is it? I think so, and childhood,
Not the door opened and the stair descended,
The voice answered, the choice announced, the
Trigger touched in sharp declaration!

And when it comes, escape is small; the door
Creaks; the worms of fear spread veins; the furtive
Fugitive, looking backward, sees his
Ghost in the mirror, his shameful eyes, his mouth diseased

Tired and Unhappy, You Think of Houses

Tired and unhappy, you think of houses
Soft-carpeted and warm in the December evening,
While snow's white pieces fall past the window,
And the orange firelight leaps.
                              A young girl sings
That song of Gluck where Orpheus pleads with Death;

Her elders watch, nodding their happiness
To see time fresh again in her self-conscious eyes:
The servants bring the coffee, the children retire,
Elder and younger yawn and go to bed,
The coals fade and glow, rose and ashen,
It is time to shake yourself! and break this
Banal dream, and turn your head
Where the underground is charged, where the weight
Of the lean buildings is seen,
Where close in the subway rush, anonymous
In the audience, well-dressed or mean,
So many surround you, ringing your fate,
Caught in an anger exact as a machine!

Parlez-Vous Francais?

Caesar, the amplifier voice, announces
Crime and reparation. In the barbershop
Recumbent men attend, while absently
The barber doffs the naked face with cream.
Caesar proposes, Caesar promises
Pride, justice, and the sun
Brilliant and strong on everyone,
Speeding one hundred miles an hour across the land:
Caesar declares the will. The barber firmly
Planes the stubble with a steady hand,
While all in barber chairs reclining,
In wet white faces, fully understand
Good and evil, who is Gentile, weakness and command.

And now who enters quietly? Who is this one
Shy, pale, and quite abstracted? Who is he?
It is the writer merely, with a three-day beard,
His tiredness not evident. He wears no tie.
And now he hears his enemy and trembles,

Resolving, speaks: "Ecoutez! La plupart des hommes
Vivent des vies de désespoir silent,
Victimes des intentions innombrables. Et ca
Cet homme sait bien. Les mots de cette voix sont
Des songes et des mensonges. Il prend la choix,
Il prend la volonté, il porte la fin d'été,
La guerre. Ecoutez-moi! Il porte la mort."
He stands there speaking and they laugh to hear
Rage and excitement from the foreigner.

In the Slight Ripple, the Fishes Dart

In the slight ripple, the fishes dart
Like fingers, centrifugal, like wishes
Wanton. And pleasures rise
                                as the eyes fall
Through the lucid water. The small pebble,
The clear clay bottom, the white shell
Are apparent, though superficial.
Who would ask more of the August afternoon?
Who would dig mines and follow shadows?
"I would," answers bored Heart, "Lounger, rise,"
(Underlip trembling, face white with stony anger)
"The old error, the thought of sitting still,
"The senses drinking, by the summer river,
"On the tended lawn, below the traffic,
"As if time would pause,
                            and afternoon stay.
"No, night comes soon,
"With its cold mountains, with desolation,
                                unless Love build its city."

In the Naked Bed, in Plato's Cave

In the naked bed, in Plato's cave,
Reflected headlights slowly slid the wall,
Carpenters hammered under the shaded window,
Wind troubled the window curtains all night long,
A fleet of trucks strained uphill, grinding,
Their freights covered, as usual.
The ceiling lightened again, the slanting diagram
Slid slowly forth.
                Hearing the milkman's chop,
His striving up the stair, the bottle's chink,
I rose from bed, lit a cigarette,
And walked to the window. The stony street
Displayed the stillness in which buildings stand,
The street-lamp's vigil and the horse's patience.
The winter sky's pure capital
Turned me back to bed with exhausted eyes.

Strangeness grew in the motionless air. The loose
Film grayed. Shaking wagons, hooves' waterfalls,
Sounded far off, increasing, louder and nearer.
A car coughed, starting. Morning, softly
Melting the air, lifted the half-covered chair
From underseas, kindled the looking-glass,
Distinguished the dresser and the white wall.
The bird called tentatively, whistled, called,
Bubbled and whistled, so! Perplexed, still wet
With sleep, affectionate, hungry and cold. So, so,
O son of man, the ignorant night, the travail
Of early morning, the mystery of beginning
Again and again,
                while History is unforgiven.

The Ballet of the Fifth Year

Where the sea gulls sleep or indeed where they fly
Is a place of different traffic. Although I
Consider the fishing bay (where I see them dip and curve
And purely glide) a place that weakens the nerve
Of will, and closes my eyes, as they should not be
(They should burn like the street-light all night quietly,
So that whatever is present will be known to me),
Nevertheless the gulls and the imagination
Of where they sleep, which comes to creation
In strict shape and color, from their dallying
Their wings slowly, and suddenly rallying
Over, up, down the arabesque of descent,
Is an old act enacted, my fabulous intent
When I skated, afraid of policemen, five years old,
In the winter sunset, sorrowful and cold,
Hardly attained to thought, but old enough to know
Such grace, so self-contained, was the best escape to know.

Sonnet: The Beautiful American Word, Sure

The beautiful American word, Sure,
As I have come into a room, and touch
The lamp's button, and the light blooms with such
Certainty where the darkness loomed before,

As I care for what I do not know, and care
Knowing for little she might not have been,
And for how little she would be unseen,
The intercourse of lives miraculous and dear.

Where the light is, and each thing clear,
Separate from all others, standing in its place,
I drink the time and touch whatever's near,

And hope for day when the whole world has that face:
For what assures her present every year?
In dark accidents the mind's sufficient grace.

Sonnet: The Ghosts of James and Peirce in Harvard Yard

for D. W. P.

The ghosts of James and Peirce in Harvard Yard
At star-pierced midnight, after the chapel bell
(Episcopalian! palian! tingled hard!)
Stare at me now as if they wished me well.
In the waking dream amid the trees which fall,
Bar and bough of shadow, by my shadow crossed,
They have not slept so long and they know all,
Both time's exhaustion and the spirit's cost.

"We studied the radiant sun, the star's pure seed:
Darkness is infinite! The blind can see
Hatred's necessity and love's grave need
Now that the poor are murdered across the sea,
And you are ignorant, who hear the bell;
Ignorant, you walk between heaven and hell."

Sonnet: O City, City

To live between terms, to live where death
Has his loud picture in the subway ride,
Being amid six million souls, their breath
An empty song suppressed on every side,
Where the sliding auto's catastrophe
Is a gust past the curb, where numb and high
The office building rises to its tyranny,
Is our anguished diminution until we die.

Whence, is ever, shall come the actuality
Of a voice speaking the mind's knowing,
The sunlight bright on the green windowshade,
And the self articulate, affectionate, and flowing,
Ease, warmth, light, the utter showing,
When in the white bed all things are made.

A Season in Hell

(1939)

BY ARTHUR RIMBAUD

Translated by Delmore Schwartz

A Season in Hell

Once, if I remember correctly, my life was a banquet at which all hearts opened, at which all wines flowed.

One evening I seated Beauty on my knees.—And I found her stale.—And I cursed her.

I armed myself against justice.

I fled. O magicians, O misery, O hatred, it is to you that my treasure has been entrusted.

I succeeded in making all human hope vanish from my mind. On every joy, in order to strangle it, I leaped with the soundless lunge of the ferocious beast.

I called the executioners that, while dying, I might bite the butt-ends of their guns. I called for scourges to choke me with blood, with sand. Misfortune has been my deity. I stretched myself out in the mud. I withered in the atmosphere of crime. And I played practical jokes on madness.

And spring brought me the appalling laugh of the idiot.

Well, quite recently, finding myself on the point of making the last *rattle*, I thought of seeking the key to the ancient banquet, at which I would perhaps regain my appetite.

Charity is that key.—This inspiration proves that I have dreamed!

"You shall remain a hyena . . ." etc., exclaims the demon who crowned me with such pleasant poppies. "Earn death with all your appetites, and your egoism, and all the mortal sins."

Ah! I have seized too much of that:—But, dear Satan, I implore you, a less petulant eye! and while awaiting the few unimportant transgressions which have been delayed, you who love in the author the absence of the descriptive and the didactic faculties, for you I detach these few hideous columns of my journal of the damned.

Bad Blood

I get from my Gallic ancestors the blue and white eye, the narrow skull, and the unskillfulness in war. I find my clothes as barbarous as theirs. But I do not butter my hair.

The Gauls were the most inept flayers of beasts and grass-burners of their time.

From them, I get: idolatry and the love of sacrilege; oh, all the vices, anger, luxury,—magnificent luxury;—above all, lying and indolence.

I detest professions. Bosses and workers: both peasants and ignoble. The pen in the hand is worth no more than the hand on the plough.—What a handling century!—I will never use my hands. Really, domesticity leads one too far. The honesty of begging rends my heart. Criminals are as disgusting as the castrated; as for me, I am intact, and it is just the same.

And yet! who made my tongue so perfidious that it has guided and safe-guarded my idleness. Without using my body for a thing, idler than the toad, I have lived everywhere. Not a family in Europe that I do not know.—I mean families like my own, which utterly adhere to the Declaration of the Rights of Man.—I have known every son of the house!

* * *

If I had ancestors at any point whatsoever in the history of France!

But no, none.

It is quite obvious to me that I have always been of an inferior race. I cannot understand revolt. My race never rose up except to plunder: like wolves on a beast whom they have not killed.

I call to mind the story of France, older daughter of the Church. I, clown, have made the voyage of holy earth; I have in my head routes of desert plains, views of Byzantium, ramparts of Solyma: the cult of Mary, the passion on the Cross waken in me a thousand fairy tales.—I, leprous, seated myself on broken pots and nettles, at the foot of a wall devoured by the sun.—Later, an old horseman, I would have camped under the nights of Germany.

Ah, more than that; I dance the witches' Sabbath in a red glade, with old women and with children.

I remember myself before this country, and before Christianity. I would not end by seeing myself once more in the past. But always alone; without family; why, what language did I speak? I never see myself at the Councils of Christ; nor at the councils of the Lords,—representatives of Christ.

Who was I during the last century? No more vagabonds, no more empty wars. The inferior race has covered everything—the populace, as we say, Reason, the Nation and Science.

Oh, Science! It has revised everything. For the body and for the soul,—the viaticum,—they have medicine and philosophy,—remedies of old wives and the popular songs rearranged! Geography, Cosmography, mechanics, chemistry!—

Science, the new nobility! Progress. The world advances! Why shouldn't it turn aside?

It is the vision of numbers. We are on our way to the *Spirit*. What I say is quite certain, it is an oracle. I understand, and not knowing how to explain myself without pagan words, I would like to be quiet.

★ ★ ★

Pagan blood returns! The Spirit is near; why doesn't Christ help me by giving my soul nobility and liberty. Alas, the Gospel has passed! The Gospel! The Gospel.

I wait for God like a gourmand. I am of a race inferior for all eternity.

Here I am on the Breton coast. How the cities light up in the evening. My day is done; I depart from Europe. The sea air will burn my lungs; the lost climates will tan me. To swim, to burn grass, to hunt, to smoke above all; to drink liquors strong as boiling steel,—as did those dear ancestors around their fires.

I will return with iron limbs, sombre skin, furious eye: because of my mask, they will suppose that I am of a strong race. I will have gold: I will be indolent and brutal. Women nurse the ferocious cripples returned from hot countries. I will mix in politics. Saved.

Now I am accursed, I detest my country. The best thing is a completely drunken sleep on a sandy beach.

★ ★ ★

There is no departure.—Let us take the ways of this place once more, bursting with my vice, the vice which has pushed its roots of suffering into my side since the age of reason,—which mounts to the sky, bests me, turns me about, drags me along.

The last innocence and the last timidity. It has been said. Not to carry to the world my disgusts and my treasons.

Let us go! The march, the burden, the desert, the boredom, and the anger.

To whom should I hire myself out? What beast must one adore? What holy image attack? What hearts shall I break? What lie must I maintain? In what blood must I walk?

Rather to keep oneself clear of the law.—A hard life, plain self-stultification,—to life, with dry fist, the lid of the coffin, to sit down, to suffocate. Thus, no old age at all, no dangers; terror is not French.

Ah, I am so forsaken that I offer to no matter what divine image my impulses toward perfection.

O my abnegation, my marvelous charity! down here, however!

De profundis, Domine, what a fool I am!

* * *

Still utterly a child, I admired the intractable convict on whom the prison shut, forever; I visited the inns and the lodging-houses which he would have made accursed by his stay; I used to see *with his idea* the blue sky and the blooming labor of the countryside. He had more strength than a saint, more common sense than a traveller,—and he, he alone! as witness of his glory, and his intellect.

On the roads, through winter nights, without resting-place, without clothes, without bread, a voice clutched my froze heart: "Weakness or strength: there you are, this is strength. You know neither where you go, nor why you go; enter everywhere, respond to everyone. They will not kill you any more than if you were a corpse." In the morning I had such a lost look, and such a dead face, that those whom I met *perhaps did not see me*.

In the cities the mud suddenly seemed to me red and black, like a mirror when the lamp glows in the next room, like a treasure in the forest! Good luck, I cried, and I saw a sea of flames and smoke in the sky; and right and left all wealth blazing like a million million lightnings!

But debauchery and the companionship of women were forbidden to me. Not even a friend. I saw myself before an angry crowd, faced by a cordon of executioners, weeping at their inability to understand, and forgiving them!—Like Joan of Arc!—"Priests, Professors, masters, you are wrong in delivering me to justice. I have never been of these people; I have never been Christian; I am of the race which sings in torment; I do not understand the laws, I lack the moral sense, I am a brute: you are making a mistake."

Yes, my eyes are close to your light. I am a beast, a negro. But I can be saved. You are false negroes, you, maniacs, savages, misers. Merchant, you are a negro; magistrate, you are a negro; Emperor, old itch, you are a negro; you have drunk an untaxed liquor, of Satan's making.—This people is inspired by fever and cancer. Cripples and old men are so respectable they ask to be boiled.—The most malicious urge is to leave this continent, where folly roves to supply these miserable ones with hostages. I am going to the true kingdom of the children of Ham.

Do I still know nature? do I know myself?—*No more words*. I bury the dead in my belly. Cries, tambour, dance, dance, dance, dance! I do not even foresee the hour when the white men will land and I shall fall to nothingness.

Hunger, thirst, outcries, dance, dance, dance!

* * *

The white men land. The cannon! One must submit oneself to baptism, dress oneself, work.

I received the mortal wound in the heart. Ah, I did not foresee it.

I have never done evil! The days are going to be easy for me, I shall be spared repentance. I shall not endure the tortures of a soul almost dead to virtue, in whom the severe light comes back to life like funeral candles. The lot of the son of the house, a premature coffin covered with limpid tears. Doubtless debauchery is stupid; vice is stupid; filth must be cast aside. But the clock will no longer arrive at the point of striking any hour but that of pure woe. Am I going to be carried off like a child to play in paradise, forgetful of all unhappiness?

Quick! Are there other lives? The sleep of the wealthy is impossible. Wealth has always been very public. Divine love alone can provide the keys of knowledge. I see that nature is nothing but a display of goodness. Farewell, chimeras, ideals, errors!

The reasonable hymn of the angels rises from the ship of salvation: it is divine love.—Two loves! I can die of earthly love, die of devoutness. I have left souls behind whose grief will grow at my departure. You choose me from among the shipwrecked: those who remain, are they not my friends?

Save them!

Reason is born in me. The world is good. I will bless life. I will love my brothers. These are no longer childish promises. Nor the hope of escaping old age and death. God is my strength, and I will praise God.

* * *

I am no longer in love with boredom. Rage, debauchery, folly,—whose every impulse and disaster I know—the whole of my burden is laid aside. Let us consider without becoming faint the extent of my innocence.

I should no longer be able to ask for the solace of a bastinado. I do not fancy myself embarked on a wedding with Jesus Christ for my father-in-law.

I am not the prisoner of my reason. I have said: God. I want freedom in salvation: how am I to seek it? Frivolous inclinations have left me. No more need of devotion or of God's love. I do not regret the century of impressionable hearts. Everyone to his own reason, contempt and charity: I retain my place at the top of this angelic ladder of good sense.

As for settled happiness, domestic or otherwise. . . . no, I am incapable of it. I am too dissipated, too weak. Life blooms through work, an old truism; my life is not heavy enough, it soars and floats high above action, that dear pivot of the world.

What an old maid I am becoming, lacking the courage to be in love with death!

If God granted the heavy aerial quietude of prayer,—like that of old saints.—The saints, strong men! The hermits, artists such as we have need of no longer!

A continual farce? My innocence would make me weep. Life is the farce which leads everywhere.

* * *

Enough! here is the punishment,—*March!*

Ah, my lungs burn, my temples roar! Night rolls through my eyes in this sunlight! Heart. . . . limbs. . . .

Where are we going? to battle? I am weak! The others advance. Tools—, weapons . . . time . . .

Fire, fire on me! There! or I surrender,—Cowards!—I kill myself! I throw myself under the horses' hooves!

Ah! . . . .

—I shall get used to it.

This would be the French life, the path of honor!

Night in Hell

I have swallowed a famous throatful of poison.—Thrice blest be the counsel that came to me!—My bowels burn. The shock of the poison twists my limbs, deforms me, throws me to earth. I am dying of thirst, I am suffocating, I cannot cry out. It is hell, the everlasting pain. See how the fire blazes up! I am burning in style. Away, demon!

I caught a glimpse of my conversion to virtue and happiness, my salvation. Can I describe the vision? the atmosphere of Hell does not permit hymns. There were millions of charming creatures, a bland concert of spirits, strength and peace, noble ambitions, I know not what else.

Noble ambitions!

And this is life still!—Suppose damnation were eternal! A man who wants to mutilate himself is quite damned, is he not? I believe that I am in hell, therefore I am. It is the catechism at work. I am the slave of my baptism. Parents, you contrived my misfortune, and your own. Poor innocent!—Hell cannot touch the heathen.

This is life still. Later the delights of my damnation will be more profound. A crime, quick, that I may fall into nothingness, in the name of human law.

Be quiet, there, be quiet! Shame and reproach, here: Satan who says the fire is mean, my rage appallingly out of place.—Enough! . . . Among errors they deplore in me, in particular, magic, false perfumes, childish tunes. And they tell me that I possess the truth, that I perceive justice: I have a sane, well-bridled judgment, I am ready for perfection . . . Pride.—My scalp is dried up. Pity! Lord, I am afraid. I am thirsty, so thirsty. Ah, childhood, the grass, the rain, the lake on the pebbles, *the full moon when the clock was striking twelve* . . . The devil is in the belfry at this hour. Mary! Holy Virgin! . . . Horror at my stupidity.

Out there, are there not honest souls, who wish me well? . . . Help . . . I have a pillow over my mouth, they do not hear me, they are phantoms. Besides, no one ever thinks of another. Let no one come near. I smell of seared flesh; there is no doubt of it.

The hallucinations are innumerable. Just what I have always had; no more faith in history, forgetfulness of principles. I will keep them to myself; poets and visionaries might be jealous. I am a thousand times the wealthiest; let us be avaricious like the sea.

Ah that! a moment ago the clock of life stopped. I am no longer in the world. Theology is serious, hell is certainly *down below*,—and heaven above.—Ecstasy, nightmare, sleep in a nest of flames.

What tricks of attention in the country . . . Satan, Ferdinand, runs with the wild grain . . . Jesus walks on the purple briers, without their bending. Jesus walked on the angry waters. The lantern showed him to us standing, white and with brown locks, on the flank of an emerald wave. . . .

I am going to unveil all the mysteries: mysteries of religion, or of nature, death, birth, future, past, cosmogony, non-existence. I am a master of phantasmagoria.

Listen! . . . .

I have every talent!—There is nobody here and there is somebody. I should not care to squander my treasure.—Does anyone want negro songs, houri dances? Does anyone want me to vanish, to plunge after the *ring*? Does one? I will make gold, remedies.

Trust in me then; faith assuages, guides, cures. All of you, come,—even little children, that I may console you, that his heart may be poured out for you like water,—the marvelous heart!—Poor human beings, toilers! I do not ask for prayers; with your faith alone I shall be happy.

—And think of me. This makes me hardly regret the world. I have a chance of not suffering any more. My life consisted of mild follies only, which I regret.

Bah! let us make all the grimaces imaginable!

Decidedly, we are out of the world. No longer any sound. The sense of touch has left me. Ah, my castle, my Saxony, my wood of willow trees. Evenings, mornings, nights, days . . . how tired I am!

I ought to have my hell for anger, my hell for pride,—and the hell of idleness; a concert of hells.

I am dying of lassitude. It is the grave, I am going to the worms, horror of horrors! Satan, you clown, you want to dissolve me, with your charms. I insist. I insist! A forkthrust, a drop of fire.

Ah, to climb back to life! To gaze at our deformities. And this poison, this kiss a thousand times accursed! My weakness, the cruelty of the world! My God, pity, hide me, I remain too evil—I am hidden, and not hidden.

It is the fire which wakes again with its damned.

Deliriums I

Foolish Virgin
The Infernal Bridegroom

Hear the confession of a companion in Hell:

"O heavenly Bridegroom, my Lord, do not reject the confession of the saddest of thy servants. I am lost. I am drunken. I am unclean. What an existence!

"Forgive me, heavenly Lord, forgive me! Ah! forgive me! What tears! And what tears again, later on, I hope.

THE COLLECTED POEMS OF DELMORE SCHWARTZ

"Later on I shall know the heavenly Bridegroom! I was born subject to him.—The other can beat me now!

"At present I am at the bottom of the world, O my friends! . . . no, not my friends. . . . never torture or delirium to equal these . . . How ridiculous!

"Ah, I suffer, I cry out. I suffer truly. Nevertheless all is allowed me, burdened with the contempt of the most contemptible hearts.

"Finally, let us make that avowal, free to repeat it twenty distinct times,—as sick, as insignificant!

"I am the slave of the infernal Bridegroom, he who has seduced all the foolish virgins. He is surely that demon. He is not a spectre, He is not a phantom. But I who have lost my mind, damned and dead to the world,—they will not kill me. How shall I describe him to you! I do not want to speak another word, not even one, anymore. I am in mourning. A little freshness, Lord, if you please, if you really please!

"I am a widow. . . . —I was a widow— . . . —why, yes, I was quite serious once, and I was not born to be a skeleton! . . . —He was almost a child . . . His mysterious courtesies seduced me. I forgot my whole human duty to follow him. What an existence! The true life is absent. We are not in the world. I will go where he goes, I must. And often he grows furious to me, *me, poor soul*. The Demon!—He is a demon, you know, *he is not a man*.

"He says: 'I do not like women: love must be reinvented, that is obvious. They want no more than a smug position. The position won, heart and beauty are put aside: there remains only cold disdain, the cuisine of marriage, at present. Or else I see women clearly marked for happiness, whom I myself could have made into good companions, devoured at first sight by brutes sensitive as blocks of wood . . .'

"I have listened to him making infamy glorious, cruelty charming. 'I am of a distant race: my fathers were Scandinavian: they pierced their sides and drank their blood.—I will make gashes all over my body, I will tattoo myself, I will become as hideous as a Mongol: you shall see me bellow in the street. I want to be insane with rage. Never show me jewels, I will grovel and convulse on the carpet. I would like to stain my riches with blood all over. I will never work . . .' Some nights, his demon seized me, we rolled on each other, I fought with him!—Often, at night, drunk, he roamed in the streets or in houses, in order to shock me mortally.—'They will surely cut my throat; that will be disgusting.' Oh! Those days when he wanted to walk with a criminal air!

"At times he spoke, in a tender lingo, of the death which made one repent, of the misfortunes which certainly exist, of painful labors, of departures which break the heart. In the hovels in which we got drunk, he wept, considering those who surrounded us, cattle of misery. He lifted up the drunkards in black avenues. He had the pity of an evil mother for her little children.—He departed with the graces of a little girl going to Sunday School.—He made believe that he was informed about everything, commerce, art, medicine.—I followed him, I had to.

"I saw all the adornment with which, in fancy, he decked himself; clothes, flags, furniture. I lent him arms, another face. I saw everything that touched him, as he would have wished it made to order for him. When he seemed to me to be of inert spirit, I followed him, myself, in strange and complicated actions, at a distance, good or bad: I was sure that I would never enter into his world. Beside his dear sleeping body, how many nights I watched, seeking to discover why he was so anxious to escape actuality. Never a man had such a vow. I recognized,—without fearing for him,—that he could be a serious danger to society.—Perhaps he had secrets with which *to change life*. No, he is only looking for them, I replied to myself. In a word, his charity is enchanted, and I am its prisoner. No other soul would have enough strength,—strength of despair!—to endure it, to be loved and protected by him. Besides, I cannot imagine him with another soul: one sees his Angel, never the Angel of another,—I believe. I was in his soul as in a palace which has been emptied so that we would not see anyone less noble than us: that is all. Alas! I depended upon him greatly. But what did he want with my colorless and cowardly existence? He did not make me better unless he made me die! Sadly mortified, I sometimes said to him:

"'I understand you,' He shrugged his shoulders.

"Thus my chagrin renewed itself ceaselessly, and finding myself quite altered in my own eyes,—as in the eyes of all who would have wished to watch me, if I had not been condemned forever to everyone's forgetfulness!—I hungered more and more for his kindness. With his kisses and his strange embraces, this was quite a heaven, a sombre heaven, which I entered, and in which I wanted to be left, poor, deaf, mute, blind. I was already getting used to it. I saw ourselves like two good children, free to promenade in the Paradise of melancholy. We were compatible. Much moved, we worked together. But, after a penetrating caress, he said: 'How this will seem droll to you, when I am no longer here, this which you have gone through. When you no longer have my arms around your neck, nor my heart on which to repose, nor this mouth upon your eyes. Because it is necessary that I go very far away one day. Then I must help others: it is my duty. Although it will scarcely be appetizing . . . dear heart . . .' suddenly I foresaw myself, when he had departed, the prey of vertigo, precipitated into the most frightful shadow: death. I made him promise that he would not abandon me. He made that lover's promise twenty times. It was as frivolous as was my saying to him:

"'I understand you.'

"Ah! I have never been jealous of him. He will never leave me, I believe. What will happen? He has no connections; he will never work. He wishes to live like a somnambulist. In themselves, would his kindness and his charity give him rights in the world as it is? Momently, I forget the pity into which I have fallen; it will make me more strong, we will travel, we will hunt in deserts, we will sleep on the pavements of unknown cities, without cares, without pains. Or I will awaken, and laws and customs will have changed,—thanks to his magic power; or the world, by remaining the same, will leave me to my desires, joys, nonchalances. Oh, the adventurous life existing in children's books, to repay me; I have suffered so much; who then will give it to me? He cannot. I am ignorant of his ideal. He has told me to have regrets, hopes; that should not concern me. Does he speak to God? Perhaps I should address God. I am in the very depths of the abyss, and I can no longer pray.

"If he explained his sadness to me, would I understand it any more than his mockery? He attacks me, he spends hours making me ashamed of everything which could have touched me in the world, and becomes indignant if I weep.

"—'See that elegant young man, entering a calm and beautiful house; His name is Duval, Dufour, Armand, Maurice, how should I know? A woman has devoted herself to loving this evil idiot; she is dead, she is certainly a saint in heaven, at present. You will make me die as he made that woman die. It is our fate, charitable hearts like us. . . .' Alas! there were days when all men in their actions seemed to him the playthings of grotesque deliriums; he laughed, appallingly, for a long time.—Then he resumed the ways of his mother, of his older sister. If he were less savage, we would be saved. I am subject to him. But his sweetness also is mortal.—Ah, how foolish I am!

"One day perhaps he will disappear marvelously; but I must know, if he should return to a heaven, so that I can see a little of the assumption of my little friend!"

Peculiar household!

Alchemy of the Word

About myself. The story of one of my follies.

For a long time I prided myself on possessing all possible landscapes, and found laughable the celebrities of modern painting and poetry.

I loved idiot paintings upon doors, decorations, backdrops of acrobats, signs, colored prints; old-fashioned literature, Church Latin, pornography without orthography, the novels of our ancestors, fairy tales, children's books, old operas, silly refrains, naïve rhythms.

I reviewed crusades, voyages of discovery of which there are no accounts, republics without history, suppressed religious wars, the revolutions of customs, the displacement of races and of continents: I believed in every magic.

I invented the color of vowels!—*A* black, *E* white, *I* red, *O* blue, *U* green.—I regulated the form and the movement of each consonant, and, with instinctive rhythms, I flattered myself with the thought that I had invented a poetic language, accessible, one day or another, to every sense. I reserved the rights of translation.

At first this was research. I wrote down silences, nights, I noted the inexpressible. I fixed vertigos.

* * *

Far from birds, from trumpets, from village girls,
What did I drink, kneeling upon that heath
Surrounded by soft woods of hazel trees,
In a mist of afternoon tepid and green?

What could I drink in that young Oise,
—Elms without voice, turf without flowers, sky overcast!—
Drink from those yellow gourds, far from the hut
Dear to me? Some liquor of gold which makes one sweat.

I made the ambiguous sign of an inn.
—A storm came, driving forward the sky. At night
The waters of the wood sank into virgin sands,
The wind of God cast icicles on pools;

Weeping, I saw the gold,—and could not drink.

⋆ ⋆ ⋆

At four o'clock in the morning, in summer,
The sleep of love continues still.
From under the groves arises.
      The evening's fragrance.

Down there, in their vast lumber-yard,
In the sun of the Hesperides,
Already swinging—in shirt-sleeves—
      The Carpenters.

In their Deserts of moss, tranquil,
They prepare the precious ceilings
        On which the city
    Will paint false heavens.

O, for these Workmen, charming
Subjects of a king of Babylon,
Venus! leave a moment the Lovers
      In whom the soul is crowned!

      O Queen of Shepherds,
    Bring to the laborers whiskey,
    That their powers may be steady
While waiting the bath in the sea at midday.

⋆ ⋆ ⋆

The old poetic tricks had an important part in my alchemy of the word.

I habituated myself to plain hallucination: I saw in all sincerity a mosque where a factory was, a school of drums played by angels, carriages on the avenues of the sky, a salon at the bottom of a lake; monsters, mysteries; a vaudeville ballad erected its terrors in front of me.

Then I explained my magic sophistries with the hallucination of words!

I finished by finding sacred the disorder of my spirit. I was slothful, the prey of a sluggish fever: I envied the happiness of beasts,—the caterpillars, who represented the innocence of limbs, the moles, the sleep of virginity!

My character became embittered. I said adieu to the world in romances
of a sort:

SONG OF THE HIGHEST TOWER

May it come, may it come,
The time when love astounds us.

I have kept so patient
That forever I forget.
Fears and sufferings
To the heavens have risen.
And the degenerate thirst
Darkens my veins.

May it come, may it come,
The time when love astounds us.
Like the meadow,
Left untended,

Overgrown, florid
With fragrance and rye,
Amid the harsh hum
Of dirty flies.

May it come, may it come,
The time when love astounds us.

I loved the desert, the burnt orchards, the second-hand shops, the tepid
drinks. I dragged myself into the stinking slums, and, eyes closed, offered
myself to the sun, god of fire.

"General, if you still have an old cannon on your ruined ramparts, bom-
bard us with hunks of dry earth. Fire on the window-glass of splendid
shops! on the salons! Make the city eat dust. Oxidate the gargoyles. Fill the
boudoirs with the powder of burning rubies . . ."

Oh! little fly drunk at the tavern urinal, enamoured of borage, which a
ray of light dissolves!

HUNGER

If I have any taste, it is hardly
For more than earth and stones.
I always breakfast on air,
On rock, on charcoal, on iron.

My hungers, turn. Pass, hungers,
    The field of sounds.
—Suck the vivid venom
    Of sour weeds.

Eat the stones someone breaks,
The old stones of churches;
The shingle of ancient floods,
Bread planted in the gray valleys.

* * *

The wolf cries under the leaves
Spitting out the fine feathers
Of his meal of poultry:
Like him I consume myself.

The salads, the fruits
Await only the gathering,
But the hedge spider
Eats only violets.

May I sleep! may I boil
At the altars of Solomon.
The broth brims over the rust,
And mingles with Kedron.

Finally, O happiness, O reason, I stripped the sky of blue, which is of darkness, and I lived as the gold spark of the radiance *nature*. From joy, I took an expression as comic and bewildered as possible:

* * *

It is recovered!
What? Eternity!
It is the sun in motion
    Upon the ocean.

My eternal soul,
Observe your vow
Through the night's solitude
And the day on fire.

Thus you free yourself
Of human supports,
Of vulgar transports!
You fly thus . . .

No hope ever,
No *orietur*.
Science and patience,
The torture is sure.

No more yesterday,
Embers of satin,
    Your ardor
    Is Order.

It is recovered!
—What?—Eternity.
It is the sun in motion
    Upon the ocean.

* * *

I became a fabulous opera: I saw that all beings have a fatality for happiness: action is not life, but a way of softening some power, an enervation. Mortality is the weakness of the skull.

    To each being, several *other* lives seemed to me to be due. This gentleman does not know what he is doing: he is an angel. This family is a litter of dogs. In front of some men, I spoke out loud with one moment of one of their other lives.—Thus I have loved a pig.

    None of the sophistries of madness,—madness which shuts one up inside oneself,—have been forgotten by me: I can relate them all, I possess the system.

My health was menaced. Terror came. I fell into a sleep lasting several days, and, waking, I continued the saddest dreams. I was ripe for death, and by a route of dangers my weakness led me to the ends of the world, to Kimmeria, the fatherland of shadow and of whirlwinds.

I had to travel, to distract the magics assembled in my skull. On the sea, which I loved as if it had cleansed me of defilement, I saw the consoling Cross arise. I had been damned by the rainbow. Happiness was my fatality, my remorse, my worm; my life would always be much too immense to be devoted to power and to beauty.

Happiness! Its tooth, sweet as death, warned me at cockcrow,—*ad matutinum*, at *Christus venit*,—in the most sombre cities:

★ ★ ★

O seasons, O castles!
What soul is faultless?

I have made the magic study
Of happiness, which none evades.

Hurrah for it each time
That the Gallic cock crows.

Ah! I shall have no more want:
It has taken charge of my life.

This charm has taken soul and flesh
And dispelled their struggles.

O seasons, O castles!

The hour of flight, alas!
Will be the hour of decease.

O seasons, O castles!

★ ★ ★

That is past. I know today how to greet beauty.

Ah, that life of my childhood, the grand avenue through all times, unnaturally solemn, more disinterested than the best of beggars, proud to have neither country nor friends, what nonsense it was.—And I see it only now!

—I was right to scorn those damned fools who would not miss a chance for a caress, parasites of the propriety and the health of our women, so that today such things are so disagreeable to us.

I was right in all my disdain: for I am running away from myself!

I run away from myself?

I will explain.

Yesterday again, I sighed: "Heavens! are not enough of us damned down here? Myself, I spent so much time already in their society! I know them all. We recognize ourselves always; we disgust ourselves. Charity is unknown to us. But we are polite; our relations with the world are very convenient." Is this astonishing? The world! The merchants, the simple fellows!—We are not dishonored.—But the elect, how do they receive us? For there are surly people and joyous, the false elect, for we need audacity or humility to approach them. They alone are elect. They are not benign!

Regaining two pennies of reason—which went quickly enough!—I see that my maladies come from my failure to understand soon enough that we are in the Occident. The occidental swamps! Not that I think the light altered, the form exhausted, the movement gone astray. . . . Good! Here my spirit desires absolutely to take upon itself with all the cruel developments which the spirit has undergone since the end of the Orient . . . My spirit itself demands this!

. . . My two cents of reason are gone!—The spirit is the authority, it desires that I be in the Occident. It should have been kept quiet in order to finish as I would have liked.

I sent the devil the palms of martyrs, the radiance of art, the pride of inventors, the ardor of pirates; I returned to the Orient, and the first and eternal wisdom.—It appears that this is a dream of gross indolence!

Yet, I hardly thought of the pleasure of escaping from modern sufferings. I had not in view the bastard wisdom of the Koran.—But is there not a real affliction in the fact that, since the declaration of Science, Christianity, man *plays*, proves his evidence, gorges himself in the pleasure of repeating the proofs, and lives only like that? A torture subtle and ridiculous; the source of my spiritual divagations. Nature could be bored with itself perhaps! M. Prudhomme is born with Christ.

Is it not because we cultivate fog? We eat fever with our watery vegetables. And drunkenness! and tobacco! and ignorance! and devotions!—Is all that far enough from the thought, from the wisdom of the Orient, the primitive country? Why a modern world, if such poisons are invented?

Churchmen will say: Why, of course. But you want to speak of Eden. Nothing for you in the history of Oriental peoples.—That's right; it is of Eden that I was thinking! What has Eden to do with my dream, that purity of ancient races!

The philosophers: The world has no age. Humanity shifts, simply that. You are in the Occident, but free to live in your Orient, as old a one as you need,—and live comfortable alone. Do not think yourself vanquished.

My spirit, take care. No violent partisanship for salvation. Exercise yourself!—Ah, science does not go quickly enough for us!

—But I perceive that my spirit sleeps.

If my spirit were wide-awake always from this moment on, we would soon arrive at truth, which perhaps surrounds us with weeping angels! . . —If my spirit had been awake up to this very moment, I would not have given in to degenerate instincts in an immemorial epoch! . . . —If my spirit had always been wide-awake, I would be sailing in full wisdom! . . .

O purity! O purity!

It is this minute of waking which has given me the vision of purity!—By the spirit one attains God!

Heart-rending misfortune!

The Lightning

Human toil! That is the explosion which lights up my abyss from time to time.

"Nothing is vanity; science, and forward!" cries the modern Ecclesiastes, that is to say, *Everybody*. And yet the cadavers of the wicked and slothful fall upon the hearts of the others. . . . . Ah, hurry, hurry a little; down there, beyond the night, those rewards, future, everlasting . . . shall they escape us? . . . .

—What can I do? I know toil; and science is too slow. Let prayers gallop and let the light roar . . . I see it clearly. It is too simple, and the weather will be too warm; they will pass me by. I have my duty, I shall show my pride in it as some others do, by putting it aside.

My life is worn out. Come! Let us make believe, let us idle, O pity! And we shall exist by our own amusement, dreaming of monstrous loves, and fantastic universes, complaining and finding fault with the appearances of the world, acrobat, beggar, artist, bandit,—priest! On my bed in the hospital, the smell of incense has returned to me so strongly: Guardian of the holy perfumes, confessor, martyr . . .

There I recognize the filthy education of my childhood. Then, what! . . . Go my twenty years, if others go twenty years . . .

No! No! at present I revolt against death! Work seems too trivial to my pride; my betrayal to the world would be too brief a punishment. At the last moment I would strike out right and left . . .

Then—oh!—dear, poor soul, eternity would not be lost to us!

Morning

Had I not *once* a youth amiable, heroic, fabulous enough to write on leaves of gold: too much luck! Through what crime, through what error, have I earned my present weakness? You who maintain that animals heave sighs of chagrin, that the sick despair, that the dead have bad dreams, try to narrate my fall, and my sleep. Myself, I can no more explain myself than the beggar with his continual *Paters* and *Ave Marias. I no longer know how to speak.*

Yet, today, I think I have finished the story of my hell. It is indeed hell; the ancient one, whose gate the Son of Man opened.

From the same desert, in the same night, always my tired eyes wake to the silver star, always, without the inspiration of the Kings of Life, the three Magi, heart, soul and mind. When will we go, beyond the beaches and the mountains, to greet the birth of the new task, the new wisdom, the flight of tyrants and demons, the end of superstition; to adore—the first ones!— Christmas on earth?

The song of the skies, the march of peoples! Slaves, let us not curse life.

Adieu

Autumn already!—But why regret an everlasting sun, if we are engaged in the discovery of the divine light,—far from the peoples who die with the seasons.

Autumn. Our bark, raised in the motionless fogs, turns toward the port of misery, the enormous city of skies stained with fire and mud. Ah, the stinking rags, the rain-soaked bread, the drunkenness, the thousand loves which crucified me. She will never have an end, then, that ghoulish queen of a million dead souls and bodies, *which will be judged*. I see myself again, my skin eaten by mud and plague, my hair and armpits full of worms and still larger worms in my heart, stretched out among the unknown who are without age, without feeling . . . I could have died there . . . Appalling evocation! I curse misery.

And I fear winter because it is the season of comfort!—Sometimes in the sky I see endless beaches covered with white and joyous nations. A great golden vessel, above me, waves its many-colored pennants in the breezes of morning. I have created all shows, all triumphs, all dramas. I have tried to invent new flowers, new stars, new flesh, new languages. I thought I had acquired supernatural powers. Well! I must bury my imagination and my memories! A beautiful glory of artist and storyteller cast aside!

I! I who called myself magi or angel, dispensed with all morality, I am cast back to the soil, with a duty to seek, and rough actuality to grasp! Peasant!

Am I deceived? would charity be the sister of death for me?

At last, I will ask pardon for having nourished myself on lies. And now let us go.

But not one friendly hand! and where shall one get help?

* * *

Yes, the new time is at best very harsh.

For I can say that I have gained the victory: the gritting of the teeth, the breathing of fire, and the sick sighs are quieted. All wretched memories are fading. My last regrets are packed away,—jealousy of beggars, bandits, the friends of death, the backward of all sorts.—You damned ones, if I had revenged myself!

I must be absolutely modern.

No more canticles; hold the step won. Hard night! the dried blood smokes on my face, and I have nothing behind me but this horrible bush! . . . The spiritual combat is as brutal as the battles of men; but the vision of justice is the pleasure of God alone.

And now it is evening. Let us accept every influx of vigor and real tenderness. And, at dawn, armed with an ardent patience we shall enter the splendid cities.

What did I say about a friendly hand! A brilliant advantage is that I can laugh at the old false loves, and put to shame those lying couples,—I saw the hell of woman there;—and I shall be permitted *to possess the truth in a soul and a body.*

April–August 1873.

THE COLLECTED POEMS OF DELMORE SCHWARTZ

Genesis: Book One
(1943).

When I heard him speak to me with such anger, I
turned towards him with such shame, that it comes
over me again as I but think of it,
    And as one who dreams of something harmful to
himself, and dreaming wishes it a dream, so that he
longs for that which is, as if it were not,
    Such grew I, who, without power to speak, wished
to beg forgiveness—

              —DANTE

"What do the dead do, uncle? do they eat,
Hear music, go a-hunting, and be merry,
As we that live?"

              —WEBSTER

To the Reader

This is the first book of a work which is almost finished. I think that it can be read as a part which is interesting in itself.

I would like to try to remove some of the preconceptions and "habitual expectations" which would condemn the formal character of the whole work.

Thus, the use of prose and verse in the same work is nothing new or strange if one remembers the Bible and the Elizabethan play.

The alternation of the two kinds of composition, for which there are many reasons, is a formal thing, like stanzas, lines, meter, and rhyme, chapters and scenes, acts and curtains, arias and recitatives.

But above all, the use of a chorus of commentators ought to be seen as the same kind of thing as the chorus in Greek drama.

Some authors are fortunate. They live in an age when their beliefs and values are embodied in great institutions and in the way of life of many human beings. These authors do not have to bring in their beliefs and values from the outside; they have only to examine their experience with love in order to find particular beings and actions which are significant of their beliefs and values. I cannot think of any author who has had this advantage and good fortune to the utmost, unless it be the authors of the Gospels, who, as authors, perhaps had only to look up or remember. For even Dante, when he walked through that Paradise which was "white on white on white," required a commentator to explain to him throughout the significance of what he saw.

It is not that the purpose of any author is merely to set forth his own or another's beliefs and values. Art abhors didacticism, although it is often present. But Art also abhors mere journalism and mere history, both popular too. The author needs his beliefs and values to give significance to experience. If one does not know what a rational being is, Socrates on the doorstep is merely a visual impression, and even a dog sees more. And yet, and this is what denies didacticism, the author's beliefs and values may be wrong in the abstract or in the living world, but "right" in relationship to his own experience, so that we may read Homer, Dante, Lucretius, or a Buddhist poem, because the views which they contain are profoundly right as generalities which govern and illuminate their subject-matter, however wrong otherwise. And thus in our own time, Bergsonianism is obviously wrong as a philosophy, but obviously right and necessary in Proust's great novel.

In any case, the present is a time of much variety of belief. Everyone has not only his own point of view, but his own view of Life. No author can assume a community of ideas and values between himself and his audience. Hence he must bring in his ideas and values openly and clearly. This necessity has shown itself many times in modern literature, but I cite one example because it is the inspiration of the form of much that I have written, the seduction scene in *The Waste Land*, which occurs in modern London, but in which the poet finds it necessary to bring Tiresias from ancient Greece, to comment and to judge.[1]

I do not understand the extreme aversion expressed for this use of chorus and commentary. What is this hatred of the effort to paint the struggles of the understanding, to show the intelligence striving to understand and evaluate experience? Such is the compulsion, so much is this need a part of modern life, that I cannot but think and hope that many other literary works will seek forms and modifications of old forms which will strive to go further and do better what is done here and has been done often before.

An analogous thing is true of the versification in this work. I have no wish to emulate Swinburne, but rather the "morbid pedestrianism" of such poets as Donne and Hardy, Webster and Wordsworth. The diction of this deliberate flatness—and the heavy accent and the slowness—is an effort to declare the miraculous character of daily life and ordinary speech. I should also like to think that I am one more of the poets who seek to regain for Poetry the width of reference of prose without losing what the Symbolists discovered. Is this not, in a way, the same purpose which Cézanne set for himself, to give to Impressionism the solidity of the museums?

"The characters and events in this work are not intended to portray any actual persons or events." Since this narrative is a mixture throughout of invention and memory, and since I cannot signify the shifts between invention and memory, it is an obvious stupidity and misuse to take any sentence as the truth about any particular human being. I hope that there is in this work some truth about all human beings: *Hypocrite lecteur!—mon semblable!—mon frère!*

---

1 Another important example is *The Dynasts*, and what Hardy says in his preface is certainly worthy of note:

> "It was thought proper to introduce, as supernatural spectators of the terrestrial action, certain impersonated abstractions, or Intelligences, called Spirits. They are intended to be taken by the reader for what they may be worth as contrivances of the fancy merely. Their doctrines are but tentative, and are advanced with little eye to a systematized philosophy warranted to lift "the burthen of the mystery" of this unintelligible world. The chief thing hoped for them is that they and their utterances may have dramatic plausibility enough to procure for them, in the words of Coleridge, "that willing suspension of disbelief for the moment which constitutes poetic faith."

Genesis

". . . . Me next to sleep, all that is left of Eden,"
—The one who speaks is not remarkable
In the great city, *circa* 1930,
His state is not uncommon in the world,
O, by no means, sleepless and seeking sleep
As one who wades in water to the thighs,
Dragging it soft and heavy near the shore;
For now his body's lapse and ignorance
Permits his heavy mind certain loose sleeves,
Loose sleeves of feeling drawing near a drowse:
He knows of dark and sleep the unity,
He knows all being's consanguinity,
All anguish sinks into the first of seas,
The sea which soothes with softness ultimate
—Thus he descends,
                    and coughs, coughs!
                                        the old cold comes,
Jack-in-the-box, the conscious mind snaps up!
—He wakes,
            his fuzzed gaze strains the dark,
And at the window's outline looks, in shock,
To see a certain whiteness glitter there,
Snow! dragging him to the window
With hurried heart. The childhood love still lives in him,
Like a sweet tooth in grown-up married girls,
December's white delight, a fourth year wish,
The classic swan disguised in modern life,
Freedom and silence shining in New York!
But, standing by the window, sees the truth,
Four stories down the blank courtyard on which
The moonlight shines, diagonal and pale
—And high, the moon's half-cut and glittering shell
Shines like the ice on which electric shines—
Says to himself, "How each view may be false!"
And then the whole thing happens all over again,
Waking, walking to the window, looking out,
Seeking for snow in May, a miracle
Quick in the dozing head's compelled free mix

—He sees the snow which is not snow, but light,
The moonlight's lie, error's fecundity
Fallen from the dead planet near the roof—

Absolute dark and dream space fall on him,
And he through dark and space begins to fall,
At first afraid, then horrified, then calm.
Then the wide stillness in which dream belief
Begins, prepared for all. And he begins
Once more to tell himself all that he knows
Over and over and over and over again,
All of the lives that have come close to his,
All of his life, much mixed in memory
Many a night through which he cannot sleep,
Many a year, over and over again!

But now a voice begins, strange in the dark,
As from a worn victrola record, needle
Which skims and whirrs, a voice intoned
As of a weak old man with foreign accent,
Ironic, comic, flat and matter of fact,
With alternation measured, artificial,
                                        moaned,
And yet with sympathy, *simpatico*
                              as if
A guardian angel sang!
                         Then other voices,
Bodiless in the dark, entered in chorus:
"He must tell all, amazed as the three Magi
When they beheld the puking child! All is
Not natural! That's Life, the Magi too
Might have remarked to one another, Life
Full of all things but what one would expect—"

And he who listened said then to himself,
"A daemon, a daemon, no doubt: who else?
Such as was heard by Socrates, perhaps,
Or an angel, the angel who struggled with Jacob,
If Jacob lived, if angels also live—"

To which one voice cried back, as if in echo,
"Rome and romance of Death, what Mutt and Jeff,
Quixote, Alcestis, Jacob, Uncle Sam,
Hamlet and Holmes look down on all of you!
What King and Queen of Hearts as playing cards?
What President or Pharaoh on a coin?
—Your mind, kept waiting by a desperate hope
For the epiphany which starlight seems
Here where Long Island like a liner slants
To the great city, Europe's last capital,
Now must suppose in Being's surprises nothing less
Than singers who have soared through many keys,
Justice, Forgiveness, and Knowledge in their cries!—"

"A number of the dead have come to you,
O Hershey Green!"
                    "Have come to me?" he cried,
He shouted out, rapt in the absolute dark,
As one who in an empty valley bound by rocks
Shouts and awaits with some hope something more
Than merely his own voice in echo bruised,
And merely his own heart,
                         "Have come to you!
Hallucination holds you by the head,
Many a night you told yourself your life,
Tell it to us, we have no more to do,
Tell it to the immortal dead in the stone
And the chill of their—O so this is it!—the conclusion . . ."

"Is this a true thing?" Hershey Green in the dark
And stillness spoke out again, leaning to hear
If once again his speech would bring back speech,
"O it is true enough! Many are dead.
Come, with your endless story," one voice said,
Hallucination leads you by the hand,
This is the way to freedom and to power,
This is the way to knowledge and to hope,
This is the way the world begins and ends,
Logos, man's inner being going out—"

"Come, with your endless story, Hershey Green,"
This was another voice, *"Così fan tutte!*
Aren't we all! only more so!" with a giggle,
"This is the way to knowledge and to freedom,
Logos, man's inner being going out,
Up! a struggling candlelight striving,
Thin leaf, slim broken knife, knife and leaf rising,
Rising ever-renewed from the sloth of fat,
Thus must the mind rise ever from the flesh,
This is a rhythm like the Day and Night,
There in the cold and limp of the breathing life—"

And then another ghost assumed the theme,
"We laugh, knowing too much; we know
Laughter's loose irresponsibility,
Gazing upon the *gaffes* and vanities
Of those who in the old life here below
Fumble at love and do not know their lives
—Convened as minstrels in an orpheum,
Rapt in the boredom of eternity,
We mock with irony and sympathy,
Discuss, explain, listen and give our minds—"

"We won't go home till morning!" one ghost cried,
In a voice joyous and cracked, "we won't go home,
Until we hear from you your endless story,
And giggle somewhat on a world-wide scale,
As ironists with several kinds of sand!
Or noble lords and ladies who have left
The city struck by plague, passing the time—"

And then another ghost assumed the theme,
"Begin your endless story, Hershey Green,
—We know (do we not know!) how some
Accuse themselves with prosecutor's zeal
In order to forestall another's word
—Hershey, you will not fool us in the least,
What you will say is *true*: we say it too,
O, we agree with you, and we will not

Deny (as you expect!), the worst self-fears
You bring against yourself: a famous trick!
A famous subterfuge of the famous heart!—"

"I love the clarity after emotion,"
Another ghost exclaimed, in abstract joy,
"With what *bons mots* we comment on an action,
Until remorse returns, too late, too late!"

"—When I interpret life, lucidity
Dresses me like a brand-new Palm Beach suit!"
Another ghost remarked, snickered, or sneered,
"Old dilettantes, nothing no more to do,
Nothing at all of nextness now for us,
This is a weekend of eternity,
We come like comic strips, speaking balloons
—I run about in death through many phases,
I go in shorts as if this were a meet!"

Hershey who listened and in dream space walked,
Willing, plucked at his mind, singing to them,
The endless story which had—many a year!—
Over and over and over again! wakened his mind—

This is the beginning of the story which I tell myself,
 Noah Green was a young man in Czarist Russia, one among many,
 He had been married for two years, and he was the father of a child,
 And he was dissatisfied because his life did not resemble the images of
adolescence. Once more Russia
 Looked south to the Balkans and the Near East. There the Ottoman Empire ruled Slav, Christian, and the great harbor,
 Constantinople. The Czar declared universal military conscription,
 The deity, Russia, took hold of Noah Green's life, he ate many lemons,
seeking the look of sickness,
 He gained a cough which lasted all through his life, but he did not convince the Czar's laughing officers,
 He was taken by the army, he suffered the humiliation of being the butt
and Jew of officers,

And then after a year he was sent home, returning with more unrest than before because he had seen much, going from city to city.

He knew then that a war would soon begin between Turkey and Russia. He would be lifted from his life once more, once more his pride would black an officer's boots—

And then the war came, and Noah Green went to Hannah his wife and said to her,

Let me give you a divorce, for if I die, my unmarried brother must marry you.

This is the strict Hebrew law, given by Moses. Hannah assented, although suspicion rose in her.

She knew her husband well and knew that he was tired of her. But she did not wish to marry her brother-in-law and other women in the community also did this.

Hence she divorced him and he went away with Russia to meet Turkey in Serbia,

And the idea grew in Noah's being, the idea sprang to the conscious mind, many a care and means

Seemed to suggest itself. The soldiers by a fast-flowing river one morning camped and went bathing.

Noah undressed with the rest and disposed his uniform where it would be discovered,

Seeming to show that he had been drowned while bathing in the fast-flowing river,

And went swimming further and further away and swam downstream, keeping close to the river bank and hiding in the bushes when tired,

Until he supposed that he had gone far enough, going away from the War and going away from his life and wife.

And then when the night came, he rose from the bushes where he had been hiding,

And walked in his white nakedness in the direction where he had seen distant smoke from chimneys rising. He sought a house in the town which he came to in the darkness,

On the door of which would be the sign first placed in Egypt for the sake of the avenging angel,

For in that house a Jew would live, against the Czar as once against Pharaoh,

He found such a house and hid in the cellar, finding bread and wine there,

He hid between great barrels for three days and nights, naked and unable
to imagine how he might appear in his white nakedness,

He listened, waiting, to the piano being played overhead in the living
room.

He knew a young girl was playing because her footsteps when she rose
were light ones.

Until he could wait no more. He made himself known. In the house lived
two rich unmarried brothers and their young sister,

They were full of sympathy for the fugitive soldier, and they were glad to
conceal him until the Russian army had moved forward,

Soon a romance bloomed between Noah Green and the young girl,

He had for her the aura of the stranger and the appeal of the just fugitive.
He was tall, lean, and handsome.

He saw in her the wondrous freshness of a new beginning for him, al-
though he often woke at night terrified by the thought of discovery,

She played the piano for Noah and in her playing he heard intimations of
the wedding night, a Balkan Prothalamion,

He was hardly able to wait, his impatience became intolerable, a wild
exaltation took hold of him,

The pride and excitement of success' early stages—

"I find this interesting," one voice declared,
"Although this Noah Green is obvious,
—I like the way Russia takes hold of him
O what a piercing power nations have!
I love to see them move through private lives
—Charming the part about the pianist
(Having light's charm and ambiguity),
—O what a concert there, music and fear,
And what a liaison, year after year!"

"The act of darkness which begins the world
Fosters what gross mistakes!" another said,
"Because the lovers lie like scissors close,
And face hides face, love's plaza absolute,
Their eyes are shut, they cannot see, alas!
And from the cache and spurt what lies are born!"
"One would suppose all hearts would learn by this
How each emotion is a house of cards!

How neither joy nor pain can long survive
All of the causes which engendered them
(I wish I knew this when I lived my life!)—"
"Variety," another one remarked,
"Is sensuality's most fleeting hope—"

"To run away is wrong," another said,
"Although this Czar is cruel and infamous,
Infamous all the laughing officers,
Running away is much more dangerous,
Fugues soon destroy the running character—"

"My boy, you are a card," one ghost exclaimed,
"To tell this story of the life we knew,
—Our minds and hearts brim over, speech flows over,
And we enjoy the intellect so much!"

"I know lucidity," one ghost agreed,
"As you begin, sleepless Atlantic boy:
Lucidity like early morning is!
A pearl-gray light upon the city street
When houses stand in all their stillness boxed,
Shaded, defended from the growing white:
I know this radiance because I pierce
The darkness of the heart! Go on, young man!"

"Lo, in the time of war man's heart fulfilled!
—How like a boxing match the heart of man!
O there is Love too, on the other hand,
But private parts fit with a certain strain
And if they yield a tenderness *pro tem*,
They make new boxers for the next decade!"

The Russo-Turkish War ended suddenly, amid Noah Green's joyous expe-
rience of the growth of success. Germany and the British Empire,
   Guided by iron Bismarck and the suave Disraeli, expressed and enacted
their nations' interest and fear
   Of the moves of Holy Russia. Britannia ruled the waves, the British fleet

was sent to the Dardanelles, ready to resume the Crimean War. The Russian army had been triumphant;

Despite many mistakes, it threatened Constantinople: the Ottoman Empire sued for peace, a peace which would have kept the Russian army in the Balkans for months,

But the Congress of Berlin convened, much of the conquered territory

Was taken from Holy Russia by Bismarck and Disraeli, the war gained little or nothing for any interested party,

Except the dead soldiers. Many of the soldiers returned to their homes, a soldier from Noah Green's town came home and told his wife

How Noah Green had taken off his clothes and escaped from the army by swimming down the fast-flowing river. It seems that few actions remain unobserved, and fewer yet remain unsuspected by human beings, of each other.

Hannah Green recognized at once the unity which existed between her husband's flight and the formal divorce he had given her, she saw the motive in a flash of insight, such insight as intense egotism alone makes possible: all her knowledge united to explain what had happened,

She had in mind, even as she possessed in her belly, the week before his departure, the week of his furlough, when she had conceived her second child, now pregnant in her, crouching in his own body.

She thought back and saw now how when she had borne his full weight upon her, in the laborious ecstasy which begins all things, even then, he had borne in himself the idea of flight, the idea of beginning a new life free from her: the fury of the betrayal moved her immediately!

With her child in her belly, five months on his way to the open air and the difficulty of breathing, she took her mother and set out on the long journey to find her fugitive husband.

The child crouched in her belly while the emotions of the greatest resentment moved in her. Her mother beside her, she was jolted south in the carriage, through Russia to the Roumanian border.

Aided by the returning soldier's instruction, she arrived in the town where her husband was engaged to be married. The marriage was to have taken place in two weeks, it was to have been a big wedding—

Everyone was shocked, even the child in the womb was shocked by his mother's anger and resentment. Not with hope,

But with a desire to justify himself a little, Noah Green explained that he had been divorced from his wife,

But no one heard him, for he had no moral stature next to the rotundity
of his pregnant wife. Soon after, the child was born,
   A premature delivery, delivered by the carriage going over the mountains
of Bessarabia and the emotion of discovery—

"Denunciations are most colorful
When character and fate blaze suddenly:
The bowl goes down the alley with a roar,
Striking the pin or pins precarious
—So delicate their stances and their falls!
The mind, being depraved, is gratified
Because the mind beneath the conscious mind
Fears the sudden abyss of accident
And with such action mocks and holds the fear—"

"The Russo-Turkish War betrays this man
With such a tick and flick, irrational:
In England it was touch and go for weeks
To send or not to send the British Fleet,
Victoria herself was partisan,
She urged Disraeli, who was hesitant,
And Bismarck, too, hardly knew what to do,
Alas! that minor Balkan characters
Should be the prey and pin of kings and queens,
Premiers and fattening imperialism!"

"After the useless war, the useless peace"
Another ghost affirmed, "Dénouement strikes
From the least match or from an Empire:
England destroys this fugitive's romance!
All these long range effects are marvelous!
And I have seen the moonlight rule the bay!"

"Here in death's cool and evening I am struck
By an insane and gay serenity,
Viewing the visits of the British Fleet:
I see the doorbell ring, the servant goes,
Mother and daughter come to show a man
How difficult to flee identity!"

"I see them all, I see the scene itself!
His face turns white, he tries to say, Hello!
—To take the pure event and touch its bones
And listen to the heart which beats in it
(Being sad doctors in eternity)
—This is a joy the mind is practiced at—"

"*Felix qui potuit rerum cognoscere causas!*
This is the happiness which is profound!"
One ghost exclaimed, pleased with these shifting thoughts,
"Although the causes are irrational,
This kind of thinking soothes the sated will—"

"He sought the to-fro wet intensities:
When War and Love, when Mars and Venus, walking,
Slip on banana peels and dignities,
Then, then, I love the laughter's foam in me,
I love the laughter from this endless story!"

To which another ghost, half-jokingly,
"How clearly now, we see, young man, *too late*,
Those mighty world-wide thoughtless causes which
Suddenly shake a dining room so much,
Shaking the dining room where a private man
Sits drinking tea with family and friends,
And eating fish, swallows a bone and chokes!
Killed by the quake prepared how many years
Motiveless in the turning globe's round shelves—"

"Yet some folks do not pray! but pout and paint
Their lips and cheeks, and look long at themselves,
As if Life were a whip the will might swing,
On Nature, that most barbarous animal—"

"Now I remember," said another one,
"How in the stupid 19th century
The pious mother often read *Ben-Hur*
To make the foetus smile like Raphael's Christ
—Did she not feel instead the chariot race

Like generation's thrust, dragging her on?
And did the new child know discovery
Fed by the silver-cord to his warm self?
Who can suppose this was of no effect?
Tell us, young man, tell us of this child's life!"

Never again did Noah Green hold up his head. The escape and the ro-
mance had been the great effort of his life,

For the rest of his life, he was a defeated man, ruled by his wife, without
the courage of ambition, forever shocked and afraid.

The family moved to a nearby town, a town by a river which flowed to
the Black Sea, a town of many churches, and an ancient university,

Here during the next ten years four more children were born to Noah
Green and his wife, all of them engendered by the sudden end of the Russo-
Turkish War,

As slowly Noah Green's life rotted. He was an agent for grain merchants,
he travelled from town to town to buy grain,

But his wife was without fear that he would not return. She reminded
him again and again of what he had done,

But she knew that she had destroyed in him the power to do it ever again.
We know, we do not know, too late now,

How the romantic cannot forget, cannot recover, cannot digest defeat.
This household lived from hand to mouth, for Noah did not earn much
money,

And sat in cafés drinking tea and smoking countless cigarettes, while the
children ignored their father, ran to their mother,

Who charged them with the intensity of her will. The oldest son Albert
inherited his father's cunning and his mother's wish for mastery,

And these traits were in Jack, the son of dénouement, also. One night
when Albert was thirteen and Jack was ten,

Jack slipped from the bed in which he slept with Albert. Tiptoed into the
next room where his parents were sleeping. Took from his father's coat as
many coins as he could

Before fear overcame him. When in bed once more, shuddering with re-
lief, beginning to relax in the darkness,

Albert nudged him, startling and scaring him. How much did you get?
asked Albert.

I don't know, Jack trembled back, afraid of denunciation,

But hearing something else in his brother's voice. Let me feel them, whispered Albert, and his fingers went over the coins, learned as the blind,

And then he said, You are a fool, they are all pennies! whispering,

And then explained to his brother how he might have taken one worth more than all the rest, less likely to be caught,

Had he but known enough to feel the coins and distinguish them by touch. If you feel how large they are, you can tell which is which, Albert instructed his brother.

The small boy began to explain that he was satisfied with what he had. But he was too relieved and too grateful, too pleased to have an ally,

While Albert enjoyed the sense of superiority and knowingness which instruction had given him. From that moment of return from theft in the darkness,

A strong relationship grew up between the two brothers. It was for Albert,

The conscious beginning of a sense of family, and the beginning of the wish to be the head of the family,

He knew then the gratification of being wise, generous, and superior,

And it was this which made him sensitive soon to the idea of America which shone all over Europe. He conceived of being the success of the family,

He ran away, and went across Central Europe, and worked in Germany until he had enough money to go to America,

And came to America, and soon prospered in New York City. But when he had been there for but a few months,

He began to send money secretly to Jack, and then one day sent him enough money to make the whole journey. Jack left without a word, to follow his brother. At each departure,

Hannah Green did not fail to point out to Noah Green that the boys were just like him, running away.

Both of them were very angry because Jack was only thirteen years of age when he left, alone, for America,

But they forgot their anger as Albert began to send them money, telling them that he wished that they would come too to the new world.

His pride and his sense of family made him an image in which he showed all of them from mother to latest child the great city of New York,

This image was constantly present in his mind like the idea of a vacation. The two boys bought a newsstand and it was Albert who put aside the money

To bring the family to America. Jack looked on, obedient to his brother's
wish, but really indifferent,
    Preoccupied as his father had been with his own intense desires: is this not
interesting, my friends: are you not curious about the future of this story?

"Hershey, your mind often moves viciously
—At least to me,—making this emphasis,
Two brothers learning brotherhood by theft:
I know, I know! I know how criminals
Find in the worst of crimes the utter need
Of many noble traits, courage, stamina,
And intellect! yet why insist on it?
What weakness lives in you through this aftermath?
What anger? what perversity?"

"I do not know," replied Hershey, "and yet
"Your observation is most accurate—"

"It is a story for the poet Gide,
"Goodness with evil mixed inseparably,"
A ghost said, who expressed delightedness,
"Hershey, you must have known unhappiness
How many times from just such tricky mixtures—"

"To think that brothers' love grows from such soils,"
Mourned one strange voice, hardly to be consoled,
"Why are such small events so powerful?
It is an insult to the conscious will!"

"Because," said one ghost, very interested,
"Some utter need, intense and permanent
Is satisfied and gratified so much
The soul thereafter seeks the self-same form
Again and again as if it were a game
With passion played before applauding crowds—"

"How such a small event conceals itself
Beneath the face, beneath the heavy head,"

Sang one ghost, seeing Hershey's emphasis,
"Yet moves the living man until the grave,
And after that! we know, in this our death—"

"America, the deity, America,
Let us now celebrate and criticize:
The growing deity, America,
Needs more men more and more to cut the trees
Of Nature, that most barbarous deity
—And cries to all who wince in Europe's pain
Would you like to start from the womb again?
Here you can leave the womb a second time!
O here the world and Life begin afresh—"

"Observe," with joy declared another one,
"The home town boy looks back when he makes good!
Sends for the folks back home when he makes good!
—So Joseph once, the typical success,—
Sends for the folks back home because at home
Fame first of all and audience began:
There mother's breast and father's brutal hand
Bred or struck in the child who is the man
The first of pieties or first of wounds—"

And one resumed, as if the footlights dimmed,
"In death's still, soft and darkening air, you sing,
Yet give a sense—strong, clanking, black and loud,—
Of the grand domed stations where the self
Made for departure a new idiom:
Travel is in your speech, trains charge the air
With guns of sound, many a liner sails
—But Hershey, say, what nextness to these boys—"

Now let me turn my mind to another more prosperous family,
    Not far off, during these years of Noah Green's poverty and defeat. In a
small town near the Black Sea
    A wealthy and honored merchant and his wife enjoyed middle age, their
children, and their prosperity.

One child was Benjamin, the son, who with energy and ambition directed his father's business, which had given the family prosperity,

And the other child was the pretty daughter, Leah, sixteen years of age, truly the apple of the parents' conscious attention.

The father had given himself to religious devotions and his place in the community, since Benjamin managed things very well.

Benjamin saw himself as a rich man in the time to come, such was the promise of the business,

And Leah enjoyed being the adored only girl of the family. Many in the town wondered what fortunate man would win the pretty girl. Leah herself looked at the future

Through the windows of the romantic novels she read with delight. And thus it was, reading in the garden on a summer afternoon,

She was seen by a young man who had come next door to visit his newly married sister. This was Noah Newman,

He was a travelling agent for grain merchants like Noah Green. He went from city to city through the year, and he was known as a young man of character and promise.

Looking down from the second floor window, he was immediately infatuated with the pretty girl in the garden, reading.

He would not rest until his sister had introduced him to the girl.

Before long, returning to the town again and again, he had asked her to marry him,

But Leah resisted because Noah Newman did not at all embody the ideas of romance she had seen in the novels she loved,

And Noah persisted, although wounded by rejection. He returned for two years until he had won the mild approval of the parents by his devotion and by the promise that, if Leah married him,

He would not take her away, but they would live in this town. The parents wanted very much to keep their daughter near them,

And to keep the contentment of their middle age exactly. At last, after three years and because of the fondness habitual return had bred in her,

Leah consented, Noah and Leah were married, Noah was given a place in the family business and promised an equal place with Benjamin in the future.

Leah's long resistance gave her an ascendancy over her husband which she never relinquished. He for his part

Never ceased to adore her, to see her as the difficult prize, to regard her among all the other later images as the image of his first glimpse, the pretty girl in the garden reading on a June afternoon.

THE COLLECTED POEMS OF DELMORE SCHWARTZ

Even when three children had been born to them, this image ruled his mind and his heart; even after he had come to hate and fear the whole world,

And now, O visitors! what have you to say to this courtship and marriage, ever a popular topic?"

A certain sadness grew among the singers;
After a pause, an unused voice commenced,
"By accident he saw her, looking down
—These accidents suggest a great abyss—
Unseeing, seen, as if *an sich*, true view!
How images may dominate a life!
So Freud has said; before him, Baudelaire:
This garden image lasted all his life
Like wedding silver, polished and kept for fêtes
—Essential silver still! This, I approve—"

To which then said the moralist of them,
"But I do not approve her last assent
Because habitual return had bred
Fondness *enough*, she said, I might as well . . .
—This 'might as well' has often terrified me!—
Thus does the heart spill its identity—"

"O he who marries thrusts into his breast,"
Lisped one voice, suddenly most serious,
"A grasping hand, as one who drags at grapes
—Drawn forth, the hand is bloodied naturally!
I know of marriage, searching experience!
It bares the body and betrays the mind,
It soils the senses and it cripples hope
Or brings banality to daily life!
I do not like affection like a stain
Or growing rust: such ways are wrong, at heart—"

Then one voice rose and sang in sympathy,
"Poor girl, how did she know, there in the garden reading,
Who might look down on her, what traveller?
Seeing her with the traveller's sparkling gaze,

By very motion freshened, like train scenes
—The face is naked when the mind goes reading—"

Then one reviewed, one to the garden returned:
"What causes novels are, in many hearts!
Novels were strong in her, many *Romanen*
Lighted her mind and heart, and would, forever after!
And in the living room of a long marriage
Upon the mantel stood, next to the flowers—"

"Suppose her obdurate? Behold, poor boy!
How the world hangs by this and that emotion!"
This was once more the careful moralist,
"And that tenacity may win a girl!
Despite imagination's rôle and rule
—Custom! custom or habit brings affection, brings
An acquiescence in a marriage which
Inner necessity has not compelled—"

"How many lives, how many marriages
Inner necessity has not compelled!"
One ghost returned, echoing passionately,
"Go on, young man, you rule your audience
With many memories and much remorse—"

For years Benjamin Harris carefully kept his brother-in-law an underling.
Conflict, at first silent, grew between the two men,
    To Noah's demands, Benjamin responded with distant promises. He paid
Noah a very small salary,
    Although the business prospered more and more, he grew richer all the
time, and all admired his success,
    Until at last Noah gave up hope of being made a partner and went in
anger to work for another man,
    But it became then only more difficult for Noah to earn a living for his
growing family, his two daughters Eva and Lillian, his growing boy Rupert,
and the new infant Ishmael,
    The two girls were sent to the convent school of the town to be edu-
cated, for this was the custom.

Because they were Jewish children, they left and went out to play when the class was given religious lessons.

The two girls loved the convent school and the nuns very much. All the schoolgirls wondered often and guessed about the tragic pasts which had made the beautiful nuns withdraw from the world.

And then the poverty of Noah Newman became such that he had to go and ask his brother-in-law Benjamin to employ him again,

He had to be grateful to Benjamin, he had to accept his complacent and triumphant smile, and he had to take his two daughters from the school because it was costly.

But the nuns were kindly, Eva the older girl was the best of pupils, she was asked to stay as a free student, and her sister Lillian too,

In return she would help to mind the kindergarten children. This grace and honor

Was told with a height of pride to the whole family. In Noah Newman existed an intense rivalry and jealousy, consoled only by such moments:

Aristocrats and critics of death, do you not recognize this?

"I do, I do! What guilt and shame revives!
Better to be a drunkard," one ghost cried,
"Than be like Benjamin, governed by pride,
For in the animal it all begins,
There, there identity has his warm seat,
O what a blaze is there, all else is far
—Better to be a gourmet or a fool,
Pride is the worst of sensualities!"

"I am depressed because I lived this too,
I knew it all!" so said another one,
"But when the party laughter rose, but when
Hearts were opened by wine, and the limbs danced,
I saw in the soft light how pride was poor
Because the dance could not be danced alone
—Yes, you are right, better is drunkenness,
It makes the self forget the self in joy,
It makes the mind run from its secret cave,
Seek out bird, beast and flower, lights and friends,
Make jokes, turn somersaults, kiss and hold hands!"

"Was it his parents? He was an only son,
Pride always wishes to be the only one,"
This ghost assumed the theme and did not sneer,
"Raisins, almonds, friendship, pleasure, knowledge,
Why are their peals so faint? I wonder why?
Be like a fist, the body cries aloud—"

"I see" said one, moving their minds away,
"The two young girls Noah and Leah fused:
They go to the nun's school, in the nuns' faces
Pale and withdrawn, they glimpse at Life's romance,
Like twilight gleams upon a lake I saw
Far off from a thick wood in the old life
—Such images often outlast that life—"

"Did they not feel as they went out to play
The famous castle ever old and new,
Christ's story, Christianity! arrived,
After how many ventures, overhead?
Making them Jews, making the living world
Conscious sometimes of *charitas* and peace"
Mourned one, speaking these thoughts slowly with pain,
"Heartbreaking castle! throned above all hearts,
How in this death I hear your mighty peal!
What anger nears in your history, young man,
Reviving Life so difficult and cruel—"

Anger indeed! fed by the years: for it became more and more difficult
For Noah Newman to endure his future in life, faced by his brother-in-
law's eminent success and his own poverty,
   Seen by the whole community. For one day Benjamin spoke with smug
irony to him, the day before he was supposed to go as paymaster for
Benjamin
   To a lumber camp he owned one hundred miles away. The jest stayed in
his mind as he began his trip to the north.
   It grew, his anger and resentment burst in him. He dismounted from the
train halfway and took the train for Vienna,
   And went from there to Hamburg, and took the first boat for America!
Benjamin's money in his pocket, aiding him. Benjamin soon found out,

And came to his sister's house with self-righteousness fat in him, saying
to Leah,

See what your husband has done, he has left you! He has taken my
money! I never trusted him!

The pretty girl who had been reading a romantic novel in the garden
replied to him:

Here! Take me and take my children, put us in prison!

Benjamin was taken aback, he took refuge in a gesture of magnanimity,
he felt in the back of his mind

Some guilt about his usage of his brother-in-law and his complacent ac-
ceptance of his only sister's poverty,

He announced with much pride that he would support her and her chil-
dren now that she had been deserted by her husband!

Judge these movements of the heart, singers and friends, all must be
judged—

"I know it all," declared a ghost with passion,
"Let me come close, I see the scene itself,
Emotion rises to a pitch at which
It is unbearable, it must take arms,
It must take action, it is not enough
To seek relief in irony or contempt
Of Benjamin, his foe, behind his back,
                    with mutual friends,
And not enough to dream of times to come,
                    revenge, success!
—Once idly and unmeaningly he thought
'I will show him he can't use me like this,
I will take arms, go to America,
A daydream thrown away like used cigars,
—Until emotion grows unbearable,
One tiny accidental joke does all
As a small match burns down a long-lived house:
Benjamin speaks with Noah of a friend
Who has lost all his money, must withdraw
His growing boys from an expensive school,
                    'You two,'
Says Benjamin, tasting his eminence
                    (in wit sublime),

'Might talk shop now!' Talk shop!
                          Noah springs back,
Pierced by the attitude defined in fun:
'Benjamin jokes about my poverty,
Now he, the cause of it, makes fun of it!
He places me with bankrupts in a shop!'
The old dream of America springs up,
Springs like a boxer's arm, blocking a blow,
—Benjamin's joke becomes his righteousness,
He flies with money to America!
. . . A certain Premier sent me: O what fun,
What heartshaking gaiety this is,
Thus to behold crime rising from the source
(The Ego slaps in the face the Super-Ego)
But nonetheless he trembles in Vienna,
Waking in panic from a fallen sleep,
In his body's disarray prepared to return
Before it is too late, until, with morning,
His body strong again, rested by cowardice,
Courage returns, daring returns, he goes!
—Is this not right, young man? do I not know?"

Yes, you are right in essence, if not in detail. It was another joke, but it does not matter much,

Surely it will not surprise you that soon a letter came from Noah Newman in America,

Asking his wife's forgiveness, promising to repay soon the money he had borrowed, and saying that soon he would send for her and the children

To come to America, for he already prospered. This destroyed Benjamin's declaration that Noah had deserted his wife and children,

And Benjamin was further defeated when month after month came equal sums from Noah, paying back the money, with cold notes in which triumph might be heard.

And then at last after a year, came railroad tickets, steamship tickets, money and exact instructions for Leah on how to come to America.

Parents, brother, and brother's wife sought to persuade Leah to stay, but without hesitation she decided to follow her husband,

The scene of parting was intensely sorrowful, for the parents were sure

THE COLLECTED POEMS OF DELMORE SCHWARTZ

that they would never again see their daughter or their grandchildren; and the children felt how they were separated from their childhood.

Again occurred the long journey across Central Europe to *Hamburg, the great port of the German Empire,*

The nervous young woman with four children arrived in Hamburg and found that the ship she had been told to board had postponed the sailing for a month, because of an accident.

Leah was afraid to disobey any of her husband's instructions, she stayed for a whole month in a boarding house, her money diminished, the landlady told her to take another ship,

But Leah was afraid, in this foreign country, and woke at night in terror at the thought that she was equally far from her parents and her husband,

So that the mother and children were in Hamburg on New Year's Eve, December 1899, still waiting for the boat,

And the children looked from the window and saw in the street the increasing excitement, and in honor of the occasion Leah allowed the children to stay up late,

And Eva was sent to the store to buy a pickled fish and all but the infant boy ate the delicacy with immense relish,

Never to forget the taste! on the shore of the North Sea, their minds turned to the dark Atlantic, while in Hamburg,

The whistles blew as they had never blown before! announcing the beginning of the new century! announcing the beginning of the twentieth century!

Was this not thrilling? Does this not inspire many a question and answer?

"It does, it does! young man," one ghost exclaimed,
"Many a question rises in my mind,
I see this Noah in the new world now,
New in New York an immigrant at night:
How many powers must have moved through him!
—When he laid down his body, when at night
He sank into his body's secrecy,
What motions rose in him, being denied?"

"O friend! as you have guessed," was the reply,
"As when the fire engines thrill the night
Often in the modern city, he wakes up!
In terror to return, fearing himself!"

"And why did Leah come across the world?
Was it her family and nothing else?
Was she not shocked and was she not ashamed
And yet excited by her husband's daring?
Nothing like that before? never before
Had character foreshadowed such a *coup*?"
This was another one, most curious,
"What motions rose in him, being denied?
Was it the family god? was this the power
Which drove him back in mind, to all else blind,
To Europe, the Europe of his crime and daring,
And failure? Was it the pretty girl, reading
In summer, in the garden, in his mind forever?
(Such images are indestructible!)
—*Felix qui potuit rerum cognoscere causas:*
This is the happiness which is profound!
What were the causes then which drove his heart?
Tell us, young man, you do not tell enough,
For the Atlantic rides between him and old times!
Many a one would turn away his mind
And go with his appetite, promiscuous to enjoy
Newness in the new world (to all things, change is sweet!)
What was it most of all which held his heart?"

With pleasure and certainty another said,
"Far off the meadow where the white goat looks,
Far off the cantor on high holy days,
But near the image of the family life,
The family god, stronger than sex itself!
And near, the aching plunge which makes the child,
—Nearest of all, passionate purple pride!
He sends for them, he pays the money back!
. . . Blows of the new world struck him, to be sure:
He pays no attention to them, he hardly sees
The new world's glories and how far he is,
Numbed by his pride and daring, numbed
By broken English, but, above the rest
Because the family god moves in his breast!"

"This is the first of spectacles, O this
Consoles in the last illness all our pain:
Gazing upon the old life's vaudeville,
Viewing the motions of the struggling will,
Seeking the causes of each fresh event,
Asking what every sore throat may have meant
And what the burnt match, what the cane,
The necktie and the boredom of the will—"

"Often mistaken! often enough in vain!"
Another renewed, knowing some pleasure too,
"Felix qui potuit rerum cognoscere causas!
We in our death this intellectual
Pleasure must seek, flying like gulls, the soaring
Persistent virtuosi, rising
And falling over the rocks on which
The seas strike blows, knowing a soda then:
What else is there to do, again and again?"

"Now let us go, young man, now let us ride
Across the North Atlantic," one ghost said,
"My interest rises, holding hands with fear,
I feel that much unhappiness is near—"

The trip to America was full of seasickness for the whole family, except the infant boy, two years old. It was the month of January, the liner rocked

As if the world were turning over. Eva as the oldest child was sent to get food for the family, the sailors terrified her with obscene remarks, she thought the voyage would never end,

Until they were in New York at last, and father was meeting them and crying in a manly way for happiness, crying to see them after the long separation,

Proud to show them the wonders of the new world and the great city, proud of his clothing store in which his prosperity grew every day,

So that before a year had passed he paid back Benjamin every cent, returning the money with a final note in which he declared his own honesty and Benjamin's injustice,

Feeling for months the intensity of triumph and justification. He had taken his life in his hands and made a success,

He worked in his store from early morning until midnight with a nervous anxiety

In which the emotions of flight and of his fifteen year contest with Benjamin continued.

The children too remained in the shadow of Europe, they stayed in the orbit of the people from the old country,

They were uneasy when confronted with native Americans. Eva and Lillian

Learned English very quickly. The two young boys hardly knew enough of the old language to remember it for long,

But the parents did not learn English well and in the household they still spoke the language of the old country,

When the girls of Eva's and Lillian's circle of friends, the children of their parents' friends, stopped going to the free school of the new world in order to take the many jobs which awaited them in the great city,

Moved by the desire to earn a dowry for their husbands, Eva and Lillian wanted to do this also. At first displeased, Noah Newman consented when they promised to go to night school.

They took jobs, they went to high school for a time,

But soon they were too tired in the evening. Most of the other girls did not go and felt no need of an education because they were girls.

Noah Newman objected weakly, but turned his hopes on his boys as he prospered more and more, and moved his family to a better neighborhood:

But now let me hear your comments, resting my mind, which brims over—

    "I see the scene itself," one ghost declared,
    "A band was playing on the deck above them
    When the lean liner moved from the long bay:
    Calm and magnificent was the onward motion,
    And happiness itself seemed vivid there,
    —The band was playing what a mighty music,
    And O two world rang out over the shifting water!
    . . . On the sixth day, a storm. All things tossed,
    Knocked, slid, jugged, knocked and jugged,
    No one permitted on the deck for hours:
    And then the sky cleared and was blue again!"

    "What causes move their hearts and make their lives
    In the new world of North America?

I see them *make a living*, as they say,
For this economy is blazing like disease
Through the thick forest of North America
(Since men are trees walking, as St. Paul says,
This trope is true): how many troops
Are drawn like them from Europe's shore and pain,
To the huge blaze, becoming part of it—"

"They rise with many other immigrants,"
One ghost observed, as if contemptuous,
"They cling to other immigrants
And countrymen, ashamed of broken English,
And since one cannot have a childhood twice,
No one begins again, nothing is lost!—"

Another echoed the thought with joy and pain,
"Hail Childhood! and hail Europe, powerful!
No one begins again! Hail the immortal Past:
Noah brings to the commonwealth his own
Nervous intensity, as some bring drunkenness,
And some bring competition, some, againstness,
And some the peasant's sense of property
—But all bring Europe with them, more or less,
The greatest thing in North America!"

"Halt now! and in this place let us now gaze,"
Said he who was the constant moralist,
"For here is Life *decided*, in the dark,
Darkness of joy and friendship! darkness in which
The class god touches them from head to foot!
For arguments informed the feelings then,
Freedom was running races in the blood,
A gull arose, (since in the mind and heart
All natural being, all Creation lives!),
Until the popular evasion showed
(A trick traditional to the famous heart!):
The soul when faced with choice tried not to choose,
The girls would go to school and go to work,
The avid heart would eat and have its cake

—Behold the slow defeat of compromise
As inch by inch choice cuts the heart in half;
The weakness of the school divinity
Cannot thrust off with learning's distant glow
The body's tiredness when evening comes,
For then the famous Pleasure-Principle
Rules tired lives and shows joy quick at hand,
For boring classes, poorly lighted classrooms,
Slow students and bored teachers dim the hour,
While inch by inch choice cuts the heart in half,
And while the mind denies the slow event—"

"What most offends me," said another ghost,
"Is powers' pressures never understood:
The girls regard the other girls: this is
Ethos in fine: *to be like all the rest,*
The social circle thus is powerful,
This is the way the social circle moves,
Only the father feels (weakly, however!)
The school divinity might give the girls
A better life, a better consciousness
(He learned this in the world of clothing stores!),
The social circle is a powerful cause,
This small divinity is made of girls,
It is itself debauched by greater powers,
Mixing, alas! in insane scrimmages!
—Go on, young man, what happened to the girls?"

Let me turn back to Albert and Jack Green, as they grew up and pros-
pered through the last ten years of the nineteenth century.

Albert continued to think of himself as a part of the family. He was the
one who sent back the money to the old country, looking forward to the day
when they would come,

The two growing boys lived with a family which had come from the old
country, and after a time Albert was engaged to marry the oldest girl of the
family.

Jack grew up to be tall and very strong. One night while he was fast asleep,
Albert looked at his sleeping form and saw how tall and strong he was,

THE COLLECTED POEMS OF DELMORE SCHWARTZ

And woke him up to tell him he ought to become a policeman, the whole family was coming to America soon, and it would be very useful to all of them,

If one of them was a member of the police force. Jack refused dazedly and went back to sleep, annoyed because he had been awakened and because Albert was always thinking of himself as the head of the family.

And then, being nineteen years of age, Jack became a streetcar conductor, after the two boys sold their newsstand for a handsome profit,

Both boys already had savings accounts, although Jack spent a great deal of money on clothes and on sexual pleasure.

When the whole family arrived, father, mother, and three younger children, Albert and Jack were too old and too used to freedom to be willing to live with them.

But Jack felt guilty and gave his mother more money than Albert did, to help to support all of them,

And Jack did not like his job, a feeling like his guilt, because in the rest rooms of car barns, his streetcar colleagues were always spitting tobacco juice:

This disgusted him, this was a delicacy of feeling which sprang from his intense sexuality—

And then a ghost reviewed, in pensive tones,
"Two young men growing up, two brothers who
Walk among office buildings as if they were
Natural as bays, carry their lives with them,
—Albert the family man, Jack passionate,
Passionate for himself and appetites—"

"I like this moment when the older boy
Sees in his brother's length the family's good
(How overpowered all perception is!
And what ideas behind the forehead blaze!)"
Another spoke, seeing the scene itself,
"Beside Jack's sleeping form, Albert looks down,
I find this small scene touching and profound:
He knows by now how the world moves, he knows
Many manoeuvres of *Realpolitik*,
He wakes his brother up to be a cop!"

"The contrast is a shock," said one of them,
"How foreign all such feelings are to Jack,
Who feels himself autonomous as stone,
And cannot yield to needs not his alone,
Hardly can think of such, for what he is
Is passionate, passionate for himself:
What better sign of this than his pronounced
Distinction and disgust with men who spit
—He cannot be a member of the team,
For he belongs to Nature's natural seas,
The leaping porpoises serenely somersaulting,
The leaping salmon, the tarpon struggling,
                    fighting like Samson!
In the foreign air, tortured and torn,
Jumping, thrashing, fighting its way to death,
He is among this class, it seems to me!"

Whence one of them, now metaphysical,
"Existence spreads itself and therefore each
Relationship is like a limb stretched far,
—Jack is a wondrous part of Albert's life,
And in Jack's life, Albert, as we have seen,
Plays what a wondrous part and brings him far
(This could not be presented on the stage!):
Space is a lie as anyone can see
Who looks at the flat earth. Time is unseen,
Time-space is what each human being is,
Time-space in a world-wide dance, Time-space
Like Krishna wound in arms so many ways
(In-ness and out-ness are important terms!):
You do not know this well enough, young man!"

When someone hurt Jack's feelings in the house where he lived with Albert, he quit his job and went to Montreal
To change his life. The trip was overnight, when Jack dismounted from the train in early morning, he was depressed.
The freshness and relief of the journey had worn off, he bought a paper, he went to sit in the nearby park, he read the want ads and became still more depressed

THE COLLECTED POEMS OF DELMORE SCHWARTZ

To find himself on a raw winter day in a northern city where he knew no one. His mind changed itself in a moment,

He took the next train back to New York, bringing with him the newspaper to show that he had been to Montreal, offended once more when everyone laughed at his proof.

And moved from this house, and did not live any longer with Albert, and took another job, a job with an insurance company, one in which he went to inspect the corpses of the insured to make sure that such an identity had actually died,

No dishonesty had been committed. This was the lowest rung of the company ladder. Going from house to house, Jack Green was excited by his many impressions of death,

Excited to a pitch where he gained a new eloquence. In the houses where death had come, he succeeded on his own initiative in selling new insurance policies,

And was promoted soon to be a bonafide insurance agent and did not see the dead every day longer, but carried with him the most vivid images of the dead ever after,

And was an immediate success as an insurance agent, because he was able to *sell* himself to people of his own circumstances in life, knowing how to overwhelm people with attention and with confidences,

Although sometimes he went too far and became too close a friend in his eagerness to consummate a sale,

And behaved badly, betraying his motive by acting coldly too soon,

The same process which went on with the young ladies he saw, whom he came to meet in such houses, for with them too he sold himself too well and too quickly,

Becoming engaged several times, and then when his mood slipped away, recoiling and fleeing, avoiding the neighborhood and the people who had been relatives of the girl,

Acting without dignity or courtesy in his flight until this became the dominant motion of the orbit of his life,

His emotions betrayed him again and again, and then made him clumsy and cruel—

"This is a weekend of eternity,"
One ghost exclaimed, "I feel for the old life
Old nausea, and would turn my mind away,
Yet at the same time I am curious,

Here on these heights at least our thoughts are free,
Like the grave starlights far above a storm—"

"Tell us, young man," another one inquired,
"What had been said where he took sleep and dinner?
Hurt feelings are important and obscene,
They show the beating heart beneath the shirt—"

"Gladly," Hershey replied, "it was a joke:
Jack Green had looked upon a photo'd girl,
And said, *Some girl*, bemused, and mispronounced
Debutante, like a German aunt, at which
Three laughed at him, two smiled, and one remarked
Not for you, Jack! that one is not for you!
(Merrily, meaning little, a plain fact
—What do you mean, not for me? What do you mean?
The pride, fat fast asleep, rose like a lion,
Wept like a high school girl, in his stoned face)
—Not for you, Jack: who do you think you are?
This makes him think of *who* he is, in fact,
This seems to speak about the whole of Life!
He mispronounces Debutante! Ha! Ha!
This laughter took him off to Montreal—"

"Psychologize, young man, all we do is
Psychologize, thinking of Might-Have-Been,
Lights of our former lives' mistakes and stakes,
Powerless, overwhelmed with consciousness,
Anguished for those who do not know their lives,"
Sang one ghost, passionate and piteous,—
"This is a weekend of eternity,
In evening's still soft darkening air we sing,
Yet have a sense, strong, clanking, black and loud
Of the huge domed stations where the self
Has for departure made a marvelous church—"

"I see the scene itself," another said,
"His grievous journey saw through Pullman glass
Only his own emotion, Montreal

THE COLLECTED POEMS OF DELMORE SCHWARTZ

Taught him what is between-ness, what it is,
How formal and how dialectical
Escape is, after all, like any bridge,
Being by two banks made to be itself—"

Another ghost was moved by this to say,
"Is not escape a major industry
In North America? Ego its separateness
Beholds upon this track, illusory,
As are the parallels which seem to meet—"

"Running away from pain!" the moralist cried,
"'The only sin is Pride,' sang Sophocles,
Running away with Pride, Identity's
Boundless and dirty sensuality!
When Mary's boy cried out, O turn your cheek,
Forgive your enemies! he made new earth,
Unutterable kindness like a May,
—He was the death of the beast, the boxing beast,
Who must strike back as see-saws rise and fall!"

"Pain is creative," added one of them,
"So was his hatred of tobacco juice,
Pain is creative more than Pleasure is,
The mother learns this as she does the split,
He learns this as he goes to look at death
—Did this intensify his sexual joy?
In any case, it made him one whose mind
Had seen sufficient instances of it
To have a heavy gold watch, strangely heavy
(As is the soft sack where the city starts),
Twined with his own initials, quite baroque
Within the mind beneath the conscious mind,
—He looks up from his pleasure as a man
At breakfast looks up from the morning news
And from the vest beside his heart takes out
The light and measure of his passing hours
As quickly melting as snowflakes and flowers!
—Go on, young man, what fate awaits this one?"

He suffered the emotions of all in whom the ego is naked. By the time he was twenty-eight,

He suffered recurrently from the desire to change his life. The round of pleasure, making more and more money, and living in a rooming house

Seemed a waste to Jack Green, from beginning to end. Albert was married and had a child. His younger brother had also married when very young, and he too had a child,

When Jack Green visited his married friends or his brothers, the longing for a home and a family arose in him. He had lived by himself since he was thirteen, he had lived by himself for almost fifteen years,

This was the state of his being when one evening in the home of one of his married acquaintances who had met him in the street that day and asked him to dinner out of good nature,

He met Eva Newman, the girlhood friend of the wife, who liked Eva very much and liked to make matches.

Eva was very much impressed by the tall strong hard-looking young man, and to Jack she seemed just the kind of a girl who would make him the kind of home he wanted,

Soon after this accident of meeting, the courtship began, with much attention and many gifts from Jack, who always gave too much from fear of giving too little,

Eva was much taken with Jack in every way, but her father made inquiries and heard stories of how he was a rounder, as mutual friends said to him,

He would not make a good husband. Noah Newman tried to persuade his daughter not to see too much of Jack,

But Noah Newman did not succeed. Eva was self-willed, as self-willed as he, the man who had taken his life in his hands and come to America,

And Noah was tired now, too tired to enforce his own will, his long intensity and striving had earned him heart disease,

The doctor told him not to work so hard, but he was unable to listen, compelled by the passion to earn more and more money:

And now it is your turn again, my friends!"

"Is Freedom then the space in which we walked
Before we died? This courtship terrifies!"
Cried one sad ghost. Another answered him,
"Because it is an accident? Behold,
Such accidents can only grow in soils

Of characters fully prepared for them
—Only the Premier falls from national power!
Only the poet finds the lucky rhyme!
Only the oak grows where the acorn falls,
Although the whereness is an accident!
—Necessity shows its disfigured face
In just such accidents! Behold now how
The ragged surd of each specific heart
Is in the midst and meets its very match,
Being itself as such, one never before,
—It is a nonesuch like essential sounds,
And Freedom is the space in which we walked
Before we died, before we knew our lives—"

"It was the creature's lies," another said,
"Just as the whole world enters through the eye,
So too the family god has entered Jack:
While visiting in married brothers' homes,
The surfaces of comforts sang to him
Many a lie of sensuality—"

"My thoughts are like a cold and driving rain
Seen in November from the windowpane,"
One ghost said then, "Necessity is there:
Yet by an accident it all begins!
—How, in the time of courtship, trembles
(As when the ball races the roulette wheel
And seems and then seems not about to stop
On the best hope) wondrous Might-Not-Have-Been!
—This thought is an abyss, when understood!
I see this marriage hanging from a ledge
Fifty-five floors above the city street.
Its slow event resembles evening school's
Slow separation from the girl's régime.
Here, too, in this pure case, the father spoke
The wisdom of his years, free of the youth
Which paints the future as an endless June:
Death in the father spoke a helpless news

When courtship seemed to daughter all of Life!
—O what unhappiness grows from the groin!
Go on, young man, what else can come of this?"

Jack liked Eva very much because she seemed to him the image of refinement and of what a good wife must seem,

Until in a few months, his unrest and his old feeling about Life returned. Returned strongly.

Jack suddenly stopped seeing Eva, alarmed one evening at the extent to which he had already committed himself. Alarmed as several times before, with other girls.

The Newman family had been living by the seashore during the courtship. It was early fall when Jack stopped coming to see Eva,

She was overcome by the sudden break. It intensified all her feelings. She would not come from her room

When it became obvious that Jack was not coming to see her anymore. It was useless for her father to say many times that she was better off without him and this action proved it,

Nothing would console her. And then Jack met a friend of the Newman family downtown and asked him to say to the Newman family that there was nothing personal in his absence, he had just decided

That he did not want to get married, he was not the marrying kind.

Jack was moved to say this by a feeling of mild remorse at paying so much attention to a girl and then going off without a word.

The message was given to Eva and only made her hysterical. She seemed to be on the verge of a nervous breakdown. Her father thought it would be best

If she were permitted to exhaust her feelings. But her mother,

Quickly moved by suffering's vivid face, asked the friend of the family to go to Jack and to tell him how severely the girl had taken his departure,

"Emotions say they are a dynasty,
Declaiming! or claim immortality
—What braggadocio! and what illusion,"
One ghost exclaimed, "I knew it very well,
Playing with an emotion is playing with water,
A looseness quintessential which corrupts,
O yes! a sensuality most desperate
Because it takes emotions serious

And lets them light the world like any dusk:
Moonlight, being both second-rate and second hand
Perhaps describes this shifting pass the best
(For thus I would refer to such emotions)—"

"Think of it as a life," another said,
"On, on, and on! first famously a friend,
And then, alas, a fugitive again
—Too many of such souls have colonized
This new America, unlike the Indians,
Noble and self-contained in dignity
—I wonder just what chutes, trap-doors, and swings
And unrest, unrest on the Atlantic rides
Learned possibly, may live on in the sons?
—Can it be true that the strange face itself
Is passed by parents in the sweetest press,
And yet these deep emotions which return
Like Day and Night, these thoughts, these attitudes,
These deathbed speeches and this nervousness
Not so? at all? O no! Does not the soul
Inherit such disease? if nonetheless
A blank check goes with it, dear Freedom's width!
—I must affirm the two, obsessed with them,
I must cry out with joy each time I view
Small Freedom struggling with Necessity,
With desperation lifting mountains up!—"

"Enough, dear friend," one ghost with courtesy
Said then, "we yearn to hear this courtship's consequence—"

The crown and climax are close. For when Jack Green heard of Eva's grief,
    He felt remorseful as he had many times before. He knew he would soon
get over his emotion, if he did nothing but let time pass. But he was flattered
    As well as remorseful, and he had been weakened by the successive occa-
sions of the same emotion,
    He went to see Eva, telling himself that he meant only to persuade her
that he was not worth her sorrow,
    But she took his return as meaning much more than that, and soon he
was in a mood to think that it was fine to have it so,

For he was attracted to Eva once more, the same image of a domestic life presided over by her returned to him,

He did not feel to her as he had felt about most of the women he had known, the distinction of the sensualist, and this too helped to persuade him,

And soon they were engaged to be married, and then one day when Jack arrived to take Eva out, he had a marriage license in his pocket,

He wanted to get married immediately, his whole being suffered such impatience always,

It was a Saturday afternoon, Eva and Jack argued about getting married, walking up and down in City Hall Park,

Eva was afraid that if she did not consent right then, Jack might go away for good,

But she felt too and with much fear how everything was wrong with the nature of the whole occasion. She did not want a big wedding,

But she felt how this impatient haste to get married so quickly was just the kind of behavior which made Jack so peculiar a person. This was why some said that he was no good at all, everything he did

Was against the norm and the custom of their kind of people, she felt this in his attitude toward everything in life, he took pride in being so:

In the midst of the argument in which both were on the edge of their tempers, each convinced that the other was outrageously self-willed,

Eva consented! they went to the License Bureau, signed and did not understand why they felt so little emotion,

And then they went back to the Newman household, amazing and shocking everyone with the declaration that they were now married!

Consider that, my friends!

> "What a stupid farce this was, in the great city
> No solemn ritual, no chanted forms, no light
> And benediction beautiful: the wedding day
> Lives on in marriages and never fades
> —As veteran sailors on firm land still rock,
> The ocean's car drives on and on in them . . ."

> "He hurried, fearing he would change his mind,
> Impatience is dislike, world without end,
> —Look, in all emptiness Might-Not-Have-Been
> Like an abyss pretends, as if the pair
> Walked hand-in-hand upon a roof-top brink

Fifty-five floors above the city street,
As in the comedies of Harold Lloyd—"

"But indecision makes man what he is
(Tigers are seldom undecided ones!)
Jack Green as undecided ought to be
Appreciated! But going back, I know,
Shows him entirely, bares the scoundrel's will
In naked cruelty turned upside down:
Sentimentality makes him go back!
One of the ego's worst dishonesties
(What monstrous lies the ego tells itself!),
It is his own pain which makes gush and flow
Such sympathy and pity for the girl,
All this will lead to greater cruelty,
It always does! Only such egoists
Make marriages like that! And then they run:
Maudlin or brutal are like right and left
Upon the ego's rather well-known track,
Fresh tears are running down my naked mind!"

New recognitions come, for soon on the honeymoon at a winter resort,
    Jack Green saw that he had been mistaken in many ways. Everything his
wife did seemed wrong to him,
    She did not behave in ways he thought becoming. She behaved rudely
and crudely because of blind self-assurance,
    She assumed that whatever she did was the proper thing to do, and no
one was able to penetrate this assurance,
    She talked too much, she did not dress with style, she had no feeling for
the differences of occasions
    It was impossible for him to take pride in her, and this was the worst thing
of all,
    So that by the time that a year had passed, Jack Green was unable to pre-
tend to himself that his marriage was not a mistake:
    He took pleasure in the comforts of domesticity, but his wife's profound
tactlessness in all matters, trivial or essential, was something he fled from,
    Going away on business trips, staying away in the evenings, paying no
attention to her, or paying the brutal attention of anger.
    Eva was unable to understand why she was treated in this way. She knew

that her husband was peculiar, but this was not enough to explain his attitude and his actions,

She felt his peculiarity most of all in his being unlike the husbands of her friends. He had nothing but contempt for the conventions of the life lived by their kind of people,

He possessed a deep-seated cynicism about all the things which surrounded this life. He had contempt for being hospitable to neighbors, relatives, and friends,

He did not respect the religion of their fathers, and he did not enjoy their leading forms of enjoyment—

"These motions and reversions in Jack's soul
Remind me of the poet Henry James!
He who was fat, profound, and ponderous,
Who saw or thought he saw how every city
Must have an actual nobility
Standing like statues, driving on boulevards
In handsome carriages, at least on Sundays!
But seen, at any rate, by the populace—"

"O, you are right," declared another ghost,
"A great nobility's *noblesse oblige*
Which penetrates all hearts, even their own!
Showing the populace to what ideals
They should pretend, for people do, we know,
Like to be moral now and then, enjoy
Virtue, Goodness, and even Sanctity
—When not too difficult nor too expensive—
For goodness is attractive, it is true;
She is a comely woman, even though
Evil, as *Proverbs* says, is pretty too!"

"But do not joke, let us be serious,
Let us not waste our death in irony,
Since understanding is available,
And through such knowledge we forgive ourselves—"

"Forgive ourselves?" another one exclaimed,
"Do not deceive yourself, we are undone,

—Return and judge Jack Green, forget yourself,
And let us not engage in hopeful lies—"

"I did not mean too much," replied the other,
"I only meant that knowledge was a joy,
A painful joy perhaps, and yet what else?
Nothing but knowledge through eternity!
And some relief to see another's sins,
—Here most of all, here in a man made strange,
Made rude, made cynical, by ego's strain
Endured apart from family, from forms
Which shift intensity to higher teams
Make pride of ego, pride of family
(Pride like the sand-colored lion stalks through the heart!)
Here most of all, in such a man is felt
A wife's demeanor: he must turn from her!"

"Let us a while comment on honeymoons,
Where blues and greens of the mind begin to be,
The blue of heaven, and the green of Nature:
Green is a noble color," one ghost said,
["]All brides, I think, ought to be dressed in green,
This would suggest, you see, flowers to come:
A little thrown rice hardly signifies,
New symbols must be made from time to time
And fresh particulars to ancient acts
Be brought, showing them ever old and new:
They throw their symbols lightly in this age
As if they had many millions of them,
And idly hang the flags on holidays
As if they did not know they played with fire!"

"Going on honeymoons is playing with fire,"
One ghost came in, as if preoccupied,
"Or playing with the sun, the force of nature,
And letting crude spring light or ghastly moonlight
Illuminate the spouse's many sides:
Before the strange wallpaper of strange rooms,
(Surprised surprising birds repeatedly!)

Deep-rooted truths emerge upon the face
Unknowingly, and from the face go down
Sensations deeply rooted evermore!
—Morphologies of honeymoons, alas!
They show the fatal chess of families,
The Knight and Queen persist forevermore,
Archaic figures in an outworn game!
I know, in general, what must come next—"

Jack Green went into the real estate business, soon after his marriage.

For now instead of selling insurance to rising and prospering immigrants, and letting the company enjoy most of the gain,

Jack Green sold them real estate lots, having enough capital by now "to go in business for himself."

The same process of persuasion, the same impress of personal force worked perfectly. These immigrants

Had brought with them from Europe the intense feeling that the owner-ship of land was the greatest material thing.

This was Jack Green's basis, this idea and the need he understood and used.

He made more and more money, he made more money every year, al-though during periods of depression and unemployment, there was a drop,

The immigrants could not be sold new lots during such times, and they tried to sell them back.

Jack Green's prosperity was tied in this way to the prosperity of the immi-grant workmen, and the continuing inflow of immigrants,

But he became more free of this bond with each new access of capital,

And his habits of life as he became richer became still more self-indulgent. During the first years of his marriage, Jack Green went away from his wife five times

With the full and avowed intention of not coming back to live with her. But in a day or two,

Remorse overtook him, he became sorry for her as he had been sorry for her when he resumed his courtship, he was unable to bear the pain of pity, unable to bear in mind the images which had made him depart:

And she in her own character was as headstrong, and self-willed as he,

But she was self-absorbed differently, in a way which made it impossible for her to correct the utter tactlessness which displeased her husband so much. She always felt that she was right,

And when her husband was displeased with an act of hers, she would cite a friend of hers who did exactly as she did

And did not anger anyone. Her tactlessness was a deep-seated thing, she talked too much or she talked too frankly, or she demanded that her husband accept the convention of their kind of people,

Or she would not accept her husband's character without a struggle renewed at any moment and anywhere.

When he brought business friends to the house, or when his relatives came to see him, this lack of tact and sense of self-righteousness inevitably appeared,

And yet amid his wide resentment and dislike, there were periods of tiredness when Jack Green enjoyed his home and was glad to come back to it,

Returning from the pursuit of sexual pleasures, pleased with his wife's native shrewdness in matters in which she was not directly involved.

During such times of peace, Jack Green spent day after day at home without going to the office. And ate with determination what he regarded as wholesome food,

And gazed for hours at his "books," the books which recorded the prosperity of his properties. But these convalescent periods

Never lasted very long. They vanished with the return of energy. Sexual pleasure was the only strong vice which attracted him. He did not drink as other men did,

He did not gamble. He had no need for that sublimation of competition, he did not understand the freedom of play,

But the one vice was enough to take him away again and again, and to enrage his wife. Such was the conflict, such was Eva's misery,

That she would have left her husband during the first years of their marriage, if her mother had not urged her always to stay,

For Leah Newman saw in Jack Green a husband worth much because he prospered and made more money than any of the men of their kind of people.

Noah Newman saw her unhappiness and wanted to ask her to leave her husband. But Leah Newman forbade this, ruling her family with the iron hand

Of the pretty girl in the garden who had not wanted the young man visiting next door. Leah Newman saw her daughter's unhappiness and Jack Green's cruelty,

But she saw too how his ability to make more and more money was a very important thing in America. He was not only a "good provider,"

He was surely a man who was going to be rich! . . .

"Let me go off upon a long cadenza,"
One ghost exclaimed, pensive and speaking slowly,
"I often wondered in the former life
What made our lives exactly what they were,
I see now how Jack Green's life by his will
Was made, yet, of necessity,
By the great causes made essentially:
Europe, America, Capitalismus,
Stupid deities in each other's arms
Locked viciously, transforming some,
Making him be himself essentially!
The young ambitious energetic man
Who in a fixed or dying polity
Might be destroyed or stopped becomes himself
Because America still grows, because
The immigrants still flee from Europe's pain
—'Walking involves the ground as well as legs!'
This lucky athlete of the passionate ego
Has found a perfect soccer playing a field;
His father who resembled him when young
Chose the wrong ground, did not flee far enough
—Even in marriage all of this is true,
Although it is less common, less outdoors,
(Half of this most profound relationship
Under the threshold of both psyches dark
Like all Sexhood comes near, Sexhood one more
Stupid divinity, an arch-divinity
Perhaps, the very warmest one, at least):
For which, of all those struggling causes, which
Sustains the marriage through unhappiness,
O desperate unhappiness, too much?
Hershey has told us, yet let it be seen
Once more in naked rule, new emphasis
—Sustains the marriage through the flights and fights
When mind must mind insult with the worst names
(What obscene rhetoric anger throws up!)
Is it not true, in this long case, that Leah
Keeps wife with husband, checks her husband's flight,
And stays the father who would take her home

(He is the man who once fled far from Pain!)?
She is the cause, only because of her
Eva with Jack Green stays, the marriage's
Evil continues, year by year. But then!
What is the cause which wins the mother's mind?
It is America which moves through her,
America's prosperity, Jack Green's prosperity
Decide her mind amid the fearful sum!
Capitalismus penetrates the heart!
—And yet! girls go away despite their mothers,
They leave their husbands seeking other lives,
Freedom remains amid necessity,
When I remember this, my mind exclaims:
Perhaps the sum alone decides the life,
And all the souls that are perhaps are spun
Just like the roulette wheel or turning globe
Under Time's utter fire and dazzling oars,
—Perhaps the all decides and nothing less,
The all immensely coiled and soiled. Perhaps
The pure event leaps from the infinite cave,
Strange child without known father, like a star!
The mother, all! obscene to Reason's gaze
—And if I say this from death's worst despair,
I know that maybe God has purposes
Stranger than any dream and wholly just,
But now in ignorant death this is a thought
My mind can utter but cannot believe,
—Perhaps Eternity will light up all,
Even the ignorance in which I grieve
—It is impossible to know at all
Until one knows causes and principles:
Felix qui potuit rerum cognoscere causas!
O friends! this is the only happiness!
Lo, in this Switzerland God has made clear
Peaks, heights, and snows! how wonderful
Is Life, O wonderful beyond belief,
Hope, and desire, on Reason's far-off heights!
—Ice cream and other sweets have gone away,
All dreams are rags, all hopes have died. Only

To see the causes which debauched our lives
In this eternity's cold cloudy light
Remains to us: let's make the most of it! . . ."

Albert became jealous of Jack. He prospered, but he did not go forward as rapidly to wealth as Jack did.

The sense of family and mastery which made him send for Jack made him wish to be first in the family more than ever,

It made him try to give his brother advice. Thus he had always enacted his superiority.

But now he spoke to Jack with more intensity and emphasis than before about how he ought to run his business.

Jack listened to advice when he was flattered by it, or when he had need of conversation and company. But when his brother gave him advice once too often about his business, his idea of himself was injured, he was struck in the nose of his pride,

He turned on Albert in rage, he gave him a piece of his mind, that piece of his mind which was blind anger, resisting

Everything anyone said to him, every word and act which did not spring from his own will.

The two brothers stopped speaking to each other, they passed in the street and grew stony-faced,

And looked away and avoided the places where they might meet each other. Albert, after such a passage,

Thought sadly of the days when they had been young bachelors in New York City at the turn of the century,

Going to lectures by socialists, atheists, vegetarians, and advocates of the Single Tax,

Going to Broadway shows and burlesque shows, campaigning for William Jennings Bryan and William Randolph Hearst, acting as passing soldiers and members of the mob in Richard Mansfield's "Julius Caesar." . . .

"No, no! O Hershey Green," broke in one ghost,
"Now with facility you move your mind,
Ignore the quarrel and move ten years back,
Enjoy the past as such, the time itself
(Nostalgia is the easiest emotion!),
And it seems easy, gay, glowing, intensely

Pleasant and interesting to have lived *then*,
A young man in New York in 1901:
The period quality attracts you there,
Hearst, Bryan, Richard Mansfield, Ingersoll,
The Floradora girls! the burlesque queens'
Rich rondures caught in tights consummately
—It moves you as the novels of Dumas
Once moved you. . . . Stop! and let your mind break through
The falseness of the surfaces. Behold,
It was not such for them, O not at all
—Anxiety and blindness, day by day,
Worked long in them and made their pleasures small,
For presentness can never see itself:
This looking back yields much too soft a glow!
Back to the quarrel, please! such paradigms
Bring with a shock what guilt and shame anew:
Knowledge is always late; feeling too soon,
Too quick, and in a rush, it trips and falls—"

"Is it not *infra dig* to view this smallness?"

"Nobility is in the point of view!"

"Feelings cannot be willed: remember that!
. . . The trees their being in October showed,
Bright in decay: the landscape was a mood,
The sky was an emotion, cloudy and gray,
(A gray and rainy day enters the mind)—"

". . . Joy is the touchstone, joy the light and power
Which makes the world how beautiful and rich—"

"The city is the only place for love,
The transatlantic city of my birth
Taught me this (never, however, enough):
There at the stadium with the populace
Roared my emotion which arose because
Community rang and surrounded me! . . ."

"Under the limen is a gold mine, perhaps
—We look as if that Breughel looked at us!"

Albert said to himself in pride and anger, He would not be in America, if it were not for me. If I had not sent for him, he would be a poor boy in Europe.

Jack was the one who was unforgiving. When his anger faded, he hated the silence and the discomfort of avoiding his brother,

But he did not know how to resume the old relationship, he hardly knew how to unbend from anger, so that for years

The two brothers did not speak to each other. The rest of the family found it very difficult and tried hard not to take sides, but took the side of the one who was present, afraid of both of them,

And Jack Green thought of the old days too, when he had lived as a foreigner and a young boy with his brother.

He thought of the time when Albert's first child had been born and of his great pleasure in visiting his brother as a married man, having dinner at his house,

And these thoughts made him sad and full of regret. He felt the necessity of pulling himself up and reminding himself of the occasion of his anger, to drive from his mind all but his brother's jealousy,

A victim of himself, victim of the immediacies of his own emotions—

"You are most eloquent," a ghost exclaimed,
"This must be close to what you are: Ha! Ha!
Intoxicating laughter splashes me!
For with your wit and heart you searched the scene
And the between-ness of those relatives:
'Twill do you good, such goodness knowledge is!"

"*Aut Caesar aut nullus!* cries all egotism,
And cannot bear another's criticism—"

I am pleased that I have pleased you. Now let us take a quick look at much that occurs in the Newman family,

Where many things are changing, growing and dying, for nothing, we know, long remains the same.

The older boy Rupert, handsome and ambitious, was going to the College of the City of New York,

Enjoying the free education of the new world. He was going to be a lawyer and all were certain that he would be very successful.

Lillian earned her living by helping a fashionable dressmaker and carefully she saved her earnings for the spouse to come. Only the youngest child, Ishmael,

Had turned out spoiled and wild, poor in school, hard to control, a truant all the time:

This is the way it was when one day Noah Newman went from his store to have lunch in a nearby restaurant where he had eaten every day for years,

And felt faint with hunger and looked for the tablets the doctor had told him to take with him all the time, tablets of nourishment so that his heart would never feel the strain of hunger,

This had happened before, his absorption and intensity at work often made him forget to eat,

He found that he had forgotten his tablets as he came into the restaurant, he called the waiter, the waiter in the noon hour rush called back that he would be there in a moment, knowing that Noah as a habitual customer might be left to wait,

But when the waiter came at last to the table, he found Noah Newman dead, his head slumped over the table, in essential and irreducible flight from the great city and America, amid the crush, crowd, and hurry of noon hour New York.

This was the failure of the heart. He was free at a stroke, it seemed, his fingers in his vest pocket still seeking tablets of nourishment.

A policeman came to the Newman household and told Leah Newman the news. She screamed, Lillian screamed, but when the funeral was held, they wept quietly.

It was a big funeral, it was given by the old country society of which Noah had been an officer, it made mother and children proud,

Noah Newman was buried in the immense Jewish cemetery near Coney Island, buried in the plot he had chosen for himself,

And in a few weeks the departure of the angry intense resentful man was taken for granted. Like a good American, he had left an insurance policy—

> "Goodbye, Noah, goodbye! Hail and Farewell!
> I know your kind, you are like most I knew
> A good man under pleasant auspices,
> A good man, if one did not look too close:
> You had your good points! you were not a saint,

You were somewhat the average family man
Made different by a livid anger which
Brought you America and early death—"

"He loved his wife and children. Which is much,
As Tolstoy said, who sometimes understood
The motives under life and death. Who sang
The lucid knowledge gained in family life—"

"O Noah Newman made his life and death
For many years, with anger and with love
—The restaurant was but a final straw—
His death clearly no accident, but made
Chiefly by character, year after year—"

"He lived by his emotions, by them died!
His heart was pounded to a private death,
The mere *pâté* of anger and of love
(The restaurant suggested this to me):
For one might say, he ate his heart and died!"
                    "By what
But one's emotions does one live? and die?
Like a romantic girl, who marries quickly—"

"See, at the funeral, many a deity:
Europe is there, green in America,
A color in each mourner's consciousness—"

"—The cemetery near the 'Atlantic stretched,
He lies with many transatlantic peers!"

"Hard lines, harsh lights, a cold vacant
Undraped scene in the house of the dead,
                    a cold glare,
And a dull white shine, the late winter look,
The sky raw, leaking the quick hard light,
—These my associations, like an old tune,
When I regard the end of this man's life—"

"Yet Life is wonderful beyond belief!
And when I think of it, I cannot weep—"

Leah Newman's children made her go back to the old country for a visit.
The change would be good for the widow,

She would see her parents once more before they died. They were both
over seventy.

She returned, she reversed the transatlantic voyage (how differently, with
twelve years living in her!), her brother Benjamin met her in Vienna, like a
Princess who had gone to be Queen in another country.

Because he was rich now and because he still felt a mixture of guilt and
anger in his brother-in-law's departure,

Proud of his wife, his children, and his wealth, he took his sister in his yacht
on the Black Sea, and to his house in the country, and to his many friends,

Proud too of the pretty widow, holding in mind the guessed-at hoped-for
image of what was in her mind, a comparison and contrast with her brother
as a young man, and now, so successful!

He was silent about the reason for her departure and silent about her de-
parted husband. She was silent too, until at last the silence became a positive
thing, as pedestrians turn heads away from dogs' excrement in the street.

And when the time came for her to go back to America, the silence made
him give her two handsome gifts for Eva and Lillian, his nieces,

A French bond for Eva, the married girl, especially because Leah had told
him with pride how successful a young man her husband was, and Benjamin
was drawn to all forms of success, however distant.

Leah tried weakly to refuse these gifts, moved by the story of America
(that everyone was rich there!), then with pride she brought back to the un-
happy marriage of Eva the French bond of her uncle. Shown with pride to
Jack Green, he sneered at it, sneered

With the cynicism of one who suspects all because he knows himself!

"Viva, the travels of the human heart,
Leah's return yields marrow satisfaction—"

"Much more to me, who wandered in the dark
Of pride and boredom, never finding rest . . ."

"—I went through Rocky Mountains where I found
The joys of effort, breathing colding airs,

I saw Sahara colored like a lion,
And I saw London colored like the fog—"

"Has it occurred to those who draw the lines
(Too straight and too Euclidean, alas!)
Of the Good Society and the Good Life
(Utopia, the first of all romances, second
Only to Eden in the Western mind!)
To make provision for commuters' tickets
Between the capital and the home town,
Between the colony and *Vaterland*,
Between the *alma mater* and Home Sweet Home?
We go away in order to return—"

"Let all profound politicos take note!
And you too, sleepless boy! who say so much!"

"Now let us criticize this boy's account
With all the classic terms (Reversal here
And Recognition like an old man's smile),
To light experience in many kinds,
And break the hurly-burly with our news!"

"When Leah went back to the *Vaterland*,
She took with her the traveller's return—"

"To go and come, a movement permanent
Among the many movements of the heart
Occurs at all times in a stadium
Crowded with cheering relatives and friends!"

"This is the backdrop, this is the frame of all,
The temple's fat white columns and the trees,
The distant valley and the twinkling lights,
The lighted Broadway and the footlights too
Are really gazing relatives and friends!
Within this scene is all Life chiefly lived!"

"Indeed, Fame is the vast infinity
Of noble and ignoble mind, the scene
And *mise-en-scène* of every human act,
The audience is everywhere like stars,
—Discusses dress and motive, making comments
Sotto voce, being both critical
And hypocritical, yet with applause—"

"Brother and sister meet and silence keep,
—The dead man's corpse lies in the living room
Where they discuss the years and make believe
Not twelve years, not America divides
Their lives from one another and *auld lang syne*—"

"But one thought full of moral chaos stares
At both of them! *Suppose he had not gone?*
Had not fled with the money, committing evil?
Benjamin sees the widow on his hands,
And Leah sees her old-world poverty,
Both see that good from evil seems to bloom,
—Abyss-like thought, full of insane disorder,
O full of terror like an accident's
Sheer imminence upon a window-edge . . ."

"Among his head, where his perceptions sail,
Are, like white columns, many highest values,
COURAGE, JUSTICE, KINDNESS, PATIENCE, LOVE,
FORGIVENESS, SACRIFICE, FORBEARANCE, LOVE,
Though like the titles on the pediments
Of long museums; also like captured lions
Noble in zoos and pacing nervously—"

"Among his head, these noble values shine,
And shine upon each thing he looks upon,
And give his mean acts an uneasiness,
And make him good when it is not expensive!"

"All of this is a recognition scene
And we have *logos* of this recognition—"

"The story has an epic movement. See,
He moves through many years with utter ease,
Quick on the movements of the soul, his gaze,
And disregarding many passing dresses—"

". . . If one can look at anything for long,
If one can look at any thing for long,
Not pause, nor blink nor let attention drift
And shift,
             what wonders, sleepless boy!"

Eva Green had been told that a child kept a man at home. She thought
that if she had a child, Jack might be different, he might stop running around
with other women, for he liked his brothers' children so much: he might
even stay home in the evening.

She was doubtful in her heart about any such outcome, but turned in
hopeless hope to any possible future. For two years,

She had wondered why she had no child. Then went to a doctor who said
she needed a minor expensive piece of surgery.

She dared not ask her husband for the money, he was on the verge of go-
ing away so often, he might say with his habitual recurrent brutality,

I don't want you to be the mother of my children! But when her mother
came home from old Europe with her gift, she thought of the child and the
doctor at once,

The prosperity of Eastern European capitalism sent the French bond
west. It went through Paris, the capital of Western culture,

And entered her marriage and entered her womb. She said nothing to her
husband, but sold her bond, hesitant a moment when she heard of the loss
involved in immediate sale,

Then went to the doctor. He with his knife corrected her, and soon she
was pregnant,

Making Jack silent, awkward, and kind as never before, of an inconceiv-
able self-consciousness and awkwardness, trying to think of himself as a
father,

While Eva knew new emotions, a heaviness, a nausea, a placidity, and an
expectancy, the oblique looks of men and women,

The aura about her of a priceless vase, poised precariously and quickly
broken. She thought all the time of the lives of the child, the child as a
young man protecting his mother against his father—

"The sleepless boy has what an oblique mind,
Thus to have emphasized a minor nut,
The French bond borne from Bucharest to Brest
And overseas, over Atlantic rides
—Surely he might have been born otherwise,
And what has that to do with what he is?"

"A French bond made the time and made the place,
And was, in fact, a relative and midwife
O this uniqueness is the naked surd
Making each thing, as such, frail and depraved!"

"The French bond moved the doctor to his art,
It is the gift which makes the *haecittas*,
It is as hideous as exodus,
Cruel and laborious, from the warm womb—"

"Twice, twice! over Atlantic rides and raves
His thisness tiptoes on Might-Not-Have-Been!"

"May we not say, given this glowing case,
Thus Life is international and long?"

"May we not say, who take the world-wide view,
Capitalismus penetrates each heart?"

"It is the gross assistant of all causes
Coming with all the players all the time
—But it is trivial here, I must admit,
The whole concatenation trivial!"

"When first the sleepless boy was told this story,
He heard it with a *new* emotion, heard
Perhaps as desperate Columbus heard
The breakers' roar upon the'incredible beach,
All the events of parents and grandparents
Stood in a fresh relation, new *Gestalt*!"

"Forgive the accident of accidents
Which made you; like the hare-lipped girl,
Forgive yourself, and like the turning world
Forgive strange God, maker of Heaven and Earth,
Who made the spring and fall with a slight tilt
Such as vain *beaux* will give their Sunday hats!"

The child was born late at night in the middle of winter.

Jack Green was overwhelmed with joy, excited and exalted as never before in his life. An hour after the child was dragged headfirst with the help of instruments

From his mother's womb, Jack Green called his relatives and his friends to tell them that he had a son. Snow had begun to fall from the low-hanging sky,

Pink-gray with the city lights, when Jack Green woke relatives and friends from the warmth of sleep: his emotion overflowed and demanded expression and required surrounding and answering voices,

He had to tell everyone! His mother-in-law said to him, They are sleeping, they will be angry. But he could not be stopped,

He spoke with warmth to people he had been cool to for years. His joy placed him outside himself,

He called his brother Albert and spoke with eloquence over the instantaneous miles, saying he had been wrong and on such an occasion

All must be forgiven. Everyone is always wrong all the time, answered Albert, wakened from sleep, too little awake in early morning

To know exactly what he was saying—

"The tears are icicles upon his cheeks
As the poor boy arrives at his first breath—"

"O Life is wonderful beyond belief
Here most of all, in parenthood's great pleasure . . ."

"What egotism is so sharp and deaf
(Sharp as the knife and deaf as rock), which lives
That it can quite resist the infant's face,
The fresh identity, the bawling life?"

"Ravished is Everyman by the small sight!
Faced by the double face and breathing twice

THE COLLECTED POEMS OF DELMORE SCHWARTZ

—The harder that the ego pained itself (like ice,
Pressed to the skin, a heavy iron-like pain),
The greater joy abounds! joy overflows . . ."

"This I always find touching, that great joy
Cannot contain itself, but overflows,
The body must run up and down the stairs,
Shout the good news and kiss the passing stranger,
—Joy drives such overwhelming energy—
Any move will express, dance out, and free
The body from the terrifying pleasure—"

"The father's joy is a new class of joy,
—First Abraham, after his hopeless years—"

"Forgiveness for his brother and his friends!
Success is kind when quite secure and sure,
Success must buy the drinks, hand out cigars
(These actions are the same as sorrow's tears!),
And is in this emotion just as blind
And self-absorbed as invalids, as cruel
As disappointment!
                    At two o'clock in the morning,
Jack Green must call his relatives and friends!"

"Thus may new goodness make the evil good
—I am a hopeless optimist, I know!"

The day came when the child was to be given a name, a name announc-
ing the unique inimitable psyche,
    And the tiny foreskin was to the cut with the knife which reached across
five thousand years from Palestine,
    Making him with this last turn of the knife even unto coitus fully a mem-
ber of the people chosen for wandering and alienation.
    Eva wished to name him Noah, after her dead father, who had come to
America with his anger, but her mother did not want her to use that name.
    Eva turned over a dozen names in her mind, unable to decide which one
she liked best until
    She thought of the neighbor's child, four years of age, fat and happy,

Whom Eva had looked at fondly and fondled during her barren unhappy
years. His name was Harold, but he called himself Hershey, a German ver-
sion, because he was obsessed with chocolate, and amused adults had come
to call him Hershey, Hershey Bar, struck by the quaintness,

Extending the smile of amusement at the child with this poem. And Eva
had vowed in a moment of delight with the child, that if she had a child, she
would name him Hershey, for, looking at him, she saw the image of what
she wanted her child to be:

She decided in a moment, Baby Green was named Hershey, howling his
pain and ignorance when his foreskin was cut,

And all thought twenty years in advance of the next generation—

"Lo, with what tenderness he speaks his name,
As if he spoke a scandal or a fame!"

"Why not? It is a sign of the self's darkness,
The private darkness of the individual,
The anguished darkness of the struggling will,
The sound which means the ego is alone,
The bass of harbor boats, alone, alone!
The pathos of departure's fogbound moan,
The self's self-exile from the womb and home—"

"The basis of the art of poetry,
The hard identity felt in the bone—"

"The basis of the art of music, too,
The self-same darkness flows from orchestras,
The brilliant congress of the instruments
Merely goes walking in what wildnerness—"

"His name might have been Noah: beautiful!
Suggests so much a boat on desperate seas—"

"Hershey, I think, is best, the Hershey Bar,
A bitter chocolate or a milk sweet chocolate
—Such is the self, knowing and gnawing the body,
When the decayed teeth of the Pleasure-Principle
Bite it, by the sweet senses' candies pained!"

"There is a joke which grows within my mind:
Here is a stadium and cheering crowd,
Pigeons pass overhead, and one lets go
(Nature's necessities are all his life),
—The one man wet amid the 70,000
Cries out, Here are 70,000 faces,
Why did that pigeon have to pick on me?
—The joke of individuality!
O what a practical joke on everyone,
Something is always new under the sun!"

"Enough, dear friend in this, the last illness,
Now let us shift the image for the boy—"

"Let us regard the deities once more,
Augment his story with our world-wide views,
He pleads for it, he looks for it himself
—Let us look down from heights, from Everest—"

"Or from a star, or from Eternity,
O from Eternity, that is, from Death:
What huge divinities move near the child,
Small as a pebble by a mountain side!"

"Lo, by a mountain range! which, lumbering,
Booming and thundering, begins to quake
—As if Creation first cracked nothingness!
Concussion's stroke rides through the city air—
No lesser trope can be as adequate,
The grandson of two Noahs, running away!
—How many other deities are near!—"

"Europe, America, and Israel,
—Israel bearing, as the boy just said,
The knife which cut the foreskin Moses knew,
Comes for five thousand years from Palestine!"

"How many other deities are near,
And soon, the Great War's shocking scrimmages!"

"—How wise in intuition of his life
The bawling baby screaming at the knife!

"But let the obsessed boy renew his story,
So interesting, leaning to what comes next—"

The new-born child cried all the time, unwilling to sleep, forever not fed enough, until the neighbors
Knocked on the radiator and shouted from their windows, Can't you shut that baby up?
At three o'clock in the morning, locked in the apartment house flats, in which the unity of modern life is obvious.
The infant would never be quiet and seemed never to be satisfied with what he was fed, he woke in the middle of the night,
And was stilled only by being given more to eat, as avid, O, as ravenous for life as his father,
Who walked about in an exaltation which lasted for weeks, and said to his worn-out wife,
To show a new kindness and to express his joy, All the women in the world are not worth that infant's little toe!
The child was the object of much attention and many gifts, given by those who wished to please his father, a rising man.
The child was the crown prince or dauphin of his father and mother, crying in the cradle,
Struggling with his body. During the cold New York winter of the new year, his uncle Rupert came often to see him,
The ambitious handsome young man who was going to be a lawyer was keenly moved to have a nephew,
And took him in the baby carriage to the park for fresh air, as if he were the child's father. And looked at him and played with him,
Thinking of himself and of the job he had just been given in a distinguished law firm, thinking of his own marriage and his own child,
Now that the years of study, and working all summer at summer jobs in Coney Island were almost over.
And then on a Saturday after he had wheeled the baby carriage in the great city park where Nature was framed, trimmed, and trained,
He went to a dance, caught cold, in two days had pneumonia, was dead in a week, unshaven to the very moment

THE COLLECTED POEMS OF DELMORE SCHWARTZ

That his body was placed in a coffin, like a limp large doll in a trunk. . . .

Leah Newman's sorrow was hysterical and boundless. Some said that she would not live through it.

He had been so promising, so gifted, so good to his mother. She cried out that she wished to be put in the grave with him,

How could God have taken him away from her? Can God be just? screamed Leah Newman, like Job, to take such a son, in the prime of his young manhood?

And the family moved, the unmarried daughter, the young boy, and the grief-stricken mother

To another borough of the great city, in order to put out of mind the associated places of Rupert Newman's young manhood,

Where he had exhausted his body, striving to become a prosperous important man in America—

"Death. Death. All flesh is grass, no more:
Nature is treacherous as quicksand, Life
May be as quickly torn as tissue paper!
All flesh is mere confetti, falling down
Joyously at the Mardi Gras!"
                            "Or snow,
The cool flakes quickly stained in city streets—"
                            "This child
Was rocked by Death, rocked by a man to die,
Uncle, young man of promise, hero,
Such as the famous fiction of the age
Brings forth to be the flower of the page—"

"Next to examples of mortality
As under the tall buildings and long billboards
Of the great city next to the Hudson River
This childhood howls, eats, and misunderstands!"

"We are as water spilt upon the ground.
Stay. Look. Cannot be gathered up again—"

"Twinly the bird flies off, snatching the air:
His wings know well Being's contingency—"

"The death of young men, like the death of Keats,
Terrifies many easy rationalists,
Gnostics and rabbis everywhere—"
                              "A light!
The spirit is a light, a sparkling star
So quickly clouded over in the sky!"

"No doubt, his death prepared itself for years,
At least for months . . . Yet who, regarding it,
Sees the hid genesis, or, seeing it,
Finds consolation thus?"
                              "Now attitudes
Spring in defense, fly in Escape
(America's most prosperous industry!)
Among the living who endure the death . . ."

"O carpe diem! cries the hurried heart
Of men of thirty, Eat and drink and play
With women and with wine!"
                                    "It cannot be,"
Says Leah Newman to herself, "It can
Not be, it is an evil dream, no more—"

"And Jack Green thinks, not me, not me,
                    him, but
Not me! And yet who knows who will be next?
He says to himself, horrified at heart,
                    facing the first abyss—"

"And Eva Green looks at her growing child
And fears that she will fear her brother's death
Each time the infant sneezes—"
                                    "She cannot
Forget one minor view: Rupert had not
Shaved on the day before he went to bed,
Hence had a ragged beard, which grew, and looked
Like Lincoln, hollow-cheeked, on the third day—"

"Rupert becomes the family saint. He shines,
A perfect paradigm: *if he had lived!*
If he had lived, what a success!
 'O what
A life his mother would have had!'
 'Poor girl!'"

"This New York boy tells us a piteous story,
I hear tears in his voice and I hear fear,
—Calm, calm, poor boy, brimming and obsessed,
 Tais-toi,
Pauvre enfant! endure your past as such:
No one, not God himself, can learn too much!
—This is an education, *faute de mieux*—"

"Tell him, a while, somewhat of pleasant things,
And take his mind far from the present case
With sterling intuitions like the stars,
—He lives by intuitions, like a bird—"

"I liked the texture of the beer and towel,
The coarseness of tobacco and of bark,
O in the former life how often these
Sensuous skins consoled me, through defeat—"

"We cannot tell him—he is still too young—
Of sherry nut-brown and pre-dinner flows
—O in the former life how wine was good
But these attractions mean nothing to him—
Like a stained tablecloth, late adolescence
Holds him, and like this darkness, youth. . . ."

Hershey in his baby-carriage was presented to his grandmother as the
new being who might take the place for her of her departed son,
 A small comfort! The physical contrast of the three-month infant and the
dead young man was too obvious,
 But here again the dead preside over the child, here again he was made
the small idol,

Scion, and heir! And then, six months after his birth, began the Great War. Eva Green shook her baby carriage, containing Hershey,

Amid the park life near the apartment house in which they lived. Heard newsboys shouting, War! War! Quickly calculated the effect on her family,

Saw that none of them would be forced to be a soldier. Then permitted herself a cool regret in the interests of humanity,

Moved by sentimental sympathy when no self-interest was at stake, moved by her own self-pity.

What a dreadful thing! she said to herself, moving past the park benches, stopping at the drinking fountain, looking at the small lake amid the spaced trees of the green lawn,

Then looking at her child. He slept peacefully all day long as he wept in anger all night, crying to be fed.

He was round, fat, and healthy, he pleased his father very much, Eva Green thought of Jack Green's avowal,

That he would not give all the women in the world for that child's little toe. She knew in her heart

That such absolute declarations were the unmeaning hyperbole of his moments of comfort and satisfaction,

And did not keep him from running around, as people said, with other women, disliking and disdaining her,

Driven by his body's appetite, as he was driven by the tiredness of his body to come back again and stop for a time,

A man for whom making money was the ultimate good and ideal of America, the great cut-glass chandelier in whose light all objects shone or were dark,

Since no other lights equalled this light in the America of his time or the mind of his being,

The other lights were fading or broken, remembered weakly or barely imagined. Fame was making a million dollars, and in that brilliance no other star could be seen!

> "After the private death, the world-wide death,
> O obsessed boy, do not regard with scorn
> The Brooklyn park scene, knowing so much now
> Your mother did not know—"
>   "She was in this
> (Remember and show proper sympathy)
> Ignorant as all presents are—"
>   "How many

THE COLLECTED POEMS OF DELMORE SCHWARTZ

Knew more than she?"

                      "Lord Grey might say in truth
And dignity, 'The lights are going out
All over Europe' . . . But he was in the dark,
The Premier did not know, not even he!
He did not understand how much he said,
He did not see, in short, ten million dead,
The whole truth of the image of the hour,
The darkness he bespoke, the uncontrollable horror—"

"Neither the senses nor the intellect,
Neither the heart, which has its reasons too,
Nor the stiff member understands the whole:
Half truths like broken dishes dine the soul!"

"Wealth to America! Wealth to Jack Green
Comes as the bodies fall on the Western Front,
At Ypres, on the Marne, and at Verdun,
—A new day blazes in America,
The business man who in the Civil War
Rose to his rule achieves nobility,
The colony becomes a major nation—"

"Jack Green in all his natural appetites
Grows with America, enjoys the blaze,
Adjusts himself like passengers on trains
Walking upon their pins to the dining car!"

"O not exact enough: he moves as if
He rode a sled downhill, and used the ground's
Incline to slide, enjoying the ride as such,
Prone as a man in sexual intercourse—"

"Giant, phenomenal, and purposeless,
How the divinities, America,
Europe, Capitalismus, others too,
Move through the life of this Atlantic Jew!"

Ever-greater troops in successive liners came to America,

The land of the refugee and of making a living, the land of the old world failure and the new world success.

All of these people prospered as a class, although some were failures for the irreducible reasons of persons. This prosperity made the opportunity for men like Jack Green.

The immigrants prospered still more because of the great event of the Great War and because Capitalism still blazed in the new world. They saved their dollars,

And men like Jack Green knew well that they had brought with them from Europe, with so much else,—and so much left behind!—

The peasant's sense that land was the most important thing and the owner of land

A king! Jack Green was one of those who took these Europeans, in whom Europe still enacted itself, to show them private property. He treated them like members of a nobility

Until he sold them what he wanted to sell them, driving to Jersey in cars on Sunday afternoons—

"America, America! O Land
Whence come chiefly the poor hurt peoples
Who for a reason good or bad cannot endure
Or be endured by the old *Vaterland*
—Being a Jew, or being a younger son, being
A Quaker, or among the wise who think
The world may end on any seventh day,
A most dynamic and dramatic view of Life—"

"That Barnum knew America quite well,
He knew the gold rush which the populace
Would run to as to fires. And he knew
The love of freaks, the hatred of the norm,
The passion for monstrosity and shock!"

"Land of the failure! land of the refugee!
Land of the gold like oranges on trees,
Land of the European man who holds
St. Patrick's Day or Budapest in him

—Moving in such a crowd, Jack Green grew fat
With this world's goods!"

                              "Lo, the relation here
Between the immigrant and immigrant
New come: just as the card sharp to the hilt
Uses his victims' greed, which is in him
Sharper perhaps, but under strict control
(Knowledge of weakness is a mighty strength!)
—Self-knowledge marks the cards and takes the pot
And gives moral dominion to the soul!"

"Thus it is, thus it has always been!
The criminal like the saint needs discipline!"

"What an America! Adams and James
Return how many times to Europe's shore
As the new troops pass them, in reverse,
(O heavy irony of all such passages!)
And heartsick go to the grave, crying aloud
—We did not know the causes of our lives,
We know at last we did not know our lives!"

"'Who is Vermeer?' asked Pierpont Morgan then,
And paid one hundred thousand dollars when
It was explained to him. He was a king!
A financier! master of many hearts!
—Mark Twain preferred cigar store Indians
To all the noble statues which he toured
In Florence and in Rome. He sneered for fun!
—'I never in my life had any fun,
I never did the things I wished to do!'
Mourned a tycoon, who owned America!
—Red caps, glass beads, and many other things
Little in value first he gave to them,
And stared for gold among most beautiful trees:
O clemens, o pia, o dulces Maria!
This was the first day of America!
All of these immigrants ruined by the ride!"

I do not think that I understand all that you have just said; but I am glad to hear it, nevertheless.

And now I will tell you of how Jack Green was not satisfied by all the money he was making. I know, you do not have to tell me,

That the living are never satisfied and always seek more and more, and that you, who are dead,

Are without desire, for the most part, and wish only to look down and understand all that you have lived through.

Jack Green engaged in new enterprises, in his unrest. During the winter, when little property could be sold, he often left the great city on business or on pleasure,

And when his wife told him that she was pregnant again, he turned on her in anger and said,

Go and have the thing cut out!

Business was poor, he felt that everything was going against him, these moods came always after the lapse of time had taken away

The joy of new successes. He was sick of everything but his plump young son. He did not want another one, one was enough.

But Eva Green refused, self-willed as he, knowing he would change and then change back: one successful business deal

And he would come home full of generosity and fine feeling. She no longer believed in the least

That children would make him a good husband to her. But since she was pregnant

She preferred the child to the abortion. Both were painful enough.

Comment on that, tell me more and more—

"Love has a suite, the act of love compels
True difficult heavy conclusions which
Must be coerced or trapped or covered up,
Stopped by the girl's hygiene for pleasure's sake,
Or by the doctor's knife expressed. Or else,
Love has a fecund will and two make three,
Love bears, augments and joins the polity,
The dark act is confessed in a pair of twins,
The heavy belly is where all begins!"

"He shudders in the dark, hearing these words,
He does not like those words, they bring him shame;

THE COLLECTED POEMS OF DELMORE SCHWARTZ

Spoken aloud, they seem like unclean linen,
Soiled by another's flesh, and not his own—"

"It is quite true, I do not like those words,"
Cried Hershey Green, grateful for empathy—
"Yours is an adolescent prudery,
One form of sex's hard intensity!"

"Not only that, but by our irony
(Although you have your own, to soothe yourself)
You are dismayed. Yet it cannot be helped,
We from our death must laugh about the living,
Just as the living, looking back, laugh too,
At the past's pastness, period quality:
The dresses seem ridiculous, that brummel
Tipping his bowler hat is certainly
Ridiculous! The dead see this, when you are dead
You too will laugh about the living ones,
Who know a matchless irony because we see
The stupid deities which make your lives
—We cannot help but laugh, laugh loud or low!"

". . . As children at the Saturday matinée,
Will not go home, but sit through many shows,
Greeted with equal interest, if not more!
The self-same melodrama, comic relief!"

"Yet sometimes tears come too, anger and hatred,
Self-hatred, hatred of Life, return,
But most of all our curiosity!
—We're dead forever, we have time to burn!"

Now I begin to understand more and more: you cannot but laugh at our
ignorance and our ignorant freedom, when to you these causes bring that
endless curiosity,
That sense of un-understood emotion, which the past does, which is al-
ways pathetic, in which you see
All that you did not and could not see when you were there. All that we
do not and cannot see, being here—

The morning after his brother's birth, Hershey was excluded from his mother's bedroom. Excluded for the first time in his two years of life,

Exiled to the living room. Grandmother had dressed him, the white lady, the nurse, had given him breakfast.

But he was ignored and neglected, left to himself. He had not even seen his mother,

Although he knew she was in the bedroom where so much was going on, where all the towering people came and went,

Carefully and deliberately shutting the door against him, not letting him come too when he tried to follow them.

This shock was the greatest he had ever been given, but he did not cry,

Unable to believe, overwhelmed with curiosity, full of desire to enter the bedroom, see what was happening and see his mother,

Grasp his exclusion from his mother herself, so that he might believe what was happening to him. He was not jealous,

He was overwhelmed with disbelief that all would thus ignore him.

And thus, faced with this problem, difficulty, and pain, the small mind became creative,

He knew that in the apartment were two bathrooms, one next to the kitchen, one reached only by passing through his mother's bedroom,

This soon inspired him. He cried out that he wanted to be taken to the bathroom, thinking that he would be taken as always through his mother's bedroom, and would see his mother and what was happening,

But the nurse came out and took him to the bathroom next to the kitchen, frustrating him.

Sorely perplexed and aggrieved, he waited until he saw the colored maid enter the bathroom next to the kitchen,

Inspired once more! He cried aloud again that he wanted to go to the bathroom, sure now that he would be taken through his mother's bedroom,

And the nurse came out and recognized the child's stratagem and was infinitely delighted,

Went to tell his mother what the cunning child had conceived, and Hershey was brought to his convalescent mother, shown his new brother, hugged and kissed, as he burst into tears, the delighted and kissed ego tasted this brilliant success,

Relieved to be the center of the world once more, in the egotism and centerdom which warmly presented itself to him,

But alarmed and appalled at the precarious perch of the ego,

And the desperate struggle!

THE COLLECTED POEMS OF DELMORE SCHWARTZ

"Touching and shocking! and yet typical,
This child who finds his brother's birth
Incredible . . . O true of all of us,
If we are candid! in the former life—"

"Mark the great speed and treachery
With which he copes with his first rivalry!
Uses his mind shrewdly and cleverly,
Cunning as Iago, cunning as Ulysses!"

"—Note that he lies: he lies about his need,
Uses the urgency of excrement
(Issue often on the *agenda* now
In this stage of his life, as Freud has mourned)
To be his Trojan horse! and what applause
Greets his tyrannical traitorous act:
Mother and nurse debauch the growing boy!"

"The ego as the ego makes the world
Glass! glass infinitely divisible:
The ego sees itself in every place
Reflected as if Nature were Versailles'
Reflexive halls and walls!—"

                              "But soon or late,
The glass will break! and on the ragged knives,
The ego cut itself and bleed to death,
O Caesar, Nero, Alcibiades,
Rimbaud, and other self-bound suicides—"

"And other worthies with a nobler fame
. . . Joseph the dreamer with the vivid coat,
Stammering Moses, curious Socrates
—O what a blaze was the sole self in them,
Although in better uses. See, in all,
The remnant not removed from infancy
When mother wiped the small child's face from jam
And Junior knew the sweet meat of, *I am,*

Just as this child who saw his brother's birth
Like a Siberia, the greatest snub!"

The new child was the quietest of infants, for a week after his birth he did not cry,

Until everyone wondered if something were wrong with him. In this way, and in all others, he was unlike his brother, he was just what his brother was not.

The time came again for the naming of the child, and though there was no such complexity as with Hershey, nevertheless

Eva's mother asked her not to name the new boy after Rupert, his dead uncle. This was death again, presiding: Leah Newman did not want to be reminded of her sorrow each time she looked at the new boy.

Consequently Eva Green announced that she would call the boy Roger. Years ago, before his marriage, Jack Green had made love to a married woman who had a child named Roger.

One day he had told Eva the brutal story, how he arranged to have a package delivered to the wrong door in order to meet his neighbor's wife,

How the woman fell in love with him and told her husband, who was nothing but a railroad conductor. How she asked to be free, only to find that Jack Green had changed his mind. How she begged her husband's forgiveness and asked to be taken back,

And was taken back by the husband because of the boy Roger. Eva Green told her husband that it was this story which made her think of the name Roger,

And Jack Green was angered as often before by his wife's profound tactlessness. He remembered that the husband had said he would kill him, he remembered

How different the story had seemed when he told it, a specimen of his Don Juan power. But the small child was given that name, named by his father's young manhood and guilt, and by his mother's foolishness—

"May I psychologize? and thus extend
—With such a light—all that the brimming boy
Already knows, and mourns? Jack tells his wife,
Smug and self-satisfied, of an *amour*
Ten years ago: pleased with himself, in mind
Too self-pleased, thinking of it, to conceive
How such a cause must seem to his wife's mind,

To her mind most of all. There it abides
With monumental place because it fits
What interests her the most, Jack's character:
Cut in her mind as on the continent
Of North America a glacial age!
Is this comparison extreme? Behold,
She names her second son her husband's guilt,
As self-absorbed, as ignorant as he
—Each to his blindness through Eternity!"

"Such egoists are so preoccupied
With their own minds, they lack imagination
Of what their pride in cleverness must seem
To someone walking in another dream!"

"Hot tears are sliding down the poor boy's face,
He sees in all of this identities
—He would divorce himself from both of them,
And from himself, a vain and insane hope—"

"O New York boy, this Life, Life in which
You can't reject the world's *de facto* shame
—This is the way to knowledge and to freedom,
Here thrashing in this depth, here in this room
From which the chairs and else quotidian
Have been removed. Keep thinking all the time,
What else is there to do? what other move?
What other play? O what activity
Can hold identity? grasping the brink
Under which utter darkness ever lies prone:
You lie in the coffin of your character,
Hopes rise and fall as the breast rises and falls!"

Hershey's ego defined itself further by means of father, mother and
brother.

During these years, when the fog of infancy, blooming and booming,
slowly lifted,

Hershey often sat in the window seat which looked out on a street in the
middle of which

A trolley passed, yellow and red in broad stripes, sparking the wire,
Delighting him more than any other object! It was to him a thing of inexhaustible interest, ever-renewed,
A kind of boat, sliding, skating, singing, stopping, and beginning again,
Presenting him with movement which is the beginning of drama, an obvious miracle passing at regular intervals:
And thus it was that when, one day, a middle-aged friend of Eva Green brought her son's fiancée to the apartment, and when the engaged girl, who was very pretty, drew the child to her
And kissed him! as if he were her future, his plump childness pleasing her, then did he cry out joyously,
"Trolley, trolley!" his first metaphor, the swift perception of a resemblance between different things. For he meant to say
The pretty lady who kisses me delights me like the trolley.
All the adults were delighted and applauded him and petted him,
Until his success grew warm in him, although he hardly knew why—

    "Come now, this is too good, too pure a sign!
    Kissed by the fiancée, the girl engaged
    In going to the fête where privacies
    Mix in the act which makes societies
    —Too pat, too easy, and too pure a sign!"

    "A fiancée; the quintessential flower:
    Who better shall draw from the little boy
    The first of all the many metaphors
    With which he will enact his hope and fear?"

    "How in this death we need the metaphor:
    We go from trope to trope like acrobats!"

    "Surprises, Being's surprises everywhere,
    —Cumuli clouds full of ontologies!"

    "We in our death enjoy this very much,
    Seeing how one thing is another thing
    In certain ways, a girl being a rose
    In certain ways, a poet being a train
    (Because he takes you where you have not been),

Painting as light, sleep as essential sin
(Being a desperate abandonment). . . ."

"Light is the heroine of all the paintings,
The camera is the hero of the screen!"

"Such metaphors are pleasant. But some come
Which show us with their light how much we missed
(Who were not those on whom *nothing is lost*)
When we were there and *could*; and might have loved . . ."

"How much we did not see when we were there,
Walking through Life self-blinded by desire
—Such metaphors like the rack torture us
With utter memory and that remorse
Forever *late*, which is the greatest pain!"

The growing child cried too much at night and the neighbors were angered.

The Greens moved from place to place because of the crying child crying at night then, as he cries now, perhaps,

Who could not be justed with the external world, nor with his own body,

Like his placid and perfect brother, to whom he paid no attention, after the first and shocking day,

And soon he grew to the maturity when he cried only when he wet the bed. And above him and outside him and yet passing through him,

His father continued to become rich, America entered the Great War, an uncle was conscripted, and went to France with the A.E.F.,

And in his own being, Hershey reached high enough to be able to play in the street

And feel excluded because boys two years older than he would have nothing to do with him,

Or when they did, asked him if he were German, and when he said he was, thinking that Jewish and German were the same,

They taunted and mocked him until the colored maid who guarded his brother in the carriage came to drive off the boys,

And Hershey wondered why and what was wrong, never before having known the antagonism of the stranger.

The colored maid named Alice was passionately devoted to Roger and thought he would one day be President,

Because the Green family lived on President Street. Hershey did not understand the War or the maid.

He saw posters in which the female goddess, Liberty, in white linen, held aloft the stars and stripes of the American flag,

And he saw high school girls garbed as nurses and making bandages,

But that was all he saw, and he did not understand these things. He played with a girl of his own age who lived in the same apartment house,

And then, the day before the Greens moved again to another apartment house, he stole two sickle pears from the cupboard,

And gave them to her, and asked her,

Will you be sorry when I am gone? The fruit had been forbidden him by his mother who when she discovered the theft, asked him if he had taken the pears?

Then he tried to lie to her, and he felt his mouth contract,

And he knew what guilt was. And soon the winter began, and he sat in the window seat on a gray day,

And saw currents of snow swept from side to side of the city street, as the wind drove them,

It was a December afternoon, there was a glow because the lights were turned on early, and expectancy was in the air not only of the beautiful snow,

But of the coming Christmas, the holiday season of holly wreath and lighted Christmas tree,

Brilliant in the lighted window—

"The snow! speaking of it, the boy grows tense,
Even as in the grave the whisper, 'God' or 'Judgment,'
Will make the waiting ones sit upright quickly,
And think, 'At last!,' though it was only
'Yes, but not now,' or 'Wait until I . . .'
A girl exclaimed, by drunken sweetness hurried,
Under a hidden tree in the dark park,
Next to the graveyard, where the summer bloomed . . ."

"What power is this of snow upon his mind?
—I do not think that it is understood—
No natural object moves his mind so much,
No game, no music, and no hope to come
—Is it perhaps because he fears the darkness?"

THE COLLECTED POEMS OF DELMORE SCHWARTZ

"O, when the snow falls, he forgives all shame,
Forgets the turning world and every hope,
And every memory of guilt and pain,
He seeks no future and regrets no past,
Satisfied by the fat white pieces' fall—"

"As one is satisfied, playing a game!
A game which makes activity pure joy,
Being itself Being itself, and more
Than striving for the absent future end—
Thus perhaps blessed souls, risen at last
To full eternity, must gaze upon
The'infinite light which makes the universe,
And know a pleasure perfect and serene!"

"Return, regard the other incident,
The theft of sickle pears, like Augustine—"

"What shall be said? Speak of the property
Stolen by the child from mother? Speak of the lie
And guilt? refer to Eve and Adam, stopped
By the voice in the garden in the cool of evening?
This is the beginning of the world again
In every heart, till the avenging angel
Drives innocence from childhood and from Eden,
Having once more performed original sin!"

Then when the summer came again, the Greens went to the seashore, Roger burned himself, learning about fire by putting his hand in the frying pan,
An Irish boy who lived in the same bungalow court hit Hershey and tortured him by pulling his hair,
And when Jack Green heard, he went to the father and demanded that this be stopped. But when the big Irish father
Responded violently, fastening his fists, Jack Green withdrew, unequal to physical violence,
But could not withdraw from his wife. She saw in his tall impressive stride, his forbidding look of power and arrogance, the weakness and the anxiety,
And with her tactlessness, she remarked, trying to be helpful, that it was

not cowardly to refuse to fight, that he was too proud to fight. Thus striking her husband with the idea of cowardice, making him think he had lost face.

During these days, Jack Green was afraid of many things, while his success continued. He came home with indigestion and feared that it was cancer, he came back from a period of dissipation with all kinds of women, as Eva called them,

And he said he was sick, and professed great gratitude for the nurse-like attentions of his wife, who did not hesitate to take advantage

Of all such occasions. The worst occasion of all, the occasion which was inevitable,

Came when a new partner in business was caught collecting funds from his former customers, the customers of former partner.

The injured man was an Italian and went to the District Attorney. Jack Green and his partner were both culpable. He had known what was happening, although he had not profited by it, because his partner was too greedy to divide his theft.

Then Eva Green was sent to the Italian man to plead with him. She went with her child and she wept. The Italian was moved and promised to be merciful because of the child,

And after days of much fear, Jack Green was relieved of the danger of prosecution, after days of much fear and the payment of ten thousand dollars in the proper quarters.

I will never forget this, he said to his wife. And was kind to her three weeks. And on proper occasions, she reminded him of what she had done for him.

"How cruel and cynical your voice, how harsh
And yet how clear, though muffled as before
Like cars which trek upon a heavy snow.
Like all the guilty, you cannot forgive—"

"We in our death can be forgiving, give
Forgiveness as a millionaire gives dimes:
It is too easy, it is not enough,
It is a sign that we no longer care
As once we cared for other hearts' harsh hurts—"

"To stop a man, to make him lose his face
And pride before a girl, not to permit

THE COLLECTED POEMS OF DELMORE SCHWARTZ

A chance to laugh it off—is infamy:
Infamous all assistants, true or false—"

"Your father and your mother, sleepless boy,
Still live in you and what you say of them
Is true of you as possibility:
This does not lessen in the least your will's
Liberty to enact both good and evil
Freshly and fully! every man is new
And every man is old; enough of this!—"

"Your mind to-night and most unnatural voice
Accuses you: let then these lives so drive
Your future life that you become, in truth,
A colonist, by the 'Atlantic voyage
Of this long night taken away from them!"

"Though every man takes all he has with him,
No matter where he goes! Though Crusoe found
The merchant's carefulness sharpened in him!
And though Magellan at the world's edge bit
His nails as nervously as in old Spain!"

"He cannot go away!"
                              "I cannot go
Away! The mind is my own place, my world,
For in the living world when I see snow,
I sit upon my fourth year window seat
—And when I see a fight, I know once more
My father in retreat under my mother's gaze,
The cruel man cowardly, fully exposed;
And any kind of fear revives in me
Fresh signs of his long insecurity . . ."

"Let us now give the boy briefly some peace,
And move his mind with images of pleasure
—Before the story starts once more, think how
The wine would tock, as from the bottle dropped,
How pigeons rose with a sound like shuffled cards,

And how birds sprinkled morning's silent width,
How the liner moved like happiness itself,
How shafts of sunlight breaking through the clouds
Looked like a revelation of God's feats!
But most, the touch and torch of rapture, yes!
Outrageous joy and secret victory!
—O in what rapids ran my heart just then!"

Then there was silence for a time, grateful
To Hershey Green, who thought perhaps his fear
And story gone away! O gone away for good!
(For he both wished to speak and not to speak).

"'Silence, you are the best I ever heard!'"
He quoted, like a child self-pitying,
Yet in his voice their voices echoing . . .
Then, as a streetcar skated through the night,
An accent of the peace, passing away,
An awe, an awe of depth of silence grew,

"Now I will really know how good it is
To have the sleep of Eden, like a tree,
I will bear this in mind like a man reprieved
(O how their voices influence my voice!)
And make myself think of the horror which
I have escaped! enjoying *everything*,
Taking keen pleasure in the smallest things,
Tying my laces, or sharpening a pencil—"

Yet as he spoke, he feared it was not true,
And yet enjoyed it all as he enjoyed
Soft drinks on summer days after a game,
Gulped down to drown the throat's pulsating need—
His pride rose with these thoughts, vainglorious,
—O like a raving fire leaping up!
He told himself all that his mind might do,
Half-doubting and half hoping it was true:

"As Adam named the beasts, with careful love,
I name the animals and the divinities
Who walk about this newfoundland, America,
(Europe the greatest thing in North America!
For instance, as one voice just said to me)
—As Socrates, who questioned everything
Because his love was great, because he loved
Life very much, but not too much, and not
Enough to accept a life without the stars,
Thus now I'll flick the salt of intellect
Upon all things, the critical salt which makes
All qualities most vivid and acute—
As Joseph, I'll enact my sweet revenge
In basic psychological reviews,
Accuse the innocents who perjured me,
Me innocent: showing sublimely then,
The Justice who uncovers innocence,
Omniscient, generous, O all forgiving
And most successful brother who displays
How he was right throughout, in his conceit,
All dreams come true, and every feat performed—"

Then said a far-off singer in his style
Breaking in suddenly on Hershey's peace,
"Let go this braggadocio, young man!
. . . *Dunamos*, dynamite, puissance, Power,
Divinity secretly close to the will
Like May beside the leaf: listen and speak,
The chorus is an ancient well-known goodness,
Like bread and wine, although more difficult. Cause
Is the secrecy and mystery. The Seed
Is marvelous. Let us look down on it. The Star . . .
Everything is a part and in the pit
Of all the nexi, darkness is cat-black,
In between sleeping and waking, part by part
(And once the sun blared like a lion, and once
The starlight fell like a petal, piercing the eye—)"

And then another ghost assumed the theme,
"Lincoln is on a penny in the mind,
A canton of the spirit! Rises and speaks!
And Jeeves and Cinderella show the boat
We all are in, the rotten ship of state!
Chaplin shuffles and tips his hat! Then runs!
John Bull and Uncle Sam are not cartoons
But heavy actual bullies boxing through us!
They move through all of us, like summer fine:
Keep thinking all the time, O New York boy!
                                        Go back,
In each, all natural being once more lives!
The subtile serpent which the apple brought
To Mamma and to Papa, starting all!
Caesar and Caesar's pal also in you,
Also the servant and the comedian,
—Lo, he has set the world in each man's heart!
And both the lamb and lion are quick in you,
The mountain and the lake, the tree and stone
All of these kinds their being must renew
—When you lie down to sleep, they rise in you!"

"Let us fly off and tour the world awhile,
Freely and frankly, going from branch to branch,
To show the boy *trouvailles* within the mind,
Many Americas found suddenly,
Surprise upon surprise upon surprise!"

"As, once I saw two nuns, like cameras;
There they were, taking pictures of modern life!"

"Remember this, young man, as we fly on,
Verdi at eighty-seven kneeled beneath
The bed to find a fallen collar-stud,
And apoplexy struck him down. Alas!
'Twas this he left out of his operas,
—Of actuality, the ragged richness!
Bend down under the bed and look for this!
O hear the children coming home from school,

And hear the gunshots of the starting car,
And hear the thin strings of the telephone,
And Sister's ennui, practicing her scales,
And see the cinders and the broken glass—"

"And yet, behold the heart within these dings:
Change jingled in his pocket like gay pleasure,
And his checked tie was what an attitude.
In his lapel a flower quoted Nature—"

"And more and more, behold the dialectic,
How light brings shadow, how the evil, good,
And how each eminence needs lowness near,
And how each eminence brings straining Iago,
And too much good makes too much sorrow soon—"

"The mind skates like a falling star! the mind
Speeds between heaven and earth like Light itself!"

"The gold, the vivid, and the actual
Will melt like flakes upon the open hand,
The mind in memory alone can live
(How many times I climbed on hands and knees
This Himalaya, depth on every side),
The memory alone can hold the self!
Logos alone can understand the blue—"

"If one but knew, if one knew Being-hood,
—This is as if we sat after a dinner,
And heard of many years in unity,
Or noble lords and ladies who have left
The city struck by plague, passing the time—"

"In us, all natural being once more lives,
—A skein of geese, a walk of snipe,
A murmuration of starlings, an exultation
Of larks, a watch of nightingales, a host
Of sparrows, a cast of hawks, a pride of lions,

                                   a sloth of bears,

A route of wolves, a rag of colts,
                                    a mute of hounds,
A cowardice of curs, a shrewdness of apes,
A luxury of nymphs, a lilt of mares,
A round of girls, a dark of plays, a jig
Of vaudeville, a crowd of joys
—Blue grapes and yellow pears beside a jar!
—All of this life and more, much more in us!
Later we will unmask, singing our names!"

"—Her privates we, yet ignorant in death,
We wait to see Eternity's worst views—"

Then said another singer in his style,
"*In medias res*, in the middle of Life,
In the middle of everything, sick boy,
—Where is the first of consciousness, where is
Where first-hand memory begins for you—"

"Eden, image of many complex thoughts
About beginning, hangs just like a picture
In many living rooms in the Western World;
Later, we might consider it; not now, later—"

"Begin in any place in consciousness,
Life and each part of Life is infinite,
Infinitely divisible, traversible,
And visible! seek out the motives there—"

"O seek, he means the depths of the Past from which
The soul's moves rise as grasses from the earth—"

Anywhere in the abyss of memory, the abyss in the darkness of the heavy
head,

Where it fades formless in the slightness of childhood, when yet the
child is carried, yet the child is dressed, fed from the high chair, fat and
helpless.

Any place in the night of consciousness which is like the night of a great
capital,

THE COLLECTED POEMS OF DELMORE SCHWARTZ

Will serve to begin for you the beginning of Hershey Green's childhood.

He had often been told of the *kindergarten*, and excited until he dreamed three times of it,

Dreamed that he walked in the cool dark cellar of a Brooklyn church while about him children passed, playing,

Perhaps because one parent pointed out to him a Sunday school in some church basement; perhaps because some obscure metaphor

Moved in the infant mind. Kindergarten was the place where thrilling games were played. So he was told,

But it was to him the advancement of the ego, his mind already climbed the ego's tower, he said to himself that when he went he could say and feel, I go to school,

Although it was not really school, but something less, and yet,

Almost the actuality, like certain toys, O like the electric train, seen in the department store.

And when he was taken at last, it was to a kindergarten kept by two maiden ladies, fallen on genteel poverty in a small house,

And he knew at once disappointment, frustration, and failure, because he could not paste correctly a design of colored papers, seeing that the other children did it with ease and with pleasure,

Until in the first week, another child kicked him, and Hershey kicked back, standing in line,

And the teacher saw Hershey, but not the first boy, and she sent him from the room, as he tried to explain and accuse his fellow,

Sent him to sit outside in the hallway upon the stair, and wait until he was recalled and forgiven, having been punished,

And as he went, he was ashamed, he was afraid his mother would hear of this, she was his audience—

Exiled, humiliated, persecuted, Coriolanus, Joseph, and Caesar, the child resumes history, each enacts all that has been.

He sat upon the stairs and heard the sounds of the children in the classroom, moving and playing,

Excluded and deprived, listening to the sounds of exile.

And when a child came from the closed door of the classroom to call him back so that he might be forgiven,

His attitude had grown to full height, he refused to return, he said to tell the teacher that he would not come, self-righteous and full of the knowledge of injustice,

So that the teacher came out for him, and the other children looked with

curiosity, and she lifted him up from his face within his hands upon his knees
as he sat small on the staircase,
   And spoke to him with kindliness, at which he knew a fearful contraction
of the mouth, the wish to cry and the wish to suppress the emotion,
      The wish to howl his cause, and yet the wish to get the kindness and not cry:
      He tried, he turned his face away, the kindness was too much,
      He burst into tears! helpless with grief and self-pity, already the actor and
victim of what a constellation of emotions,
      Injustice, paranoia, bursting tears, and most of all, deliberate withdrawal
to show his strength and pride—
      Already active in the fifth year; for this was the beginning of his childhood.

"School is the wide world, at five years old:
Release from mother's rule, and a vast game
Under a circus tent until, so soon,
The Nero ego finds out once again,
Now more than ever, that the world resists
Its wishes everywhere—"

                    "Blackboard in playroom
Where the chalk screeched, where small shoes wore the floor
And the small chairs where the children sat and sang;
A garden in the back; between two trees
A swing (not unlike sexual intercourse
When Jack swings Jill, glimpsing the dress flown up!);
Pasted upon the windows simple forms
Cut by the children, bird and beast and flower,
Life imitating Life with much delight,
And by the strict attention growing strong—"

"Two maiden sisters, gentle and genteel:
I knew this kind in the former life, I knew
The growing hidden nervous strain in which
Sex slowly dries, and the body, once a pear,
Becomes a lemon, pleasing through bitterness—"

"And then the children, drawn from many cradles,
With different angers planted in the seed!

—Congress of thirty Ids, like a convention
Of a small radical party in some respects:
This was the nature of the kindergarten—"

"Children and fools will often play the senses
As if they dallied with xylophones—"

"When any human beings from five to ninety
Are brought together, every unique will
Feels like an itch the need to show itself
Tenacious and pugnacious! when suppressed
By higher irresistible authority,
Must make the firecracker of a joke
While the Law's back is turned.
                              Hershey was kicked,
Kicked in the ego by another child,
And learned injustice, felt like Monte Cristo,
Sought to become the hermit of his wrath. . . ."

And then one day Hershey played by the door of the apartment house,
when three of the other boys, always friends before now, members of the
kindergarten class,
    Took up the janitor's hose, coiled serpentine on the sidewalk, and sud-
denly turned it on Hershey, crying,
    You are a Jew! a Jew! Hershey ran away all wet from the baptismal flood
of the communal mind,
    He ran away to his mother, asking her what was wrong, what was being
a Jew?
    But she did not answer, he did not know so well, wetly, and sensuously,
until far later years.
    She took his hand and rang the doorbell where one of his opponents
lived,
    And protested to his mother in a loud self-righteous tone, which made
Hershey ashamed, although he hardly knew why,
    But knew that more than he understood defended and offended him,
    And knew with passion that laughter thrown at him by boys pitted
against him was one of the worst pains, and that other boys turning on
him

Stripped him, even if he ran to his mother, stripped him and left him alone, naked, wet and ashamed.

And then one day when his father gave him a fountain pen, and he lost it the very next day,

Playing in the empty lot behind the apartment house. He went and told his mother and begged her then, securing her promise,

Not to tell his father. But when in the evening his father came to see him go to bed, his father asked him and asking smiled,

Where his fountain pen was? When Hershey began to lie, Jack Green smiled still more broadly, the lying child was a joke, or the lying child was himself,

And said to the poor pajama'd boy that he knew he had lost his fountain pen, and gave him another one, his own, a better one, the best, and for some time admired by him,

And then Hershey knew such joy as Adam might have known, had his father brought him back to a greater Eden,

Making his loss his gain. But in the midst of his joy, Hershey saw that his mother had betrayed him,

He saw there was a communication between his parents which would always betray him.

Because he was a child.

"Poor boy, how education comes to you!
Learning to be a Jew, attacked because
A Jew, born to the long habit of pain
And alienation, of the people chosen for pain. . . ."

"Attacked for the first time because you are
A kind, a class! as you were not yourself,
The pain of the sole psyche insufficient,
The naked surd's self-torture not enough!"

"Thus to begin, in sudden dripping shock,
Abstractions' mastery, as if a teacher
Taught species, genus, higher genera,
Slapping his student's face as if to say
This is what faceness is, learn it through pain:
How better than in shock to learn of terms?"

Hershey felt now as when his hands and arms
Fell asleep, powerless, too weak in strength
To hold a cigarette, or hold a pin. . . .

"Now of betrayal, now these far-off singers
Will speak of parents' and betrayals' first—"
Hershey prepared himself, speaking these words,
Once more in mimicry of what he heard—

"The loss of faith's virginity, the sense
That anyone might lie, as when the earth's
Flatness turned out to be a curving lie,
Falseness objective in the turning world
—The sense that always underneath the face
Many a motive hid the truth, prepared
Illusions, made the mirage, deceived!"

"Life is a lie! Life is a long long lie,"
Another far voice cried, "Death is a news
Life painted differently! What have we now
But this eternal knowledge and regret,
Not an oblivion . . . at best, a sweet drugged sleep
When we are lucky! the sleep of hospitals—
True, one gets *used* to pain as one gets used
To living near a waterfall or trains,
But I cannot believe I will become
Used to regret, return, the infinite
Apocalypse of all that might have been,
Millions of instances shown in these lives,
Every future untrue and every hope,
Even in satisfaction, vain and false,
Since no success is terminus, serene. . . ."

"The hanged man like a sack upon a tree
Cannot believe the freedom of the will—"

His mother took him to Macy's department store just before Christmas
came; there he saw Santa Claus,

Much moved and afraid and dismayed, for he was seated on a throne,
White-bearded, rouged, and hoarse-voiced, hideous in his disguise. He
cackled, he laughed, he rang his bell, and all the children gaped,
He told them to be good and he would come unto them, the Providence
in children's terms, the unspeakable unknowable
Nameless *Ahhhhhh* of Abraham, in a department store!
A blackboard was bought for Hershey, and many colors of chalk. It
seemed to promise him an endless field of play,
But the interest faded quickly in a few days' experience.
Yet on that blackboard he inscribed in the tall crude print of the child
His parents' names, his brother's name, Anna the servant girl's name, and
his own,
And as the very finest thing, WOODROW WILSON, on top!
For this, the child who wrote before he went to school, his mother praised
him, praise which moved him
As nothing else could. Visitors and relatives came and he enacted printing
again for them,
And the pleasure of praise also was renewed again, the visitors praising
to please the mother,
And the child heard or overheard and climbed the ego's tower,
A prince of the wide world, expecting to be a king!

"A notable and just epiphany!
God in the great city, seen where else
But a department store? Thus through the dark's
Harsh elemental and white-buttoned roar
You rode, O Hershey, to meet Santa Claus,
Holding your mother's hand, which held the lamp,
Aladdin's lamp to you, of father's purse—"

"God through the World War! for this year was the year
That Woodrow Wilson went to La Belle France
With the A.E.F., being his father's son,
Minister of the Word, vocational—"

"I think this Santa Claus could but have been
Some poor fat man unemployed all year long
—Christ rode a jackass to Jerusalem,
Setting such standards for embodiment:

Who then can criticize Macy's because
They chose a poor fat failure for the part
Famous forever, of strange Providence?—"

"—Used by the business world, for God is used
By everyone. Is used for every purpose
As water is. Makes new the flesh, makes fresh,
Fertile and flowering all things in soil,
Bud, bird, and beast!"
                              "God amid many gifts,
Though business life dresses and places him
In the show window just at Christmas time!"

"The blackboard too is just and most exact:
It is the native night on which the boy
Inscribes with a child's hand, crooked and large,
His crude and loving sense of identity!"

"Praise for the small boy's quickness! kissed by praise:
What action and what satisfaction can
More than this action make a child depraved?
How wise the Greeks who saw Pride's foolish height—"

"Wiser the Christians, praising Humility!
A virtue which the Greeks could never see—"

One morning Hershey went with his mother marketing, and she left him
on the pavement when she went into a store,
    And was gone so long that fear rose in him: he cried in the foreign street,
he turned in the midst of loss,
    Until a small crowd stopped to ask the crying child, What was wrong?
Where did he live?
    Between his tears, he drew on the sidewalk square the numbers of the
apartment house, knowing its look and form, but not its name,
    Until his mother appeared and he wept still louder tears,
    Suddenly purged of loss, and yet appalled perhaps
    By apron-string or navel cord, the shadow of the womb!
    And he heard in this time of the World War and the Armistice, he heard
his aunt tell his mother

How his uncle, their brother, nineteen years of age, had come home ut-
terly drunk for the first time in his life

The morning of the Armistice, celebrating the peace or celebrating
himself.

He heard the neighbor shout the good news up the dumbwaiter, who had
a brother in France,

Relieved, not overjoyed. His father took him one day downtown to his
office near Wall Street, a place he loved to see,

And when they went back in the subway, a train awaited a few more
passengers,

But his father turned to the newsstand to buy the latest paper, letting the
train close doors and move away,

And when Hershey asked his father why, Jack Green said to him, he
wanted to read the newest lists of the dead,

His youngest brother Martin was Over There, and some men were still
being killed,

Surrounded by history, the growing fusing child ate and drank from the
tables huge as America,

What a child's consciousness feels, and never understands!

"The War again, Cain's everlasting sin. . . ."

"And Europe's guns, heard in America,
Dull thunder of the Fourth of July, heard
In thickwalled hospitals. Thus to the boy
Only a loud event, a subway ride,
And yet, fixed in his consciousness, until
In ten years' time, he slowly understands!"

"My mother's loss: my lostness! What of that?"
Hershey's increasing interest spoke out,
"Interpret that, O you who know so much,
Each tireless as the Ancient Mariner,
Learnéd and sick as Hamlet Coleridge,
And like him full of generalities—"

"No loss is like the loss of Mamma's womb,
Never again to be so snugly warm!
Not in a thick wood, not in the mountains,

THE COLLECTED POEMS OF DELMORE SCHWARTZ

Not on the rocking seas is anyone
As lost as when the doctor slaps his rump
(A hale and hefty slap, the first of Elks)
As if to say, breathe the harsh air, but know
Doctors and friends surround you—for a time!—"

"Is not the womb the South Seas of the Id?
A kindly matriarchy, motherland,
And every man like Crusoe, after that,
Makes out as best he can, makes friends, joins clubs,
Marries like Oedipus, honors on Mother's Day
The belly which fed him for nine eternities,
While he rehearsed the million animal years
Lived by his fathers through the ice and caves—"

"Yet some supposed children are innocent!"

And then, early one morning, Hershey slept and dreamed that he had to make water,

But could not, until the toilet was repaired. He stood in his dream in the white bathroom, regarding the janitor at work, waiting and impatient, pained by his need, fearing blame, if he let go,

And just as the janitor finished and told him he could now begin,

He was wakened from his dream by his parents, they stood by his child's bed and looked down on him,

Distant with years and with their emotion's heat, and asked him to choose with which one he wanted to live?

They had been having a brutal quarrel, the children had become a prize and an issue on which his mother fell back,

And in some pretension or abstraction of justice, an action read about in the newspapers, of some court of law,

They felt they must present the older child with choice; the younger one slept on—

He said with ineffable tact and practicality, he had to make water, he had to make number one.

What a unique fusion of choice, of the animal's need, and the parents' conflict was thus engraved on his mind,

Man's freedom, making water, and the anguished conflict of wills forever united for him!

He accepted this conflict of mother and father as he accepted their presence,

An ultimate natural fact of existence, overwhelming as the air and the sun,

And like the huge rock-face outside the living-room window, across the street, on which he often gazed,

Supposing or fancying it an immense human face, the face he sometimes thought of an Indian, centuries dead!

"Take sides, Antigone, take sides,
Orestes and Electra or the ghost
Of Hamlet's father will cry, Swear! Swear!
Under the boardwalk at Far Rockaway—"

"Not that way, not that kind of speech:
Too quick a universal will perplex him,
Seem merely a *mélange*. He has just learned
To name the essence with the famous names
That stand like statues in the Western mind—"

"I know enough by now," Hershey replied,
"Go on and on: now that my mind has reached
Those vivid scenes of childhood, scenes which I
Know well as anyone (except for God,
If He exists, if He, in fact, exists?)
My fear is light, narcissist interest
Engages me, as if I played a game—
A game of tennis, close, hotly contested
—Yet, at the same time, gazed from the grandstand, cool!"

"Choice cuts the heart in half as the lungs breathe,
Those ultimate balloons! Choice cuts the heart
In half and throws away one half as if
The unelected half were useless rind!"

"Wakened from sleep by choice: how true that is!
Wakened too soon, premature by ten years,
Afraid to wet the bed! Is not this boy
Made paragon, a very Fauntleroy
By the need to urinate?"

THE COLLECTED POEMS OF DELMORE SCHWARTZ

              "I did not know
As I begin to know," Hershey exclaimed,
"That everyone is wrong and everywhere
At all times!"

              "Righteousness is the unicorn,"
Another deathly voice replied to him,
"Living nowhere but the imagination,
Let every judge but the one Judge resign!"

"Virtue is far away, Goodness is difficult,
And, at its peak, almost unbearable!
The air harder to breathe, the climb almost
A cliff, and looking down brings vertigo,
Also disgust and hate, more than the plain's—"

The child was always listening, he heard of death, his mother spoke of a friend's grief, whose niece had died,

Whence Hershey asked his mother why the dead were not kept in the house, in a glass box or a vase,

Since they were loved so much? The dead must go to the blue sky, his mother said, and then he saw in the sky

A huge apartment house! somewhere within the blue. This was the time of the World War's exhausted aftermath,

From overseas came the influenza, moving in on the weakness of body and psyche, international illness!

Walking one morning with Anna, in a May day's mild and sunny air, Hershey came, holding the Polish maid's hand,

Where a small crowd stood by an apartment house, a line of black cars by the curb,

And Anna explained that a young lady had died, they were going to carry her from the door to the hearse,

Thrilling Hershey because he thought the dead were naked and he wished to see a naked lady very much. But when the coffin was shouldered through the door to the hearse,

He was left there on the sidewalk intensely disappointed, and from that moment there, in the sunny May morning, waiting on the sidewalk,

Love and death have lain by each other in his mind, Eros and Thanatos, the beginning and the end, Romeo and Juliet forever composed!

"There are more things in heaven and in earth
Than any philosophy! And Death holds all.
We look up when we hear that word as one
Looks up to hear of his profession, his home town,
Or as all human beings when they hear
Of sexual intercourse!"

      "Here Love and Death
Meet in a metaphor: love is a kind of death
On Venusberg, as Tristan might have said—"

"A child can think all things and do all things,
O he will take advantage of the dead
As of the living, pinch his sister, kick
The nurse, wet the expensive carpet, put
His hand in the frying pan because the sound
Is interesting! Will climb into the coffin
And touch the private parts! All later life
Seems—I say, seems,—at times only a long
Vain effort to diminish and control
The violent childhood living in the man
Like Katzenjammer Kids!"

       "Return, return:
What is the first vacation? sleep? Utopia?
Childhood is far more popular! why not?
Go down the Mississippi with Huck Finn,
Escaping from small-town America
With Rousseau in the heart, and a colored boy
Who from green Africa inherited
All glowing summer spontaneities—"

"Revert, free of responsibilities,
Naked at the swimming hole with other boys,
Or in dark dormitories mix the sex
Until you hate all girls or hate all boys:
Hershey amid a million juvenile
Delinquents only wished to gaze upon

'September Morn,' nude on the calendar,
Her pink-brown private parts shown off to him!"

In the same surrounding illness, Roger, three years of age, was taken with scarlet fever, like many other children,

And Hershey was taken to stay with grandmother, aunt, and uncle, his first departure from home,

And on the very first night, his aunt was moved to wean him of his bogus nipple. She said it was left at home,

He cried a while, unwilling to let go of mother and of infancy. But soon the animal's tiredness adjusted the ego,

And he fell asleep older. In the morning when he woke, his aunt smiling explained to him

That his need had been in the dresser drawer all the time; had he cried longer she would have given it to him,

But he had not, he was a big boy now. Hearing this, the knowledge of betrayal arose once more, but faded in the pleasure of praise.

And then on Sunday his father came to see Hershey and took him back in the car to the apartment house where Roger lay sick,

Stood with him in the empty lot behind the house, pointed to the fifth-floor window where his mother waved,

While tears rushed to his face and he was afraid. And on the next Sunday, this far-off interview was renewed,

But now the convalescent Roger, held in his mother's arms, waved to him also from the fifth-floor window,

And Hershey burst into uncontrollable tears, and knew abyss-like fear. And thus will wave and know fear, from an empty lot to a window, his father no longer beside him,

This the image of distance and separation to him forever, looking with Helen from the tower, seeking the distant ones!

Yet during this first vacation, Hershey played with three girls in the apartment house

Where his grandmother lived. They were a year older than he was, they went to public school, and hence looked upon him as an infant,

But asked him one day to choose the one he liked best and thought most beautiful. His choice had long been made, the little girl who lived next door,

She knew it very well, his looks had shown his heart. But she, when she saw Paris about to choose her,

Took him aside and asked him for her sake to choose another, the fat and wistful girl,

And he obeyed, utterly pleased by her appeal and by the secret between them, feeling the sex in the secret,

And by the ancient choice. But most of all by the thought which suddenly came, that the other girl loved him and he had not known.

And yet his own chosen girl knew, and knew him as one who was loved,

An enthralling delicious thought with which he went to sleep, dancing through the forms of love,

Appeal, mystery, recognition, sympathy, the stations of the heart; dismissed, denied, and passed under the very next evening when

His aunt came home from her business with a pretty young lady friend, who stooped and kissed the cunning child,

So that when she went to the bathroom during the evening, he went to the hallway and saw her shadow on the glazed window door,

And the untaught Id banged and banged on the door, demanded admission, wished to see the woman naked,

Frustrated once by death, excited by the neighbor's children, not yet knowing enough to hide his naked desire,

Until grandmother drew him away, saying, Shame on you! Shame on you! The far-off cries of the Super-Ego!

"Jesu, Jesu, the days that we have seen!"

"The bathroom is, in modern life, a kind
Of monk's or nun's retreat. For there some read,
Study the face upon the glass which hides
The medicine chest, cure the loved body,
                                        sing!"

"Yet is it, on the other hand, a North
Of white sterility, marble repose."

"Is it not true that this boy of five years
Was most exact to bang the bathroom door
In sexual attack? Is it not there
In modern life that Venus paints herself?"

"O penetrate this surface deeper now:
See how the Super-Ego grows in him
And how the adult's point of view is learned
Against the grain, against the animal
Harshly and slowly and with much surprise—"

"These episodes bring out primordial
Forms of the will's procedure, never quite
Pulled out and cast away. Thus, when some dine,
Distant reflections of the high-chair dinner
Can be perceived when they reach out for bread—"

"Never free of the past, not even in death!
And never free of childhood, childhood's crime,
Though intermissions rest you for a time:
All things forever live, nothing is lost!"

To which for the first time a brand new voice
Spoke out (but Hershey was far far
Beyond surprise): "So it is, so it has been,
Sex flows within a childhood as the Hudson
Beside the great city, bringing distant things—"

"Everything happens once in a lifetime,
Except the falling rain, fresh on the gazing mind. . . ."

"My senses blaze, hearing of childhood sex,
It is a most attractive nakedness—"

"He clambered up the heights of Venusberg
As I . . . with wine-stained, wine-awakened mind!"

And his aunt had a new victrola, Galli-Curci and Caruso
Soared, cried, and pealed, and touched the fusing child with intuitions of
the beauty of formal sound,
   And hysteria or aspiration of emotion, *Pagliacci*, *Ave Maria*, Verdi's melos,
mixed with his wonder
   At the mechanical miracle, the voice in the box, the dog which stood
attentive by the curving horn,

His Master's Voice, on the red seals of the Victor records! But his young
uncle played different voices,
  Al Jolson sang for them of going to the sunny South, where the Negro,
the enslaved peasant, and Dixie, the defeated nation,
  Furnished for the immigrant Jewish genius metaphors for his maternal
emotion,
  And reached to touch the fusing boy with the lyricism flowing from the
profoundest sources,
  From the Ghetto, from the Civil War, from the warmth of Nature in
summer,
  Of the suffering nations and people who had made him a living child!

  "Everything happens in the mind of God!"

  "Scenes of your life and of the life which made you,
  And the immense powers, Europe, America,
  Nature, Capitalismus, New York City—"

  "Almost as if you were about to die
  When the violet light touches curtain and pane—"

  Hershey fell back once more, in the worst despair—

  "Your father is in Eastern Europe now,
  A letter comes to him, his brother writes
  Thousand of miles away, summoning him;
  Your mother is the Jewish girl at the nuns' school,
  Loved by the sisters and the little children;
  Her father is the man you know full well,
  You who inherited his deathly anger,
  Growing, as his wife's brother grows more rich:
  He takes the money, trembling, crosses Europe,
  The long migration to America begins. . . ."

  "Everything happens in the mind of God:
  Thence is the blueness of the quality
  (Perhaps, *that is*, perhaps all of our thoughts
  Are versions of perhaps) we think we feel
  In every living thing. . . ."

"We from our death
Have lived through such a night how many times
In our own lives and in a million lives:
Our interest never fades! We are the children
Who stay all afternoon to see the pictures
How many times! and with the same emotions!"

Hershey, though breathless resting, cried right back
"Everything happens in the mind of God?
—This news is thrilling and I hope it true!
It is like looking at the sky's round blue,
Blue within blue within blue and endlessly
And does the angel Gabriel know it too?
All of the scenes of my life?

       my intimate emotions?

     And in the summer,
 The Green family went to the seashore, to avoid or lessen the heat of
Nature,
 Hershey saw his father striding home from business in the daylight saving
evening,
 Coming from the suburban train or from his car, tall, broad-shouldered,
powerful, and paternal,
 Bringing candy and toys, and bringing the relationship of fatherhood,
so that Hershey admired his father very much, the emotion of admiration
arose and shone when he looked at his father,
 And thus when late one afternoon Hershey played with a little girl, asked
her to play doctor, took her behind the garage,
 Knowing intuitively that this must be hidden, and lay down with her, near
the garage door, where the ground was soft brown sand,
 And caressed her belly, seeking he knew not what, remaining unsatisfied,
the fifth-year libido far in advance of consciousness,
 And went still further, and lay on her belly, and was still, by what he did,
 Unsatisfied, even as his father came for him, sent to call him for his supper,
 And saw him on the girl's belly, smiled faintly and far-off! as never before
to Hershey,
 But with unmistakable pleasure, as Hershey recognized, even as he
sprawled off, perplexed by being ashamed,
 Perplexed by his father's smile, for how could he know

He would be haunted forever by his father's smile, smiling with a Mona
Lisa faintness? How could he know
Nature smiled at itself that day, his father smiled
Faintly and profoundly at himself and at his grandchild?

"Why must I tell, hysterical, this story
And must, compelled, speak of such secrecies,
. . . When by the seaside for the sexual act
Vaguely I felt? Speak of my father's face
And make comparisons with famous paintings?
Where is my freedom, if I cannot resist
So much speech blurted out, of obscene shames?
How long must I endure this show and sight
Of all I lived through, all I lived in: Why?
Why? I know, I have been told that one
Gets used to anything and every pain:
I feel like one before a hundred doctors,
Stripped of my clothes, ugly in nakedness,
Walking from infancy up to this night,
While all the white-gowned antiseptic men
Lean down to hear my beating heart, stare down
My throat, touch all my limbs, and try
My eyes, my ears, my breath, feel the strange skull,
Look for my mind, seek for my thoughts!
                                    When will
I sleep? when will I be allowed to close
My mind, and look no more at my long life
(I feel as if I had lived hundreds of years,
Assisting in his pain the Wandering Jew),
Be the warm beaver of a winter's sleep
And feel the warm bath of unconsciousness?"

"This you must face," a voice unmoved in tone
Replied to Hershey, whispering as before,
"This you will not evade. Like Time and Space,
All memory holds the mind. In Life, in Death,
O in Death most of all! Like Oedipus,
No one can go away from genesis,

From parents, early crime, and character,
Guilty or innocent! Though he cut out
His eyeballs, though he kill himself, no man
Escapes the Past, nothing is lost,
—There in the ultimate pit, rising and falling,
Lie all the deities which make our lives—"

"*Ride, si sapis, O puella, ride!* Be gay!
And in eternity's cold cloudy light
Giggle somewhat upon a world-wide scale
—The West was dying and my hopes in bed
—Pressed with what flowers, bon-bons, and fruits—
Their lingering mortal illness indifferently
Regarded, and I was gay!—"

                "But I was not.
The wine stain on the book moved me to tears,
I in the slump and slum of the former life grew dark
Because I did not say to every state,
Emotions pass, evil as well as good
—My heart dashed like a fiacre often in June
When lightning's fiat displayed Being's quick powers,
But each such exultation quickly passed,
—Spray! spray of the mind! in a November gloom,
Knowing that no fiesta can quite hold
The midnight in a lighted dining room,
Boredom and disappointment moved in me,
Sneering like many fiends with rough raw rumor,
Whispered behind my back as I passed by—"

"Where Knickerbocker once his comforts took,
A sofa of a life, my life was bled:
My face was mushroom-white in adolescent
Sickness, uneasiness, and deep-dyed need—
But early morning when the great city stilled
Turned for the last time in the tumbled bed
Then, then! did I know happiness like birds—"

And now the memory which keeps the self from nothingness, or from the lakes and seas the body often swims,

Grasps in my mind scenes of more length and depth and width. For when towards the summer's end,

A minister of the religion and of the stamina which to ancient Judaea still bound and still brought back

The world-wandering race, stayed with some relatives one weekend at a nearby hotel,

There on the porch Jack Green and Eva Green met him, a refined and eloquent man, skillful in easy reasons

And facile sentiments. He much impressed Jack Green, speaking of how Jewish children should be taught in this modern day,

As in the Ghetto, as always in Abraham's bosom! Jack Green was so much impressed, he wished very much in turn to make an impression,

He declared in the loud dominant declarative tone he used, when he felt his intense selfhood most consciously,

That *his* child would get a genuine Jewish education, in the old way from the very start at any cost!

Hershey listening nearby heard this with pleasure, any promise of going to school was a voyage to the Indies,

But as the family of three walked home, Eva Green, also pleased, but always unable to permit another person his pretensions,

Told her husband how she was pleased, but recalled to him his frequent cynical Ingersollian remarks about religion,

To which Jack Green cynically replied, cynical about most things because he thought to be cynical was to be intelligent,

And to defend his tone and his attitude from his wife, cynically replied that he had not meant a word he had said about the child's education,

And Eva Green saw then the egotism in the cynicism, this was what made him so different

From husbands of her friends. Between the two in a moment a brutal quarrel grew,

By the time they had reached the bungalow, both were enraged, by the end of the evening once more,

Immediate separation became the purgation which Jack Green's psyche declared!

And yet the next afternoon, after all morning long Hershey had gazed on his mother's misery and fear,

Jack Green called from the city, told Eva Green to come to town immediately, ignored the quarrel utterly,

Eva Green willing that he should, although unable to suppress a single sardonic sentence at his sudden shift in mood.

I have seen, said Jack Green, a new house. It was a real bargain, he was thinking of buying it,

He wanted her to come and see, in a harsh voice, if she wanted to come and live in it? If she found it suitable?

It is easy to see what had happened, knowing Jack Green. The movement of his heart shines and is clear in the light that the years throw down,

Turning, glittering and sad as the weak moonlight, the after-light of knowledge.

Jack Green had tired of the seashore before the summer's end, as in the romance of the romantic ego

He was too quickly pleased and too soon tired by every *milieu* of his life. And when, haggard in this mood, his wife offended him,

He had to hit back and hurt her as much as he could. But in the fresh new morning,

And in the freshness of his body in the morning, his mind had swung back, he had been sorry, he

Had felt the appeals of family life strongly and clearly, now that the end was near, and graspable,

And when he went to the city, this mood arose and became obsessive, and he wished compulsively to make amends,

And when he saw the actual prospect of the new house, his emotion brimmed over, he acted,

Thus from Jack Green's heart fell the new house of the family's life!

The child was impressed, the child did not forget this, the child bore

The truck and burden of the actual event, for his sensibility was quick and avid and ravenous, avid for news of Life,

Just as his parents were insensitive in the sickness of their marriage—

> "How clear and typical is that man's mind,
> The movement of his heart seen as through glass!
> Tired of the spa before the summer's end,
> —Too quickly pleased and too soon tired
> By every *mise-en-scène* of life, as always
> —Fugues and romances of the barbarous ego!"

"He did not see that such depressions were
Hardly objective adjectives, but only
His body's tiredness and disbelief
—He did not understand the falls of love—
This forced the monstrous in both characters,
And the sick child who wakes up and who whines!"

"'O God! O God! that it were possible
To undo things done, to call back yesterday,'
As the old play says. But would that help?
How can the will reverse itself, arise
From paths and passion such as these? Cannot
Go back, cannot begin again, *brand-new!*"

Hershey chimed in, separate in thought from them:
"I must be patient, how patient I must be
To speak these years which I am, which are in me
Like an incurable disease—"

                    "Go on,
Go on! no news, no nakedness, no truth,
But it will help you live, if you must live,
There in the last of Europe's capitals—"

"The autos move with goggle eyes dead-white
And in the glasses of the wet streets draw
Slanting pillar-like rays which slide with them,
The while the rain on roofs makes cracks of sounds,
The driving autumn rain in the sick city!
—This is an image of the city life—"

So the small waking animal was thrown about by towering father and
mother,
    Giant and giantess to him: they went to live in the new house in Brooklyn
on the Parkway
    Which moved to Coney Island, Manhattan Beach, and Atlantic Ocean,
over which twenty years before,
    Eva Green's heart and mind had floated to the dark, supposed as golden,
    Of America and of the future. And now neighbor's marriages move

through Hershey, next door in another new house lived a newly married couple,

The husband Jewish, the wife Gentile, a difficult alliance: the husband a short fat man who had just made a fortune

In a small store on the Great White Way, selling greeting cards; the wife a Ziegfeld Follies girl until her marriage.

Eva Green was thrilled to have her for her neighbor and soon her intimate friend,

Because she was Gentile, because she was beautiful, because she had been on the stage

For which Eva Green retained her girlhood feelings, of glamorous footlights. Eva Green was soon telling her new friend how beautiful she was,

And Mrs. Rinehart in turn would tell Eva Green that she should have been and could have been in show business!

Every day after her husband left for business, Mrs. Rinehart, in the intensive sorority of women,

Came in her kimono across the adjoining backyards, and brought with her, her marriage, for an endless discussion.

She suffered from a guilty sense that everyone was always thinking she had married her husband for his money.

When she stood next to her short fat husband, knowing her own image, tall and dark and beautiful,

She felt their contrast, and was sure it was present in the minds of those who saw them,

Obvious and obscene! When her husband's relatives came to visit them, she knew or thought she knew what they were *thinking*,

When they were due to come, she came to Eva Green, saying, Jerusalem is coming to the house!

And Eva Green was flattered to hear her speaking as if she herself were not Jewish, and she mildly complacently protested

That she too was Jewish; but after all some were common. The growing fusing boy, listening and looking always,

Heard and in his soft head his sense of persons grew.

Hershey too admired Mrs. Rinehart, and when he gazed from the glassed sun-porch, waiting to see his admirable tall powerful father,

Striding from his car, while Mrs. Rinehart too awaited her returning husband on the lawn,

Hershey saw his father's distant nod to Mrs. Rinehart, and saw the indifference and the unawareness of her beauty in his father,

And wondered why his father did not fall in love with her, and wished
that his father would fall in love with her,

And was, by that identity which made his wish,

An adulterer at five! Vronsky, Oedipus, Hamlet! prince of the king his
father,

Freely sinning with all! And because he was so interested in the pretty
lady,

He told the laborers building a house nearby that Mrs. Rinehart had been
a Ziegfeld Follies girl,

Observing them, brick by brick, not knowing what Follies meant, but hav-
ing heard his mother proudly mention the word many times to her friends,

Then quickly through Mrs. Rinehart's chauffeur, mocked by the laborers,
in *their* adultery,

The word came back to Mrs. Rinehart, and she came straight to her
neighbor,

Raging, demanding that Hershey be spanked in front of her, telling
amazed white scared Hershey, always prepared to be guilty, that the police

Would come for him and take him away! He did not know what was
wrong, having been pleased as always

To see the beautiful lady coming to the door. Eva Green sent him up-
stairs, but he stood halfway up the stair,

And listened to the Follies girl's rage, and to his mother's replies

When the Follies girl suggested, begged and then insisted that the child
be whipped in front of her,

Until he bawled and howled! Eva Green tried to soothe her, soothingly
she said,

There was no shame in being a Ziegfeld Follies girl, and even if there
were,

How could the child have known? But Mrs. Rinehart would not be ap-
peased, the indecent workingmen

Had said the most indecent things about her, of so much she was sure,

And Hershey heard, halfway up the stair, terrified more and more,

By her rage and by her police and by her past! by the morality which thought
the actress wrong, and by her guilt in her marriage, and by her ancient need

To make the child the scapegoat, to whip him for her sins!

And then when she had left and taken away her guilt, Eva Green came to
the boy and told him he had done nothing wrong,

He had been sent upstairs only to soothe the lady. Not to cry, not to be
afraid.

THE COLLECTED POEMS OF DELMORE SCHWARTZ

She spoke with such sympathy and knowledge of the boy as she but
rarely used.

Yet Hershey was terrified for days, and then for the next six months,

Terrified each time a policeman passed the house, running and hiding in
the garage,

And his fear and anxiety did not lift until one day at the end of autumn,

As he slid back and forth through the late cold bright afternoon, upon the
sidewalk squares where they had frozen over,

In the black and orange sunset amid the rising wind. The ease of sliding
and skating pleased him and relieved him, he triumphed,

Sliding when a policeman came into view, skating without the least fear,
amazed at his freedom and radiant joy.

The beauty of form which made his body light moved him as Galli-Curci

Singing *Ave Maria!* from the fat brown box which was the victrola in his
grandmother's house. . . .

> "Beauty, dénouement, and denunciation!
> By this strong mixture he will be so scored
> He will forever after find it hard
> Not to fear guilt in beauty, not to fear
> Sudden ignorant unexpected crime
> In all his passages with pretty girls—"

> "And if the child is struck for others' sins,
> His mother by her child is also struck,
> Deprived of glamorous friendship by a guilt
> Which heard all tongues whisper behind her back—"

> "Here too we see the sense of audience
> Ugly and necessary as the nose—"

> "These children everywhere walk in the gun-room,
> Play with the guns, I mean; at other times
> Run to the parents' bedroom, seeking a game
> Early on Sunday morning, only to find
> Mamma and Papa wrestling and moaning in bed,
> Naked, startled, and angered by the heir:
> *Coitus interruptus!* by the plump fruit
> *Of an old joy*—"

"These revelations are
Frequent enough in the lower middle class
Without a maid to keep the untrained child
From running wild—"

                "Your irony right now
Is hardly proper—"

             "This Mrs. Rinehart too,
She was a victim too, her mother's toy,
Impressed by her with the Almighty Dollar,
And by newspapers singing of actresses
Who married millionaires. Made by her beauty
Narcissist, like so many by sweet flesh,
She turned aside the short fat man's pursuit
For several months
            —I know, I see it all!—
Until she was seduced by gift and ease,
And custom made her used to fat physique,
And the heart's indolence said, *I might as well!*"

"This *might-as-well* has often terrified me:
Thus does the heart spill its identity!"

A girl six months older than Hershey lived in a nearby house. She was a
Catholic and already went to parochial school,
    Hershey tried to get her to play the games he had played the summer
before with his seashore belle.
    But she refused. He gave her an apple, O Adam, he divided his candy
with her.
    But she refused to divide her sweetness with him. She promised to kiss
him,
    But ran away, and when he said, You promised! I took it back under my
breath, she replied, anyone may do that,
    And Hershey wondered, struck by the holy nature of the promise, and
his curious mind was keen,
    And he wished to know what Catholic was. But she refused to tell. He
asked about God, he paid her many times
    With all the goods he had, pennies, candies, and toys, for such was his desire,

To tell him what she was taught, and not to withdraw by speaking under her breath,

To tell him of God and the angels and the castle where they lived.

But she would only tell him that the white mushrooms which grew on the lawn sometimes

Were the work of the powers of evil *down below!* a thought which forever remained and lived. When he ate mushrooms for the first time, years after,

Disgust took hold of him, feeling them on his tongue and touching in their taste,

The enchainment of past and future, the immense presence

Of the Past in every moment, waking or asleep!

"The little boy, like curious Socrates—"

"O Nature is a view of Paradise:
The snow, the lilacs, and the dripping fish
Drawn from the sea by man's technique show what
Profuse prolific inexhaustible
Variety provides *down here, below*—
And yet each tiny thing in Nature's vast
Bouquet is but a minor tiny clouded
Species and sample of Heaven's plenitude—"

"Did Hershey at five years feel this somewhat?
Is that why he asked questions, stopped the game?
Feeling much more in riches everywhere?"

"Rather the night, before he fell asleep,
When like a candle going down the stairs
Borne by a servant-girl, his consciousness
Flickered and blackened on the bedroom walls—"

"Just like to-night," said Hershey, taken up
With the *expression*, that it be exact—

"From such experience his questions came,
The boy thus grew to know that Life was, everywhere,
More and much more in principle, and full
Of mystery, no matter where he looked—"

"What! from a nebula came forth man's mind?
—It is not true, it is a stupid lie!"

"Now that you hear much more, though otherwise
Than you had wished at five or later times,
Now that you hear the dead speak of strange Life,
Living beyond their lives and ignorance,
Do you still wish to know of God? do you
Still wish to hear of his angels? of the castle
In which they live? of all the passages
Between them and the Nature where you live?

"Whether I do or not," Hershey replied,
"Such news will come for me throughout my life!"

"Alcestis, Lazarus, Eurydice
And Orpheus, returning from the dead
—They knew the strangeness we have come to give,
They knew that in all Life the dead must live!"

Eva Green took her two children when she visited friends, when she vis-
ited Mr. and Mrs. Eastman,
   A couple in their fifties with grown-up children, an unmarried daughter
and son.
   And much was made of the two small boys, the little child was the idol
of this middle-class,
   Center of poetry, center of comedy, so much else having passed—
   Excited by the attention and the praise he received, Hershey cried out,
Woman talk too much! delighting everyone, amusing everyone,
   With incongruity and precocity, although the remark itself but echoed
what he had heard,
   Listening to an older conversation between his mother and her friends.
   And then eighteen-year-old Amy, daughter of the family, began to play
the piano as young girls often used,
   Evening began to darken the wind-blown autumn light of this Sunday
afternoon in the lower-middle class,
   Hershey sat in the corner glowing warmly with praise, listened as Cho-
pin's sadness was tinkled and tapped in tone,

Until his joy disappeared, in the darkness and the sounds
Of the romantic ego, Chopin's or his own. . . .
What an occasion! how that family visit was to the growing child
An image of the world! society as audience! towards which his wish and act
Prayed and played for praise and winning it, fell sad
In the returning darkness of Nature, and the ego's solitude . . .

"The emptiness of Sunday afternoons!
Especially when autumn's shows begin
With heaving winds in the quick dusk and city lights
Grow sharp, so soft all summer long,
Sharp-bright in street-lights, shop-signs and marquees,
And on the glaring fronts of passing cars:
A certain gloss prevails, as if ice shone!"

"Children may feel this most of all, and most
When the light fails more early and more quickly
—They played till nine o'clock all summer long
. . . Perhaps that's why Chopin broke through the child's
Pleasure in praise and applause, as evening fell:
Music is dark, darkly from the piano
The bird-like notes fly out, fall in the mind
—Pathetic fallacies fume forth from this,
The ego's darkness is sufficient cause!"

"None can long live free of the worst despair,
Anxiety, boredom, and the worst despair,
—Not only does it teach the heart to stop,
Not only does it keep the heart from breaking
In obvious sensational delight
In all the glories of the turning world,
But it brings doubt, doubt is intelligence,
—Brings criticism and serenity,
Calm gaiety and careful conscious
Contemptuous indifference to all Life,
Inseparable from utmost seriousness
—Lo, in some great men, such serenity,
Inseparable from anguish and from doubt—"

"O Life is terror-full, beyond belief,
—How difficult it is to know and live—"

"Seldom in Sodom had they the stamina
To thrust a toothpick through the crevices
Where lodged some poor chick's torn saliva'd flesh,
Until, that is, this move became a pleasure:
Everyone liked to pick his rotten teeth—"

"—Would we laugh now, if but we could? We would,
These family lives offend and anger us,
So full of what we were, shameless, obscene:
This you shall not escape, O Hershey Green!"

"O what a sense of relief I felt! as one,
Long standing at attention, might go home,
Sit in the arm-chair and take off his shoes
—Thus did I feel in the first hour of death—"

"When I looked down at Life for the first time,
It was as if I turned to the comic strips,
And lit a cigarette for the first time,
And in deep relaxation, started slowly
To smile, then roared! at the mere black-and-white
Unlikely slots and strips of comedy,
Speaking balloons! as if they did not live,
Had no true being (somewhat Platonic then
My frame of mind). But, as the clowns slid on,
Perceived the universals in the art,
Saw Jiggs as Everyman and Jiggs' wife
As the harsh criticism Everyman endures,
No hero to his wife: at least, that is,
In lower-middle-class America,
Among the Joneses rising in the world,
Among that Mutt and Jeff, or Sancho Panza
And Don Quixote, deathless in this life—"

"Soon Laughter turned to Irony as milk
Turns sour: when I saw such average scenes

As have just passed, told by that helpless boy,
Tears filled my mind and made my spirit weak,
And several of the older dead nearby
Suggested that I look at the starry sky
Above this life, the moral law within
—For such sublimities redeem the man
Sad in his underwear, ridiculous!
The woman also, who, most self-absorbed,
Crouched over, cuts her toe-nails carefully
(Does dusky Rembrandt's picture hold my mind?)
As if naught in the wide world were worth
Such sharp attention, but her much-loved body
(Great art comes dimly back, I see the boy
Who draws a thorn from his bare foot, concerned,
Contorted, self-concerned with the poor body . . .)"

Pre-school ended, a period was over, Hershey was taken to begin to go to the foreign world each day,

No longer wholly within the scan and appeal of mother or servant-girl,

The struggling ego faced with longer relationships. All over the great city, Education set up the public school buildings,

And when he passed one, riding in the car next to his father,

Aspiration seized Hershey, he felt his life would be transformed and illuminated,

When at last he went to *real* school, and *more* than kindergarten. When at last he was taken, and his impatience was ended,

He was taken too soon, on his sixth birthday, when the fall term was almost over,

Beginning for him another left-handedness of his irregular life, beginning at the wrong time.

And he loved to go to school, his pride was most intense, he thought that all who looked at him saw him as somehow *more*,

He loved the primer read by the class, he looked with jealousy

At children in the higher class, who had a different book, the story of a pig, which he would read next year—

And thus one evening in mid-winter, in pajamas prepared for bed, he read from his primer proudly and loudly,

Seated with father and mother on the sofa, proudly and loudly until his mother observed

How Jack Green had been mistaken to think that his son would resemble
him
    In nature as in feature; and hate, as he had, to go to school; for look, he
loved it now.
    Jack Green replied to his wife that in the end he was sure the boy would
be just like him and would not want to go to school,
    And Hershey heard and disagreed, and yet was very pleased
    To hear the identity his father with pleasure declared!

        "The school divinity exerts its power,
        Much like the big city on a farm boy—"

        "Against the parenthood, against the life
        Made by the family divinity. . . ."

        "Elucidate, go on, make lucid all,
        For it will do him good!"

                        "What do you think
        You have been doing all this while?"
        Cried Hershey Green against the foreign voices
        Which tutored him in what he knew or what
        He did not wish to know, wishing to sleep,
        Yet at the same time brimming with the story—

        "O teach him of the causes of his life,
        Showing the guilt and freedom of his will!"

        "Saw from afar, riding in father's car,
        The buildings of the school divinity,
        Almost an Indies to the little boy,
        A new world full of news and thrilling games,
        Against the other boys and with the girls!"

        "Schooldom in conflict with the family!"

        "Look how his father sees identity,
        Insists on it! Facile analogy

Which rests, however, on the first abyss,
Death! Death and the countless dead, such as we are:
The boy will be like him, renew his life!"

"—Fatal rotundity! on which we turn,
And where the plants are fresh or dry, and where
Many a one has tried to get a statue,
And many a one has wished, at times, to die—"

"The boy hears the identity: it please him!
His father has impressed him very much!
Reads to his father from the primer proudly,
And they much moved! moved without knowing why,
Not knowing that, in the end, he'll read to them
Judgment and revelation! Condemnation
Like Hamlet's and Electra's, tragic and true!"

"Amid the 70,000, one man rose and howled,
Howled with absolute cries, *That's my boy!*
(The crying of the needle in the haystack)
—It was his son, there on the broken field
He fled in fame, the fame of the roaring crowd!"

Because it was snowing, Hershey was not wakened for school. And when
he woke up, he broke into angry tears,
　　Because he loved school so much. But when, from the window,
　　He looked and saw the white advent, softly and wholly
　　Settled on all, roof and parked car, sidewalk and lawn, a coat and bloom
at once upon the next house,
　　Disappointment snapped in a twinkle, he was neither
　　Happy nor unhappy, he was illumined, he was transfigured and quiet be-
fore the whiteness which seemed
　　An unknown stillness and faëry visit from a new world, the evident Par-
adise or Nirvana
　　For which sleep yearned and dreamed!
　　But then, the next day, in school, not knowing how to raise his hand and
ask to leave the room,
　　He tried to hold in, he tried to wait, as the class morning neared its end,

But could not, but wet his pants, and disgraced himself before all,

And even when the teacher forgave him, the giggling girls ran through his heart,

And he knew insuperable shame, he knew the sex in the event,

The letting go of the flood of need and of feeling,

When inhibition failed . . .

And then it was the week before Christmas: Hershey was told to write to Santa Claus. The letter would be mailed to him, and then, if Hershey were good,

Hershey would get what he asked for. A bicycle was his wish, he wrote for one and described the kind. He did not know whether or not

He believed in Santa Claus, but he was prepared to believe. But not convinced,

Even by last year's Macy Santa Claus. But wanted him to exist, and wanted to believe in him. And as he wrote his letter, Eva Green said to Hershey and her husband

That they were Jewish, Christmas was not their holiday. But neither father nor son

Paid any attention to this repetition of her self. The day before Christmas all day in vain Hershey waited for the snow to arrive,

The white décor of the holiday had grown vivid in him, having been seen in popular pictures.

He thought that without the snow Santa Claus could hardly come,

Driving his reindeer'd sled through the sky, the bells tinkling the epiphany, even as a music-box.

He could not come; it would hardly be Christmas at all without the snow. And as the growing fusing boy prepared for bed, all his excitement mixed

With disappointment because so much was lacking, this time as in times to come

Nature had failed the unnatural imagination and the hopeful heart!

Then in the darkness of the child's bedroom, annulling the wide world with whiteness,

Blown against the window with tiny ticking sounds, endlessly falling,

The clean clear shining good in itself Hershey saw in his sleep and dream,

(Amazed from the window seat in the apartment house two years before),

Haunted his dream and his sleep which skimmed the surface of waking,

In his expectant eager soul that Christmas Eve so that he woke up just before morning,

And heard someone moving in the hallway, going downstairs. And thought, surprised,

And surprised at being surprised, So: there really is a Santa Claus,

Grateful and moved! and fell asleep again and later woke and heard

Sounds of his father shaving in the bathroom, stropping his razor,

Then fell asleep again, and Anna woke him and wanted to dress him,

But he ran from her and ran downstairs in his pajamas. And there in the living room,

His bicycle! before the fireplace big and brand-new, and a shining green,

Stood by packed stockings with the heart's outline, hanging down from the mantel. He seized it,

He tried to mount it, his mother protested the carpet, his father looked on, pleased at the boy's joy,

As Hershey teetered and tottered, trying to gain his poise, pedal the wheels and ride about the living room,

And struggled with balance until he came to the window and saw,

And stood stock-still, shocked and overwhelmed,

That the whole world was white! Excitement left him at once, he forgot the gift, he put the bicycle to the side, he felt once more

Hallucinatory calm, utter quiet pleasure (as falling towards the depths of sleep, the grateful coma)

At the actual presence of snow, the apotheosis of winter,

The death of the colored world, the final fineness of Nature.

And then ec-stasis faded, and rose up Ambition,

Older and growing, he began to dress himself, to put on his stockings and tie his laces,

Part of the event of mounting the bicycle and trying to keep his balance,

While riding it in the cellar all through the Christmas week which was the beginning of his sixth year—

"What themes return! what deities!
                    If sleep would come!"
Cried Hershey Green, "if but my mind would cease!"

"The body, unable to control itself,
Guilt, as once at the seashore on the sand
With a little girl, prone behind the garage,
Shame, and the body brimming over, cup,
Profoundest cup, never controllable!"

"Christmas and Santa Claus, the ancient story
Throned in the heaven of the Western World
And every living room . . ."

                         "The nameless *AHHHHHHHH*
Of Abraham, seen in a department store!"

"Nature not good enough, and not precise
(Hence gardener, doctor, and engineer!)
Not adequate to winter's festival,
Full of much disappointment or rude shock—"

"And snow once more! what does it mean to you,
O sleepless boy, that you look everywhere,
Hoping to find it, wishing nothing more?
Ecstatic when it falls from the gray air!"

"There is the snow once more! How long and strong
—'It looks like silence and it looks like sleep'—
How deep in the boy's mind, some feeling which
I cannot understand, even in death
—It has a tie, whatever it may be (what is it? what?)
With all the deepest generalities
Which rove the living world for images!"

"The Id or daemon sleeps like a great river,
On it the ego, rowing back and forth—"

"He is as happy as a Beaux-Arts winner,
An hour after the news by telegram,
When the snow falls, and on the street composes
What lucid criticism of the sick city!"

"Happy as some in May, in the May morning,
When sunlight stamps gold coins on the blazed gaze,
And on the river does the diamond-dance,
—These sensuous skins, alas, obsess the life—"

"O Sun of Nature! source of all the forces,
All blooms, all snakes, and Botticelli's views
Of both of these, and Nature as a dance:
(Light is the heroine of every picture—)"

"O what a glory has the turning world!
And that is why some say that God himself
Took on this flesh:

                              to be God was not enough
To feel in blues and greens of natural life
Immediacies they have, like any kiss—"

"I hardly know just what it means to me,
But when I hear the word, my soul soars,
Strong as a gull over the evil shores
Of this unending terrifying night—"

"Hear how he speaks like us, now more and more—"

"Again, go back, see how Christ's story lives,
Born in the winter, risen from the year
As once in Palestine—

                              "If you were wise!
Like the three Magi all your attitudes,
Expecting any kind of Paradise,
In any poverty or paradox!"

"See how the Bible rules the consciousness
Of the West for two thousand years:

                              O, what a book!"

"Bible and Ovid too! who brings to us
Leda, Medea, Psyche, she who wished
To look at Love's forbidden hidden face,
Long before Sigmund Freud looked down on it,
And saw the serpent climbing up the stairs—"

"Psyche arrived after the birth of Christ!"

"The Sistine Chapel is the Western mind!"

"The snow: obsessed with it! This we must know
And understand; his love of it unceasing
In the deep mind beneath the conscious mind
Whence many motives rise up to command!"

"The gift! the bicycle! the gift of motion,
As he had loved the streetcar years ago,
Since motion, as the Stagirite once said,
Is being's deepest wish, most general form. . . ."

"Gift from the doubted wished-for nameless *Ahhhhhhhh*
—Amid snatches of sleep, dreaming of snow!"

"Yes, is it not most profound that he should hear
His father or his God in the living room?
Are not mistakes like these a dazzling news?
Now I remember a poor joke I heard
In the breathing life: a small boy, Hershey's age,
Asked by the company on Christmas Day,
'Do you believe in Santa Claus?'
                              'O yes!'
The child replies, 'I heard him late last night,
He walked in the living room and came upstairs,
And went in Mamma's bed!'"

                    "Shook the bed!
                              Ha! Ha!
Let that detail be added to the story!"

(This was a voice which Hershey recognized,
Who told with anguish and delight the truth
Of how the children everywhere sometimes
"Run to the parents' bedroom, seeking a game
Early on Sunday morning, only to find
Mamma and Papa wrestling and moaning in bed!")

THE COLLECTED POEMS OF DELMORE SCHWARTZ

"Here is the snow once more, in ecstasy,
Death of the colored world, and super-Nature,
Hallucinated calm, and utter pleasure
Calm and controlled! what does all of it mean?
Is it aesthetic joy, no more?"

"Much more!"

"Much more!"

Winter's staleness and coldness in February, June and October inconceivable

In the knifing wind and the overcoat, took Jack Green to Florida,

Nature depressing him, shifting his appetites. Friends and relatives of the family were told in euphemism

That Eva Green did not go with her husband because she could not leave her children.

Everyone knew the husband went off alone where he wished with his will, driven by appetite and sadness. Eva Green and the children

Went to the station with him, walked in the train, heard all the shuffling chuffing shaking sounds of the monstrous black beasts,

In the great shed through whose skylight dome fell the sooty light,

And felt the pure romance of going away, until

Doors shut, a whistle blew, the beating wheels began,

Wife and children waved goodbye, and were left behind, and turned to go back home,

Let down, empty, faced by all monotone.

Aunt and grandmother came to stay for a weekend, after Jack Green had been gone for six days,

And on the second day, Aunt Lillian who made much of Hershey, even as she had taken away his child's nipple, after the supper-time

Took Hershey to walk to the business street to buy him candy at the corner drugstore,

And when they returned in ten minutes, they found that Jack Green had come back, ten days before he was expected,

In a terrifying anger. Grandmother was packing to depart, Eva Green stood stony by her, and said to Aunt Lillian,

You must go, he has ordered both of you from this house, he wants you to go right now,

(As if to say, You see what a monster I married. Now you see.)

Aunt and grandmother went away in silence and dignity, the children were sent to bed,

Hershey who had listened and looked, shocked and offended by his father's will and emotion,

And yet impressed by it, felt a child's pity for all the adults,

And looked and listened, and could not understand, but tried, but fell asleep.

"Easily as a king he takes his pleasures. . . ."

"As once I saw, upon the silver screen,
Richard the Lion eat of a chicken leg,
Munching with gusto, slouched upon his throne,
Playful and powerful: is that what you mean?"
Thus from his interest cried Hershey Green—

"Here how he mimicks us, our influence:
Just what I mean. He goes away for joy
Even as any king and finds the truth:
The insecurity kings must endure
Or any climber climbed to any peak—"

"The shell shoots forward—slows . . . shoots forward, slows . . .
Under the human will, in concert there,
And by much artifice contriving strain
Not to be bored! and this complexity
Makes God regard the tiger as a trope
Too obvious, though striped and murderous—"

"Kites which I flew from empty lots in boyhood:
So I would do again, and touch some angels!"

"Left in the boy departure's fugue or poem,
Sadness and joy of railroad stations which
Display a fictive view of liberty
In the glistening parallels of the receding track—"

THE COLLECTED POEMS OF DELMORE SCHWARTZ

"Fictive, since each goes with himself. Arrives
At the far grand hotel, the weather warm,
June in December; yet in the lobby glass
Nonetheless meets himself, sees all he is
Rise like a traitor, betraying identity!
Thus Jack Green meets his heart in Florida,
Like any king, like any man of power!"

"O let me add to this!" cried Hershey Green,
"Freshly I see my father's will obscene,
Then merely shocked, no more. When I returned,
Holding, like a party thing, my candy bar,
Love Nest its name, O happy irony,—
Joy in the *Love Nest*, joy to see my father,
Turned sour, stopped and shocked by angered looks,
I was *surprised* then not to want my sweet,
Yet by my father's will impressed—"

                              "How good!
You did not want your candy: very good!
Priceless particulars are always present—"

The next day was a Saturday, no school for Hershey, and all afternoon behind the closed door,
   Hershey heard his parents' loud quarreling voices rise and reply, until his mother shrieked,
   Then wept loudly. And Hershey stood halfway up the stair, trying to hear,
   Anna beside him, Roger on his knees, following his brother, as if it were a game,
   When suddenly the door opened, both issued from the bedroom,
   Passionately angry, too absorbed to take account of their shocked witnesses. Hershey was afraid, and Anna was afraid, and they discussed it with each other, the child and the servant girl,
   That Jack Green would go away again, the fear his mother often mentioned. And the two were certain when they saw Jack Green's face,
   And they were right. Jack Green went away. In Florida a man met in the hotel had said to Green,

No woman would let you go on trips like this, unless she had a lover!
    This, Jack Green believed, and when he came back, the presence of sister
and mother, and the evidence of his senses,
    Could not hold down the paranoiac ego, prepared to believe that all, in
the secret incestuous adulterous heart he knew himself,
    Enacted Iago, Brutus, Judas, Clytemnestra, Delilah, or Gertrude,
    Always betraying him! this was the cynicism he knew in himself.
    Thus, as from the shadows on the silver screen, the audience
    Takes home the Hollywood stars, admits their influence,
    Which dwells in them then, and enters, look, gesture, and love,
    So did the motions of the parents impress the child,
    And will impress him forever! under the moment, under the present, under
    The conscious mind, when feeling looks out for what Life brings:
    Expectancy and dread, hope and despair, the ancient boxers,
    Struggle before an ultimate landscape which covers and surrounds city,
and sky, and sea,
    Created like a natural epoch by such events of childhood, for forever
    Father and mother struggle behind the bedroom door, Hershey stands
with the servant girl and his brother halfway up the stair,
    Trying to hear and understand, ignorant and curious, full of hope and
despair—

        "Junior Orestes, as I said before!
        Children by Papa and by Mamma made
        In many senses. So you, O Hershey Green,
        Declare so *feelingly* that evermore
        This *heartscape* was the background of your life
        —As a ruined mansion in a small town stands,
        Scandal and scarlet of the family known—"

        "But do you not exaggerate somewhat?
        A hundred million very different scenes
        Will follow with their most impressive shows
        To win your gaze and win your imitation
        And be to you a world-wide education?
        Is this not personal? an obsessed trope
        With which you try to fly from Freedom's trap?"

THE COLLECTED POEMS OF DELMORE SCHWARTZ

"You ought to know, being learnèd in death,"
Hershey replied, "it is forever more!"

"Too true!" (This was a voice heard many times),
"Although I knew a different childhood. Felt
Mother and father against me in a fort—
Not shown explicitly—but always strong:
I was a foreign task amid their harsh
Ravenous need and freshened satisfaction
—An accident made by their hurried joy:
Father, once too impatient, would not wait
While Mother turned aside and fixed the guard
Against Love's true conclusion. All my life
I felt my self's lack of necessity,
Often afraid that I had stayed too long,
Or come too soon, or come quite uninvited—"

"O shyness stems from childhood in this woe,
Flows from conception's second! See, then, how
Orestes is the name of every son,
Bearing the guilt his forbears have begun,
Forced to fresh crimes because of it, and tracked
By the deathless Furies of the family life . . ."

"O pain goes ringing through me like alarms:
Go on and criticize and let me rest—"

"Unlike this sleepless boy, the fortunate play,
Express their natures sweetly and serenely
In tennis, company, and love. But this
Is not for him: though what, I cannot say—"

"How long, in fact, the act of procreation
Endures! Endures through childhood mixedly—"

"I turned a corner once, and saw two girls
Wearing their parents' hand-me-down looks—"

"Let us once more soothe and console the boy
And take his mind a while from all these shames—"

"I could throw up my being now, compelled
As in the aftermath of drunkenness,"
Thus spoke the agonist, wishing relief
And curious to hear fresh sudden shifts—

"Panting and breathing hard, the runner halts:
Garbed in his shorts he is a fantasy!"

"Give him a cold shoulder or a high hat.
Give him an apple, sin's first metaphor,
That he may turn on Life with attitudes
Which free him for a time from his confession—"

"Let him have one neat attitude which is
A closed umbrella quickly opened up—"

"O let him have daring insouciance
Such that he runs upon the edges of roofs
Like a child hurrying downstairs! Let him
Drive on with joy and hope as easy speeds—"

"Strength of attention! let him study long
Lenin, Picasso, sleepless Edison,
Phenomenal inventors of the Age,
Students of friendship, power, light, and space—"

"Spotted by good and evil, like a giraffe,
Let him yet eat the flowers of highest trees
And gain a monstrous neck by aspiration,
Accepting laughs, awkward and dignified—"

Far far away. As from the park one sharp cold night,
One might have seen the lighted trolley, skating and singing,
    While under the gala ads the seated passengers, quiet, empty in revery,
reading, stiff as the dead,

THE COLLECTED POEMS OF DELMORE SCHWARTZ

Moved toward eternity (this is a version and sample of eternity!),

So this scene seems from this view: far far away. And perspective fails,

The unique warmth returns, this view and voice speaks as if from the small boy's ultimate mind (such the inner knowledge),

He is in the divinity of public school, his heart takes for granted his father's departure,

And it is February: the teacher, seeing the small boy's cleverness,

Promotes him with the rest of his class to the next class, 1B, instead of keeping him in 1A because he had started late in the year.

Thus it was that began the long ascent of the school hierarchy, and thus Hershey was six months ahead of his fellows,

And his mother spoke of it to her friends and Hershey knew his distinction and felt himself as famous.

And Jack Green seemed to be gone for good this time, he did not return as he had before,

He sent his lawyer to ask her to sell the house. The Anglo-Saxon law of the New World gave her the power to refuse,

She took her savings, the savings gained by the clenched hands of her sense of life,

And paid the first installment of the mortgage, going to another lawyer and taking with her Hershey,

And rehearsing to the stranger, her whole marriage, while Hershey sat by and listened once more to the same story, told to many friends and to relatives,

All of Eva Green's wish for sympathy indulged, incapable of reticence, prepared to see every act directed against her heroism.

But Hershey heard other notes and gained other knowledge. In Woolworth's for a nickel, Anna bought for him a packet of seeds of radishes,

And Hershey planted them behind the garage in the backyard, and looked day after day for the growing, in the wet brown ground,

And gave up hope because nothing happened. But Anna said, You wait, you see,

And then when at last came the small green shoots and then the small red bulbs,

Hershey felt the wisdom of the Polish farm in the servant girl,

He felt the thrilling and the inconceivable power of growing Nature,

Yielding green life.

"Cupidity and stupidity of the self!
Souciant to the fingertips in flows
Of nervousness which make one bite one's nails
—Or the confession like Niagara Falls!
(This is a shift extreme. But Man contains,
As Pascal says, this monstrous symmetry,
Being at once infinite and a pin!) . . ."

"The need to tell the heart ever recurs!
—Permit me to refer to Augustine,
Rousseau, Raskolnikov, and other souls
Who had to blurt out all, being oppressed
By what they lived like nausea. See, here too,
Something as necessary as the nose!"

"The boy tells all his heart as Mamma did:
Perhaps he learned such hebetudes from her?"

"Not hebetudes in the stricken boy. See,
Ugly and necessary as the nose!"

"Jack Green, son of dénouement, goes away
(This too is one more of the repetition):
He lets between his self and family
The long law of the city intervene
—It is as when police come to a house
To stop a family fight: all are ashamed
And lifted momently from conflict's hits,
—It is as if the court came to the house:
The city travels through the living room!"

"Many varieties have now been seen
Of how these deities enter the heart
And carry it away, abstract as trains
Passing through small towns in the growing dusk,
Or bob it like a buoy, or write on it
Like rest-rooms marked by adolescent boys—"

THE COLLECTED POEMS OF DELMORE SCHWARTZ

"Yet Freedom is the space in which we walked,
Never exhausted by these foreign powers
—Sleeping and unforgiven, Coriolanus
—One of the ego's proper names—still treads
The playing field of conscious being which,
Rising and falling, is named Liberty!"

All summer long, Eva Green held out, resisted every effort,

Made by Jack Green and by his lawyer to persuade her to move from the red-brick house,

But when September came, more money was due on the mortgage, and Jack Green promised to come home, if she would move from the house,

And sign the agreement, which permitted him to sell the house at a profit,

And Eva Green consented, although she but half-believed Jack Green's promise to return,

And Jack Green himself did not know what the truth was, for he was full of a tiredness of another evening lady.

And thus on a warm and drizzling day in late September, the family moved from the red-brick house on the Parkway,

Jack Green came for his family to drive them to their new home in his car or machine,

And Hershey cried out because his kitten was being left behind, and both parents promised him that the moving van would bring the kitten,

And then, after driving through the autumn rain, they came to the cheap dark apartment hurriedly chosen by Jack Green,

Who felt that he had already spent too much money. Grandmother met them there, to help them unpack,

And when the moving van came, the kitten was not with the moving men,

And Hershey cried with great bitterness, depressed by the rainy day, and the dark apartment, and the loss of his pet,

And one more deception upon the part of his father and mother. And then after supper,

His father put on his coat, and his mother asked his father where he was going?

And his father said that he might as well stay out the week he had paid for at the hotel where he had been living,

And Eva Green saw and her mother saw and Hershey saw, trembling with disappointment, that he was lying,

But Eva Green kept silent, a self-control unknown to her, inspired by the indestructible hope that silence might help to bring him back,

And Hershey sat in his chair and rooted vainly

That his father would change his mind and come to live with them, and buy him toys,

And be the powerful presence moving Hershey as a king once moved his soldier boys,

And Hershey felt the presence in the darkened air of these relationships, the family divinity,

The great city, the America in which Jack Green made his way with his will,

He felt them as the sailor feels the rocking sea under him, vast and abysmal,

Endless and disappointing!

"Is it this year that Chaplin in 'The Kid'
Performed his miracles of sentiment?"

"It is next year. But I know what you thought
—O how appropriate to the event
Which just has passed and shaken our used hearts:
The poor boy tricked by adults' promises,
His pet and kitten taken away from him—"

"How well I know the dark apartment house
—Type of the unity of modern life!—"

"This is the new place, this is the seat
Of the defeated middle class,
                                O city, city—"

"O what a box for souls! O what a tomb,
An obvious tomb of lives! Makeshift and pleasure
Conceal the slow defeat of hope. Hope most of all
Conceals defeat, postpones the recognition,
Night most of all awakes the guilt and truth—"

"The small boy felt in his heart the city's worth;
He knew this was a going-down. He knew
The social scale in sensuous terms. He saw

THE COLLECTED POEMS OF DELMORE SCHWARTZ

The dirty light from the backyard as truth—
Capitalismus penetrates each spot!"

"No wonder, then, that Hershey felt depressed,
As the rain drizzled on that autumn day—"

"A cloud-gray intuition entered his mind,
He felt the orders and the cruelty
Of the tall boxes of the great city,
He felt, unable yet to understand,
The roots and powers of private property—"

"Poor boy, who with a tired tireless voice,
Moves between ecstasy and irony
—See how he needs our tutelage. He saw
Little enough despite his anguished gaze . . ."

"He did not understand each feeling's cause:
This leads to such an endless night as now—"

The motors of the great city which ran the subway, placed the bridges, lighted the avenues,
  And painted the billboards, poured water in the tub from distant Croton,
  As natural as a tree to Hershey: for now he began
To mix Narcissan pleasures with his pride. There in the white bathroom, warmly flowing
Flushes of touching water covered the naked flesh. And from the ambient aura reveries rose,
  He went to military academy and was a story, he marched to Sousa's music in a uniform,
  Commanding troops, saluting troops, leading his fellows,
  And in his intuition found the very suit
  Which fits the ego best, the soldier's uniform!
  And now his widening wakening gaze saw and did not like the neighborhood, felt the contrast
Between the suburban street on the Parkway and the old city-block of apartment houses,
  He wished for the first time to be where he had been before. He was not good in school, in his new distemper.

His teacher scolded him, and he wished he was in the school where he had been advanced quickly,

And he told his mother this regret when she came to school with his lunch on rainy days, and she said, Tell your father.

But the boys on the block accepted Hershey and made him a peer,

And he learned the great street games for the first time, *Buttons*,

(On which the faces of Cox and Harding looked at them from the campaign for President,)

Pitched to the wall, the player coming closest to the wall winning,

Beautiful vari-colored *Marbles*, spun from the thumb, to hit the other player's; both games of skill, and difficult;

And *Picture Cards*, small cards with the faces and names of baseball players and Hollywood stars,

Successively put down, one after another, until one player or the other matched the top card's first initial,

And took the sum which had arisen, waiting for identity to fall like chance, breathlessly waiting, moved by the postponement which made the sum grow larger and larger,

Drunk with contingency and private property, the deepest motives that surrounded the playing boys,

And among the deepest motives in the United States of America!

"I too in the *aesthesis* of the warm bath
Lived a dream-life before I came to this:
I thought of tired Romans, made believe
That in the classic day I owned Greek boys—"

"Perhaps a shower would be best, perhaps
If rye's illusion is prohibited
(Soon, in the years which in America
Begin to be) the long warm bath should be
Also prohibited. Makes introverts
Or rather helps them to their sweet defeat,
As novels' baths, the self-abuse of minds—"

"Yet is this growing boy in school and in
The street, in games between passing cars,
Dragged from the rottenness of revery,
And struck by competition everywhere,

Struck by the teacher's strict authority,
Thrilled and depraved by picture games of gain—"

"Capitalismus is not mocked! O no!
The children feel it keenly. Lo and behold,
They root for politicians. And they strive
Just as their fathers strive, to gain a sum
Which never is too much—"

                "Never enough!
I used to make a point of seeing this,
I saw corruption seize the playing boys
In school as well as in the city street:
I taught the young, an intellectual,
Shabby-genteel, pitied, viewed with contempt
Because I was not as their father were
Rich and hence powerful with true success
—Capitalismus is not mocked! O no!
It crowns the fixed idea of wealth as such,
Makes maniacs of this fixed idea—which must
Deny all other gods—captains and kings!"

"I knew this well, I lived through all this too:
Did I not flunk at Naples? Did I not fail
At the Staats-Oper? Life is like that,
The treason of the cliques will never end,
The meanness of the manger dog remains,
(All of these evils propagate like flies!)
He cannot bear another's newcome goodness,
Although his breakfast food is just as good
As when his neighbor did not have a car,
—This is the famous heart, world without end,
Do not deceive yourself with periods—"

"I managed to get by by drinking wine,
In drunken-ness I knew that Unity
Of Being named by Lawrence the dark god,
The god of darkness or the act of darkness
—And not that indecision and revision,

Stammering, hesitating, waiting at the door,
Holding the knob as if one held one's heart,
In dread that maybe there beyond the frame
One might fall down the stairs, or in the dark
Behold the secret sin which made one go
A furtive fugitive to a foreign country—"

"My worsted soul at last is comfortable:
It knows the stillness of the sated will!"

"Death's trauma holds us stiffly, as who rode
In the funicular! Spray of the mind!
This irony is nervousness in us,
—May God have mercy on your living soul,
May God have mercy on your wish to know!"

Values held them, like day and night; glittered like chandeliers. Jack Green stayed away, drawn by his appetites and held by them,

Leah Newman came to persuade her daughter to live with her, her unmarried sister, and her brother,

She felt that Eva Green ought not to be alone with the children, but she wished most of all to secure for Lillian, the unmarried daughter,

A better apartment, a better neighborhood, Eva Green's furniture, with which to welcome suitors.

These values of the middle class shone for Leah Newman, but under them

Fulfillment of womanhood, fulfillment of Nature, supported the social feelings moving her conscious mind.

Eva Green, however, was persuaded by the wish to save money on the rent.

Money assured identity, money made strong, no matter what happened she saved money every week.

And thus they moved from the dark apartment to a new and better one, and Roger and Hershey slept in the same bedroom as Mother,

And Mother was often sad at night, and asked her children, lying in the darkness as they dozed to sleep,

Did they think their father would come home to them? He would, he would! Roger and Hershey replied, knowing that this was the answer their mother wanted.

Children know best! Eva Green said to them, sighing and echoing Rous-
seau on Washington Heights,

    Appealing for sympathy in every quarter, moved by the pathos (made by
herself and then to friends recited)

    Of children full of pity for unhappy mother. Roger would fall asleep,

    But Hershey would strive with his emotion, all of the maudliness his
mother meant,

    And pick upon his heart the tender scab of pity,

    Self-pity, pity for all, pity forever to make him endure a lasting falseness

    To avoid a month of pain!

"It took some time for Jean-Jacques Rousseau's thoughts
To reach the populace. But when they did,
How the heart fed on them, fed foolishness,
Self-pity, sentimentality, weak tears!—"

"Even as Christ's pure sentences are mouthed
By Billy Sundays under circus tents
Above the sawdust trail, crying aloud
Guilt! Guilt!
        Are you washed in the blood of the Lamb?"

"The child as innocence and sibylline:
What a contempt for the adult, what a sense
Of his adultery and ignorance
—When an age dies, all the grown savants seem
Part of corruption and senility,
Child wonders star in all the Sunday papers
And many primitives come from afar,
From Africa! and are as new as May
Amid the monotones of industry—"

"This Rousseau was a foolish egotist,
His was a version of Arcadia,
Really no more than a trope, really no more
Than metaphors with which to fly away—"

"Mock on! mock on! Captains of the modern age:
O when you saw the strong divinity

Whose birth you helped to bring, did you approve?
What did you think then of your angry love?"

"Call them to come here and speak for themselves!
Call them. But it will take too long. They are
With Buddha, Augustine, and Lao-tzse,
Just punishment! even as Swedenborg
Is forced to listen to Democritus!"

"I hardly understand your irony,"
Said Hershey Green, relieved to be released
Though only momently, from his long life
Which in increasing nausea rose in him—

"Reason
And Laughter loll in each other's arms,
               Ride, si sapis, O puella, ride!
Reason and laughter are man's unique possessions,
Their sunlight is the glory of the world!
What *chichi* handsomeness, what chic and flash!
—Dentist, barber, and hangman are in us,
Painter and actress, all the old professions,
And if all things are always from some window
Viewed, and if the senses smear the dings, and if
This story has in it much that is sordid,
Nobility is in the point of view,
We bring to you a noble point of view,
We help you rise with heavy irony!
La! La! Life is a breathless ride and jig,
And irony is full of citrus fruits,
And there are other lofts and lights to bloom,
. . . . The Great Bear as a dotted paradigm
(Even the Lamb had need of parables),
The clishmaclaver of the living dead,
Anna Karenina's adultery,
The Quartet running down the chopped stopped road
Doubt, hesitation, doubt, a moment's joy,
—We come to give you this, O New York boy!"

"Thank you, junior Platos! where I go,
The din is deafening and my gaze is mussed,

                     and one gray winter day. . . ."

"O Reason's far-off smile! from ugly Socrates
Who thought only of love, conversing sharply—
But I must still myself, and let the boy go on!"

    One gray mid-winter day, Jack Green paid his family a visit,

    He was going to a winter resort near New York for a weekend, he said.

    Eva Green, ready as always to make whatever appeal, to yell, to scream, to say that she would kill herself

    In order to gain the sympathy she wished, said to her husband that Hershey too

    Needed a vacation: look how pale he looked in mid-winter. Then Jack Green answered that he would take Hershey with him,

    Astounding and confounding Eva, who had not expected his duct of pity to be so quickly opened,

    And who was sure that he was going to the winter resort with some woman, her mind's recurrent phrase.

    Hershey was prepared, burning with joy. He was kissed and given to his father,

    Father and son rode on the train and came to the winter resort, and when they walked on the Main Street,

    Hershey read aloud to his father the ads on the great billboards,

    And his father said to him, You like to read, don't you? You are a smart boy! And Hershey glowed with pleasure.

    And then on this business street of the winter resort, they met a pretty lady, as if by accident,

    And Jack Green was not at all surprised and spoke briefly with her, and then went on with his son,

    But Hershey looked back at Delilah, struck and attracted and pleased by the pretty lady, wishing that she were coming with them.

    And Jack Green stopped in a jewelry store and bought for Hershey a wrist-watch, whose second hand, thin as a hair, Hershey regarded for hours with fascination,

    And in the evening after dinner, Hershey sat with his father in the card-room of the hotel,

And gazed at the game of poker, and held his father's stack of chips, red, white, and blue,

And rooted for his father to win, although he saw that his father was hardly interested,

But stared long at Hershey, smiling, and gazed at Hershey's pleasure in the holiday,

And explained to him what WHITE ROCK was, and gave him a taste of it from one player's bottle,

And left to make a telephone call, and then Hershey heard one player say,

This is some place to bring a child, this is some kindergarten—

But then Jack Green returned and took Hershey up to bed, and gazed on him as he undressed and prayed

For father, mother, brother, asking with child's intuition the King of Hearts to be good to all souls,

Self-tortured, self-diseased, self-deceived! in the freedom which breaks the heart!

But when Hershey's prayer was ended, Jack Green said that he must go, surprising Hershey,

He must go back to the card-game, to go to sleep like a good boy.

Hershey tried in the darkness to stay awake and wait for his father's return. He listened to the ticking of his wrist-watch under the pillow,

He looked at it, the phosphorescent hands glistened in the darkness, like ghosts, between the moving hands,

He listened and looked, he listened to Time and Nature, Mother was there in the bedroom, Father was there, their marriage was there,

The Pretty Lady too was present in that darkness, while also present moved the America

From which Jack Green drew the power of his ego, the energy and money to indulge his unsatisfied will. All these entities

Arranged the bed, prepared the room, paid for the watch to which the boy was listening and looking,

Hardly knowing Time, ignorant of all that thus surrounded him and held him and passed through his mind and heart,

Until the small animal's natural tiredness

Brimmed over, he fell asleep and was a plant once more.

But energy rose from the earth, fell from the sun, moved in the air, turned through the day and the night,

And North America leaped like a runner at the line forever,

Upon its hemisphere!

"Vacations are true life. *You really live*
In this sick city just on such occasions:
Work is the dungeon of pure means, alas!
Justified only by the holiday—"

"Jack bares his moral life. He loves his boy,
His sympathy, his trip, and his *amours*,
—Confronted by a choice between the three
(Exclusion seems to cut off each of them,
As looking forward cuts off looking back)
Takes all of them upon the sweet weekend:
Thus is his appetite pure infinite,
As Augustine, I think, once said of all,
—This is his ethic and his way of life—"

"He did not know that he who cuts in two
The pie that faces him, with choice's knife,
Has gained the bigger portion in all truth,
May get a fresh piece, and have some tomorrow,
Not sicken with too much, lose definition
(Renunciation freshens and sharpens *things!*)
Nor have to fight with many boys for *all* . . ."

"Is not the wrist-watch *too good to be true?*
No one of all the deities that then
Presided over the little tired boy
Free of that first dominion, Time, which gleamed
In the hotel bedroom darkness. All made of Time,
Father, Mother, Pretty Lady, and Child,
Night and America, all made of Time,
Made of their years, not made of flesh and blood:
The wrist-watch he is given signs this truth
Which moves and leaves the mind far far behind—"

". . . . How true and fleeting is this very truth!
Each was his only years, each nature there
Became itself, and otherwise was not
—The boy, being a boy; the pretty lady,
Being full woman, realized; the place

Quite qualified, being a winter spa
(O Time and Place, locked in each other's arms!)—"

"The being of America which gave
Men like Jack Green Power, Possession, Place
(As firemen are made, when fires rave,
Chiefs of the city, most important men!),
Each of these souls is at an only age,
Burns in Time's fire, or in Time's darkness hides—"

"Regard each only time, and not each face,
Often merely a use and wood of Time!"

"Time's forms surrounded Hershey, manifold
As if he rode the seaside's carousel,
Where, by the central motion circumscribed,
Many a horse went up and down, many a child
Of passion rose and fell next to his rise and fall—"

"See, then, the boy was wise because he gazed
Long at his gleaming wrist-watch in the darkness
—His father elsewhere, in another rhythm,
But by the same globe carried to his death
Engaged the pretty lady, riding her—"

"Please do not use such words," said Hershey Green,
"Let me return now to my endless story—"

"Death and astonishment! how small these souls
Seen from our point of view: O what stupidity,
Self-stupefied, self-blinded and unsatisfied
While everything happens in the mind of God!
Go on, O boy, return to your endless story—"

Now Hershey was in a new public school, and in a new class, moving up
the scholastic stair,
    And the great city's growing populace crowded the schools with children
and made necessary

Rapid Advance classes in which the smart children advanced three terms in a year,

While the remaining host advanced but two terms in the same time. Hershey was chosen as one of the elect,

And placed in 2B Rapid Advance, confirming his pride once more. And on the very first day,

He saw in the seat beside him a beautiful girl, of a beauty dark and extraordinary and new, making him feel

As snow made him feel. Instantly he strove to create a relationship, by borrowing a pencil,

Give me something, will you? his utter nature asked, And she gave him a pencil,

But looked at him with disdain, and said to him that he should have known enough to bring a pencil with him,

This is just the first day, he trembled back at her,

Hurt and humiliated, and immediately in love with her!

And then, at the end of this winter, Noah Green died, after a long illness in a sanitarium in Manhattan Beach, overlooking the Atlantic,

The end of the broken romance in Eastern Europe forty years before, when he had died his first death,

And Jack Green sat with his brothers in mourning on the floor with shoes off,

And Albert Green said to him, Who will mourn for you when you die? Ever the head of the family, and the source of morality.

And Jack Green said in a rush of feeling made possible by the week of death,

Yes, you are right, Albert, who will mourn for me? Go back to your wife and your children, said Albert,

I will go back tonight, said Jack Green to his brother in the immediacy of feeling,

And thus Jack Green came back to his family and told his wife why he had come back, and lived in the apartment with Leah, Lillian, and Ishmael,

And when one Sunday morning Jack Green lounged in bed, reading the Sunday paper, while Hershey read the jokes,

Eva Green straightened the bedroom, and said aloud as if only to Hershey,

Your father will go away again, soon enough! for she knew with what unrest his will filled him,

And Jack Green laughed and pooh-poohed what she said in a good-
humored voice, relieving Hershey,
Who wondered why his mother must always say the most unpleasant
things, and awaken strife with his father.

> Then there was silence, then the agonist
> Oppressed by new emotion spoke like them:
> "In primy nature seeds of many beasts
> Wait and are warm in the thick and heavy dark
> —'Twas bitter chill, and I was sick at heart
> At duskfall trembling, skin against skin chafed
> At the hard knuckle's nub. Sirs, in my heart
> There was a kind of fighting, blow by blow
> Of deep-rooted desires: what did I know?
> What had I ever known? the senses tear,
> Smear, and wring out each luminous thick thing,
> Break the nut, tear at the plum and bloom!
> —What were they before I touched them? Before
> My shadow fell on them? what did they say
> In the secret mystery and pulse of being,
> Going on and on? I knock at the door
> Of the *ding-an-sich*, and all that I hear
> Is the vain shower of a telephone ringing,
> No one at home. Coiled is the inner being,
> Never to be untied. I felt my emptiness,
> I felt my self's lack of necessity,
> I held with frenzied hands upon the brink
> Of the 55th floor and knew the tensing strain
> High in my arms as in my fingers' joints,
> Knuckles hysterical! the lamb and the kid,
> Bounding and happy, had gone! Gone was
> The savor of the oranges and roses,
> And the *gemütlichkeit* of the brown evening
> About the dining-room table, cracking jokes
> With friends of the age, and the belle girl,
> And splashing laughter and soon drowsiness,
> Thick fat long sleep to come. Where was this lost?"

THE COLLECTED POEMS OF DELMORE SCHWARTZ

"Accept yourself, sleepless Atlantic boy,
And in an infinite repetition rise,
Return and surmount, in the midst superior
To that which is the earth your being knows,
Bituminous bony black underworld,
—Go back along the track, say what you know
And are, and do not know, and wish to know
Until at last the belle girl dances with you
Who cannot dance, until the lime-gray morning
Seems like a true beginning, peak, and success
—O an infinite repetition, from the pit
Of your being rising, part by part, blow by blow,
The unknown modes and moods which rule your life
—You cannot run from yourself, O no!
To go to Portugal, to go to Sweden,
To go to sleep, useless variety:
All the celebrity and fame of light,
The burst and bush which rules the daytime sky
Will rise like a looking-glass. And this is Life—"

"In this cantina one may gain *katharsis*:
I love to sing, how irony makes free
And gives a clarity and radiance
As if illuminated by Vermeer!
—We walk with freedom and intelligence
As if we waltzed, there in the former life!
Go on, O New York boy, your endless story—"

One evening, Jack Green, still in good humor, took his family and his mother-in-law too

Downtown to the Capitol Theatre, just like The White House, to see an old film, "The Birth of a Nation,"

And Hershey was greatly enthralled, and just when Lincoln drew his shawl about him, troubled by a sudden chill, suddenly sad in his box, while the play continued,

Hershey heard his mother say to his grandmother in a low voice, You see, he knew, he had a premonition, he knew what was coming!

Making Hershey afraid of the powers of Life, and then Booth fired and leaped from the box and gestured on the stage, limping,

And Lincoln's head slumped, and Hershey felt beside himself, gazing upon himself in the middle of Life,

The actuality of Life and Death, seen from the distance of form,

Entered and moved in his heart! But later, when the family rode home in the car, and Hershey sat next to his father,

Riding home in the early spring evening, he told his father he did not understand the Ku Klux Klan in the picture, nor how the Civil War had been the birth of this nation,

And Jack Green explained to his son the reasons for the Civil War. The sheer experience of being given a reason

Delighted Hershey immensely! He asked his father to tell him more and more,

He undressed in the bedroom while his father gazed and smoked a cigar and smiled at the curious boy,

Hershey asked his father who lived on the moon and the reasons for a later conflict, the Great War,

The long mild twilight faded in the bedroom window, a soft blue spring night grew beyond the lighted room,

Hershey heard the reasons his father knew and felt the clear

Health and pleasure of coming glowing from cold water:

Plato's starlight shone on the fusing animal!

"Let us go off on a candid cadenza,
For the great man still grows in the boy's mind,
All those events live in the national fable,
Expressive of America *an sich!*"

"Manic-depressive Lincoln, national hero!
How just that this great nation, being conceived
In liberty by fugitives should find
—Strange ways and plays of monstrous History—
This Hamlet-type to be the President—"

"This failure, this unwilling bridegroom,
This tricky lawyer full of black despair—"

"He grew a beard, becoming President,
And took a shawl as if he guessed his rôle,
Though with the beard he fled cartoonists' blacks,

THE COLLECTED POEMS OF DELMORE SCHWARTZ

And many laughed and were contemptuous,
And some for four years spoke of killing him—"

"He was a politician—of the heart!—
He lived from hand to mouth in moral things!
He understood quite well Grant's drunken-ness!
It was for him, before Election Day,
That at Cold Harbor Grant threw lives away
In hopeless frontal attack against Lee's breastworks!"

"O how he was the Hamlet-man, and this,
After a life of failure made him right,
After he ran away on his wedding day,
Writing a coward's letter to his bride—"

"How with his very failure, he out-tricked
The florid Douglas and the abstract Davis,
And all the vain men who, surrounding him,
Smiled in their vanity and sought his place—"

"Later, they made him out a prairie Christ
To sate the need coarse in the national heart—"

"His wife went insane, Mary Todd too often
Bought herself dresses. And his child died.
And he would not condemn young men to death
For having slept, in weakness. And he spoke
More than he knew and all that he had felt
Between outrageous joy and black despair
Before and after Gettysburg's *pure peak*—"

"He studied law, but knew in his own soul
Despair's anarchy, terror and error,
—Instruments had to be taken from his office
And from his bedroom in such days of horror,
Because some saw that he might kill himself:
When he was young, when he was middle-aged,
How just and true was he, our national hero!"

"Sometimes he could not go home to face his wife,
Sometimes he wished to hurry or end his life!"

"But do not be deceived. He did not win,
And, it is plain, the South could never win
(Despite the gifted Northern generals!)
—Capitalismus is not mocked, O no!
This stupid deity decided the War—"

"In fact, the North and South were losers both:
—Capitalismus won the Civil War—"

"—Capitalismus won the Civil War,
Yet, in the War's cruel Colosseum,
Some characters fulfilled their natures' surds,
Grant the drunkard, Lee the noble soldier,
John Brown in whom the Bible soared and cried,
Booth the unsuccessful Shakespearean,
—Each in some freedom walked and knew himself,
Then most of all when all the deities
Mixed with their barbarous stupidity
To make the rock, root, and rot of the war—"

"This is the way each only life becomes,
Tossed on History's ceaseless insane sums!"

The divinity of Nature brought the heat of Nature to the great city. Take the children, said Jack Green to his wife,
Go to the mountains. But Eva Green was suspicious, she knew him, she feared that he would go away again,
But after arguing she took the children to the summer hotel in the mountains, their first visit to the country,
And Hershey smelt the warm baking smell going through the kitchen into the sweet cool of the summer evening,
He heard the guests in rocking chairs on the porch discussing many things, he listened,
A man had killed his sweetheart, finding her in another man's bedroom. He was at Sing Sing now, a model prisoner
For the rest of his natural life. And a man's ears had fallen off,

Because of a dreadful disease named syphilis. Hearing this, Hershey was sickened by Life,

Afraid it would happen to him. He walked through the kitchen into the country evening,

Meeting the rancid sour cream smell of the refuse cans, and then the wondrous cool and the darkness.

A newly married couple became good friends with Eva Green, and fondled Hershey and Roger

As if they played with the future. And then one day the bride received a telegram that her father was very ill,

And that she should come home at once. The bride was sure that her father lay dying, Eva Green was all sympathy,

She told the couple that she would go back to the city with them in a car privately hired, for they were poor and she too would save some money,

The trip back by car took them over hair-pin turns on mountain-sides, Hershey was afraid, hearing the talk of death,

Eva Green tried to reassure the bride that her worst fears would not come true,

They rode all day and came at sunset to the Jersey shore of the Hudson,

And had to wait for the ferry in the windless wet heat after a scorching day,

And then they were home at last, and Eva Green saw something was wrong the moment the door opened

On her mother's face.

He is not here? said Eva Green, a declarative question. Maybe only this week, said Leah Newman to her stony daughter,

For she always took the most hopeful view of all that happened. But Eva Green moved past her with her stony face, went to the bedroom,

Took drawer after drawer from the dresser, finding them empty, one after another, turned to the closet,

Empty also, all of Jack Green's clothes gone. Gone for good! said Eva Green to her mother and children, meaning for evil,

And sat upon the bed, too angry to cry, faced with the fulfillment

Of the long day and the bride's fear and the tiring trip, Jack Green, the son of dénouement,

Gone away for good, making his son Telemachus or Orestes, altering the nature of the family divinity.

"Let us have irony for some relief,
—Irony is release, caricature
Yields momently a freedom from strict pain,
As in the August heat, lightning and rain!"

"O in the depth and height of this long look
To see the deities and causes which
Brought him from baby carriage to this night,
Is not the family god within the self,
The self as such born of relationships,
The weak top card upon a house of cards?"

["]Mercy and freedom are new each morning, yes!
This should reject remorse and bring on care—"

"And in the New York country summer, he
Knew natural delights, and all his senses
Stood open as French windows do in June:
The Gentiles and their poets sang of this—"

"And like a badly-taken photograph,
He heard of Life, discussed from rocking chairs—"

"You hear the rhythm, sleepless boy? It is
A kind of boat . . . Better to cross the seas
In shapely boats than wade the raves and rides
Ridiculous in motion. Comes, from depth on depth,
Fast in the mind, because this order draws
And drags, many a handsome light as if
Tulips live there, and order plucks them up—"

"Let him go on, humility when joined
With honesty, and honestly, wins all,—O Hershey Green,
From darkness to darkness proceed; depth has decrees
No one has dreamed! As one, trembling from fear,
Escaped from seas in which the ocean liner
Sank, reaches the sure, dragging the last furs
Of death dripping from goosechilled legs

That shook a moment since,—as he
Might halt, stand on the sand, look back
(Feeling perhaps he has died once, he now
Begins a second life!), so you, poor boy—"

"*Me too! Me too!* by saying that you know
Guilt and humility! *Me too*, at every sin
Beheld and criticized in other hearts:
O how the blood will club your forehead then!"

"The middle-class delights are not for you,
The handsome furniture, the set of silver,
The Sunday dresses and the cunning child;
And not the pleasures of the innocents,
When monarchies of light blaze in the window,
Or when the early morning is a saint,
Or when the sunlight like St. Francis chants
Glory! Glory! Beauty! Love and Wonder!
—For you belong with us, remorse's troops,
Gaining through pain and through unhappiness,
Knowledge, freedom, hope, forgiveness, love!"

The children were soon accustomed to their father's absence. Hershey
slept on a cot in his mother's bedroom and heard her weep at night,

Stricken with pity! And once more, in the darkness she asked her two
boys, Did they really feel sure that *He* would come back?

And the boys assented and affirmed and said what was expected. And
Hershey's mind began to grow wildly, an unweeded garden,

He read the comic strips ravenously, unable to wait from day to day

For the next slot of fabulous figures, speaking balloons; Jiggs, struck by
his wife with a rolling-pin, because he stayed out late,

Or bored by the opera, or appalled by his British bemonocled son-in-law,
or resisting the effort to keep up with other members

Of the upper lower middle-class. And the Katzenjammer Kids who bored
and perplexed Hershey with their endless destruction,

Presenting the adult vision of childhood, the vision of freedom, the anarchy

Adulthood yearned for and could not have. But more than that, Hershey
was taken one afternoon to the ball game at the Polo Grounds,

He walked with his uncle Ishmael down the runway into the great stadium, under the shadow of Coogan's Bluff, next to the Harlem,

He took in the smell of cigar smoke, sunshine on the diamond, smack

Of bat on ball, and ball in glove, the cries

Of *Scorecards, Cigarettes, Chewing Gum, Peanuts, Popcorn*, and saw the outfielder running back,

Gauging the arc of the fly ball, and the infielder scooping up the grounder, and the black and white scoreboard, framed in the horseshoe arena, on top of which

Pennants were blowing in the breeze, under the blue-and-gold sky. The sensuous scene

Soon burned in the drama of the game. The Giants were playing the Reds, Rixey and Toney were the pitchers,

The Reds scored early, all game long the Giants strove back, trying to overcome their early lead. In the seventh inning,

With one out and bases full for the Giants, Young hit a smashing grounder, which looked for a second like a hit,

Into a double play, a ballet of ordered movement, shortstop to second baseman to first baseman,

Bringing swiftest disappointment. And in the eighth inning, a Giant was thrown out at the plate,

By the right fielder's perfect throw, as he tried to score from second. The nervous sweetness

Of rooting seized and ran through Hershey. Partisanship took him and held him,

Shouting and hoping for a single or even an error,

Amid the contingencies of the bounding ball or flying ball, swung at, fielded, and thrown and caught

Before the runner reached first base. The Giants' rally failed in the ninth, and as Hershey walked home with his young uncle, Ishmael,

His sadness was almost tears. From that day forward, he followed the pennant race every day with passion,

He learned the names of players and manager, Bancroft, Irish Meusel, John McGraw, Frisch the Fordham Flash,

The Odyssey of the Giants' Western trip soon obsessed him, he ran to the stationery store newsstand to see the latest scores,

And trembled, seeking good or evil news. Not roulette, not the cards with medieval faces

THE COLLECTED POEMS OF DELMORE SCHWARTZ

Taught him the drunkenness of chance and liberty. But major league
baseball, going on like a life,
  Victory and defeat, a daily progress and drama, a sacred egotism, a gam-
ing patriotism in which
  The heart fell in love with an entity too big to know, a moving entity
made by many powers, made by
  The teams of capitalism. For there in the light of the stadium,
  Great symbols enacted the age! with strength and with passion—

      "These national games are always interesting,
      And yes, as the boy says, how they express
      Many strong motives of the sick city
      Hidden, unknown, deliberately ignored—"

      "Now I remember it, in the former life,
      Now looking back, I think I understand
      Not only partisanship, which makes the game
      Intensely interesting, as if one saw
      In brief, the ego's fate in days to come,
      Striving upon a team against a team
      —Not only the beauty of the medium,
      The foul lines like a compass to the stands,
      And the green outfield like a yachtsman's bay;
      Not only the swift contingency of loss
      Or gain, rally or error; not most of all,
      The quick spontaneous drama of the game,
      The unexpected homer or the catch,
      Leaping high in the air! of the line drive
      By the trained shortstop, cutting off a run,
      His intuition moving like a bird!
      But now I see, under the surface which
      Held me like melodrama, how I was wrong,
      How much I was deceived, how all the stars
      And actors of deception were deceived,
      Each in their kind, as all in the old life:
      Capitalismus struck the horsehide ball—"

      "These games are made in nature to enact
      Sweet sublimations of the people's need,

Babe Ruth was merely a masked millionaire,
And vicious competition ruled the stands—"

"You too, O Hershey Green, became a fan,
And through your heart and mind this drama passed
In which the national life performed itself
As a toy train runs through the Christmas child!"

"When great prosperity came to America,
The batting averages were bank accounts,
And salaries were paid to the great stars,
To suit the crowd's emotion, when it roared:
Capitalismus struck the horsehide ball!"

And Hershey played in the street games with the other and older boys,
Prisoner's Base, Tag, Cops and Robbers, and *Punchball,*
Which was baseball, played with a rubber ball in the gutter, pausing for passing cars,
And in these games Hershey took with passion all he did in the game as an instance of his fate,
An omen of his gift or failure. Played with so much fear and trembling that he became
The butt of the older boys because he was too serious and his passionate play was ridiculous,
And he was teased and mocked, and made the bewildered baby, until he was ashamed,
Cowed by the audience, afraid that he would never be a great star or hero.
But when bedtime came and the light shone in the hallway pinkly from the pink lamp-shade,
He talked to himself as if he were a Giant star and also the President of the United States
For whom the brass band played the thrilling martial marches, Sousa
Heard in the school assembly, "The Stars and Stripes Forever," the United States of America always triumphant,
Hershey as the hero in all and center of the world. And yet, during the same bed-time, appalling fear appeared. From the fifth-floor apartment bedroom window,

He heard sounds in the courtyard, and was afraid that someone had fallen
from the window,

And was afraid that he might fall himself or feel the impulse to jump.

Or he saw figures in the half-darkness, or heard them in the closet, behind
the closed door,

For he knew now fully and thought again and again of the truth that all
human beings must die. And then one night,

A person died in an apartment on the courtyard, hysterical shrieking was
heard, window glass was broken,

Hershey shuddered awake, and cried out too, not to be reassured or
consoled

Until the light was left on in the bedroom, dismissing fear with false day.
The growing fusing boy

Told himself soon that if he lived long enough, Science which had done
so much

Would do away with Death, a thought from some Sunday Magazine sup-
plement in the newspaper's objective mind. The idea consoled the conscious
mind, but under attention

The fear of Death, the desire of the ego to be a king and live forever
Stayed with him deeply, like the cold farms
Under the city where the buildings have risen.

"Old themes return and go in brand-new places,
The Game and Fame, Science, Night, and Death,
Divinities of different stature, yet
Important in their times. The Girl and Sex
Seen in the school divinity, adored!"

"A boredom of the plane was overhead:
To such superiority, technique—"

"Who cares to listen to this endless story?"
Hershey exclaimed, ashamed of what he said,
"Each comment which you sing goes through my head
Like a deadly expanding bullet, fired
Into the brain, which has so many lives!"

—To him a voice, as if just come, as if
One of the new and unused dead, replied:
"Old wives perhaps; O my God, my God!

                                whoever he is,
By what name justly known,—better anonymous—
Abraham's *Ahhhhhhhh*, or Moses' burning bush,
The nothing of the saints, or Aristotle's Thinker—"

And then another voice spoke out, replying,
"*He, he*, indeed, if no one else, has and has had
The sympathy to listen to this story,
Look at this life, going backward and forward,
Which does not 'grip the interest,' compel
The mind for 'what comes next' because
It lacks beginning, lacks an end, and has no plot
But Life itself, weird, wasteful, wild, without limit—"

"Life has more order than you think, O friend!
Even this life, come to decaying youth,
Between our Heaven and Hell, our consciousness
Like the old life's consumption, burning pain
Tortured by the worst knowledge, Might-not-have-been!"

"It's great to be dead, O, O, what fun!
Like an amusement park, or New Year's Party,
—Death, I could dance with you forever,
Knowing eternity has just begun!"

Now was the seventh year between heaven and hell, the womb and the grave,

The boys on the block made more and more fun of Hershey, mocked him as a smaller boy than the leaders,

And mocked him as his uncle Ishmael's nephew, because Ishmael quarreled loudly with his mother and his sisters,

And would not go to work in the morning and came home late at night after gambling away his salary,

And the sounds of quarreling were heard in the apartment house courtyard, and the other neighbors felt the unrefinement,

           THE COLLECTED POEMS OF DELMORE SCHWARTZ

Feeling minutely a little higher in the lower middle-class. The boys on the block mimicked Ishmael's shouting or his mother's shouting at him,

And saw that Hershey was much hurt and disturbed, and were delighted and amused by the small boy,

Who could not bear to be a butt, day-dreaming of grandeur! And now at bedtime, he made believe so much, and so long, that he did not fall asleep,

He regretted Germany's defeat in the World War because it was the end of royalty's hierarchy.

And told himself and tried to make believe that it was true, that Una the beautiful girl lived next door,

And slept in the bedroom with him and let him kiss her lips. And chose a cabinet as President of the United States,

Until Eva Green saw how the boy lay awake and did not sleep enough, and took him to the doctor,

Who told her to change the boy's diet, not to give him heavy foods at supper-time,

For a boy is what he eats, he is his body. But when his suppers were changed, he still did not sleep enough,

Mind and heart thick with wishes. And when one of his mother's old friends paid a visit,

A lady renowned in her circle because she read poetry and admired very much Ella Wheeler Wilcox,

Asked Hershey with insight what it was he thought about when he was not sleeping in the darkness,

O I think of flowers in meadows, said Hershey. A deliberate lie made for his audience, whom he knew well,

And he almost fainted with pleasure, hearing their praise and applause,

And wished it were true, but knew that when he lay awake in the dark bedroom he only extended

The habits of mind he had learned on Saturday matinées, gazing at the silver screen, rationing his candy for three hours, seated with the other boys—

"O Hollywood! new Milky Way! and last
Capital of the Western mind!"

                    "Objective trauma,
        Week after week, forth from the angels' city—"

"Forth from how many milky marvelous poles
Glittering like Annunciation in the dark,
How many hearts from Iceland to Australia
Get what they want, no more. The revery
Becomes an institution and industry—"

"All that they want: all life's dishonesties,
The happy ending in insensate moonlight,
The lightning rise to Fame, Fortune, and Fun,
The bathing beauty warm beside Royal Palms,
The serious gunmen raging in their cars
And letting go the violence all would bang!"

"The pie against policemen's faces spilt,
The bar and broncho of the Far West new,
Monsieur Beaucaire like Mozart for the dumb,
And Jesus Christ, in fact, strolling the seas—"

"The Mark of Zorro, leaping from car to train,
From horse to train, from roof to garden wall,
More agile than electric lights or birds
—And Robin Hood restoring to the poor
With banditry, the wicked really good,
A dialectic loved like fairy tales—"

"And Moses actually miraculous,
The Red Sea opening up for bald DeMille!"

"The West's imagination utterly
Fulfilled in most spectacular and trite
Magnificence, corrupted to pure trash
—From this continuous show all boys must rise:
Who can recover actuality?
And who can win his way to criticism?"

O what Saturday matinées upon the silver screen, when Chaplin and
Jackie Coogan played in *The Kid*,
    When Chaplin was the shabby-genteel bowlegged little man born every

minute in the lower middle class. Who trembles before the boss, who fears the landlord and the cop,

And yet with deftness and with agility rises and strikes them and runs away . . .

He has now found an infant upon the church steps, left there by a beautiful girl tricked by her lover, in the middle of winter, snow everywhere, an icey wind blowing through the modern city,

Blowing against the street-lamp's whiteness, blowing against the swinging doors of the corner saloon, where it is warm—

> "For unto us,
> A Child is Born,
> For unto us
> A Child is Given—"

Christmas Christian echoes moved through the dark, racketing like ashcans on the sidewalks of modern life,

While from the piano tinkled the maudlin Magdalene heart, and Charlie lifts the child, tickles him, takes him home,

Diapers and nourishes him in the dingy drab rooming house, until the landlady, a practical business woman, expels him, denying children and dogs,

> "For unto us,
> A Child is Given—"

And Charlie departs in the bowlegged shuffle and dance, tipping his derby hat and straightening his tie. His dignity totters but is maintained by his cane,

Desperately elegant. And Years quickly pass as subtitles on the screen. The child is now a little boy, Charlie is now a glazier,

The waif is his assistant, dressed in pants too long, and cap too big: he mimicks Charlie's shuffle, he mimicks Charlie's kick,

And with a slingshot breaks windows, David all over again, thus to create for the glazier more and more business,

Profits from the chaos and destruction of a Katzenjammer Kid, and profits from the contradiction and poverty

Property brings as its shadow. This most of all, this accurate cunning deceit

And forced anarchy to win a living in modern life delighted and rocked the darkened audience,

Although their being shook as helplessly when Charlie flipped with ineffable skill

Pancakes on the frying pan! striving to hide from the landlady's nose and knowledge. Or when he slept

With the cute clever orphan harbored beside him in the brass bed of the drab rooming house to sate

The easy wish for goodness of the maudlin Magdalene heart—

"Piano in the darkness tinkling tirelessly
Always brings back wholly the silver screen to me—"

Until in the end the young and beautiful mother, long loved secretly by shy Charlie, who hopes to marry her

(The insane inexhaustible hope of the Sweepstakes' ticket), meets and is met by the fortunate young man, the boss' only son, an Arrow collar star,

And marries this handsome young man in a beautiful church, while the Kid stands by, dressed up and respectable,

And with Huck Finn's nostalgia looks at and gauges the stained-glass windows,

While Charlie pressed with the crowd outside, in pathos, waits for the perfect pair to make a hurried exit,

Laughing rice thrown after them. Admires, shrugs and sighs and turns away,

And down an empty converging road walks his bowlegged dance, and swings his cane, and shrugs acceptance,

A wanderer forever, infinitely hopeful, helpless, and homeless,

As the lights go on and last laughters ascend, and the dazed sleepwalkers turn to their overcoats

As if to keep from them the chill of the actual world—

So the sick city, focussed in complex images, relieved in some the strain of living life as ego. And I blinked at these stars, and I enjoyed and loved

The constellations of plots. But I never saw or knew the genesis of their motions, the frustration,

Suppression, hope and anger imposed by modern life: So through the life of symbols, Life makes its way,

Such emblems are the bread and wine of night and day! . . .

The sharp-eyed tailor who sews at twilight, cross-kneed, stitching,

Such as Hershey might have seen any day on the business street between the candy store and the drugstore,

Fixes the concentration with which this story must be viewed, and the human hearts surrounding this boy,

Power and divinity boxing there, striking, feinting, and dancing. For now the growing fusing boy read more and more,

And seized the printed trees, magazine, book or paper,

For the fiction or sport in them, on which the ego rides. The thrilling day came when Hershey was at last allowed

To go to the Public Library by himself, dreaming as he walked across the streets

Of his playing consciousness, dreaming of the grandeur of the life to come.

And he borrowed books from the other boys, and one accused Hershey of not returning his book to him,

And made Hershey pay him a weekly sum in marbles, pictures, and pennies,

An interminable repayment aspiring to two dollars and fifty cents, enforced by Hershey's fear that his mother would hear of the loss,

So that Hershey sat in the window seat of the living room overlooking the Avenue and gazed as the Fifth Avenue bus passed,

And wondered why he had not been happy in the days when he was not oppressed by debt and the guilt of loss,

Until one day his oppressor bragged to the other boys of how he had deceived and used Hershey,

And came with the other boys to show them how Hershey trembled and paid him,

And one of the other boys saw how Hershey's mouth contracted with fear of his creditor,

And was moved by justice or pity to say, Agh, stop it, Hershey gave you back your book,

Betraying the villainous one and lighting up for Hershey

A street of suspicion he walked from that day forward,

Bearing in mind the oppressor's deliberate dishonesty, fraud and glee at the cleverness of his evil,

Forgetting the other boy who had helped him and undone the villain!

"In Hearst's sheet, the images appeared . . .
John Bull and Uncle Sam were scratched in black
Near editorials; la Belle France, too,

And Justice, barefoot and in classic linen,
Like a Barnard girl playing Antigone
In Central Park . . ."

                "Never mind what profound
Movement in the national consciousness
Drew to itself from cartoonists' minds
These easy images: the growing fusing boy
Inhaled them credulous as any savage
Unable to distinguish symbol from thing . . ."

"This seems a thousand years ago, at least:
The year was 1921 and the event
An Allied Naval Conference: the Past
May be a dinosaur; or it may be
All that is seen, no matter what one sees,
As one sees in the sons, the family face;
Or as one sees the daughter in the mother,
Plain image of the middle age to come—"

"This juvenile, this hero, thus for years
Looked at the history books in public school
And what his mind saw was cartoons in Hearst,
The concrete universal makes it way
As sunset's vivid glory tours the world!"

"A hundred years ago are understood
Now in this darkness. O how many causes
Move in their courses underground, overseas,
Or flying through the air like meteors
—And when we see what vileness they perform
How reason is offended! as by Luck . . ."

"As when a boor inherits a million dollars,
Or foolish girls are beautiful: vile luck!"

"See yourself, Hershey, eight years old, reading,
Delightedly, of Tarzan of the Apes:

Darwin and Huxley hold the book for you!
Child of the century, this is your life!"

Jack Green came to see his children and asked Hershey what he wanted,

Guilt and generosity always at work in his heart, and Hershey stopped with his father at the stationery store next to the subway kiosk,

And Jack Green bought for his son a year's subscription to *St. Nicholas Magazine*! Twelve months to come, like an income to an adult,

Deep deep absorption in the evening in the serial, wondering what would happen the next month,

Until Hershey came to think luxury was going to bed and sinking deeper and deeper, wet with interest,

Into the soft hours of a long book, a memory of the womb, perhaps? But in the active world, in the school divinity, much was more difficult,

Hershey climbed from 3RA, the second term of rapid advance, to 4A, the first term of the fourth year,

Una, worshipped from afar was in another 4A class, but he looked with love toward her, standing in line,

In the school basement during recesses. The 4A teacher was an old woman, gray-haired and annoyed for years. On charts on the wall, each pupil was given a box,

And sent to write his sins, talking, not paying attention, coming late to school,

Chewing gum, cheating. Hershey committed all of them, and was sent to write them in his box. Now four charges in any month equalled a D in conduct,

And the parent was sent for to come to school, and Hershey trembling wrote on his box, rewriting the same sin again and again,

While the near-sighted teacher gazed at him and did not see what he did and did not actually care very much.

Hershey had learned this deception from other scoundrels in the class, boys who stole pennies from newsstands,

And lifted girl's dresses sometimes and looked under them, while the girls screeched,

And Hershey was afraid that he would become like these boys in all things,

But without their bravado; fearful, cowardly, fugitive, the nice boy seduced in his weakness. Thus he was taught of falsehood,

Evasion of authority, guilt. Thus he became more learnèd in fear. But another learning persisted and increased,

He walked home from school with a Catholic boy, and asked him, as three years before he had asked the Catholic girl next door,

About the Catholic Church; for one of them reigned at the south end of the block, and this boy went there all Sundays.

But the Catholic boy would not tell Hershey anything, he would mention the bread he ate, but say no more,

Which made Hershey look at the bread he himself ate; and the prayers he spoke to the Cross,

Which he must keep secret from such as Hershey. From overseas, from silent Palestine, from so many centuries,

Dominion of the sepulchre! touching the schoolboys. For he kept faith and silence, although Hershey offered him gifts,

Pictures, pennies, marbles, being curious and intent
To know just what the bread was, what the Cross meant,
For all men desire to know, as Aristotle said,
All children too sometimes would like to understand bread!

    "A wise man says, Religion is what man
    Does with his solitude: what a remark!
    —We know, do we not know? what some men do
    When left alone: Arnauld declared that Man
    Was capable of any monstrous act
    When left in solitude in his own room
    —Pascal, his pupil, on the other hand,
    Observed that all our trouble and our pain
    Sprang from the failure to stay in one's room?
    —*Les extrêmes se touchent*: these poles which meet
    Define a circle of uneasiness,
    Somewhat a swaying sea. We are but sailors—"

    "The early morning light becomes a sign:
    It is the snow! Even as sometimes snow
    Stands for the early morning light. These shifts
    Show Baudelaire and Freud were well-advised,
    Saying, Man walks through a dark wood of symbols,
    All his life long, no matter what he does—"

THE COLLECTED POEMS OF DELMORE SCHWARTZ

"I when I heard of God from black despair
Rose always like a bird; quickly, lightly,
Prone in the former life to utter sadness
Because my efforts fell short many times:
I said to myself, 'An infinite God!
If such a being really exists, he hears
What I am saying now. Does He not know
All, look at all, see all with perfect views?
And if He hears me, is it not possible
—Although I am not sure—that He will help me?
Is it a profanation of the pure Idea
Which makes me think that He really exists
To think that He will aid me in my pain?
                              Can I be sure?'"

"I too would think these thoughts, also unsure,
—And yet, thinking these thoughts I always rose,
I was less desperate, I could endure
My dark body's awkward brutality,
I could endure my soul's black guilt which hoped
The world would end, and all things, screaming, *die*,
Because I was in my ambition stopped
The while my brother, friend, and enemy
Succeeds with seeming spontaneity,
And wins the girl, acclaim, the world's applause!
Yes! when I thought of God Himself *an sich*,
It was *enough*, although I knew He judged,
Judging the world in me! . . . Infinite joy
Flooded me then, as if I came to the shore
Of the cold sea upon a summer's day,
And let my dear dark body be by water's silk
All over touched and known! This was my stay,
My hope, my wish, my ground, my good, my God!"

"Will Hershey Green go down this old abyss
Of thought in days to come, since now he asks
Questions and answers of the Catholic boy?
—How can he help but go, being what he is?"

"The Sunday-looking people, like big flowers,
Know many shades, however secular:
They know the heart hangs down, a Christmas stocking,
They feel strange drafts, however warm the May,
They know that Nature sails like a Zeppelin
Precarious aloft in a dark void:
The fool hath said in his heart, There is no God!
—He marks the fall of sparrows, verily!"

"Everything happens in the mind of God,
This is the play it is, ever since Eden!"

"Let me revive my passions, far from this,
Although as relevant to the agonist,
Let me go off upon a candid cadenza,
Running through memories as shuffling cards:
—Branded by parents with identity,
(Mamma and Papa who with private parts
Most irresponsibly began this *crise*,)
I sailed the seven seas, I saw the Czar,
Millions of mighty men sang through my soul,
The stars stretched out senseless as alphabets,
I thought the world was anybody's fun!
Gemütlichkeit was like the sunlight then!
The golded charging and electric earth
Appealed to me, full of such plants and sweets!
I saw the infamy which made me rich,
Capitalismus native to the heart,
Nothing like that before for egotism,
Never such forms and such fine playing fields!
I saw the evil of the average man
—Clio! between your legs obscenities
Performed and pushed! Jesus and Socrates
Downed by the populace with happiness,
—I saw all modern life in Street & Smith,
Promised virility, and social charm,
Strong muscles and trapped breasts hailed in the ads,
Yet Life was wonderful, beyond belief,
Wine was a light, and all the arts were lights,

THE COLLECTED POEMS OF DELMORE SCHWARTZ

The dancers with their discipline destroyed
The chaos and the waste of Broadway crowds,
They with their limbs an inner order knew,
They took it with an easy willingness,
I took it too, from an orchestra seat
—But when will the houselights of the universe
Go on? You! You! trapped in your childhood!
Let us go back to the past, quickly and smoothly
The dark water closes its lips on today—"

And the summer came again, and Hershey and Roger were taken one weekend to the seashore,

There a friend of Eva Green, a friend of her girlhood days owned a summer house. Her youngest daughter

Had been born the same week as Hershey, and they had been present like John and Jesus at many conversations of the two young pregnant wives,

Loving jokes of the foetuses' later friendship. Now the child Elsa played all day with Hershey and Roger

On the boardwalk and on the beach and in the house. When bedtime came, Hershey and Roger and Elsa decided to sleep in the same room,

The natural conclusion it seemed to Hershey of the day's playing. But the two mothers smiled the smiles of matrons,

And commanded the children to go to different rooms. But when the two boys were in pajamas, Hershey sent Roger, forever his lieutenant,

To go and bring back Elsa to sleep in the same bed as he, while Roger slept in her room. She came, but would not stay alone with Hershey,

And as they argued, Hershey turned aside a moment, and Elsa cried out

That she had seen his secret parts between his pajama fold, carelessly buttoned,

O no, said Hershey, you did not, feeling that the denial of his voice might be sufficient, horrified,

Turning to Roger for help. But Roger was moved by the truth and betrayed him and affirmed Elsa's glimpse,

And Hershey leaped into bed and hid his head, feeling deprived of his dressed virginity,

And sniffed at the pillow's musty smell, and felt ill at ease,

And shrugged, falling to sleep, the Eden where Venus fused with all seas. . . .

And then one day in the June New York summer, Hershey walking on the Avenue with a friend met his Uncle Martin, his father's brother,

Who had gone to France with the A.E.F., and Uncle Martin gave him a half a dollar to buy sodas,

And Hershey told his mother that his uncle had given him only fifteen cents, for he knew that she would take the remainder from him,

And the thirty-five cents he kept became a precious fund which he held for some unknown purpose,

But he lived in fear from month to month, as he had been afraid of Mrs. Rinehart's policeman,

That his mother would meet his uncle and learn how much he had been given, and that he had lied to her,

And when he walked on the Avenue one day with his mother and Roger, they met Uncle Martin and his wife, and Hershey terrified ran away,

Certain that he was discovered as liar and thief. But Roger said when they came home

That they had only spoken of Jack Green's absence, except that Uncle Martin had asked her why Hershey had run away,

And if he did not like his uncle? And Hershey knew that his uncle's feelings were hurt, and he felt an intense guilt

Thus to repay his uncle for the fifty cents of his gift!

"The boy seems to encounter concrete abstractions
When merely idling Sunday afternoons,
Or by the seaside, whence his parents came,
Playing the summer like a sailboat toy,
Which wanders out beyond his will on the vast
Atlantic minuscule, even as he cries out—"

"Napoleon, the absolute on horseback:
He was the type of egotism bare,
He was the Corsican against the world,
He was the celibate of his own will,
Yet he too everywhere met helplessly
These causes, these most powerful abstractions,
These deities we seek throughout this night,
Gazing upon your life, O sleepless boy!"

"Russia and England were the deities
Who stopped the little fat man, in the end—"

THE COLLECTED POEMS OF DELMORE SCHWARTZ

"And every soul within historic terms
Finds his life tossed upon these insane sums,
Just as the merest infant when he walks
Steps on the whole earth, treads the universe,
Takes up another stance, locked in the laws
Of Time and Space, whether he stands or falls!"

"Some deities are born as quick as flies,
And yet, longer than many monuments
They live, and like some monuments they shift,
Good to the father, evil to the son—"

"O like Vesuvius some causes are
Dormant for centuries and then alive
As vast catastrophes! O like the Cross
Which melts the hardened heart and the tough sword
Of soldier boys intent upon the will
Of men who would maintain their pride and place—"

"Behold once more the prowess and the struggle:
This is what makes Life cruel. Makes all
Things flow, downs every captain soon or late
—That all the deities each other strike!
Strike desperate blows, even in the small child—"

"The school divinity against the family
Strikes desperate blows within the very child,
The city god against all Nature strives,
Tying the bridge upon the river banks—"

"Children are taught in school how to behave
In contradiction of the family life!
And in the city street, the children learn
Brutalities which shock their relatives—"

"The boys hit boys from other blocks with rocks,
Because they come from other blocks, because
Partisanship creates these minor clubs
And every club would down the other club—"

"Each club, cause, deity, and private soul
Seeks to extend itself until it dies,
Seeks to become an absolute itself,
The soul becomes the broken battleground,
And the will's suffrage is the victory,
When there is victory! not Pyrrhic end
No one foresaw or wished, a stupid sum
Irrational to all, utter defeat—"

"Yet many goodnesses are also present
—The school assembly sings the city's good!
After the teacher shows the children's minds
The Gettysburg Address and Valley Forge,
Jefferson, Jefferson Davis, General Grant,
The famous dead who moved in America
... And now are high schools, statues, postage stamps!"

And in the heat of the summer, Hershey was sent with his aunt to the country.

Aunt Lillian was on her vacation from making dresses, this was the period when unmarried girls went every year for two weeks to the country,

Hoping to find a husband to take away their maidenhood and make them important.

And the country came back to Hershey like a memory, the smell of leaves in the wind,

After the scorching sun burned forth their sweetness; the adults on the porch on rocking chairs,

Talking or playing cards; at night at the Casino the popular songs of the year,

Which greatly perplexed and charmed Hershey, "Yes! We have no bananas!" and "That Old Gang of Mine," nostalgia fixed in the banal air,

All of these objects and motions passed through Hershey and made an increasing impression—

"Grand oh! extreme surprise! dénouement's boom!
On, on, and on! we lift you up, poor boy,
We help you rise from your experience,
As the plane rises high above the city
(And in a new *Gestalt* perceives the parts)

Above the clouds and to the bluest air
—Significance is like the sun itself
And from true causes truly seen shines forth!"

"O make believe this is your education;
Lo, how these powers come to be and live:
The people make a city when they come
To a new place where fertile fields abound,
Where water goes, where with the rock and tree
They can erect the fort against the beast
And enemy, nature and foreign man:
The city then becomes a *thing* itself,
Not living, but a deity because
It has laws of its own of growth and strength,
Laws hardly known or meant by those who first
Came to join need and weakness, and from the knot
Gain satisfaction and gain company—"

"Illusions and conclusions hardly meant
By anyone who started the whole boon—"

"You are a New York boy, O sleepless one,
The cause is quick in you as on the moor
The Scotsman dour, or in the vivid sunlight
The known Italian, singing and vivacious,
Crying out *Viva!* the name of all his operas!"

"Some deities are born as quick as flies,
Yet last as long as all the Pyramids!"

"The family which in the city joins
Is of like nature, being made by it:
Under the shadow of the city god
Two human beings join their need and weakness,
And from the knot produce the brand-new child!"

"These are the players in your life so far,
Which dominate the scene, all-powerful—"

"The wind blows in the curtains, as of old,
Being a hint of emptiness and doom,
Absolute darkness full of sound and need,
And I go back, O New York boy, forever,
—My heart went up and down, like cyclist's knees,
Power, ongoingness and thoughtlessness
Pumped at the pedal with thorough happiness
—I kissed the bride I would have wed myself,
I knew the joy which is self-sacrifice,
Some of the benefits of actresses
(The make-up and the glamorous footlights' gulf)
Shone in my face when I for goodness lied,
—My body by desire whipped! The amateur
Never forgets the tie, the nurse's brush
—Being a ghost is not a picnic. I
Know in my mind nostalgia like brown beer's
Glow, fuzz, and mounting warmth, another lie
(I am bewildered by these memories!).
My body ridden like a horse forever
In an expensive coffin rots, but I
Tic and tick with my life, revived forever,
                                        Shall I relax?
Shall I forget? Will the dead sleep? O no!
One must tread water, paddling as if mid-seas
Of the Atlantic slopped about one's flesh,
After the burst and wrack of the sinking ship,
One must hold on as if one climbed a peak,
Struggle and effort are the endless need,
After events like Christmas and like War
(My wild and whirling words seek to be clear),
—All this is meant to help you, New York boy—"

Hershey heard all the time of his father's absence, his mother tensed and
paled with her anger,
    She heard from his lawyer who told her how Jack Green would provide a
sum each week for the support of her and the children,
    She went to his relatives, to his sister and his brothers to tell them of his evil,
    And talked avidly and passionately, and was so self-absorbed that she did
not know or feel

THE COLLECTED POEMS OF DELMORE SCHWARTZ

How they resented her and were loyal to Jack Green and admired him because he was successful and made a good deal of money,

And now boys on the block began to ask Hershey, Is your mother divorced from your father?

And since Hershey had been told many times by his mother what a disgrace divorce was,

Hershey lied to boys on the block, trembling, unable to hide his falsehood,

But then one day two boys playing in the apartment with Hershey heard Eva Green speaking on the telephone loudly,

And telling a friend of Jack Green's desire for a legal separation. The two boys looked up and smiled to each other and Hershey saw this,

And when they had gone, he came to his mother and asked her why she had said so much and revealed so much in the boys' hearing,

And she told Hershey that it did not matter. But the stigma of his father's absence, which she had impressed on him,

Turned now to the light in which Hershey saw his mother,

Wanton with her emotion, "contradicting herself."

And now the boys on the block had a new way in which to tease and taunt Hershey, knowing him sensitive,

Finding another wincing wound. Until they forgot, drawn to new interests and new targets,

Or finding another use for the cruelty of the heart. Then on a soft and sunny Sunday in August came another girlhood friend of Eva Green,

She came with her small meek husband in his Ford to take Eva Green and her children for a ride,

The characteristic play of the lower middle-class in the day to which America had come.

They drove to City Island, admired suburban scenes, while Hershey felt contempt for the Ford, so unlike his father's expensive car,

Roger and Hershey licked ice-cream cones, and looked at Long Island Sound,

And half-listened as their mother's monologue obsessed the afternoon.

Then they were riding home in the late afternoon through expensive suburbs, and on the national highway which led to the great city,

And then they passed the back of a roadhouse, full of parked cars, half-hidden by shrubbery,

And Eva Green, although she talked on, seated in the quick-moving car,

Saw,—such was her interest!—Jack Green's car parked in the back of the roadhouse,

And demanded that the car be stopped, while she went to see if her husband was in the roadhouse,

And with whom he had come there. Mildly arguing, weakly protesting, husband and wife both said, How can you be sure it was his car? We passed so quickly?

Eva Green's anger was stony at once, she said to stop the car and let her get out, she would go home alone,

Someone would help her! The car was turned about, Eva Green asked the small mild and meek husband to come with her into the roadhouse,

He stammered once more, asking her not to go, instead of answering her. Until at last,

Impatient and self-righteous, she took Hershey by the hand, the other available man,

And mother and child walked up the cinder path marked by whitewashed flagstones, surrounded by a lawn,

To the large white roadhouse, once a Colonial Mansion, from whose roof

The Stars and Stripes were blowing in the daylight summer evening, like an accordion.

As Hershey and his mother came through the door, the headwaiter came up and asked Eva Green,

Was she waiting for anyone? Because she looked intensely through the dining-room, and because she was an incongruous figure, holding a small boy by the hand.

Yes, she was waiting for someone, she replied, standing there in the lobby, holding Hershey with a grasp which hurt his hand,

Casting her glances about, almost ready to give up because she did not see Jack Green anywhere,

Until, just before she was going to turn to go, she saw Jack Green at a table in a corner next to the window,

Seated with a woman, dining and chatting, amid soft music from the musicians. Quickly she moved to his table,

Turned to the rest of the long dining-room, the headwaiter beside her, helplessly polite,

Begging her to sit down, and cried out and spoke aloud

Her passionate righteous anger, inspired and shouting phrases she had read in the Hearst papers about divorce cases,

Pointed to Hershey, his hand still clutched in hers, his joy at seeing his father destroyed at that moment,

THE COLLECTED POEMS OF DELMORE SCHWARTZ

Shouted to the diners on the mezzanine floor that her husband had left her and her children to dine with a whore!

And no one was able to stop her until her rage had been exhausted, even though the waiters convened about her,

But Jack Green arose and took Hershey by the hand and walked outside with him,

And lighted a cigarette, and stood with Hershey silent upon the cinder path, his face hard and cold as he looked down at the boy in the daylight saving evening,

So that Hershey felt sorry for his father and admired him, tall, towering, of a dignity increased by mastered emotion,

As a waiter came out and Jack Green paid him and apologized curtly to him,

And then Jack Green asked Hershey, Who brought you here? and Hershey told his father what had happened,

And Eva Green came out from the Ladies' Room where she had been restoring herself, and Jack Green turned aside, and they did not speak to each other,

And Eva Green took Hershey home from this Sunday School in the 'twenties. Passion, self-possession,

Shame and shock, and yet a certain interest, a certain joy

Witnessed the roadhouse scene, and strove in the boy, saw what the public means and what the private,

And yet admired most of all his father's poise and dignity, after Medea cried aloud and Clytemnestra struck!

> "The husband trapped while dining with a whore
> —Here matrimony is a ground for her,
> The sacred nature of the family
> Enforced by feelings of the polity,
> Grew from the deepest source, the actual child
> The mother knew enough to bring with her,
> Holding him by the hand, her righteousness!"

> "The other diners dining with their whores
> Hardly, I know, regarded her as wrong,
> And if they felt that they were guilty too,
> Were *glad* they were not caught; and in their hearts
> Affirmed, despite their place, her view; rejoiced,

As she cried out, to hear, loudly pronounced
The sacred nature of the family!"

"You give them too much credit: they rejoiced
To hear the scandal, feel the shock, relieved
Because they were not caught. Felt that this was
A novel floor show, most dramatic, perfectly
Cried and enacted by the characters—"

"Poor Hershey Green, for whom this scene becomes
Arch-typical of every living room
Until he shouts himself, denouncing all,
Himself, his parents, and America!
In just such intervention, shockingly,
Until the very dead come to cry out
And from their death denounce the former life,
And like a wife speak with self-righteousness,
Hold Hershey's hand, who listens and is stunned—"

"Childhood was ended here! or innocence
—Henceforth suspicious of experience!"

"This hideous scene presents the biggest truth,
Man's Nature is this being-in-the-world,
This in-ness is the warmest thing in Life,
This in-ness is the widest thing in Life,
This is the space in which you live your Life!"

"Although a soul may travel or may flee,
Moving from Europe to America,
No one departs from being-in-the-world,
This space goes in and out of every soul
As light which penetrates the heavy head
—This space goes everywhere and is a part
Of the sole self in every kind of thing!"

"This in-ness lives as mother holds your hand,
As father looks at you, and looks away,

Anguish and shame, anger and guilt enact
The in-ness of your being-in-the-world—"

"This is the way all are political!
This is before and in all images,
This is the first of images, poor boy,
This in-ness is in every feeling, full.
This is the first of feelings: Space itself
With what varieties and richness whelms—"

"Here is the Super-Ego wholly grown,
Upon your temples it will live forever!"

"And here is where this very night begins,
For here you learned to cry aloud your life!
Before a staring mezzanine audience,
Superior, wise, thunder-struck, apart,
Yet guilty too, alas! being in Life:
How many times before your life is lived
This hideous scene will make fresh repetitions!"

"Your mother's oratory will abide,
Whence what a senate, what a court becomes,
What a profoundest theatre holds and will hold
Your being as a being-in-the-world!"

"The growing fusing boy takes it all in,
The strong divinities, this vision of himself
Surrounded by many relationships and little else,
But anger, irony, self-pity, all the emotions
        self-absorption brews and begets—"

"O Father of all hearts, give this poor boy the power
To speak his naked heart without excessive nausea,
O Dream behind the Dream, give him the strength
To see himself with disgust full depth and full length!"

"The history of Life repeats its endless circle,
                    over and over and over again,
In the new boy, in the new city, in the time forever new,
                    forever old,
—All of the famous characters are glimpsed again,
All the well-known events; yet something new,
Unique, undying, free, blessèd or damned!"

"Everything happens in the mind of God:
                    This is all
You need for wondrous hope, and this we give,
                    Sleepless Atlantic boy!"

                    "O no!
You do not give that, but give greater darkness,
All this is but a fixed hallucination
Made by the passion of imagination:
This may be false, if I know anything,
I do not know that all is in the mind of God,
I do not have that hope miraculous,
I am more certain of all other things,
The bed, the darkness, and my dear dark body
Are with me, certain,
                    God is a dream! And this is what
I do not know and have to know. O *if*
I only knew *that*! then what other lights on all—"

Thus Hershey Green, drawn in the opera,
Thrilled and enthralled by each new aria!

"Poor New York boy, with what finality
You will in time say,—and triumphantly!—
O what a metaphysical victory
The first morning and night of death must be!"

from
Genesis: Book Two

"—Rilke and Yeats, unknown to each other,
Seek with Stravinsky for the moving doll
Who has won out over the natural world!
Over the child, the sex,
                the need to make a living
—And this is all because the artist is
An exile in his Age,
             exiled from The City,
Exiled from Nature too, in his illusion. . . ."

"And in America, while these great men grew up
In Europe's pain, O in America
Art sought its bearings in an Age
Of quake-like change. After the Civil War,
The decades have about them the disorder
Of mining camps, gold rushes!
                The landed gentry
Died, or decayed, or else united
With leaders of industry, men on the make,
Aggressive, merciless, uncouth . . .
And when the landed gentry fell, there fell
In slow decay, the mild genteel tradition
Which had a mild good taste, and which now seemed
A cultured aristocracy, although
It never had been large, or sure of its taste. . . .
The booming industrialists arose
And roved, brash individualists
In a hurry to wealth and power,
                barons of mill-towns,
Mining towns, coal, steel, and oil towns,
                  builders of railroads,
Speculators, land-grabbers, carpet-baggers,
Prospectors and gamblers.
            America
Was on the make. . . . wasting and destroying

The rich Nature of a continent . . .
The Public which existed wanted only
An art which flattered its pretentions, thoughts
Of a careless individualism,
                            blowing up, wanting more and more,
Caught by the ideal of ever-mounting wealth.
—In this America, in this *milieu,*
The serious artist had no place, driven
To isolation, forced to accentuation
Of personal peculiarities,
                            bohemianism and defiance,
                                        shocking the middle-class . . .
Hence rose the Age of solitaries and exiles,
Whistler went to Europe and stayed there,
Everyone went there for a time and stayed
In some sense, forever . . . And yet some stayed
Behind, remained to accept and try to master
The new America blooming in grime,
Though Eakins suffered long neglect and solitude,
And Homer, in the end, withdrew from all men
To a small shack by the eternal sea,
And the life of the sensitive Ryder
Centered about the one room in which
Says Lao-Tze, somewhat too hopefully,
A man may see the entire universe . . ."

[8.]
_____

"In Hearst's sheet, the images appeared . . .
John Bull and Uncle Sam were scratched in black
Next to the editorials,
                            la Belle France too, and Justice
In classic linen, bare foot and blindfolded
Like a Barnard girl playing Antigone

In Central Park . . .
                        Never mind what profound
Movements in the national consciousness
Drew to itself from some cartoonist's mind
These easy images: the growing fusing boy
Inhaled them, gaping, credulous,
                              and like a savage
Could not distinguish symbol from the thing . . ."

"This seems a thousand years ago, at least:
The year was 1922, and the event
The Washington Naval Conference: the Past
May be a dinosaur; or it may be
All that is seen, no matter what one sees,
As one sees in the sons, the family face,
And as one sees the daughter in the mother,
                              twenty-five years to come . . ."

". . . This juvenile, our hero, thus for years
Looked at the history books in public school
And what his mind saw was cartoons in Hearst,
The concrete universal makes its way,
                              just like a chain letter. . . ."

"A hundred years ago are understood,
Now in this darkness. O, how many causes
Move in their courses underground, overseas,
Or flying through the air like meteors . . .
And when we see what vileness they perform
How reason is offended! as by chance. . . .
—See yourself, nine years of age, reading,
Delighted and amazed, of Tarzan of the Apes,
                              half-ape, half man:
Darwin and Huxley hold up the book for you!
Child of the Century, this is your Life!"

[IDENTICAL TO PAGE MARKED 9A.]

"We rode to City Island on a Sunday,
Before my father left the house again—"

"We saw upon the oblong billboard, huge,
A Broadway play,
                            to the wide world advertised
In most deliberate accepted lies—
Called *The Bad Man*: mother and father had seen it. . . .

"As we rode on and on through Sunday suburbs,
My mother told me what the plot contained:
In Mejico, a bandit, Pancho Villa
—Someone like that—captures Americans,
Holds them for ransom,
                            captures, as the curtain
Rises, a young man and his pretty girl
Engaged to marry. He, a brisk brusque
Aggressive and self-confident young man,
And she devoted to her crippled father,
And not in love with the self-assured young man,
But marrying for poor crippled papa's sake,
Who uses pity as his capital, like many
Invalids, with brutal cruelty . . .
And soon the other young man enters, also
Taken by members of the robber band:
He's the defeated suitor, really loved
By the young lady, but offending her
By poverty and irresponsibility—
And too much charm, indolence, and conceit!
But look! it seems The Bandit and the loser
Were buddies in the World War.
                            He will not

Shoot down in cold blood the girl and the girl's father
He will restrict himself to her fiancée—

So on and on, as we drove on,
                                 through Sunday's suburbs
(Unto Long Island's liner, sailing on)
Until the bad man bandit in the end becomes
Good angel, Santa Claus, and Robin Hood,
Or Cupid, finding gold mines, finding millions!
For the poor young man rejected by the girl

The so-called Bad Man makes the girl accept
His services as Cupid, showing her
How cowardly her fiancée, how brave
The poor young man wrong rejected by her—
And how she was in love with him throughout. . . .

"This is the theme of Robin Hood, this was
The lower middle class release, to hate
The brisk efficient business man, rising
To greatest power in that post-war day:
—But for the growing fusing boy it was
A sign of how complex all good must be,
And how the outer villain might be saintly,
As how the ugly duckling was a swan,
As Cinderella rose, married a prince!
He learned the power of these paradigms,
He learned the fascination of the plot!
He learned the ambiguity of good and evil!
He learned the dialectic taught by Hegel!"

"Look how these fictions soon were fabulous
—At early silver screens, he saw the villain
Attack the ingénue or Mary Pickford
Rescued from shameless shame *at the last minute*!
By the poor young man or by the rich
Young man or by the stranger (as the wish
To make a ritual of the common mind's

Deepest emotions about society
Might at the moment *need*):
                    O Life performed
By forms ancient and modern! what a gift
To man and boy, to logos, man's
Intimate being, learning of Life by such
Vivid and unmistakable cartoons. . . ."

[10.]

"Love me, love my snake! or other vices:
So shouts the ego's hoarse and barbarous voices. . . ."

"An eye for an eye! Forgive your enemies!
And love them too! Two ethiques which remorse-
-ful Jewry from its pastoral passionate
Intercourse with Nature and with Man

                         engendered . . ."

The light which never was! on land or sea,
Shone on the second Law, delicate
As starlight in the silkiest growth of dusk
. . . The moment when all arms relax and fall,
And purest humanism has a chance
To lead the ego in a gentle dance. . . .

"But black night after! when the separate soul
Fall endlessly through an endless wall-less hole,
Wakes very anger! Brings the vicious fear
Which makes all energy into a fist
Striking against the wide world,

                         every face!

". . . Then morning, irritated by what night
Brought forth, yet subsided, quieted
          and

Since now the worst had been and been endured
Morning brings forth the smile of reason,

                                patient, profound,
Soon, after coffee's force, the soul can bear
The globe's great burden and like Atlas feel
It's but a basketball, to throw in play,
Effort and satisfaction following each other
Game after game, but in the adult's day . . .
A soft and lucid ease, as toil begins . . .

"Forgiveness, Charity, Humility,

                             Mercy, Pity, Peace!
This was the starlight strong at the Calvary,
Handsome as Valentino, daring

                         as Western heroes
Leaping from horse to train: He walked the sea,
And changed to wine the water,

                        a metaphor
At marriages worthy of William Shakespeare!"

Mercy, Pity, Peace, He brought the world . . ."

[12.]

"My whole life long—my life mature, I mean,—
I tried to win—like this boy's vast Idea—
A miracle of reason! O, a change
Making merely a change of dress of what
Industrialism did to Western Man—
Namely to show *that God exists*!

                       To make
It clear and obvious as cold lake water
Touched by canoists with an idle hand
Immediate to the flesh and consciousness . . .

What would be proof like that?
                                For all would see
A sign, no less! a blazing sign, a star
Palpable in the pure brew of the evening—
—Now first, after some thoughts of method,
I sought to fund the probability
That this wide world would from a trash
Of spinning chemicals or lesser bits
Evolve, as we said then, that painful glory
A conscious being! Hamlet, black with thoughts?
The probability that chance has done it *all*,
Forth from the whirling atoms Nature & Man,
Was such a fraction, such a long shot as
appalls the mind,
cannot be understood,
Is inconceivable to sense at least!
One chance among chances whose number would
Reach the city of New York unto
The farthest reaches of known stellar space!
A fraction whose denominator would
Make of The Milky Way rather an inch!

—'Just think of such a number!' I cried out
To meager audiences on lecture tours!
'One chance among a billion billion chances
That this big beautiful world should be
Only the product of a chance event
And not a mind that knew it all,
                                and made
The tree look for sunlight with its leaves!
Or animal sleep through the winter snow!
Or breast be nippled for the infant's mouth!
Or eyebrow grow to stop the forehead's sweat
From blinding the farmer, falling in his eyes!'

'Candide!' they cried at me, 'Pangloss! Leibnitz!'
Was the nose made to bear a pince-nez's clasp?
Ingersoll! Darwin! Voltaire! Democritus!
And they refused to believe my argument . . ."

". . . There primitive peoples without money,
Or private property or 'things like that';
But none without ornaments and trinkets:
The sense of dignity, and the sense of beauty,
Rule, you can see, the living dying world . . .

"—The pygmy tribes in Africa build bridges
Made of rope-cords with labor which takes days—
But never think of building rafts or boats
To cross the rivers, although many have seen
Others swimming across, or riding across—"

"Then there's initiation of the boys,
As often elsewhere, Months in the forest
On small rations, and then the great day when
The boy is circumcised—the utmost pain
In which he must show how he bears it all
—Keeping his face, keeping his dignity,
Keeping his courage,
                    shouting at the end
Three loud brave cries, the triumph of his manhood—"

"Hardly like you, O Hershey Green, who cried
Merely the ancient words, the ancient prayers
Pained merely by self-consciousness, no more—
Ignorant relatives, an indifferent priest . . ."

"At birth the skull is soft, easily shaped;
Wrapped in thick folds, an elongated firm
                              a kind of pair,
Which to these primitives is beautiful!
The head and mind are bound around and around—
By such ideas as—getting ahead! making
A living! dressing well! being healthy:
But then the world moves on, quicker, my boy
Than in America! and the young man cannot

use or endure,

The ideas wrapped about his mis-shaped head:
Hence with that head made in the middle class
He hates all other heads shaped in that shape
He hates himself; like some Jews, hates the Jew,
This is the artist in our modern life!
The artist is a Jew modern!—"

[15.]

"'Just think of such a number!' I said then,
To meager audiences on lecture tours,
Old men afraid of death, old ladies bored. . . .
And a few students! mocking and skeptical,
Present to heckle, feel superior,
Laughing at me, mind from another age—
Later, I took with me, a kind of cage
Containing building blocks, the children's toy;
On each of their four sides were letters, red,
Or black or green, no matter! 'All are here,
Many times over!' I cried loudly out,
'And yet suppose this cage of building blocks
Were big as the Atlantic!
                     big as the moon!
And with more letters of the alphabet
Than sands upon the shores of the seven seas!
Suppose they shook a million years or more:
                         long as you like—
Do you think that, by accident? by shaking?
By merest chance? *Hamlet*, by William Shakespeare
Would be produced, as it has been produced,
A monument of careful consciousness?'

. . . .This never brought conviction to those who
Were not for years convinced, wished to believe,

willed their belief!
'Reason compels!' I cried, 'only the will
denies belief!
                    It is an evil act
Thus to refuse the knowledge of God's being:
Life is so bare and harsh until his glory
Is seen like sunlight,
                              bringing all the colors!'

—And then by reading old philosophers
I found old arguments, as fresh, as new,
As genuine as gold,
                          and wrote each day
Long letters to the papers, arguing;
Printed sometimes to go with auto ads. . . ."

[17.]

"'Think of all the conditions,' Karl Barth says
'That poor Man knows' (still echoing Pascal!)
—'Nature's wide muteness or unmeaning sounds,
The accidents or shadows which befall
All things that live in Time!
                                  the fate of nations!'
(Speaking in that defeated Germany!)
'The fate of peoples! Death, the one abyss!
The one and irredeemable conclusion! . . .

—For Man desires to live: this is the whole
Of his effort, even when he, despairing,
Attempts to die . . . Man is his own sovereign,
His world is but a shapeless chaos, struggled
By man natural and social forces,
                                  sexual need, social need,
Need of mouth to be fed, and body dressed . . .

This is the world of time, the world in time,
The world of out-of-one-another,
                              near-one-another,
Towards-one-another,'
                    —the wound of existence
Flows from these harsh propinquities!—
'—Broken humanity, always unfurnished—'

. . . Back to Pascal again—our minds run on—
'The furthest reach of reason,' he cries out,
Triumphant, blazing, anguished! 'is to know
What an infinite sum of things utterly
Surpass it, and resist its feeble light!'

'—Broken humanity, always unfinished—'

'God speaks, Man hears; Man speaks, God hears';
                                        This is
A dialogue before and beyond the stars . . ."

". . . The bears are quiet in the pit next door . . .
Players come out, platform walk
                        a palace gate at Elsinore,
Two guards upon patrol. They meet:
                              'Tis bitter chill,
                        And I am sick at heart . . .'
The tragedy of Hamlet, prince of Existenz,
Waving thinking reed, always unfinished,
                              walking through Life and Death . . .
—More things there are in Heaven and Earth, my dear,
Than all philosophies! dream of!
                        and all the dreams,
                              however mixed . . ."

[490.]
[18.]

"Let us speak of the city of New York
In which this boy has lived for sixteen years . . ."

"But did he live and does he live, in truth
In a city or a place with unity?
In the whole truth which is like a young girl
Who will be married soon, whose whole truth is
Her pregnant belly and her distorted body . . ."

"O no! this city has no unity,
Such as a body, such as a school or house,
Such as a stadium might have!
                              and has . . .
It is a sum compounded by the mind,
A vast abstraction, like a sick monarch
                                        who
Rules without reason like an untrue god,
Believed, ruling through an untrue belief—"

"It is a sum of living neighborhoods;
Each neighborhood defines itself in this way:
Is felt as being from Downtown removed
A certain distance,
                    subway, car, and bus
Count this relationship and no one walks,
For walking distance *is* the neighborhood—"

". . . The skyscrapers, the long office buildings
Were a pure product of expansive will,
To get the most from what the city names
                                        "the land values"
                    the real estate,
An accident made by the long and narrow island . . ."

"The bridges laid across the rivers seem

Fire escapes! in sublimation seen,
Escape to suburbs and the countryside:
No one can fly to New York *sans* crossing water,
The two rivers, the two bays, the great Harbor
Which made the city eminent and key . . ."

"The movie houses overwhelm one's gaze
With all the vulgar swag of nouveau riches,
Designed like Moorish temples, Egypt's tombs,
Versailles, Byzantium,
                                        and one I saw,
On the Grand Concourse grand, whose ceiling was
A blue sky, banal, crossed by too-big stars
To make the people feel an out-of-doors. . . ."

[492.]
[20.]

"The city was defined by visitors
As well as citizens . . ."
                                        "'this is,'
                                                        one author said,
'A big apartment hotel, nothing more' . . .
'I like to visit it, but live there?
                                        Never!'
Said Middle-Westerners. The poet said,
'Accessibility to experience,'
That is its strength, its wealth, and glory,
                                                        what a rich phrase . . .

'Coal from Pennsylvania,
                                        labor from Europe,
Oranges from Florida and California,
Tea from China and coffee from Brazil
—The power of finance, Wall Street, so-called
Because the mind must think with images

THE COLLECTED POEMS OF DELMORE SCHWARTZ

Surpasses every physical barrier
(As if they were not there or hardly there)
And reaches out like the radio's flashing cries . . . '"

"—No one could know before The Civil War
The'incalculable outcome of the ingress
Of factories and immigrants,
what troops,
what a grim era,
the Brown decades
Destroying Federal New York,
                       the small handsome
Self-contained city Edith Wharton sang,
Child of the abdicated, mourning wisely . . ."

"Nineteen thousand horses,
                  three hundred thousand dogs
Five hundred thousand cats,
              one million trees,
                      one million sparrows,
Six million human beings,
                six million psyches in New York
                         by 1930 . . .

"—Brownstone houses off Fifth Avenue
Where Hershey saw them as a little boy
Already were defeated rooming houses,
              signs
Of a decade outlived,—smiled at as quaint . . ."

"—The Age like Tartar hoards consumed
Each period, each neighbourhood . . .
                  Fifth Avenue mansions,
Limestone in chateau style were boarded up
When Hershey rode north on Fifth Avenue buses,
Green schooners with two decks and a blunt nose!"

"Brilliant moving romance,
                romance and poetry of railroad stations,
Auto as well as train and boat,
               harbor
As well as terminal, caroch, droschky,
And sleeping car,
          it is, how many times!
                 how often here,
—In moving vehicles! that Life is moved
More fully than at any other place!"

"—Do you know why? I do! It is because
The moving vehicle takes man away
From family and other fine divinities
Which hold and hurt the ego's utter wish—
Nowhere else is this modern life so quick
And powerful, so organized in forms
Purely for motion from a place
               to a place

Whether another block,
              another theatre, restaurant, and friend,
Or Asia! train and harbor wait
With the long arm of car or ocean liner
To take away the man from where he is!"

"O city! city! city of refuge and of power,
                 and of despair,
. . . Narrow and vertical from north to south
Succeed the inner fists, Wall Street,
Washington Square surrounded by a park,
Fourteenth and Union Square, Fifth Avenue—
The garment district west where Israel
Finds in new dresses the problems ever old—
Broadway north to Columbus Circle,
              then the park

Where joy is organized, though nervously,
Yet brightly—
                    Central Park from 59th
To Harlem where another continent,
Green Africa, also has found boxed houses
—Because the harbor took the whole world in!
                                        this is the world city!
                                        this is the last capitol of Europe!
Long Island sails in like an ocean liner . . ."

[22.]

            "O City! city!
'The indolence of sun, of sky, of water'
Exiled by office buildings,
                            apartment houses,
The green tree trapped and boxed,
                                the place of work
Become a place of business,
                            reached through the loud
White-buttoned subway dark!
                            Here tenements
'Which reproduce the foetor of the slave-ship,'
And on the next block, or crosstown, as if
The other life did not exist, and strive,
Stand the apartment hotel city,
                            where Life is lived
'Brittle as glass,' some say,
                        as quickly broken—
Or I would say, like chromium, brightly dead!
But not by stones cast at adultery,
And not by the exile and the curse declared
Against the rich man's journey to rich Heaven . . ."

"—The Jews came with the Dutch,
                        and soon were banned

By Peter Stuyvesant; later, 'shawled refugees'
From Czarist terror in a dying Russia . . .
Came to the tenements of railroad flats—"

"The office buildings' utter heights arose
'By a tough bed of rock made possible. . . .
Abrupt ledges of rock, limestone, sandstone,
Granite and brick and brownstone,'
                              O stony city!
O city of two rivers and the great sea—
'The massed upthrust' of office buildings
Makes Manhattan look like a monstrous warship,
A dreadnaught! seen from the slowly widening
                              harbor. . . ."

"O what an aggregation!
                    what a concussion
And collaboration of strength and power
Drew up the world city from the cold farms
Where once the Dutchman throve!
                              What energy
And mastery! and nothingness, in truth,
the naked sum presents,
                    lived through for years!

[23.]

_____

"That old man says, Religion is what man
Does with his solitude: What a remark!
—We know, do we not know, what some men do
When they're alone . . .
                    Arnauld declared that Man
Is capable of every monstrous act
When left alone; and yet, his pupil, Pascal,
Speaks of how most of our trouble and our pain
Springs from our inability to stay at home,

To stay in one's own room: these two extremes
Define a circle of uneasiness,
Somewhat a swaying sea, of which we're sailors. . . ."

"Who says: buy a notebook for courage?
                                        What
Does that mean? Does one by writing gain
Courage, as well as light and darkness? . . .

. . . The early morning light becomes a sign . . .
It is the snow! Even as sometimes snow
Stands for the early morning light,
                                        these shifts
Show Freud and Baudelaire were well-advised,
                                                    saying,
Man walks through a forest of symbols
                                        all his life,
And this is why language is breath and mind. . . ."

". . . Everything happens in the mind of God . . .
                                                    that's all
You know, and all you need to know!"
                                        "O no!
I do not know that in the very least,
I am more certain of all other things,
The chair, the table and my dear dark body
Are with me, certain,
                        He is not!
                                    That's all
I do not know and wish to know,
                                    O if
I knew that! Then what other lights
                                    on every side—"

"That's why I said one day, triumphantly!
O what a metaphysical victory
The first day and night of Death must be!"

"Was it not neo-symbolist de L'Isle Adam
Who said that as for Life,

                 our servants
—Butler, and cook tied in each other's arms—
Could do our living for us. O let us
Leave it to them!

             This was no joke
And not an epigram, although *poseurs*
Might quote it in their buttonholes
As they quote God in Nature or their *chic*
With certain flowers, certain handkerchiefs . . .

This was a grand refusal of the world
Where industry painted the changing heavy air
And stressed the pulses of the human heart
With automatic continuity:

           The city cut off the light,
           The city cut off the water,
           The state declared the war
           Which took away private life—

Flight to the will and the world of art

                    wherein
Law and disorder are supposed and known,
And all enacted in clear consciousness
Whatever dream presses from the mind's pit,

                   sexdom's abyss . . ."

"Although Wilde said Nature must imitate
Great paintings (as the eye does, if it wants
And looks for long, and looks with love at it),
He who arrives, a child, in such an Age
Falls in this pit when he reads any book
Or picture delights him, holds him warmly,
Greater than do the customary things
Of merchant industrial

and last
—Most powerful!—financial Capitalismus . . ."

[25.]

"It is that Art no longer serves a use
As milkmen, druggists, doctors, scientists,
Bellboys and postmen do. It is not
                              needed
The way that coal is needed in this city
Except to paint the billboards,
                              and paint girls
For national cigarettes or moving cars
—Or if the millionaire is won to Art
Having heard of its pure and lasting glory,
Old Masters from old Europe seem the best
Bargain, it's obvious, for such a man—
His taste for getting money soon becomes
His taste for getting what will cost the most—
See Henry James, who saw it all! and yet
By his much seeing and his noble heart
Was brought to ignorance in fiction's truth:
He thought that millionaires were innocent,
Though crude, if natives of America,
Betrayed by Europe's noble dignity
Decaying, which, moving to death, became
Corruption of the heart and ruined those girls
So beautiful in feature and in heart,
So much in love with Europe,
                              Isabel Archer,
And Milly Theale, dying, a lamb, a dove! . . ."

If you live long, O Hershey Green, if you
                              —through courage—
Outlive the witness of this night, so harsh,
You will read in these books and recognize
The world in which your childhood grew and knew

FROM GENESIS: BOOK TWO

—Atlantic boy, who, in the lower middle class
Become the monster, prophet, witness,

                              artist and scribe . . ."

[26.]

"Romantic artists were, I think, like those
Shot from a cannon at the moon!

                              like those
Who walk trapezes at the circuses
Where all the people satisfy their hearts
By seeing norms,—of flesh, of mind,

                              of poise—
Defied, destroyed, denied in monstrous sights,
Pin heads, lion tamers, fat ladies, and tall men,
Clowns and careerists of the tight-rope's thin:
Look at Pablo Picasso, fusing boy!
Atlantic borne, whose mountebanks profess
A sadness which springs from the insane place
The artist had achieved in modern life
By 1900 and by 1905—
The heart of art held in contempt went off
Unto Tahiti with Gaugin from banks
As cool as ice, or with Cézanne refused
To entertain a personal view of *things*,
Offended by all other hearts,

                              though some suppose
All that he wished was to deny the light
Seen by Impressionists,

                              light of shop windows,
Vacation scenes of country sides, breakfasts outdoors,
In soft and unexamined sunlight,—

                              boating light
Upon the river Seine, the tourist views
Which sees the object in a tender haze
Because he does not need to work on it,

THE COLLECTED POEMS OF DELMORE SCHWARTZ

To hit at wood like carpenters,
                              or strike
The soil with farmers, who with sweat
Must earn the daily bread long begged of God—

. . . These were the sickly saints and visionaries
Who lived like criminals within the Age
Amid the strong divinities and powers
Which brought about your genesis, O boy!"

"Think now of your own consciousness, O boy
Atlantic-borne, made in America
                              and made in Europe,
Hearing, seeing, remembering, expecting,
                              feeling
—And magnify this consciousness of yours
A million times! a million million times!
Infinitely! so many times that you
Know you have no idea of what it is,
(Only this guess and this analogy,
This state of being and this state of mind . . .)

Since there is no concept if no percept,
Since there is no percept without a concept
Or no idea if no impression (Kant
And Hume, two wise men,
                              yet not wise enough
Once said, the one bringing the other's thought),
Only this state of mind, thus inconceivably
Magnified, only this consciousness
Without a body—and without a place—
Without a limit and without a need,
Sans problems, tiredness, and all the hurts,
Knowing all things with instantaneous light!

—This is the great *idea* vouchsafed to you
Of what God's nature is! what better warmer
Percept or impression than your own warm mind
At any moment able to leap to Asia
Or 1908 with light's velocity!"

"O let this be your hope and only hope,
The sole stay of the heart and mind at last
In the long run or the short run,
                              awake,
Asleep, through birth, sickness, and death,
Marriage and conjugation, thrill and despair,
Study and indolence:
                    it turns to straw,
It turns to nothingness as the great man
Said with the deathbed truth, of what he made,
The Two Summae, reason's lucid sunlight,
A monument equal to all of Europe's churches,
Unto the greater glory of God,
                              the nameless One,
Maker of Heaven and Earth,
                          He who knows all . . ."

[28.]

"I when I thought of this from black despair
Rose always like a bird,
                        quickly, lightly,
Prone in the former life to utter sadness
Because my efforts fell short many times—
I said then to myself, O God, in this idea,
If such a being really exists,
                          he will hear!
What I am saying now: does he not know it at all?
Does he not look at all with utter light?
And if he hears me, is it not possible

THE COLLECTED POEMS OF DELMORE SCHWARTZ

—Although I am not sure—that he will help me?
Is it a profanation of the pure idea
Which makes me think that he really exists
To think some more? to think that he will come
Quicker than light to help me in my pain?

                    Can I be sure?
—O when I thought these things I was not sure,
And yet! thinking these things I always rose,
I was less desperate, ready to endure
My dark body's beating, eating, breathing,

                    moving and desiring ways,
And ready to endure my soul's black guilt

                  which wished
The world would end and all things, screaming, die!
Because I was in my ambition stopped,
The while my brother, friend and enemy
Succeeded,
        as if spontaneously,
And won the girl, acclaim, the world's applause . . .
—Yes! when I thought of Him in this Idea,
it was <u>enough</u>, although I knew he judged,
Judging the world in me! . . .

                Infinite joy
Flooded me as if I had come to a shore
Of the great sea upon a summer's day
And let my dark body be by the water's silk
All over know and touched!

             This was my stay,
My hope, my wish, my ground, my guard,

                my God!"

[Some Schools]
[42.]

___

"THUS does the growing boy and the living man go on,
Passing from club to club as through a train,

walking from car to car,
His motion moved by their motion. But are they clubs?
And are they cars? All of these entities
                              surrounding him?
Are they a train? Now names are dainty delicate lies
For the inexhaustible darkness of any thing,
Which travels from town to town from year to year
                              with many pseudonyms:
Ding, ding, innumerable *dingen-an-sichen* flow in the dark
Past the howling dog mind of man! Let them be called
Some schools perhaps,
                      since now our hero goes to school,
Let them be seen in every act of the boy
Entering into the freedom of the will,
                              thwarting and aborting his liberty."

Now through the sharp cold evenings of fall
                              I played with Joel
The boy whose bearded father owned the candy store
                              "around the corner"
And looked at the evening papers on the stand outside,
From habit, (though baseball scores were gone for months),
And saw one evening that Woodrow Wilson was dead,
Whose name I had printed on a blackboard once,
President through my nativity and early years
                              an agent of my age.

In the empty lot next to the apartment house,
The boys burned mickies at twilight
                              drawing with sticks from the fire
(Which flickered shadows on the tall side walls of the house)
The charred potatoes. And if a bearded man passed by,
The boy who saw him could pound his colleague's arm
Until he saw him too and cried aloud *Bourgeois!*

Marbles, pictures, election buttons, a secret club
Run by the older boys; with a hut on the empty lot;
To which the small boys paid *dues*, marbles, pictures,
                              a dollar bill,

Getting the *password*, candy sometimes, a sense

                                 of groupness closed,

And of belonging and of being accepted

                           by the community.

I entered into the club with too much joy,

Too much enthralled, one of the small boys who

Played butt and errand boy to the masterly older boys,

But most of all, an alien already,

                        afraid of his being apart.

[54.]

12. He was buried in the immense Jewish cemetery near Coney Island
and the Atlantic Ocean, buried in the plot he had bought for himself,
13. And in a few weeks the departure and absence of the angry intense
resentful man was taken for granted. Like a good American, he had
left an insurance policy.

[Child Helen]
[61.]

AS HOMOSEXUALS in their estrangement sometimes possess

The sensibilities which grasp the *milieu*

                          with a sharpness which

Shows the familiar face in an astounding light,

Cracker mirror, too much sun, or softening shade,

So on a weekend trip, the growing fusing boy

Went with his grandmother, looked back

                      from Philadelphia

                            two hours far

Toward his own home, his block, his school,

                    his relatives,

And Mona most of all, who on the Friday before he went

Gave looks of fondest friendliness to him until
From the intolerable sweetness he turned his face away,
                                        shamed by his pleasure.

A distant cousin was marrying. Grandmother with the boy
Was sent as representative. Then in the private house
Where lived the family patriarch and his children,
New thresholds opened, another sense of life was seen,
For these were German Jews: one cousin,
                                a mature unmarried young lady,
Asked the grandmother at dinner, making conversational
Why one might drink *milk things* before meat dishes
But not reverse the order.
                        Meanwhile upon the table
Stood milk, butter, and meat in prohibited profusion
Far from the pastoral economy which made the Law.
Grandmother was pleased to answer, be authoritative,
Speak with the sageness of those who have eaten [them,]
Because meat sticks between the teeth, grandmother [said]
But milk does not, an explanation which
Pleased everyone, combining fact, reasonableness,
                                        and dentistry.

Later, my second cousins, two wild brothers, came for me,
To take me to the silver screen and to their house
Where an immense pot of cocoa simmered perpetually,
Beneath a coat of cream, beside the cookie jar
Although no sum of candy would ever quiet
                                these Katzenjammer Boys.

[Made in America—handwritten—appears here]

[Child Helen]
[63.]

Who, who, and where? Patience upon the train,
                              upon the transience,
Upon the pure means, shaking from side to side,
                              the dance of wheel on wheel,
                                    of wheel on track,
While sides slip back and take away
                              tree, stream, and cinder bank,
Frame-house and farm and cloud-curved mountain side,
                                    sponging green masses.
I looked into the mirror and did not see myself,
Nor see the face imagined most by consciousness,
Did not connect the glassy essence with the unending
Interior monologue,
                    which, in a way, resembles this whisper.
Actors and actresses must know this nothingness,
Since all the world's a rage against identity,
Despite the statutes built for clever cunning statesmen,
Despite the bride's pumped crotch, which makes the son.

Ah but my years are fabulous, despite myself,
Every river of nature, every passage of man:
I am this history which I rehearse so much,
I am my years, rather than flesh and blood, my blood
A wine of time pressed from its flying leaves,
                              green, brown, or white,
                                    or black and white.
Let each one seek his name or his many names,
Joseph the dreamer's coat was many colors, many things,
Because of dreams perhaps, which slip identity,
                              perhaps because
His father changed his name after his wrestling match
With God or with God's angels all night before the river bank,
Where his enemy waited to murder him,
                        to take his life, his name.

Identity, authority, society! All things move on and on,
Absolutes dwell among the relationships
                                    which make them absolute,
Just as the sobbing child, sent to bed supperless,
Lies on his parents' heads in his emotion's absolute,
Till on the ride, the river, and the train,
                                    in the MEN'S ROOM mirror,
Who am I? shouts an insane second,
                                    snubbed by the image in the glass,
Life's natural son, history's orphan, working through the night.

[Child Helen]
[65.]

The telephone is ringing and ringing! What time is it?
December 1923 in a quickly-built region
Of New York City, the northern tip of the finger
                                    which is Manhattan,
The heights which rise up between two rivers
Rise slowly to Fort George, then fall in a ravine
                                    to Inwood, and Riverdale,
                                        an upper-class suburb.
On one side lolls the Hudson, spreading gray and wide,
On one side the narrow Harlem runs in the channel
Which moves past Coogan's Bluff and the Polo Grounds
                                    to Hight Bridge and Spuyten Duyvil.
Many apartment houses were built in twenty years,
Upon cold farms, old pastures, and old highways
To make a modern neighborhood
                            conveniently located
Thirty-five minutes from downtown New York
                            Wall Street and the garment center.
Now Jews have come here most of all, moving North from Harlem,
Prosperous, ambitious, concerned that their children
Should live near a park and play with
                            a better class of children.

In an apartment house, people nod to each other

                                 in the elevator,

Nodding their ignorance in isolation, wall by wall,

Making love and children over the heads

                         of those beneath

Under the feet of those above, physical nearness

Inversely proportionate

                  to the separation of hearts.

Sounds in the courtyard, sounds of shouting next door

Anger, excitement, a rowdy party Saturday,

                             banging the piano,

Brings this relationship, the nervous man nearby

Knocks on the radiator, calls up the janitor,

Hardly much more occurs, except that wives with children

Talk idly in the afternoon,

                minding their baby carriages,

Discussing the price of meat.

                 This is the box, the hospital

Fashioned by private property, containing lives,

Keeping them near their business and their living,

Holding them up, floor upon floor, while many divinities

Fly as great birds near them,

               and eat their hearts.

[184.]

"Man is was er esst, a painful laborious pun

Man is what he eats, said unfunny Feuerbach,

A John who made the way for Marx,

                and who explained

By this physical principle,

           the English rule in Erin:

The Irish ate potatoes, the English ate roast beef

Which made them stronger soldiers, Erin would fight free

As soon as dinner was better:

             what shall we say of this?"

"Metaphysician, who are you? Much too
Facetious, to *my* taste:
                         Who'll answer him?"

One voice cried out, "Some like potatoes best,
Some do not like roast beef! Man is what he takes in,
But chooses from a bill, selects, rejects, decides—"

Another voice sang out, in reedy tones: "Then too,
                              'Tiny and cheerful,
                                And neat as can be,
                              Whatever Miss T. eats
                              Turns into Miss T.'
While her brother the butcher is fat as a pig!"

"Let us consider this," replied the former voice,
A waste of time perhaps, the history of thought,
Yet wisdom, Aristotle says, wisdom
                              is knowledge of causes,
Our greatest need perhaps: let that justify awhile
This parley which renews itself,
                              like lascivious flies—

"Now if, in the life which breathes this sleepless boy
Ate deer and birds, quail, pigeon, and gull,
Might he then gain the peerless poignant grace of them,
Flying and running the troubled sea and the dark wood?
And if he ate fish only, would he then acquire
That sleek adjustment to the silky *milieu* which
He lacks so much sometimes?
                              Why not eat rocks perhaps,
To be less sensitive. Let me confess the truth,
I ate men most of all, men and the trees in which
Consciousness lives forever, Plato, Sophocles,
Dante and Shakespeare too have fed me many times,
Until I lost, at last, the taste for what was not
Printed, put in a book,
                         the toad-chill and the moist warm hand
Of actuality ten years before I died—"

"Now see Frank Merriwell, a telltale image,
The perfect boy and man, who hits a homer,
Rescues the heroine from the Johnstown Flood,
And foiled the villain,
                              even reforming him!"

"These fiction writers, Burt L. Standish,
Like Alger, near growing America's
Objective hope and need, listened and lay
—Like courtesans with Premiers, in a way—
And give symbolic action to the need
In simple crude enormous paradigms—"

"—It is like baseball, as we said before—
Capitalismus tells the story
Which wins fans for its power and its glory—"

"The drama of the bet is very good,
It shows where Hershey's point of view is false,
Analogy deceives him, Roger helps him:
How much he lost,
                          betting on the pennant race. . . ."

"—And guilt returns, conflict returns, the boys
Are boys and taunt each other just for fun,
Oppose the adult world just like Huck Finn
Or like the Katzenjammer Kids play tricks,
Accuse and strike the good boy since he is
A traitor to the boy-world's anarchy—"

"Thus does the growing boy and living man go on,
Passing from club to club as through a train,
                              walking from car to car,
His motion moved their motion. But are they clubs?
And are they trains? All of these entities
                              surrounding him?

Are they a train? Names are dainty delicate lies
For the inexhaustible darkness of any thing,
Which travels from town to town from year to year
                                    with many a pseudonym:
Ding, ding, innumerable *dingen-an-sichen* flow in the dark,
Let them be seen in every act of this boy,
Entering into the freedom of the will,
                          struggling with liberty. . . ."

[206.]

"He knew a Helen once!"
                    "No, that's not right,
Not Helen, Beatrice,
                    Dante's pure girl,
Black-haired and ivory-skinned. It is well-known,
This pure experience, in juveniles—"

"—This type of sexual experience
At nine years old is not unique, and not
Impossible,
            even at five or six,
Childhood encounters this transcendent love!"

"The city divinity was here involved,
The school divinity was filled by it,
The ego blew up like a big balloon,
And friendship was nearby,
                    a confidante!"

"Transcendent love: that's rather strong?"
                                "It is,
And yet it fits exactly. Hershey felt
—Did you not, Hershey, is our *insight* wrong?—"

But Hershey gave no answer to that voice—

THE COLLECTED POEMS OF DELMORE SCHWARTZ

"A poise of being in that girl of nine
Which made him feel there was another world
A realm *above* somehow,

                    from whence she came:
Her quiet carriage was an absolute,
It seemed to him like the round sky above,
He could not think of something *more, in kind*:
Her quiet carriage and her perfect face—"

"She looked like Norma Talmadge I thought then,"
Said Hershey to explain,

                    "The silver screen
Affords comparisons. But more, much more,
O sleepless boy, is in your life contained,
The snow, I mean! death of the colored world,
Hallucinated calm and utter pleasure,
Annulling the wide world with utter whiteness—
She was of super-Nature, like the snow—"

"How do you know all this?" cried Hershey Green—

[209.]

"Recites the young Republic's easy trope
And falls by accident into a part,
Comedian,

               center of laughing attention,
Glad to be foolish, if the cause of mirth—"

"What did he do with 'Old Ironsides'?

                          Give us
The given, let us present directly, quote—"

"'Old Ironsides,'
        by Oliver Wendell Holmes,
          Ay, tear her tattered ensign down,

Long had it waved the sea'
            —*on high*, the teacher said
'And many an eye has *danced* to see'
            teacher corrected Hershey;

'Beneath it burst the battle shout'
            rung the teacher said,
'And rung the cannon's roar!'
            and then the whole class laughed
                and laughed and laughed—"

"Ah, yes, we see it now; not funny here.
Now give us of the names of Russian towns—"

"Lodz, Brest-Litovsk, Vladivostok,
Przemysl, Dneiper, Smolensk,
                            Minsk, Pinsk,
And Omsk, Udinsk, Yakutsk,
                    all mispronounced,
The triumph of America in them—"

"The Atlantic rides between them and their fathers,
The Slav, the Jew, the Rabbi,
                    and the horsemen,
The goldsmith and the cantor,
                    crying aloud:
They did not hear, laughing Americans,
                            innocents abroad . . ."

[212.]

_____

"So that was what it was!" said Hershey Green,
More and more moved to comment too,
"It's true. We felt a special feeling when
Our Mrs. Curtis, whom we liked so much,

THE COLLECTED POEMS OF DELMORE SCHWARTZ

Scolded our manners, told us that she was
Descended from a Founding Father,
                                   proudly—"

"Always in every scene divinities
Are present under all: hence surfaces
Are half-truths often, often make a lie
Or an illusion when no more is seen
—The earth as flat, a half-truth and a lie!—
When no one knows the flesh beneath the dress,
The mind beneath the hair,
                                   the Trojan horse
Of every mixture of the flesh and mind!"

"The class-room, now a Lovers' Lane, of sorts,
Had long blackboards in front, and colored maps,
Rolled up, attached to it.
                                   At one side stood,
The clothing closet with a sliding door,
And at the other side, long windows were,
Where many a child would look, to go away . . .
The teacher's desk stood at the head, whence she
Presided, faced *against* the class,
                                   the children's desks
Stood in six rows. Each desk grew to the one
Behind it, like a Siamese twin . . .
Under the desk, the place for books. A well
For ink, a groove for pens and pencils
Carved in the desk:
                       now these minutiae,
Do they tell much? Do they not, in a way,
Conceal the powers which the children felt?
Each brought his family to school with him,
As each took home his school? As Mrs. Curtis
Rode on an "L" above the children's heads,
With aunts and uncles, many genteel souls,
In a defeated part of the middle-class!"

FROM GENESIS: BOOK TWO

"O, I love you? Do you love me?
                              Will you
Love me when my hair has turned to silver
At three o'clock in the morning,
                              All Alone,
                                    so all alone!
The songs called popular sang to the mind
Of the populace just what it wished to hear,
Amor was broken up like bread and wine,
A Tin Pan Alley transubstantiation
Of Ovid's, Solomon's, Arnaut Daniel's,
Petrarch and Shakespeare's vaunted
                              vaulting value!
A little inexpensive, in a way,
                              as we might say,
By the time it reached this schoolboy in New York—"

"What open tactics manifest his love:
Would changing his seat, move near, that's it,
Move nearer all the time, love's very pulse—"

"Blue grass beside the river. Willows too
Brushed by the wind. And in the stunted orchard,
Played with apples, flung them, heard the plump
Soft in the thick grass. This is the being
Of this Atlantic boy in great New York—"

"She came before him dressed in crimson hue,
He trembled greatly, heart and pulse afraid,
His mind marveled immensely, whence it cried:
Here now your blessedness appears for you:
From that time forward, love possessed him, king:
King with assurance and with mastery,
Imagination's power, perfectly:
He sought Love's pleasure first in everything!
She seemed no mortal; but of God,

As says the poet Homer, wholly good!"

"Often in childhood went he seeking her;
This is no idle tale; Love said to him,
I am your Lord, and bore his naked heart—"

"Don't see this as a Pre-Raphaelite Art—"

[218.]

"An ill-bred boy, bred as we have said before
By the romantic ego, playing Timon, Hamlet,
Byron, O the romantic day, after
The French Revolution burned, when men
Of sensibility, no longer held
By their society at heart, ran off,
Ran off to Nature or themselves, their own
Emotions, lakes and despair, seeking
A dignity and mystery in Life,
A sense of being which no longer ruled . . ."

"Yet Hamlet was *that way* long, long before—"

"The ego when offended will not pause,
At any crime, at any accusation;
The Nero ego burns the whole world down—
Casts saint and virgin to the ravid [sic] lions
In circuses that bore it soon enough—"

"Cézanne, I'm told, from his sulking retreat
From human beings who had hurt his feelings
Sought to restore the world as solid,
                                        hard and clear,
Free of the vagaries of personal
Impressions and hurt feelings, clinical,
—This shows how the individual's

Private and bedroom self prepares him for
A most important part in painting's history—"

"—This shows how Historydom uses the man
In his most private self and liberty—"

"Pedantic dead, sententious dead,
All this is merely talk!" cried Hershey Green,
"And hardly relevant. When I hear this,
Shame rises hotly to my face and mind,
I have this little pride, that in the end,
I saw the moral rule, I judged myself
Harshly and justly then."
                                    "Then did the same,"
A dead one said, "the same your whole life long!"

[221.]

_____

"Tears, paranoia, guilt, revenge, self-pity,
Tears and hysteria, all in a day,
And then the other side of schoolroom life,
His comedy, his courtship once again,
His vanity, his *bon mot*:
                            this is rich!"

"O what a boy becomes, what a genesis!"

"Yet who is not appalled, seeing in this
The naked ego nakedly erect?"

"The ego is a penis: that's profound—"

"I wish you would not use such words!" cried Hershey, then
"Though I mind penis less than Anglo-Saxon ones . . .
I'm not the only one, and not, you know,
You know it very well, the millionth one,

Or billionth one! *you* once behaved this way—
Don't think that I don't know what others are!"

Yet as he rose to his defense, could not
Conceal a fond smile at the incident
When Valley Forge made comedy for him!

"Look, how he touches on economy:
Capitalismus is not mocked, O no!
She feels and fears her insecurity,
The ruling emotion of the middle-class!"

"Part of the dread which holds all human beings,
No matter where he is or where he goes,
And thus a metaphysical donne [*sic*],
An aspect of the death no man evades!"

"Do not forget the bread-and-butter wound,
You with your metaphysics! Living room,
Standards of living must be well maintained
Or members of the piteous middle-class
Feel shame O feel disgrace so much
Appears, to rid the pain, cold suicide!"

"Thus butlers, other servants, kill themselves,
When aristocracies are nullified,
In Petersburg, in Paris,
                        and elsewhere
Sooner than you may think! Economy
Holds over Life a shameful mastery!"

"—More than economy: Identity!
The part the soul gets from Society!
The way of life becomes the soul itself! . . ."

"Place! Place and Condition! Powerful!
Did you see then, sleepless Atlantic Boy,
The family circle's power?
                          How it became
(Like everything which lasts near human beings
And causes in their being spot, or shade,
Or light, some difference, however slight)
A strong divinity?"
                    "It is like snow
(Let me expound this thing once more to him!"
—Falls piece by piece, merely a pin or kiss,
Down past the arc-light, driven by the wind
Will-less, shiftless, powerless until
The fallen sum becomes a thing itself,
Become a white god newly come to the city,
Makes the cars slow and all movement hushed
Under the window outside the stoop,
Brings the blue white color's cool shine everywhere,
And the cool freshness snuffed in the blowing air!
—Then rots or freezes at the curb,
                              struggled against,
Picked dug and scraped by janitors
Suburban homeowners or unemployed—
Thus a divinity becomes!
                    The family
Coheres about the light, *Gemütlichkeit*,
And strikes the boy with sharp comparisons—"

"Yes, and look at the facts of point of view
Bequeathed to him two hours from New York—"

"How just it is that at a marriage feast
He should see this! how just that he should come
With Leigh Newman, young and pretty girl
In long eternity's complete possession,

Who might, with luck, have been the matriarch
Of such well-grounded pleasures, moral joys!"

"No, not with luck. For strong divinities
Made her life what it was, though not with ease;
Struggling against her choice and liberty!"
The *what I want* which is identity!"

[229.]

"The telephone is ringing and ringing. What time is it?"

"December 1923 in a quickly-grown region,
Of New York City, the northern height of the boat
                                    Which is Manhattan Island,
The Height which rises up between two rivers,
Rises to Fort George, then falls in a ravine
                                    To Inwood and Riverdale,
                                         An upper-class suburb—
On one side flows the handsome Hudson, beneath its cliffs,
On one side the slim Harlem runs in the channel
Which moves past Coogan's Bluff and the Polo Grounds
                                    To High Bridge and Spuyten Duyvil:
Many apartment houses built in twenty years
Upon cold farms, old pastures, and old highways,
                                    where once the Dutchman throve,
                                         leaving only his name—"

"This is a modern neighborhood,
                                    conveniently located
Thirty-five minutes from downtown New York
                                    Wall Street and the garment center
Now Jews have come here most of all, moving north from Harlem,
Prosperous, ambitious, concerned that their children
Should live near a park and play
                                    with a 'better class' of children—"

"In an apartment house, people nod to each other
                                        in the elevator,
Nodding their ignorance and isolation, wall by wall,
Making love and children over the heads
                                        of those beneath,
Under the feet of those above, physical nearness
Inversely proportionate
                        to the separation of hearts—"

"Sounds in the courtyard, sounds of shouting next door,
Anger, excitement, a rowdy party Saturday,
                                        banging the piano,
Brings this relationship, the nervous man nearby
Knocks on the radiator, calls up the janitor,
—Hardly much more occurs, except that wives with children
Talk idly afternoons,
                        minding baby carriages
Discussing the price of staples.
                        "This is the box or hospital
Fashioned by private property, containing lives,
Keeping them near their business and their living,
Holding them up, floor upon floor,
                                while many divinities
Fly as great birds near them, above them, between them,
                                eating their hearts and lives—"

[232.]

—————————————————————————————

"Who, who, and where? Patience upon the train,
                                        upon the transience,
Upon the pure means, shaking from side to side,
                                the dance of wheel on wheel,
                                        of wheel on track,
While sides slip back and take away
                        tree, stream, and cinder bank,

Frame-house and farm and cloud-curved mountain side,

                sponging green masses—"

"I looked into the mirror and did not see myself,
Nor see the face imagined most by consciousness,
Did not connect the glassy essence with the unending
Interior monologue, which, in a way,

                resembles this whisper.
Actors and actresses must know this nothingness,

                before they die,

                  and many another I,
Since all the world's a rage against identity,
Despite the statutes built for clever cunning statesmen,
Despite the bride's pumped crotch, which makes the bawling child—"

Ah but your years are fabulous, despite yourself,
And every flow of nature, every passage of man:
You are this history which we rehearse so much,
You are your years, rather than flesh and blood, your blood
A wine of time pressed from its flying leaves,

                green, brown, or white,

                summer and winter days—"

"Let each one seek his name or his many names,
Joseph the dreamer's coat was many colors, many things,
Because of dreams perhaps, which slip identity,

                perhaps because
His father changed his name after his wrestling match
With God or with God's angels all night before the river,
Where his brother waited to kill,

            taking away his life,

              taking away his name—"

"Identity, society! All things move on and on,
Absolutes dwell among relationships

              which make them absolute:
Even as the sobbing child, sent to bed supperless,
Lies on his parents' heads, in his emotion's absolute,

Till on the ride, the river, and the train
Who am I? he howls insanely and truly,

                                      snubbed by the image in the glass,
Life's natural son,
                    deprived of his name by the flowing of time,
                                    the flowing of Nature—"

[235.]

"See a divinity's peculiar nature
Confer a different dress on Jack Green's flight:
Not as his father's flight in nakedness
But ninety thousand dollars go with him!
Money is free in certain ways,
And air-like, going from hand to hand
And place to place without losing its precious
Priceless and perfect power!"
                        "O like the sea!
It makes a kind of sailor of the man,
Takes him to foreign cities, foreign girls,
                              the home town falls,
It cannot hold him! International,
its interest and its love!"
                        "Capitalismus
Cuts down all trees except the tree of gold!"

"Have I not heard enough?" said Hershey Green,
"Myself, my father, mother, history,
Subjected to this abstract commentary
                            —if I could sleep!
If I could sleep and end this comedy!
Let me alone, I say, O let me sleep,
What good is this for me, or anyone,
                          what purpose does it serve?
Or am I being punished for my faults?

THE COLLECTED POEMS OF DELMORE SCHWARTZ

Or am I dead, maybe,
                    let me alone!"

"Sleepless Atlantic boy, you are not dead—"

"I almost wish I were! If I could not sleep . . ."

"No, this is Life. Death amid Life speaks out,
Yet in the forms used by your Age, your time,
—The editorial, the columnist,
The book review, the play or silver screen review,
A thousand miles across the vibrant air,
The news report, all objective minds:
Here in your Age objective forms perform
                                        each in their way
The comment of the mind on the event
A most important thing,
                    for this is Life,
Man is the animal who speaks, remembers,
Judges and weighs all in his mind and heart:
O this is what man is, this is his part!"

[238.]
_____

"Back to your question, sleepless Atlantic boy:
We tell you why this night's Logos is necessary—"

"The sand upon the Red Sea shore, or on the beach,
Far Rockaway, where I admired the waves,
Pleased me because sterility and movement seemed
The sum of the green world
                    when the end and the and are known . . .

"Nearer the city, the subway rises to the 'El,'

Comes to stop called, Gravesend, justly named,
Here in a great cemetery wait the Judean dead
For that Redeemer other peoples have enjoyed,

                      katharsis or kingdom come
                            fictive or true, who knows?
But anyway, *enjoyed*, except by these stiff-necked

                          poor and passionate folk
In whom I participate, though ignorantly,

                under the threshold of attention
                    and in my beating heart
In the long trek and track from Palestine—"

"The main thing, Atlantic boy, is to see Life,
To see it as a progress and waste of days,

                      that is, as a story,
In which are certain scenes which seem to show

                    all that is, as a story,
The glittering attractions of dignity and pleasure,
Which made the man and the woman

                tiptoe on the window sill—"

"The mind is the greatest tourist, never at home,
And hence freely we pass through the places where Life

                    has agreed or agonized,
So we go on, seldom satisfied even a while:
But when we think of that Consciousness which sees all
When then our minds like larks at heaven's gate sing,
Sing out sing out

          our endless memory and hope of all things!"

[241.]
___

"O Love is difficult and beautiful!
How wise the stories of the ancient Greeks:
Do you know that one, Hershey Green, which tells

How Love in the true guise of a small boy
Came to Anacreon one autumn night,
Woke him from sleep, begged for a night's lodging,
His wings wet through, and chilled by wind and rain?
A kindly host, Anacreon took the boy
Warmed him at the fire, chafed his hands,

                                    dried his blond locks,
But when the strange boy was made comfortable,
'Let me try out my bow,' he said, 'I want to see
If it has been warped by the heavy rain,

                                    made powerless'—
He spoke with a child's utter charm and lisp—
And put an arrow in the bow and drew,
And pierced the poet's heart,

                            then laughed aloud,
And flew away, crying triumphantly,

                                'Thus Love
With utter unexpectedness amazes you,
Tricks and destroys the heart on silent nights

                            during the wind and the rain,
                            when the West Wind doth blow,
                                and the small rain falls. . . .'

"These acts and elements were in the air
Amid the school divinity,

                        the schoolroom life,
The trembling boy who pressed the note of love,
Logos, man's inner being, had yet been pierced,
Although from far, yet many times by what
Love meant to Abelard, and many knights
And troubadours,

                arrived,

                        after what passages
Unto the silver screen, shining for him:
Ah, but the climax was the best of all,
Logos, man's inner being, scribbled, then scored
By lines through which affection could be seen;
Dear Hershey, dumb, upon the schoolroom blotter,

Just and appropriate . . ."
                              "How do you know,"
Hershey cried out, "Just how I felt those days:
Sure that she loved me when I looked at it,
I saved that blotter like the Holy Grail!"

[243.]

"Here we are in the lower middle-class:
What mastery it holds over many hearts
—*To make a living* is the rushing sound
Signed by the blood in souls who have been fed
From birth in middle-classdom's dining room—"

"The ads that Hershey read in a child's monthly,
St. Nicholas, bespeak the taste inside
Of Life in middle-classdom lived as in
A penetrating climate,
                              Iceland, Samoa!"

"'Get Wrigley's after every meal,
It is both *good* and good for you
                              and best of all
The cost is small. The sugar packet
                              melts in your mouth,
The gum center remains to give you all
The usual Wrigley benefits of gum:
Your stomach will thank you!'
                              Just think of that,
How secular, how naturalist in the mind,
Appealing to digestion's pasture smile—"

"'O come to Camp Winoka, in the Woods:
Say Boys! Here is a camp right in the timber
Of the real wilderness.
                              It's woods like your great great

Daniel Boone trapped in, right bang up against Nature'"
                              "right bang up against Nature!"
"'You learn the woods' ways, make your own clearings,
Build your log cabins while you bunk in tents,
Play the game straight in the Adirondacks' heart,
Live like a guide and O, boy, you live high!
Your character is built in real camp life,
Fishing, canoeing, swimming, hiking,
                              is it safe?
Safe as your own home! What's the cost?
Only two hundred dollars: mighty little'—"

"Ah, what a mind! with tones and words like that!
The cost and safety build his character
Where once the Indian knew dignity!"

[246.]
_____

"I know Vienna rolls in the former life
Which breathes and sweats: I liked them very much,
Am touched to hear how this boy looked at them!
Seeing his aunt's lunch at the breakfast table,
An image which will live for long in him . . ."

"As Adam named the beasts, with careful love,
We name the animals and the divinities
Who walk about this newfoundland, America,—"
"As Socrates, who questioned everything
Because his love was great, we question all—"

"As Joseph, once I knew a sweet revenge
In basic psychological reviews,
Accused the innocents who perjured me,
Me innocent,
              showing sublimely then,
The justice who uncovers innocence,
Omniscient, generous, O all forgiving

And most successful brother who displays
How he was right throughout, in his conceit:
All dreams come true, and every feat performed!"

Hershey cried, "What has this to do with me?"

"A boy once died, and wandered through the scenes
He lived, saw them again, not living them
But *seeing* them, within their background,
                                    ground and earth
The flashback of the cinema,
                          fadeout, dissolve, return. . . .
Wandered through memory's halls,
                            through all of his life,
Saw what he lived and what he did not know,
Enjoyed and travelled through the whole of life,
Passionless, piteous,
                  then he understood
And held the whole of life within his hands:
And you, O Hershey Green, who are not dead,
You may attain to this, go back to Life
If you have the strength!
                    if your heart does not break:
O what a glory then,
                    patience and purity,
Labor in joy in knowing self-identity!"

[248.]

"This was for Hershey as for all the boys."

—This was the foreign voice, in different measure—

"A new divinity! deeper than school
With deeper roots in day and night because

The boy did not go home, he ate and slept with it
Far from appeal to father or to mother,
Who when a boy came from school might re-assure them
In what the family divinity had made them. . . ."

"Letters were written home,
                              but must be passed,
Looked at for statements of unhappiness,
Corrected by the counsellor.
                              Quickly, dancing,
The train took Hershey north to the Adirondacks
Where many new relationships were waiting—

"And the train's long and shaking length contained
The counsellors given boys, boys whom they called,
Seeing them for the first time, by their first names,
An act full of strangeness,
                              very moving!

"After the excitement of sleeping overnight
On the Pullman, Roger beside him, Hershey
Stood with the thronging boys
                              In the early morning
In the cold dark small railroad depot,
Waiting to ride by bus to camp
                              Waiting in the cool sunshine
Unlike the stilled wet fog of the day before
                              in the great city—"

"In any society men who dislike their lives
Begin to dream of Nature as a dairy valley
                              full of calm lakes and lawns,
Or as a village in green thick Africa
Where the tom-tom pounds the leaping shaking heads
Beside the leaping fire all night long,
                              or whiteness!
White immense horizons and ice mountains, white,
In absolute cold, where life becomes effort to breathe—

Or some may dream of Heaven, where no one sweats,
                                          Nature negated,
                                          that is nature too . . .
—Some of these feelings surrounded the growing boy—"

[250.]

"Poor boy! Thrown headfirst into camp's
Divinity! as one is thrown at birth
Howling into the brave new world,
                              so cruel!
(This new to you, said Prospero, a wise man)—"

"The New York Central took him north from one
Divinity to the other, a brutal train
Hardly revealing what a gulf it made
Between metropolis and the North Woods,
Between the parent's gaze, the teacher's rule,
And the strange strict discipline of camp
Which mimicked army law because, some said,
It 'built the character,'
                              because, in feet,
It was convenient with a hundred boys,
And handsome too,
                              marching at dress parade—"

"How fresh and cool the sunlight in the woods,
The glittering lake was like a capitol,
There the boys swam, paddled canoes, and rowed,
Fished on the pier, and though they did not know it,
Drank in an image of the mise-en-scène
Of all societies,
                              O waters' passive might
Is near the life of man as kinds of light!"

THE COLLECTED POEMS OF DELMORE SCHWARTZ

"Two counsellors," Hershey joined, once more
Full of deep interest, and free of pain,
Pain and despair and care, "pointed to me,
And to another boy, named Lester, 'look,' they said,
'They look identical!'
                              I looked, I saw
How Lester looked like me, troubled for weeks—"

"O what a paradigm! Identity
Sinks in a black night when analogy
Compares the painful self with just one more—"

"Hence tennis, handball, other games like that
Are played with passionate intensity!"

[254.]
_____

"Struck! struck! the Cain of accident indeed!
A fusion of the new relationships
Which struck this poor boy's forehead until then—"

"The fact is," Hershey said, elucidating,
"The blow did not hurt me. It knocked me down,
Yet did not hurt me, though I don't know why.
But all thought I was hurt,
                              hence I arose,
My whole being arose, to the event:
I knew myself the center of attention,
I felt how serious it was, I meant it to be
Not as I had been till then, a crybaby,
I felt how I might be here, show them all—"

"How interesting it is to hear of this,
Hear how the subject felt,
                              continue, Hershey,
Sleepless Atlantic boy, give us your point of view:

Adds to the roundness of the long story,
                              the roundness, the wholeness!"

"I meant to show that when I wept to see
My mother, not my true being showed itself—"

"A deer ran past, heavy, heavy, and graceful,
The grace increased by the heavy body, running,
—An early world not known to city boys,
Such images may last through death itself!"

"And shocked again by Mrs. Baker who
Thought him not fit for friendship with her son,
Because he was his mother's son,
                              a membership,
Though everyman is nonesuch, in the end:
Here was identity with family
Blocked, struck, as just before it sunk
Before the comparison with another boy
—How long the ego struggles with the world,
How many ways, how newly, vainly,
                              painfully,
                                    to be itself,
And yet it just begins, this ancient fight,
The ego never free from the world's might!"

[256.]

_____

"Again! socked in the nose! the nose which is
Ego's northwestern part.
                    Boxing, profound
Image of egotism, thinly masked,
                         if masked,
If not, in fact, the perfect medium,
As bathing suits on girls are nudity's
Increased aseity! And quiddity!
Essentially increased, pointing to what

Is not revealed,
                    But barely barely covered—
Like the fat gloves which cover striking fists—"

"Yet Hershey broke the frame, denied the game,
Was justly criticized, could not contain
The ego's penis, like a two year old,
And older men,
                    were the whole truth declared—"

"The National pastime shows its influence,
Shows its divinity when Hershey plays,
Enacting underneath the conscious mind
His utter wish to be a major leaguer
And all the motions he had seen performed
Upon the diamond at The Polo Grounds
—This gave him strength, talent, and passion
Some of the other boys did not enjoy
Who were not baseball fans,
                    Rooting for the The New York Giants
                              passionately for six months. . . ."

      "'Where will we be
      A *hundred* years from now?'
An old camp song, sung on campfire nights
Which made him feel the blackness of the woods,
And the slipping slicking lake against the shore
Wednesday were campfire nights,
                    on Friday nights
Services were conducted. The campers heard
As once on every coast, the ancient cost
Of being Jewish, played by a well-known cast,
God and old Israel. . . .
              'Thou shalt love the Lord thy God
              With all thy heart
              And with all thy soul
              Which I command thee this day,
              Shall be upon thy heart—'

Effort to win the ego's pain and love. . . ."

A mind which hovers over everything
And sees the motive move the moving man,
Sees the car move upon the tar-paved street
Where men and women lift their covered feet,
And pick them up again, then put them down,
In the long waste of Life by love and need . . .

A mind that like a bird flies over all,
Dipping, picking, singing, going away,
Coming again to sleep, but never known. . . .

To the apartment house where an unhappy boy
Works out the structures which his love presumes
Might give Life what a game contains,
                            joy, form, and chance
Ever renewed and fresh,
                     to the apartment house
Where early in pre-morning now and then,
                         now and then,
The elevator whirrs, ascends, stops,
                  then descends:
Racing ropes knock against the shaft, the wheel
Clicks, letting go the sounds which make the hearer
Picture the latecomer tired, leaning toward bed
Full of the night's events in his timely head . . .

A mind which sees the chaos which the sum
Of living beings, unliving houses, many lives
Accumulate in the actuality of place,
And sees that no perspective yields an order there. . . .

Between the earth and sky, two opposites,
Between the stars and the seas, both going on,
Turning and spilling their natures on the air,
Before they marry or before they die,
Between the teeth in the mouth, between the hair

On the head, between the heartbeat and the thought,
And the blood in the belly and the falling rain,
Under the grave, under the womb, under
The pavement, under the clothes,

                                  under the heart,
We seek to understand, all our death long
All things as they are and might be,

                                  all things in themselves. . . .

[341.]

"As many times before, he makes his way
Forward in Life, through book and school,

                                the two
Learned divinities which change the mind
—Each new stage holds the old somewhat somehow,
Anachronism is a mark of time
Permanent as the nose which sucks the world!
Cain's jealousy and Nero's insane will
Grow in him as his mind grows,

                            strangest flower,
And strangest light!

               And he rejoices,

                    and he enjoys
Riding in the streetcar, the pure instance
Of the industrial divinity,
And most of all, drawing away in place
From scenes and acts of family life,

                        his mother's lunch—
When he eats lunch in school, he eats his freedom—"

"I know! I knew in the old life, just how
Ambition works, romance deceives, though I
was older than this boy when I began
To let its forward hope make me relax,
Rest and collapse before the daily task

—Tomorrow and tomorrow and tomorrow
Flashed on my inner eye as the new day
When I would start to be the very soldier,
Study from dinner time to half-past twelve,
Wake up at six and study until eight
Before I went to earn my livelihood
—How in the [indecipherable] evening drained away
Because my body's tiredness would make me go
To silver screen or billiard table, play
Or friends at beer, The body's tiredness, I thought
Does this, after my office work all day,
I cannot help myself,—determinism!
Just as a thought at last made me give up
(And yet let me admit, the Pleasure-Principle
Wins when the body's tired, less other times),
I said, Tomorrow, God I hope will understand,
Forget that Life is somewhat in the will's command—"

"Never mind that," said Hershey Green, "this is
My night, my life, I have not failed like you,

not yet. . . ."

[345.]

"Lo, we descend like light. Light. Light.
Through the windowpane and through the eye,
Find out the private movements of the heart
And move with them. The hatred and the love
Color us, yet release us, like the scenes
Of the enacted play, in a like dark—"

So said a freshened voice, joyous,
Synoptic of the parts that the dead sung—

"Before the apartment house, set like a tomb
Among so many tombs, now, late at night

I hear the passing of an occasional car,
                            now and then, now and then,
On the Avenue. I hear the silence
                    like a wide sound,
Full of the ticking of hearts and clocks
                            in bedrooms and in lives—"

"Ah, if they were but wholly wholly there,
Contained in the body's box, separate from all
Divinities and all superior powers,
Free of the school. the street, the city, and the sea!"
                                        can become
"Great authors sometimes are superior powers
And small divinities. As Spengler here,
So Machiavelli in the Renaissance,
Rousseau in the Enlightenment, Byron
Luther, Goethe, whose Werther killed young men
                                    a while
(Though they were fertile for the death he made):
O anything you see may be a cause,
Although elsewhere it is itself a thing:
Make the distinction! Any thing's old acts
Go on and on in time and place,
                        beyond its will,
Beyond its knowledge, overseas,
                        in the air,
Like the great lights and like the radio's voices,
There in the air although you cannot hear—"

"The causes moving in their many courses
Mix in a struggle whence each day arises—"

"Man is a liberty [indecipherable] the causes,
Rather weak liberty in Time the darkness. . . ."

"O what a mess of judgment we have made,
Like many stricken birds they are arrayed!
The flying thoughts which from our last dismay
Issue like deathbed speeches, just as false,
A bit more hopeless, but as special too,
As different from the speech of everyday
Passing as handkerchiefs and newspapers:
I too in the old life evaded all
By this or that device, like Hershey Green's
Telling the doctor that he's sick.

                        —A fresh start!
How that white paper freedom ruins the heart!
—Not to accept one's fault, but turn from it,
As if it never was, not to endure
One's imperfection as the very ground
Whence grows the fusing summer, full and green!
And to play new-born child or freshman thus
As if you washed with your blood your sins away:
This is the cowardice which is the first,
All else a mode of it, and not the glued
Flypaper which one cannot throw away,
Other retreats merely a piece of this—"

"All night, all this hardly bearable night,"
Said Hershey Green as if to boring guests,
"No one but failures speak to me,
                      did none
Of the great succeed, or are they quiet now,
The great successful ones? and was there nothing
That with pure pleasure you remember when
You lived in the old life of hope deceived,
—Deception must itself have brought you joy—
I don't hear anything pleasant at all,
I don't hear one word which would help my hope,
Or at the very least, let it endure—"

"Sleepless Atlantic boy, what else would you
Expect? most men are failures and most men
Remember evil more than good,
                              dead or alive!"

[354.]

"Caesar and every cur are like that,
They cannot bear the least comparison,
It makes them think that they do not exist—"

"Yet, on the other hand, anonymous
The very greatest shine; seem, now and then,
Hardly to have existed, Jesus, Shakespeare,
                                    Homer,
—They fade to nothingness as living persons,
They turn to ashes at the question, was it true?
What was his beating heart beneath his dress?
And these men were among all men the most
Unique, their individuality
Blazes like diamonds in the studied text!"

"—Caesar and every cur in Time the darkness
Seek to regard themselves and no one else:
What happened every time? They take the darkness
—Even as you and I, a shameful illness
Hid from the relatives, sickening the nurse—
They take the darkness as a great relief
From the long agony of conscious being,
—Only to find that consciousness becomes
In the new life, all that there is to do!"

"It serves them right! Let them live on like that!
Faced by their vagueness through eternity,
Tortured by twins of their identity

Whichever way they look in the wide world!
Narcissus was the one who knew the way
And only route to final satisfaction:
Stared at himself all day in the soft pool,
Until in the enchainment of the water,
By the horrid softness of the liquid limbs
The homosexual was stuffed to death!"

[359.]

"Please speak of something else awhile, let go
My horrid childishness and Caesar ego
A little while. Let me look at some joys
In your rich minds, rich with all the views of life—"
So Hershey begged, greatly ashamed of himself,

                                        the story told of him . . .

"This is the way to knowledge and to love,
This is the way to knowledge and power,
This is the way to freedom and to love,
This is the way to knowledge and forgiveness!
Beyond remorse, beyond regret, the light—"

"Although as one has said, after such knowledge,
What forgiveness? Self-forgiveness least of all—
This night will like an endless cold assume
A weeping feeling tone, charging the mind
Beneath his conscious mind, a vivid rule
(Otherwise he would be a bigger fool!)
If he lives on! if he survives his fear—"

"Boys on the block would often tease and taunt me
Boys elsewhere too: for I was tender-skinned

                                        as you have heard

THE COLLECTED POEMS OF DELMORE SCHWARTZ

Made soft and sensitive by pride and dream,
By praise and by attention,
                              but this is
Worse than all boys, worse than my dreams of death
When someone died in our apartment house,
When the darkness made me afraid,
                              just as he said,
—That foreign voice who saw and knew it all,—
At bedtime when my mother turned the light out,
I begged her to leave on the hall light still,
Until I fall asleep. This is the same,
But worse and endless. Will it ever end?
—I came to hate the sight of picking teeth,
Sucking at cavities,
                    O, it became for me
The ego's blind absorption in itself,
Seeing it in the older people with disgust:
This night is just like that, you suck the teeth
Of your unhappiness beside my bed,
                              beside my life—"

"You want to eat your cake and have it too,
—You want to flee your life,
                              but you will not,
No more than flee yourself on any sea . . ."

[362.]

_____

"Now what divinities made me the fool
Of this absurdity? Or was I on my own
In this, as nowhere else in my long life?"

"O, no! all of the old divinities
Were there in power and in glory—
New York, America, and powerful science,

Nature and Fame mixed in your soul as on
A battle-field!
                The car, the plane, the train,
The tallest building in the greatest city,
Moved through your soul as light about the globe
Around and around and around the track
Of the growing fusing mind which took them in
—Thus you were left depraved, like the small town
For two months in the summer, making the year
Apart from them seem dead and boarded up
Like Coney Island in the midst of winter . . ."

"Lindbergh flew the Atlantic on a day
Of drizzling rain in May. At eight o'clock
The twentieth of May in 1927,
He took off,
          all by himself,
               that was
What made him glorious! to go alone
To be the brilliant individual
In this America of 1927
—The whole country rose in exaltation,
As at The Yankee Stadium, during a bout,
The crowd of 40,000 boxing fans
Rose as a man when asked to pray for Lindbergh,
And bared their heads in silence to the heaven
Before the boxers hit each other's faces
                     a few more times—

[363.]

"When in the papers hurried minds came word
Of Lindbergh's pure success, descent in Paris
Mobbed by the French, modest behavior,
Millions took him in image into their minds,
As they had taken no other human being

In living memory. The New York Evening World
Sold on the news of his complete success
114,000 extra copies!
The World said too that Lindbergh had performed
'The greatest feat of a solitary man
In the long records of the human race!'
A cruiser of the Navy went for him
To bring him home and bring the plane home too
—Greeted in Washington by Calvin Coolidge,
Before a vast crowd in the open air,
55,000 telegrams were sent to him,
One had on it 17,500 names
Signed in sweet personal congratulation!
18,000 tons of paper were thrown
                              gaily, from office buildings,
To make a snowstorm of greeting on Broadway
(Only 150 tons greeted the Armistice)!
He was offered two and a half million dollars
To go on a tour of the world by air!
—And to appear upon the silver screen
A mere seven hundred thousand dollars!
A town was named for him, 'the largest dinner
Ever given to any individual
In modern history' was eaten then,
To honor him, feeling his fame in food:
Such was the admiration and the love
Risen from all America because
A man had given them a perfect hero,
The pure romantic ego flew in the Atlantic,
Such an event, so loud in praise and applause
Moved through the quickly moved heart of Hershey Green,
—Is it a wonder then that he cried back
His own belief and hope in his own terms?"

"I hardly paid attention to that flight,"
Said Hershey Green, "much more engaged in what
The Giants had done. But thanks,
                              thanks anyway,
For showing that I was not utterly

An ape of self-abuse in an abyss,
A maniac of my dream in a pure void—"

[363.]

"When in the papers' hurried minds came word
Of Lindberg, pure success, what vast applause!
In Paris, mobbed by the French, perfect
His modest quiet shy behavior,
Charming ambassadors and journalists,
Charming hundred and twenty million readers,
Who in this image took him to their minds
'As they had taken no other human being
In living memory'!
                    The New York Evening World
Sold on the news of his complete success
One hundred and fourteen thousand extra copies!
The World said then that Lindbergh had performed
'The greatest feat of a solitary man
In the long records of the human race'!
A cruiser of the Navy went for him
To bring him home and bring the plane home too.
Greeted in Washington by Calvin Coolidge,
Before a vast crowd in the open air,
Fifty-five thousand telegrams were given him,
One of them signed by seventeen thousand names
In sweet sincere open congratulation!
Eighteen thousand tons of paper were thrown
Gaily and whitely from all office buildings
To make a snowstorm of greeting on Broadway
(Only one hundred and fifty tons had greeted
The Armistice in 1913!)
Two and a half million dollars were offered him
To go on a tour of the world by air!
But only seven hundred thousand dollars
To appear as a star on the silver screen!

THE COLLECTED POEMS OF DELMORE SCHWARTZ

A town was named for him,
     'the largest dinner
Ever given to any individual
In modern history' was given him
—Such was the admiration and the love
Which rose from all America because
A man had given them a perfect hero,
Vicarious in the *The Spirit Of St. Louis*
The pure romantic ego flew the Atlantic!
Such an event, so loud in praise and applause
Moved like a shock through Hershey Green's new heart,
—is it a wonder then that he cried back
His own belief and hope in his own terms?"

"I hardly paid attention to the flight,"
Said Hershey Green, "much more engaged in what
The Giants were doing. But thanks,
     thanks anyway,
For showing that I was not utterly
An ape of self-abuse in an abyss,
A maniac of my dream in a pure void—"

[366.]

"What a relief, like coming to the shore
Of the fresh sea (whence once rose Love and Life)
After the wet heat of the summer city,
O what a freshness to go back to small
And rather normal moves in this boy's heart,
Not giant ambition like an office building,
     the Chrysler Tower—

But season's return, the draw of memory,
Like migratory birds returning South,
The sweet hot rumors sexual action gave
To the growing fusing boy, looking at girls,

FROM GENESIS: BOOK TWO

Looking at adults' lives, feeling from head to foot,
The long outstretched and wincing wound of wounds!"

"And yet the wide world is not barred, the boy
Hardly was unaware of social death,
Too innocent Italians burned, alas!
To say the face of an angry ruling class!—"

"I hardly paid attention. I tried hard
To study Shakespeare and the Bible when
Others danced in the Ballroom or looked on,
                              while the band played,
Sickened, as that voice said before, because
My interest never rose, I could not see
Why these were famous and profoundest texts—
And in the morning, seizing the paper's mind
I sought the baseball scores, as that voice said
And cursed with utter hatred Nature's ways
Because It rained for five days 'in a row'
                              in the city of New York,
That uncontrollable divinity,
Nature, as you would say,
                    and say so much.
Stopped the Giants' games. Their pennant rival played
And won, and won the pennant. This, I thought,
Was the injustice of the wide world's ways!"

"Hear how he knows our lingo! Gifted boy,
Quick at an idiom—"
                    "Never mind the praise!"

. [369.]
_____

"Interpretation! that's the act of mind
Which we began, which now this sleepless boy
And from the very start that foreign voice,

Though intermittently except implicitly,
Have practiced with no little satisfaction—"

"It is the sunlight shining through the window,
It is the sunlight shining through the leaf
Showing as in analysis the veins—
It is the sunlight shining through the stained glass,
Bringing rich colors to the ancient figures
Of the Bible tales which are the Western mind—"

"It is the teacher teaching in the classroom,
What the text means and how to take it in,
Whence rise the classics or the classroom books!
(Just like the preacher! just like the sunlight too!)
—yet what, O sleepless boy, shall be replied
To those who say, interpretation's free,
Free and licentious, anyone can say
Just what he wants to say, Satan himself
Quote scripture for all crime and each mind find
What he brought with him, in the book or act?
What holds interpretation in its flight,
                              and makes it good or evil?
—O glory of the turning world! it is
The future whose events show true or false
Empty or relevant, senseless or sure
The inner structure and the inner future
Interpretation found in book or act,
                              or things:
The bare bones of *ti to ov* move on and on,
Reveling in the grave the whole of truth!
We who are dead know what is now to come
In your sick life—"
              "Tell me!" cried Hershey Green—

"Now was the lawyer right? Was Jack Green's act
Like Teapot Dome, Warren G. Harding's cost
To be the President? like business men
Lying about their good, their goods, their land,
Their product, prize, bon-bon, cold cream or cake?
Was Jack Green's act like theirs? A little worse,
Let's say, than what was recognized
As legal, justified and enterprising,
—Yet, on the other hand, the line is vague,
Who shall say Jack was wrong in what he did,
Since it was but a minor prolongation
Of what he had learned from his *milieu*, what
Making a livelihood, justest of motives,
Entailed, made necessary? Business men
Have business men's morality. This was
A polity of business men all else
On the frontier, merely endure a while
—Capitalismus is not mocked my boy,
It penetrates the man from head to foot,
It dominates this boy's America,
Kicks all the other strong divinities,
Until they are merely its servitors:
The forests of [indecipherable] become the lies
Printed on paper better used to wipe—
And girls' lips lewdly on the billboards part
To make Sex serve the sales of cigarettes—
As Motherhood increases florists' trade
When made a holiday,
                              as Western Union gains
By the vagina's long remembered pains,
As Christ becomes the greatest business man
And Notre Dame becomes a football team!
Capitalismus is not mocked, O no!
But like the greatest Gorgon every maid
And every boy is fed it, every day
—Forgive my anger, now that I am dead

I see what infamy my life endured
In this old newfoundland, America!"

[374.]

"More than a million dollars! what a sum
With which to pay a boy from Eastern Europe
For being cunning, clever,
                    full of energy—"

"Capitalismus rises to a height
Never before this known in the wide world
—Many an immigrant becomes a lord—"

"And Edgar Allan Poe, is he still here?
How just that the romantic ego finds
A cast of characters including him
Who went across the seas to France in black
Robes garbed, singing for Baudelaire—

"Back to America, a later boy
And in a later day, far from luxurious
Despair and melancholy finds a word,
Eureka,
        what he wants who wants the morning,
Blueing and graying the bedroom windows, wan
And snowy light like the light in mirrors echoed—"
                                "—the sounds
Of clapping acts and coughing cars
                    before the city wakes,
Marking the snowy quiet like a ground,
                    like a wide sound—"

"He fails! he has been judged and truly judged,
He is unable to submit himself
To tasks imposed on him by classroom laws—

His consciousness flies to an utter morning
Or flies to fiction's womb which is so warm,

                                 Pleasure itself

Immediate, spontaneous, and free,
Nothing but that can with his will, poor boy,
All by himself in piety and law
For no divinity appears to him
As teacher and as kind, though one or two,
America, The New York Giants, far off
—Needing no effort, only admiration—
Win his attention as he flies from school:
Such is Romance in 1927!

[379.]

"Well I never! what the sense of glory
Will sometimes bring about in a young boy!"

"I hardly hope to sleep," said Hershey Green,
"Before I die, I hardly hope to know
Freedom shame or from your constant voices,
But is it necessary to pronounce,
In such detail, a young boy's foolishness,
Moved to a megalo-childishness so vast:
Will not that Foreign voice let me alone?
—I was inspired by Spengler's book, he was
Responsible as much as I for all—"

"Trying to shift the guilt will do no good,
O no, sleepless Atlantic boy, not he,
Not he alone, nor you alone, but all
The strong divinities were necessary!
America, Capitalismus,
Powerful science, childhood prestige and praise,
The wonder boys who in the paper's minds
Broke the world's record in progressive schools!

Lindbergh, as we have said, flying the Atlantic:
All these divinities were necessary!
But none sufficient! none enough to make
Your mind and heart rise to such vast intent,
O no! nothing compelled:

                you were a liberty,

                       even as now you are,

You were yourself the one sufficient cause!
You and your Caesar ego brought the thought,
This guilt you must accept before you die—"

"Let me alone," cried Hershey Green, ashamed,
Shamed beyond shame, desperate to hear no more—

"I must say that I find this most engaging,
This True Republic is a good idea,
Fuses most [indecipherable] fights of this poor boy,
And gives expression very well, I think,
Too much of man's essential nature,

                      yes!
Plato and Thomas More here had a new
Voice for their choir, singing, What Should Be!
O man's desire, Kingdom of Heaven On Earth!—
O lasting image of this life's poverty!"

"It is a boy's Utopia in every way!"

[381.]

"Una returns: that's as it should be, true
To the small world and puberty's good luck—"

"His knees knock once again, as Dante's did,
He feels faint and he feels the ecstasy,
Quiet and calm, of finding all in snow,
The great city suddenly white, awaking,

(As if an inner essence showed itself,
Miraculous, or super-Nature dove,
The Holy Ghost concrete in winter's white
When all the colors come, all Being thus . . .)"

"Never mind that! let me hear more and more,
Let me see how your interpretive light,

                          so voluble,
Illumine this renewal," Hershey said,
"Why did I meet her thrice? or even once?
Among six million souls, anonymous—"

"Merely pure chance, sleepless Atlantic boy,
No more than that, the irreducible
Crossing of ways. But there where chance has struck,
Nothing much happens most of the time, if not
For all the strong divinities in act
And the unique character of what, I think,
Sometimes is called, 'the two parties concerned'—
You were the nature who saw in the girl
Something like snow, the greatest kind of beauty—
How many chances struck you in the street,
School and a thousand places of the city
Sans growing to a church, as Una did?"

"But if one were by lightning struck,

                        in the park
Or in the wood, would that not be a pure
Event of chance which showed the world insane?"

"No, no, O sleepless boy; what drew the one,
There to the park or wood? A love of Naturedom?
The strong appeal of some divinity
Which won assent from the free and wanton heart:
Such is the nature which makes rational
The hurly-burly of events and years
For Man the liberty in Time the darkness. . . ."

THE COLLECTED POEMS OF DELMORE SCHWARTZ

"This is as good as walking home from school
To show Spengler was wrong, the West not
Dying,
       seeking to see the swan and princess
Of his ninth year, after five years had passed
His pure emotion is in no way abated—"

"Her father in the dress business: how good!
How very good! Forth from the middle class
Divinity two fusing hearts enact
Dante and Beatrice,
             helped by the silver screen!"

"If I had not been shy, if I had spoken!"
Said Hershey Green, moved by the old emotion,
"Is it too late? will I see her again?
I heard her voice once, climbing up the stair
Behind me, speaking with another girl,
It seemed somehow a sharply ripening whistle
From a cold star whose twinkle reached two senses!"

"Look how this love affair unites, like most,
Many a strong divinity: they mix,
The school, the family, and great New York,
love, which aped egotism in his heart:
He writes an essay with his love and dream,
Gives it to the school paper, waits to hear
That he is famous, must be introduced
before the school assembly to the swan—"

"—The mind is, in a way, all things, and all
Things pass through it, never the same again:
It is like water, in a way, it is the water
Ultimate, whence Love and Life once rose,
All things once wet by it never regain
Their linen, sand, or innocence:

The mind of Hershey Green passes through all,
All things pass through the mind of Hershey Green!"

[388.]

"What strangeness lies in puberty's first blush!
It is untaught, though others speak of it—
Even the desert island must, I think,
Make the sole growing boy feel in himself
The need to augment, grow hard, be touched,

> be pushed

Until he stretches out upon the sand
And fondles coconuts with ignorant hands!"

"Why did I separate her from the girls,
Feeling for her no sexual desire?"
Hershey inquired, purely curious:
A different hardly heard hoarse voice replied:

"The ice cream parlor near the high school held
In pumps, of adolescence the great sweetness,
The flavors, vanilla, chocolate, pistachio,
And tutti-frutti, too, mixtures baroque,
The puff of whipped cream, cherry on the sundae,
But most of all the soda's surged orgasm,
Sucked through the straws,

> a drained sound at the end—

"A Frenchman owned this place and on the walls
Next to the booths cheap murals of the Alps
Showed snowy over a dairy valley where cows grazed.
The counter fellow studied law at night,
And freely chatted with the dallying girls,
As if he might be part of their affair
If he but wished! did not ambition hold:
The radio danced on and on above the booths

The marbles tables and the candy cases,
Providing airs or rumors of all to come,
General emotions, an obvious sea for them
To splash in gaily, taking of each other
The possibility in every joke, quick look,
[Indecipherable] boys and girls perform—"

"What does this scene, this mise-en-scène reveal?
And from what points of view must it be seen?"

"Come now, no playground, holiday,
Party of lovers' lane can equal this
Fusion of coldness, sweetness, and intuition:
This is the place where boys and girls first learn
That in America sex is quite cool,
Here souls are fixed in forms that will last long:
Of all the causes pleasure is most strong!"

"I did not go there, though I looked at it,
Going from school," augmented Hershey Green—

[388A.]

"The ice-cream parlor near the high-school held
In pumps, of adolescence the great sweetness,
The flavors, vanilla, chocolate, pistachio,
And tutti-frutti, too, mixtures baroque,
The puff of whipped cream, the cherry is on the sundae,
Sucked through the straws,

     a noise at the end—

A Frenchman owned the place and on the walls
Next to the booths cheap murals of the Alps
Showed snowy over a dairy valley where cows grazed.
The counter fellow studied law at night,
And freely chatted with the dallying girls,

As if he might be part of their complete affair
If he but wished, not three years too old.
The radio danced on and on, above the booths,
The marble tables and the candy cases,
Providing airs or rumors of all to come,
General emotions, an obvious sea for them
To swim in, gaily, talking of each other
The possibilities in every joke, quick look,
And struggle boys and girls always perform—

What does this scene and circumstance reveal?
And from what points of view must it be seen?
Come now, no playground, holiday,
Party or lovers' lane can equal this
Fusion of sweetness, coldness and intuition:
This is the place where boys and girls first learn
That in America sex is not much,
Here souls are fixed in forms that will last long:
Of all the causes pleasure is most strong—"

[392.]

_____

"Consider this poor boy, haunted by quantity,
Trying among a hundred million souls
In subway, stadium, school, street, and house
To feel the 'unique identity' no gaze would see,
Classing him in a class with all the boys—"

"The vertebrae which holds the body up
Has at its head a likeness, a great question,
Curved like a scythe to cut down all of Nature:
Who am I? What is my name? Who made me?
                                    Am I different?"

"Everything happens in the mind of God—"

"Moonlight faintly shining; as in the mirror
Beneath the hat rack in the hallway, faintly
Gleams the vague light reflected from the window
At the other end, in the living room,
A kind of ice lost amid shadows near the door:
Such is the ego's sense of itself when it
Has tried to grasp itself apart from all,
'O Cassius, for the eye sees not itself
But by reflection, by some other things' . . .

A voice screamed then, then quieted,
                              then said,
I should not have done that, screamed, but sweat,
Brought back my own mind, I forgot
That I was dead, the dignity of the dead:
I'm sorry. . . . the snow made small sounds
Of scratches on the window. The lamplight fell
Bright and full on my lap and on my book,
A false image of ease and interest. . . .
It was too late. . . . nothing is ever wiped out,
No matter what Jack Christ says. *Caritas*
Would be wonderful, but modern life's
Racket outside, ashcans moved by the janitor
Destroyed the silence in the winter night
—This was the time when I first knew my own
Lack of identity in the full sense.
—Ten years have passed. Time is the unforgiveness,
                              and the darkness,
And the lost irreparable. But guilt abides . . ."

"Everything happens in the mind of God—"

[394.]

"—Something is going to happen fairly soon
Of the very greatest interest to us all!"

FROM GENESIS: BOOK TWO

"I see this boy as if made flexible
By what but the strong family divinity,
His soul stretched out a thousand miles between
Chicago and New York: Orestes, Hamlet!
Children divided by their parents' love
                                    and hatred!"

"Never mind that: look at his mind spread out
Upon the continent! he is inventive,
Let's say at least that much for him, poor boy,
The names he chose are very interesting—"

"O yes, I was inventive," Hershey, pleased
By praise, declared. "And in detail—"

"Never mind that: let us move on this trip,
—The boys get in the Lincoln car and go,
Something is left behind just like remorse,
Something is always left behind, that's Life;
A violin this time, as if his heart,
Played by his mother many many times!"

"They eat ripe cherries all the morning, this
Is purely holiday.
                    Let us attend
And concentrate upon the passing scene,
For all of Hershey's growing pains grow here
Increased, this is like other trips before,
Other apartnesses and separations, going
To camp,—tortures the silver cord!"

"And now he breaks Moses' commandment, eats
Bacon! and finds it very keen
After five thousand years!:
                            and now he hears
A strange thing from his father, *girls*!
Women, his father means, as he knows well,

It is an older lingo's euphemism:
Girls will live with them,

                through their unhappy summer . . ."

"Capitalismus drives the flowing car!"

[399.]

"How rich, how very rich all this was!
All the divinities were dancing there,
About the head and heart of Hershey Green!"

"The family divinity and sex
Appalled him, faced with his father's lady friends,
As long before, going to the winter resort,
Given a wrist-watch which shone in the dark!
But then he was as innocent as snow!"

"O Sex! which made him see the newlyweds
Giggling at the white Falls, at tying laces,

                      how rich, how rich!
Mother! who from afar a small divinity
But powerful, who'd painted his father's life
On the long walls of his mind, forbidden bacon,
Glumly perused and dropped!

                    The hard silence,
Sulking Achilles, independent
Being's great Chinese Wall to show his anger,
As at the kindergarten long before—"

"And Roger's contrast, happy and thoughtless boy,
Untroubled by all the deities,

                  this shows
The unique ego in its liberty—"

"And O the negro waiter on the boat,
Fresh from forty years of vaudeville!
Who brings the game of chance which brings
The accident and ends the poor boy's heart!
A game of dice and ice cream are the means
Which bring about the victory!
                              What wins
In Hershey's heart, triumphs over his mother,
over his shock, his shame, and his *tabu*?
—Marriage [indecipherable] doth the Polity's
Sheer values, shining chandeliers!
                              I see
Society is never mocked for long,
This boy was won by custom and by gold!
                              how rich, how rich!"

"You make it simpler than it really was,"
Said Hershey Green, wincing in memory
"There was a struggle in my mind until
I could do nothing more: what could I do?"

"That's the whole truth and infamy, poor boy;
When every choice is wrong for liberty,
                              in Time the darkness. . . ."

[401.]

"Jack Green sees in his son identity
Twice over,
              in the likeness death
                              is leaped—
Nature is quite defeated by itself—"

"My father stared at me as if I were
Not wholly credible," said Hershey Green—

"Your soul stretched out a thousand miles, Chicago
Unto New York, you wrote those letters home,
Mere violin, as many times before
Of your mother's sick emotions—"
                              "Luxury!
Capitalismus lifts the fusing boys,
Ten dollars' spending money every day,
Won from America's true real estate,
The immigrants from Europe's struggled shore!"

"Do you know what I found out then? I learned
What satiation was, could not regain
My appetite for sodapop, joy and like things.
I said to my father then, 'I guess
Everyone only wants a thing until
He has it! if he has it all the time,
It hardly gives him pleasure any more!'
'You're a smart boy,' my father said to me,
Smiling at my well-known psychology—"

"Smiling over your head: he knew quite well
Some appetites are never satisfied!
He learned this day by day until he died!"

"How different now this family life became,
And how depraved, in fact, to go about
And then to back to mother's rule, meager
In the very middle of the lower middle class!
Like the small town mentioned a while ago,
Corrupted by the summer visitors,
So that the winter seemed a closing down
Of all the carnivals and carousels—"

"Such is the nature of all the vacations
In the divided hearts of modern life!"

"Look, how the riot on the darkened green!"

"No! that's another life, you silly ghost,
Two lives nearby in Jackson Park, a man
And woman fondling one another's parts
Upon the grass in 1928!
Get your gaze straight, there's Hershey,

                  at the window,

Gazing upon the flatness of the Lake
Fading to indeterminacy—"

                  "Perhaps

This is inane Nirvana, Hindus' hope,
The wish to die, the nothingness of saints?"

"Perhaps it is the mysticism egos

                  project, prolong,

At least propose,

          the ego, as I said,

Is but a penis! wants to be enclosed,
And this explains the pass of pantheists,
Mistaking Nature's unity for God,
Because they wish to find the biggest womb!"

"Give the boy credit, foolish as he is—"

"Yes, give me credit, foolish as I am,
Keeping me sleepless,

           till I wish to die!"

"All right, here is your credit: that, in a way,
A wish to understand was mixed in all
Your vanities composed and dreamed in you.
You rose, in fact, your feeling was much more
Than just the ego as a Zeppelin,
Travelling across the brilliant summer's day
As millions cheered and doffed their hats to see:

Your feeling rose until it was a sense
Won from the deepest memory! the sense
Of infinite extent and warmth
                            within the womb!
Both indistinction and that unity
Which many saints have dreamed rose in your head,
Both blazing light and black darkness,
                            vanity
And intuition, in your foolishness,
Tortured by incomplete identity—"

"I studied hard in Spengler," Hershey said,
That was a wish to know, to understand,
Give me some credit, foolish as I am!"

[406.]

"Although the new ideas this boy had made,
Adding to his strange dream, The True Republic,
Are very interesting, and call for comment,
This is the thousandth or ten thousandth time
Another thing has happened: we have seen
Pasthood repeated in the Present,
                            differently,
Significantly and richly.
                    Is it not time,
Long over time perhaps, to speak of this?
—Thus Sex made Jack Green curious about
The new experience of his son's flesh,
A curiosity profoundly *selfed*
In self-identity's concern with sex:
He saw his young son as a second self,
He wished to know if he had touched a girl
There in the darkness where all life begins
—And Hershey, hearing of his father's query,
Returned with his whole being to the time

His father found him *on* a little girl
In his fifth year and smiled far off at him!
—This continuity, this river flowing
Between the Past and Present,

                      like the Hudson
Beside this boy's life, always the same,

                         and different,
What is it? What sustains it? Is it not
The self itself which thus brings forth the Past
As it accepts or it rejects the other
Divinities? prehends the Pasthood's vast:
Each selfness in itself chooses, takes hold,
Selects from that deep-welled divinity
What it needs most. Takes with its liberty
From Time the darkness what it wants or needs,
—The taking makes the moment; the taking is
Itself the self in act!

                  How deep the Past!
Earth of all growth! soil of all consciousness!
A queen of queens! queen of all thinking things! . . ."

"I am left bored," said Hershey Green, "by this
Voluble and abstract analysis—"

[409.]

"Again the father and the son combine
To show how deeply selfed the family!
How it rests on the pain, identity,
And yet surrounded by divinity,
Which stretches it and takes it far away—"

"The Future rides into the father's mind:
Is, to the boy's mind, different as Eskimos
From deep-dyed Africans!

                The father warns the boy. . . .

The boy will not believe, sees on all sides
Riches that he will have to make his own life
Obedient to his will as his own car—"

"The quick hurrying *dynamos* outside
Of passing cars upon the Lake Shore Drive
Were obvious images of life to come
For Hershey Green when he was twenty-one—"
"And one divinity above the others
Convicted him and his imagination:
Capitalismus moved throughout the city
Like streetcars coming close to every house
With regularity and certainty
Piercing the head, even the sleeping head,
Open all night like certain restaurants!
Always on tap, like the electric light,
Which came unseen from the great company
Immediately, as if spontaneously—"

"Capitalismus moved through America
And pierced the dreams of the whole populace
And brought the beds they lay in, the houses
That held the beds, the food from Florida,
                              Kansas or California,
Digested through the night, the kinds of life
Prepared for them to seek, as bottles wait,
Prepared with the emotions, at the druggist's
                              or at the liquor store—
O everywhere you look this monstrous cause
Spreads out like trees in air its heavy branches,
From which men with slumped heads hang down like sacks—"

"Soon from that tree Jack Green's slumped head will hang!"

"See the divinities dance in a ring
About the boy, shunt him about me as if
He were the medicine boy of seashore play
—The family divinity stretches him out
—The family divinity stretches him out
A thousand miles, as we have said,

                                  Chicago
Unto New York! And this bears repetition
Because it is an old and new condition—"

"A million dollars tortures Eva Green!
Jack Green admires Edison: Just so,
Just right, for one of just his generation—
The man who lighted up the world, a star!

                                  a very sun!
Also admired by that Henry Ford—"

"The family divinity advances now,
New Thresholds, new complexities, and old
Motives like swords! attack the boy,

                              even as he
Attacks himself,

                pierced by his father,

                         shocked,
Because he seems of red-haired Judas' kind,
he pours a version of his fantasy—"

"My father said, when I had told him why,"
Said Hershey Green, in wincing memory,
"I wrote such letters to my far-off mother
In her unhappiness, 'you have been made to feel,'

                              he said,
'Too great a burden of responsibility,'
Even as later to his relatives,

he said
'He's a peculiar boy! I don't know why,
Unless living with women all the time—'
Why did that knowing voice leave all that out?"

"A mole grew on your face above your cheek-bone:
It was a sign, peculiar boy, of all—
Your weakness, vanity, and fantasy . . ."

"My father did not want me. I was struck
As by a lasting judgment, by that news!
I saw myself objective in his gaze,
For a brief while—"
                              "Faded in a few days!"

"Everything happens in the mind of God—"

[416.]

"This mysticism of the early morning
And staying up all night: what does it mean?—"

"Is it not just the wish for a beginning
—Oldest of wishes, old as the Creation?—
Is it the ever old and new attempt
At utter transformation, which we see
When Jacob alters his name to Israel,
After his wrestling match with God,
                              or with God's angel
The whole nightlong beside the dangerous river?
Is it not Saul, also changing his name
After Damascus' blaze?
                              It is this boy
Returning to his home town with a lisp
Which meant to show what richness in a newness

Had entered him,
                    breaking down every time:
The self is not denied, it is the wings
Of every fugitive flying from himself!"

"'*History is the bunk!*' said Henry Ford,
Mentioned a moment since. His statement rose
From the same wish in new America,
To find the morning and the new beginning—"

This Ford became an *antiquarian*
Of his boyhood's *milieu*, destroyed by him:
The horse-and-buggy day, the hardship farm!"

"Never mind that: look at poor Hershey Green—"
                                        "yes! look at me!"

"Tortured by a large mole and by the school
Divinity, imposing foreign law
On his romance and hope.
                            How at the silver screen
Thrilled by the images of Faust, he saw
The endless darkness of the Western ego,
Striving forever like the famous spire,
Infinitely unsatisfied! denied!
—And deified by power over Nature:
Though finding only fresh fields of starved desire—"

"Capitalismus drives the flowing car—"

[420.]

"Sleepless Atlantic boy! born in Brooklyn,
                                that is, Long Island,
Which seems to head for North America
Just like an ocean liner coming from Europe,

THE COLLECTED POEMS OF DELMORE SCHWARTZ

The greatest thing in America,
                                        as we have said—
. . . What freshest dreams bloom from his heavy head?
—What is a dream? A vari-colored map,
Moving itself and showing hope and fear
(The two resistless tigers of the heart),
Or like the mustaches a wanton boy
Will draw on actresses in photographs,
Expressive of what hatred of the real?)"

"Roger of Colonel Snowflake was the same
Being, in species, as camp Richard was,
Model of poise, 'great calmness and great sweetness
Of temper,' generous,
                                        good-looking, happy—"
The dream of aristocracies.
                                        But look!
How snow once more is under all obsession,
Imagination's utter white possession,
Matrix of every good: what does it mean?"

"Tell me now what it was!" cried Hershey Green,
"It is quite true, snow was my utter dream—
                                        I don't know why!—"

"You were the poet of your fear and hope!
You saw your brother as a sign or trope!
With tongue and mind, as if things were but words!"

"Everything happens in the mind of God,
Thence is the quality of every man
Realized as none such in a Judgment Day
Perpetually in session, like the blue
That over-rides the world, O Hershey Green!"

"You lie in the coffin of your character,
Or like a fly, trapped in a treacherous sweet,
Trapped by each move made to escape and fly—"

"Everything happens in the mind of God!"
Hershey cried out, appalled to hear the word,
Coffin, feared above all,

                crying in hope—

[422.]

"We have not said it yet, but it must come,
Implicit as it is, as lighted rooms
Imply the night outside,

                   that, in the depth
Of the whole mixture of the struggle which
The strong divinities wrestling in this boy's mind
Like lions, what monstrous cause among them
Triumphed,

         but anyone can see,

                   needless to say,
And how we must announce it, guilty boy:
Capitalismus moved you most of all!—
Made you the monster of that fantasy!—
(This does not free you from responsibility—)
Yet you are not free of your guilt, of your shame,

                     Identity
Knows itself here, as barbarous as ever!
Nonesuch as clear as blue! For, look!

               the other boys
Surrounded by the same divinities
Did not conceive and never entertained
Any such dream! And Roger most of all,
Subjected so much to the same *milieu*
Of monstrous causes was as unlike you
As black and white or the two famous brothers,
Isaac and Ishmael, William and Henry James,
—Many another pair: but never mind—
Even the dead grow tired in the end

Of saying many times, You are your guilt,

                      —for you are free!"

"I know it; I have never doubted it,"
Said Hershey soberly, almost mature,
"I know my liberty, although but vaguely,
I feel it every conscious moment ever fresh
And new in me,

                as in the morning, waking:
What else is there to say? Except, again,

                      'I wish to die!'"

"You lie in the coffin of your character[,]

                    You wish to die!"
"Nothing is ever wiped out, no matter what
Jacky Christ says! What can I do? deny

              that I am I?"

                    "Call him Ishmael!"

[426.]

"The girls, the World War guns, and business man's
Morality,

          what a mélange, deep from the Past,
Yet with a new old one apparent at the edge
Of this most moving picture, quickly passing,
Karl Marx! attorney of eternity,
As one might say, accusing history . . ."

                "Never mind that,
Never mind that right now! Is it not like,

               —that foreign voice,—
The Ancient Mariner, quietly speaking, damned?
Is it not like the famous book of Job?

Though this poor boy is not a righteous soul?"

"O my life, my only life!
What have I done with it? . . .

"Now after this long night, I am like one
In a dentist's chair. I am prepared for pain,
Ready to pay for it, passive before
The white-gowned expert,
                              —click down the seat,
                                        dead everlasting voices,
Begin to take away the teeth which are
So near the ego, the penis ego which
Made me take Roger's girl, and made that good
And natural boy burst into passionate tears—"

"Give the boy something pleasant for a time
To rest his mind's eye which has stared so long
                              —and if unwillingly,
                                   who, who would be brave?
—Sing to him of the glory of the world!"

"O Atalanta, the apple of the eye!
O Eve before the tree which is this world!
O bird, O beast, O flower everywhere,
All the *richesse* of being through the year,
For the earth turns like a carousel on which
All sensibilities ride horses, grasp for rings
—Which crowds with too much sweetness,
                                        too much blaze,
And blare the ear,
                    as torsos up and down
Are taken and around and around and around
Until the outer scene is whirling too,
Faces blurred and repeated, blurred and repeated,
Upon the benches by the ice cream stand—"

"The pleasure turns to pain, like all
Extended sensuality! And yet you see,

Poor boy, from certain surfaces in May,
Why God, some say, took on man's flesh: to be
Great God was not enough! before this world!"

[428.]

"Everything happens in the mind of God—"

"And everything re-happens many times,
The father tells the son, Beware of women,
Even as he had told him, Marry young,
Even as he had asked the chauffeur, Allen,
Had Hershey ever touched a woman wholly?
Identity still seeks to free itself,
Faced by the young boy and appalled by death—"

                                        "Death!" cried Hershey,
"O Death!" cried several voices of the dead!—

"—Excrement left by dogs upon the sidewalk,
And in the gutter by the milkman's horse,
The ashcans in the gutter, the sewer open
To suck down dirty rain, the smoke,
                            blown out
In gust and gout, like handkerchiefs,
                        or sleeves,
From stack and chimney lifted aloft away—
And the refused, the refused of the fire
And if the human body,
                  so, pieces of Nature
Are broken down, picked of their use and meat,
And carried off, the city's tendency
Acts the negation which inheres in Life,
And places everywhere small open forms,
Sewer, basin, chimney, ashcan, gutter,

That Death may be well-organized!
                                    like criminals
In penitentiaries: it does no good!
Death no less runs with Life on every side
Like that small death of light, the shadow!
                                    like that vast death, the night!"

"My father said, Let's all go out to-night,
                                    have a good time!
—That night when he came back from the funeral—
Let's have a real good time! We went, just think,
To The Rodeo! and my father said, [illegible handwritten note here]
A strange unheard-of thing,
                                    Get inexpensive seats!
Giving me money to buy tickets: he
Who always bought the best seats in the house!
And then with intense interest he gazed
In Soldier's Field in 1929,
At the barbarous animals conquered by cowboys
As the crowd cheered. And with strange appetite,
He ate our peanuts—hardly ever before—
As if he had not fed himself for days!"

[432.]
_____

"That mole begins to be Original Sin—
O, if all men might in the looking-glass
Find such a mark of something wrong with them!"

"And now he learns to drive a motor car,
And now, as that voice says, he feels his will
Multiplied many times when the car flows
Ignorant of its basis and *anima*
As of his belly which takes in the world!"

THE COLLECTED POEMS OF DELMORE SCHWARTZ

"Capitalismus drives the flowing car!"

"And fatherhood, looking at death, as one
Might look at the black thunderheads,
                              like chariots
Waiting the race upon a summer's day,
                              in the sudden stillness, of tree and air,
Bringing torrential rain,
                    and violent blows,
                                    so, from afar,
The fatherhood in Jack Green speaks of death!
And of his will, so-called, and of his life,
And of his property, so-called, and of the death
He half-knows in the world whence money comes—
. . . O what a scene! repeated many times,
I do not doubt, wherever father is
A powerful man respected by his son,
But here inviting such a flood of feeling
—Deep from abysses of the mind beneath
The conscious mind,—
                        that father and son are most
Embarrassed as they talk! They hardly know
Why they should feel so *weakly* what is said!
But I know why!
                    the knowledge of the dead!"

"Back to the sex, however, which goes on,
There in America-in-1929
(Say all of that as one word, for we know
That time and place are indivisible
Or so that Einstein says conclusively!):
Hershey moves to the April of a boy,
The spring-sick April of the city life—
A girl sits on his lap, he touches her
Hardly-grown breasts—Nature in both of them
Rises, the colored chauffeur looks, *voyeur*!
For all men, Aristotle says, are curious,
The ego cries on a great street of the world:
Capitalismus drives the flowing car!"

FROM GENESIS: BOOK TWO   [413]

"O it was bound to come! that perfect fall
Of the erected prides, like office buildings,
Of this America! naught could avert,

                           evade, avoid,
Capitalismus could not rise forever

                       and ever!
The Tower of Babel was the final story
Of all those office buildings everywhere
Throughout Eternity—

                God is not mocked!"

"Everything happens in the mind of God—"

"Few understand the scope of the event—
Not the capitalist, Jack Green,
And not the daughter of the socialist
Who sees the doom as possibility—
Few understand what monstrous causes mount
More than an earthquake to shake down this world!
For none foresee the Germany of Hitler!
And none foresee ten years in America,
America tired out! and none foresee
The Second World War and The Fall of France—

"What do you mean," cried Hershey Green,

                    "Will War
Come once again? And will France lose?

                   Tell me more and more,

                       and more!"

"Never mind that! back to the black day which
Reversed, in such a peripety
As Aeschylus, Dante, Shakespeare,
And Aristotle never dreamed! a world!

"How grim my father looked upon that day!"
Cried Hershey Green, breathless with interest,
"Will Socialism come, as people say?
What countries will fight in the Second World War?"

"Back to your guilt, O Hershey Green,
                              you are
Not dead, the future not yet yours,
                              the past
Fallen and falling with you, for you too,
                                   O New York boy,
Fell with the market that October day,
In new America in 1929!"

[438.]

"Still lives the pride after the vast Fall,
And will live on for years, as Hershey drives
The big Lincoln on Riverside Drive and tries
Vainly with car sounds to make Una see
How he is rich! and has a chauffeur too!"

"How recognition often is delayed,
Even as Oedipus for long,
                         grasping
At every straw, dodged from the obscene knowledge,
And then, when he could not, put out his eyes!
The boy does not know Una goes away
And never to return perhaps!"
                              "Never again?"
Cried Hershey Green, "Will I see her no more?
                              no more?"

"Never mind that, O guilty boy!
                         The future is not yours!
But I will tell you this,—un-understood

In any case, that Delia known as Daisy,
The girl with the fresh-colored and Dutch beauty
You will see more and more,—
                                    forever more!"

"What stumps and fragments I am given now,
And all this sleepless night, no matter what,
                                    with sickening joy,
I ask for. Yet I know this cold comfort too,
That this cannot go on much longer. For
You come, and that foreign voice comes near
This very night,
                    there'll be no more to say,
If you must hold the future from my gaze:
Will I sleep then? or will I die? my God!"

"Perhaps he will begin again! and touch
On incidents omitted here and there—
Perhaps he will repeat it all again,
Each word, each incident, each strange event,
So full of meaning and divinity!"

"*Am I like drowning men are said to be?*
Who see the whole of life before they die?
Stuffed with the water whence Life's mother rose—
Perhaps he will repeat it all again!
O what a nausea that black possibility
Raises in me: to see it all again—"

"Each thing lives in itself. Forever recurs
                                    over and over
And over again, in the mind of God!"
                                    "My God!"

[441.]

"Some warm details are irreducible,
No matter what divinities we see
Holding them up, as water holds a boat
                              (prepared to flood and drown),
—You know how, Hershey, that this was the last
Time you would see your father in this life:
Just think of how the scene shines for you now,
And in what lights! the lights of memory!
The lights of death! The revelation
That every future brings unto the past!
Perhaps this is the reason for this night,
Besides your guilt! I do not say it is,
I only say, Perhaps it is! The future
Cannot be yours! not even the coming hour
When all in this endless night will show its power!

"Note, guilty boy, now, as that voice
Wisely remarks, you bear upon your flesh
—Bear it forever! that sandpaper wet
Brush of your father's cheek upon Broadway:
The sensuous thing by death made everlasting!
All light into death's great shadow bows!—

"The chorus girl just like an odalisque
Is one more repetition; note it well,
How much *develops* from that seashore day
When the small boy and girl went out to play!"

"The garish whites of New York lights shone down
Upon the farewell scene. Their very daze,
Blinking and shifting, advertised the gap
Between the modern night and private lives. . . ."

"Look, Jack Green hardly seems to understand
Capitalismus in its broken ride!
The manic-depressive roller-coaster tour!

He gives his niece a rich man's gift,
                          a thousand dollars!
How the mind lags behind the great event,
And how the heart lives like Grand Dukes in Paris,
After Lenin's profound compound affair!"

"Capitalismus drives the taxi there!—"

"You lie in the coffin of your character!"

[445.]

"Thus an awareness of the Fall begins,
Thus must have been, I guess, but do not know
The gradual awareness of Christ's death,
Until the mind began to seek his life
And finding it, three times, two times, four times,
(In words which haunt our Western consciousness!)
They came to know and say at last with pulse
And breath, the way in which he shone,
                          he blazed
On every living moment of their lives;
In birth, in copulation, and in death,
No matter what we do Christ stares at it!
No matter what we are, he stares at us!
This most extended figure on The Cross
Should show, despite the difference of degree, mutatis mutandis,
How the Depression, so-called of the vast
Divinity, Capitalismus, grew:
Hershey saw it in intellectuals,
For clerks are sensitive as fish to cold
And heat, their thinking and their blood, adjusts
And shifts itself momently to the clime:
There was a growing twilight in the air,
Quickly their minds turn to a new old view of Life,
To suit the different mood of their *milieu*!"

"Smart, cynical, sophisticated,
The civilized, inquiring mind, so-called,
Which from the Armistice began to grow,
The Post-War period, debunking all,
Died like a fly! Slapped absentmindedly:
They turn to the need for Order,
                                    need to retrench and check,
Need to go back to discipline and knowledge
Rejected [Forgotten] when they issued forth from college!"

"Hershey lived on like a Grand Duke in Paris!
He looked at this great shift, but did not know
How much was ended,
                    how his dream was done:
A crisis ten years long had just begun!"

[Two largely illegible lines follow here]

[449.]

"Nothing is left unsaid, no shame forgiven!
Nothing that I escape in common pity,"
Cried Hershey Green,
                    "Who knows so much about me,
Yet does not let me fly from agony,
Except, like tortured men to convalesce
Before the rack once more is placed upon
His hands, his mind, his pride, his private parts!
—All of the order that my life has known,
Every disorder, together or alone!
I take my guilt! I know it very well:
Was *I* the only one like that? Do they,
Like me, rehearse it over and over again?
                                    all of it, every shame?
Whether they do or not, *I wish to die!*"

"Now we are coming to the very end,
Through every end is but a new beginning!
Now we approach the consummation which
Fulfills and justifies this shameful story,
Until it must be justified again,
As human beings, however satisfied,
By dinner, come for breakfast, until lunch
Renews the process and prolongs the life,
                              the vanity!"

And yet, O New York boy, harsh as this is,
This is the way to knowledge and to power,
This is the way to knowledge and to freedom,
Though as the poet said, After such knowledge,
What forgiveness,
                    yet will you be forgiven
Though you do not forgive yourself!
                              This is
The way that you must live! By this attention,
The utter writer's concentrated gaze
On every kind of thing from fly to mountain,
On every living moment of the movement
Of the breathing hoping soul among
The great divinities which struggle with
His waning liberty in Time the darkness
                        before you die!

"Not God himself can quite destroy the Past!
What's his forgiveness then? All men, Macbeth!"
So cried the tortured boy, crying for death!

[455.]
_____

"Death is unequalled in the midst of Life,
Nothing can touch it for its revelation
Of all the private parts of the poor soul—"

"—This was the end of Jack Green's earthly life,
If ends are genuine or if beginnings
Genuine,
        this is the end of that poor soul who rode
South with his mother from Russia to Roumania,
Warm in her womb, hot with her utter anger,
Seeking his father and the blazed dénouement:
Jack Green, dénouement's son, the son of anger,
                        the song of passion!
—A few weeks after that, the child was born
Who now decays with heavy years in him
In a shaking hurrying train which from Chicago
Unto New York,
             shakes somewhat as the carriage
Shook when his angry mother carried him,
                    so warm!
Was it for this? one well might say; for this?
Would it not have been better if he had never
Seen daylight, left his mother, breathed?"

"Look, how the news comes instantly, look!
The relatives huddle, congregate, close in
About the corpse. Death is a living thing,
The troops of living beings assume an order
About the irreducible disorder
As some men build a bridge above a gulf!"

"Death merely heightens Life in those who live!
Hershey cries out his whole relationship
Unto his screaming mother,
               while his brother,
Being the natural boy, weeps natural tears,
—Then Hershey with the full of Life in him
Brimmed over by the nothingness of Death
Wonders how rich he is?"
              "How rich! how rich!"

"Between the death and hour of funeral,
Between the split second when the last breath, hard,
Returns to the empty air, wasted and burned,
And the heavy clumsy laborious
Entrance of the coffin into the turning globe,
What emptiness ensues! much like the vacant
And waiting interim between the lightning's sword [whip]
And the loud thunder's breaking boom!
                                        —relief!

"The food digested in those waiting hours
Is wet by juice [modified]/made different by no less
Than the extra emotion which pervades
The being of the mourning relatives
—And if the teeth at the dinner table click
Against each other, missing the warm tidbit
What intimations sound! of emptiness,
                                of nothingness!
In diners' mouths: Piano! in a way,
Of the harsh ego's hold on life, so sore!"

"Much as the beard on the dead face still grows,
A letter comes posthumously. How rich!
How very good! We who are dead rejoice
In just such incidents, so full of Life's
Interminable and countless consequences!"

"Capitalismus moves the relatives,
Death's poverty seems to bring wealth to them—"

"But why are you so silent, Hershey Green,
Who have not said a word these many thoughts!"

"I am just waiting hopelessly to see
What will be said after you reach to-night

—Will it begin again? Or will I die?
Then to become a singer just like you
Over the lives of those who breathe and hope—"

[464.]

"'O Death, great captain, lift anchor!
                                                it is time!'
And lift away this passionate ruined man:
This guilty boy shows how *he* does not die,
This boy is but one act of his, in dying . . .
                                        Will move with you!
This gulf, Atlantic boy, will move with you,
As with Pascal and Baudelaire, henceforth—
You will fear Death as one fears a great height
Full of vague horror leading who knows where? . . ."

"You will see the infinite at every window,
Desiring always insensibility,
Which is your wish throughout this shameful night . . .
—Across the black depth of your nights, God's knowing hand
Will draw more nightmares, greater terror
                                        and horror,
Without an exit and without conclusion—"

"Thus all is a gulf,—'action, desire, hope,'
Language and thought. Silence is under all,
Appalling and empty space surrounds you now:
You lie in the coffin of your character,
Trapped by each effort to escape from it,
Just like a fly caught in a treacherous sweet—"

"Everything happens in the mind of God—"

"We know O Lord, we know it very well,
Your Judgment is a righteous one always,
However monstrous to the human mind!"

       "ever the silver cord is loosed!
       Ever the golden bowl is broken!"

"The soul of every life is in your hand,
Your hand is full of righteousness and truth!
O pure and righteous Judge! blessed art Thou,
Who know our guilt, forgive and understand,
After Eternity's impatient wait,
When we have lived it all again,
             how many times!
May we pass with some others through the Gate,
Whence all may see Thy Face and see enough!
Who hardly are yet sure that Thou Art, yes!
             and not a dream!—"
"Free of all monstrous made divinity,
Face with Your Face and with Your Matchless Face,
Patient at last with self-identity!"

[468.]
_____

"Capitalismus brings the consequence!. . . ."

"Never mind that! let us keep to our thoughts,
We who are dead have our own life to live,
Which is this abstract comment on all life,
          and irony and regret—"

"*One and one make three*: this is a law
Among all animals;
       but one and one
Among two spiritual beings brings the mind,

Logos, great conversation: such is Life,

                                    Being is rich
Here at the very top; more painful too!
For where the mind is greatest, pain is strongest!
As where the good is tall, the fall is most—"

"As pearls grow from a sickness in the shell,
So will, perhaps, from this long sickness come
Some pearl, some glittering light, O guilty boy,
"—Lying in the coffin of your character,"
"—And lying in the coffin of your guilt—"

"What shame to go into the silver screen
The week your father dies. Just as he did,
The week his father died! thus it goes on!

"This is the way the world begins and ends,
Thus it goes on: Jack Green's life is not dead,
His lawyer and his friend, chosen by him
Arrives after a trip like a retreat!"

"Capitalismus brings the consequence!"

"Everything happens in the mind of God!"

"He lies in the coffin of his character!—"

"Capitalismus gives this death its décor [dress],
Containing it in its inclusive death.
As when a ship goes down, the private life
Is quite contained in high seas' large event!"

"All of his hope and his desire die!
His childhood now old age and soon a ruin—
Nevertheless he still cries,
                    I am I!"

"Capitalismus rules the dying boy!—"

"They were all in the same boat!—"

"One gets used to everything—"

[470.]

"Now we approach the darkness of to-night!"

"Now we have almost seen the causes' play
Their arbitrary work in many hearts,
Who in [with] their freedom consented to begin with,
And when they would withdraw had gone too far!

"—Have we not seen just how a private life,
Mack and Mack's wife, mixes, just as before,
As always everywhere with the great causes?"

"Now we approach the recognition scene!
The scene of scenes: all has been recognition!
Lucid obscenely, of the human condition!"

"Hershey, you see the true sufficient cause:
Capitalismus fell and you fell with it!
Even as financiers,
                          leaping exactly
From office buildings,
                          images of their world!"

"But hope can tell more lies than fabulists,
The human mind can run away with light's
Velocity to Asia, America,
And to the future, even as you dreamed.
And you who think that what fell down will rise

Lie to yourself! Capitalismus rules—
But it is ruled by one Cause infinite
In might and strength,
                                in power and in glory!
Everything happens in the mind of God!
This is what we have come to tell you now!"

"And you, O guilty boy, who with your freedom
Took to your heart the monstrous infamy,
Capitalismus, and made your fantasy
Equal to it, just like an office building,
Must bend and break before the only one,
                                my God!"

"I lie in the coffin of my character!"

[473.]

"At last! the present darkness! all is known!
of what the past was! all its private parts
Have been *in principle* shown clear before you:
Your freedom and your guilt is the whole truth,
Sleepless Atlantic boy, son of two Noahs!
You are your guilt, you are your liberty,
Made of your years,
                    in Time the darkness,
                                Time the turning fire,
                                which brings the day and night—"

"Your act is chosen by your rich poor heart
Among the living dying stupid mindless
                                and strong divinities;
No matter what compulsion they enact:
Your act is yours, you are your liberty,
                                your self-identity!

—Here hearts are tried as gold is tried in fire!"

"An age is ended and an age begins!
This is New York in the year 1930,
This is the end of the world and the beginning,
For there where freedom breathes the empty air,
                                     changing, shifting, burning,
                                          in Time the darkness,
                                               Time the fire,
Beginning and conclusion in every moment
Wait for the freedom which creates anew
All the divinities and all the freedom,
                         all the fathers and all the children!"

"All is forgiven when guilt is accepted
Like a hard task that must at least be done,
And all begins again amid your guilt
When you see freedom heavy in your hands,
Heavy as the wide world! light as the air,
Breathed in at will by him who wills to breathe!"

"Everything happens in the mind of God!—"

THE COLLECTED POEMS OF DELMORE SCHWARTZ

Vaudeville for a Princess
and Other Poems
(1950)

—I think that now we who are together this
evening cannot find anything better to do than
to praise Love.

I propose that each of us, speaking in turn,
going from left to right, make a speech in praise
and celebration of Love.

—Who can have any objection? said Socrates.
Certainly I cannot since I profess to understand
nothing but matters of Love.

For if I have not been talking about Love
all the time, what have I been talking about,
anyway?

I

Vaudeville for a Princess

*Suggested by Princess Elizabeth's
admiration of Danny Kaye*

Vive la bagatelle.

—SWIFT

Imagine for my purpose that you are
a squad of urchins.

—JOYCE

On a Sentence by Pascal

"True eloquence mocks eloquence."
    Did that Frenchman mean
That heroes are hilarious
    And orators obscene?

Eloquence laughs at rhetoric,
    Is ill at ease in Zion,
Or baa-baas like the lucid lamb,
    And snickers at the lion,

And smiles, being meticulous,
Because truth is ridiculous.

"My Mind to Me a Kingdom Is"

The mind to me a North Pole is,
Superb the whiteness there I find,
The glaring snows of consciousness
Dazzle enough to make me blind,
Until I see too much, in this
Resembling James' governess.

* * *

The mind and self in Civil War
Are locked and wasted, blocked and forced.
Desire raids the heart once more,
As scruple counts desire's cost.
Each day betrays the night's last dream,
While night confuses same and seem.

Now Jackson raids the Shenandoah,
Now ironclads block the Southern coast,

Sharp England keeps shop, seeking power.
At Gettysburg both sides are lost.
From London, Marx computes the cost,
Young Adams finds it all a bore.

Perfidious Albion hesitates.
Brady takes death's true photographs.
Charles Adams' tact transforms the fates.
Lincoln tells jokes but no one laughs.
Grant gets drunk as the rocking sea:
Ulysses longs for his family.

Who pardons the weak who fall asleep?
Lincoln forgives the Gorgon's commands,
Procrastinates, and fears to leap,
Knowing how little he understands.
Triumph appears ambiguous:
How nervous are his shaky hands.

Davis protects his friends to the end.
The Negroes chant in the promised land,
The Negroes jig at heaven's gates,
Lincoln explains why he hesitates,
What right which wrong attack defends,
And who with what will make amends.

This is the famous Civil War.
Assassins stop in Baltimore.
Grant closes in remorsefully,
Longing for home and family,
As Lincoln sighs for unity
Until Booth kills him pointlessly.

*   *   *

The mind resembles all creation,
The mind is all things, in a way:
Deceptive as pure observation,
Heartbreaking as a tragic play.

Idle, denial; false, affirmation;
And vain the heart's imagination—
    Unless or if on Judgment Day
    When God says what He has to say.

I Did Not Know the Spoils of Joy

When that I was and a little tiny boy,
    With a hey ho, the wind and the rain,
I did not know the truth of joy,
    I thought that life was passed in pain.

And when I came to thought and art,
    Shame made my naïve flowers wilt,
I glowed disgusted with my heart,
    As cynicism salved my guilt.

When youthful hopes proved true and false,
    As hard-earned riches fool or pall,
I thought the mind lied like a waltz
    Which chants love as a brilliant ball.

And when I followed where sleep fled
    I woke amid the mixing dream,
My self or others hurt my head,
    Making the frigid Furies scream.

And when I fled from this estate,
    I drove the quickest car to bliss,
With drunken fools I struck at fate,
    Charmed at the falls of consciousness.

A great while ago the world began,
    With a ho ho, the fog and the mist,
The Pharaohs are enthroned again,
    The endless wind and rain persist.

Illusion and madness dim the years
    Mere parodies of hope, at best,
And yet through all these mounting fears
    How I am glad that I exist!

How strange the truth appears at last!
    I feel as old as outworn shoes,
I know what I have lost or missed
    Or certainly will some day lose

And yet this knowledge, like the Jews,
    Can make me glad that I exist!
        with a hey ho, the stupid past,
            and a ho ho, and a ha ha at last.

True Recognition Often Is Refused

We poets by the past and future used
Stare east and west distractedly at times,
Knowing there are, in fullness and in flower,
Chrysanthemums and Mozart in the room,
A stillness and a motion, both in bloom.

Or know a girl upon the sofa's ease,
Curved like a stocking, being profoundly round,
As rich and dark as April's underground.
We see in strict perception probity,
The lasting soil and good of all our art,
Which purifies the nervous turned-in heart.

And when we hear in music's empty halls
Torn banners blowing in the rain and shame,
We know these passages are surfaces,
Knowing that our vocation cannot be
Merely a Sunday with the beautiful.
There is pace and grace we must fulfill.

For we must earn through dull dim suffering,
Through ignorance and darkened hope, and hope
Risen again, and clouded over again, and dead despair,
And many little deaths, hardly observed,
The early morning light we have deserved.

The Passionate Shepherd to His Love

Come live with me and be my wife,
We'll seek the peaks and pits of life
And run the gauntlet of the heart
On mountains or the depths of art.
                We'll do the most that thinking can
                Against emotion's Ghenghis Khan.
And we will play on Hallowe'en
Like all souls on the silver screen,
Or at a masked ball ask for fun
Dancing dressed as monk and nun.
                We'll ride a solemn music's boat
                When humors cough in breast and throat.
When snow comes like a sailing fleet
We'll skate a ballet in the street,
Though poor as saints or rocks, immense
Our chatter's rich irreverence.
                And sometimes speak of endless death
                To quicken every conscious breath.
If one becomes too serious,
The other can bring down the house
With jokes which seem hilarious
About the self's pretentious Ows.
                I'll be your room-mate and your hoax,
                The scapeghost of your gentle jokes.
Like Molière's bourgeois gentleman,
You may discover you have been
Speaking blank verse all your life,
And hence you must become my wife.

For you will know of metaphors,
If I say aeroplanes are bores.
If these excursions seem to you
Interesting as a rendezvous,
Rich as cake and revenue,
Handsome as hope and as untrue,
And full of travel's points of view,
Vivid as red and fresh as dew,
Come live with me and try my life,
And be my night, my warmth, my wife.

The Masters of the Heart Touched the Unknown

For thirty years what madness I have known;
Of solitude the blankness and *longueurs*,
The nervous doubt which thought and art assure,
Causeless despair, or causeless joy alone.

But when I thought of the masters of the heart,
And of the mind and of life's long disease,
And the majesty and fury of great art,
I was renewed like April's wooden trees,

And I was *parvenu* and green with hope.
They pacified the underworld in me:
—What are we? what are we not? when touched by them—
And I rehearsed their passion's history.

His senses great palms stormed by fury,
Keats left for Italy to burn away.
Emerson lived in Eden's innocence,
Thinking the world was like a summer's day.

He did not understand Hawthorne's dark works,
His endless guilt, his passion for the snow.

Mozart knew comedy's great melancholy,
And spoke of Thermidor in Figaro.

The glib, the clever, the fluent, and the vain
Pompom chrysanthemums like Oscar Wilde
Destroyed themselves in witty drawing rooms,
By earnestness and epigrams defiled.

Hugo in Jersey like a sunset shone.
Baudelaire slumped in a deadly tiredness
And saw his own face in the tragic play
Of Poe's face which like drowned Ophelia lay.

Emily Brontë gazed awestruck to see
Passion consume her brother on the moor.
Emily Dickinson went to Washington,
Falling in love like flowers to the floor.

She learned, like heroines in Henry James,
Renunciation like a tower remains
Of Christ's great castle in the Western heart.
And sang. And made a notebook of her art.

Wordsworth on walking tours found innocence,
Harked to the mariner who talked all night
Of the real world, pure consciousness as such,
As if he understood the world of light.

The poet Dostoevsky cried and sang
Of penitence, since he was criminal,
And of forgiveness, wishing to be forgiven
The crime of making love to a little girl.

These masters used their lives like Christmas trees,
They skinned themselves alive to find the truth,
They gazed upon their vileness like excrement.
They ate their hearts to sate the need for love.
They fingered every coiled snake of the mind,
Searching for choice and chance and wish and memory.

They stood upon their heads. They thrust their hands
In furnaces to find what they could bear.
They climbed down pits and wells, and praised
The wilderness, the future, and the truth.
And in the end their separated heads
Glared from a plate and criticized this life!

To Figaro in the Barbershop

From him to me what services,
Clipping the mussed hair on my head,
—He does not know how near he is
To what is under, living or dead.
Sir, in my mind there is a need
To know your intimate profession,
Figaro! not the fattest weed
On Lethe's bank in endless session

Knows more than I monotony's
Gungray and endless empty cars!
But what are your immediacies
Amid the thick and curl of hairs?
Now, through horn-rimmed glasses, you
Blink and look straight ahead of me
To what warm coast of brilliant blue?
(O tourist mind of revery!)

How shall we come to terms at last
And talk like friends with ease and poise?
All men are strangers dark and lost,
All are deceived as girls and boys.
There is a gulf which I detest
Between the self that clips my hair
And the warm beasts lounging in my head
Where past and present soil the air!

Starlight Like Intuition Pierced the Twelve

The starlight's intuitions pierced the twelve,
The brittle night sky sparkled like a tune
Tinkled and tapped out on the xylophone.
Empty and vain, a glittering dune, the moon
Arose too big, and, in the mood which ruled,
Seemed like a useless beauty in a pit;
And then one said, after he carefully spat:
"No matter what we do, he looks at it!

"I cannot see a child or find a girl
Beyond his smile which glows like that spring moon."
"—Nothing no more the same," the second said,
"Though all may be forgiven, never quite healed
The wound I bear as witness, standing by;
No ceremony surely appropriate,
Nor secret love, escape or sleep because
No matter what I do, he looks at it—"

"Now," said the third, "no thing will be the same:
I am as one who never shuts his eyes,
The sea and sky no more are marvelous,
And I no longer understand surprise!"
"Now," said the fourth, "nothing will be enough,
—I heard his voice accomplishing all wit:
No word can be unsaid, no deed withdrawn,
—No matter what is said, he measures it!"

"Vision, imagination, hope or dream,
Believed, denied, the scene we wished to see?
It does not matter in the least: for what
Is altered, if it is not true? That we
Saw goodness, as it is—*this* is the awe
And the abyss which we will not forget,
His story now the sky which holds all thought:
No matter what I think, I think of it!"

"And I will never be what once I was,"
Said one for long as narrow as a knife,
"And we will never be what once we were;
We have died once; this is a second life."
"My mind is spilled in moral chaos," one
Righteous as Job exclaimed, "now infinite
Suspicion of my heart stems what I will,
—No matter what I choose, he stares at it!"

"I am as one native in summer places
—Ten weeks' excitement paid for by the rich;
Debauched by that and then all winter bored,
The sixth declared, "His peak left us a ditch!"
"He came to make this life more difficult,"
The seventh said, "No one will ever fit
His measure's heights, all is inadequate:
No matter what I do, what good is it?"

"He gave forgiveness to us: what a gift!"
The eighth chimed in. "But now we know how much
Must be forgiven. But if forgiven, what?
The crime which was will be; and the least touch
Revives the memory: what is forgiveness worth?"
The ninth spoke thus: "Who now will ever sit
At ease in Zion at the Easter feast?
No matter what the place, he touches it!"

"And I will always stammer, since he spoke,"
One, who had been most eloquent, said, stammering.
"I looked too long at the sun; like too much light,
So too much goodness is a boomerang,"
Laughed the eleventh of the troop. "I must
Try what he tried: I saw the infinite
Who walked the lake and raised the hopeless dead:
No matter what the feat, he first accomplished it!"

So spoke the twelfth; and then the twelve in chorus:
"Unspeakable unnatural goodness is
Risen and shines, and never will ignore us;

He glows forever in all consciousness;
Forgiveness, love, and hope possess the pit,
And bring our endless guilt, like shadow's bars:
No matter what we do, he stares at it!
What pity then deny? what debt defer?
We know he looks at us like all the stars,
And we shall never be as once we were,
This life will never be what once it was!"

II

The True, the Good, and the Beautiful

He Heard the Newsboys Shouting "Europe! Europe!"

Dear Citizens,
I heard the newsboys shouting "Europe! Europe!"
It was late afternoon, a winter's day
Long as a prairie, wool and ashen gray,
And then I heard the silence, drop by drop,
And knew I must again confront myself:
"What shall I cry from my window?" I asked myself,
"What shall I say to the citizens below?
Since I have been a *privileged character*
These four years past. Since I have been excused
From the war for the lesser evil, merciless
As the years to girls who once were beautiful.
What have I done which is a little good?
What apples have I grasped, for all my years?
What starlight have I glimpsed for all my guilt?"

Then to the dead silence I said, in hope:
"I am a student of the morning light,
And of the evil native to the heart.
I am a pupil of emotion's wrongs
Performed upon the glory of this world.
Myself I dedicated long ago
—Or prostituted, shall I say?—to poetry,
The true, the good, and the beautiful,
Infinite fountains inexhaustible,
Full as the sea, old as the rocks,
                    new as the breaking surf——"

The Silence Answered Him Accusingly

"Don't fool yourself," the silence said to me,
"Don't tell yourself a noble lie once more!"

Then to the silence, being accused, I said:
"I teach the boys and the girls in my ageing youth,
I try to tell them the little I know of truth,
Saying, In the beginning is the word,
And in the end and everywhere in love,
In all love's places and in the mind of God.
Three words I speak, though they are bare and far,
                              untouchable as a star,
The true, the good, and the beautiful,
Shifting my tones as if I said to them
Candy, soda, fruits and flowers,
And if they hear, what thunderclap uproars,
                              unanimous applause,
(Extremely gratifying signs of pleasure).

'Behold the unspeakable beauty,' I say to them,
'Arise and lift your eyes and raise your hearts
In celebration and in praise because
Plato's starlight glitters amid the shocking wars.'"

Such Answers Are Cold Comfort to the Dead

"What empty rhetoric," the silence said,
"You teach the boys and girls that you may gain
The bread and wine which sensuality
Sues like a premier or a president.
These are illusions of your sense of guilt
Which shames you like a vain lie when revealed.
The other boys slumped like sacks on desperate shores."

"But well you know the life which I have lived,
Cut off, in truth, by all that I have been
From the normal pleasures of the citizen.
How often in the midnight street I passed
The party where the tin horns blew contempt

And the rich laughter rose as midnight struck,
The party where the New Year popped and foamed,
Opening like champagne or love's wet crush,
The while I studied long the art which in
America wins silence like a wall.
—I am a student of the kinds of light,
I am a poet of the wakeful night,
In new and yet unknown America.
I am a student of love's long defeat.
I gave the boys and girls my mind and art,
I taught them of the early morning light:
May I not cite this as a little good?"

Some Present Things Are Causes of True Fear

Dear Citizens,
Some say this age is hardly worth a sneer,
Yet let us applaud and cheer for certain things,
Let us not use the mind merely to jeer.

Come, let us praise the noble lies which were
To justify the millions dead in war.

Does not the honor of man appear in this,
He must deceive himself in waking consciousness?
He must have reasons noble as Jesus Christ,

Chanted like anthems in great stadiums,
Sung to Justice, Hope, and Charity,
Crusades, charades, parades, and masquerades
To guard democracy or hypocrisy.

And if the gold rush is the true career,
And if the economy has made it clear
How manic depressive Uncle Sam must be,
This metaphor is mere analogy.

Yet let us praise the noble sentiment:
That every poor boy can be president.

Come, let us praise the life in which we live
(Pretend no more that happiness does not exist!).
Have we not television and Broadway,
Victrolas, coca-colas, powerful cars?

And every principality and power
Which gives dominion in the earth and air?
Balloons, buffoons, crooners, and fine cartoons,
While every boy can be a millionaire?

When Tin Pan Alley formulates the heart,
When Hollywood fulfills the laws of dream,
When the radio is poet laureate
To Heinz, Palmolive, Swift, and Chevrolet,

(Eloquent operas soaring night and day!)
Pretend no more that happiness does not exist.
Let us not be embittered, citizens,
Because the beau ideal once glittered for us.

And if some students of the age declare:
"As for this age, it's hardly worth a jeer,
Hitler and Stalin rule our ruthless time,
This is the age of matchless worldwide crime!"

Let these romantic critics go elsewhere,
Elsewhere pretend that happiness is not like this.

Do we not have, in fine, depression and war
Certain each generation? Who would want more?
O what unsated heart would ask for more?

Lunas Are Tempting to Old Consciousness

Dear Citizens,
You are a summer people, all year long,
The seashore is the lyric of your lives,
And all hearts quicken when the breaker strives
To curve and fall, like love, forever wrong.

The strong rocks also serve the fickled soul,
The sand is rough with goodness like a towel.

Cartoons, come true, run forth in bathing suits
Cheery as flutes, spontaneous as brutes.

The self-enjoyment of the flesh is full,
The nakedness is warm and admirable.

Nevertheless the Luna Park is near,
The roller-coaster soars and dives to fear.

Hark, from the coiling track come screams like jazz,
As if they jumped from brinks of a burning house.
How much some love the gross and plunging shock
As if the screeching broke the block to luck!
                    Why do they hate their lives?
                    Why do they wish to die?
                    Believing in vicious lies,
                    Afraid to remember and cry.
Nearby in little caves a little train
Seeks mystery and darkness like a vine.
Upon a wheel the couples are revolved,
As if tomorrow's blank had been resolved.

Not far, before a door, and with a roar,
A girl's skirt is blown up! showing her hips,
Her drawers, her giggles, her belly and—surprise!
Panic like rape shudders and shakes her eyes.

Soon at the boardwalk sandwiches are rich.
Apples and cones are sticky, licky, lush.
The sated summer people now may look
At abnormality's crude picture book.

Perversity attacks the mind like a storm,
Seeing the fat lady with the gashouse form.
And as the Sunday wanes, and the flesh tires,
How the unconscious stretches, yawns, rises, wanders,
                    aspires and admires!

A Negro's face appears, to grin, if hit,
And hurt by baseballs, sublimation sweet!
Last is the gallery where the guns are neat:
The hearts not satisfied and still denied
Can win a mamma doll with a good shot.

This is the Luna of the heart's desire,
This is the play and park we all admire.

Disorder Overtakes Us All Day Long

Lo, from the muff of sleep, though darkened, strong,
I rose to read the fresh news of the age:
"Elizabeth would like to be a horse!"
(Though she'll be Queen of England, in due course.)

While in the South Pacific Southern boys
Upon a flagship raised the Stars & Bars
As if the South had won the Civil War.
Meanwhile in Washington Ickes declares

That every plant owned by the government
Should go to G.I.s when they come back home.
—What does he think this is, Utopia?

He should have stood in bed and read a poem.

These politicians have an easy time,
They can say anything, they have no shame,
Kiss babies and blow promises to all
And chant that everything is wonderful.

Awed or indifferent, bemused or ill at ease,
We who are poets play the game which is
A deadly earnest searching of all hearts
As if we struggled with a puzzle's parts,

Making the huge assumption that there is
A lucid picture which these fragments fit,
Disheveled in our clumsy pious hands,
A picture true, good, and appropriate,

Raised up, like Joseph, from the unjust pit.
—And yet suppose that we are wrong? and in all pathos
We handled foolishly essential chaos?
                    What then?
What but with patient hope to try again?

Most Things at Second Hand Through Gloves We Touch

                    Dear Citizens,
How little we have to say to each other. How much
We have, if we lay bare our hearts,
                    how much, if we
But take away the masks which hide us
From our gaze and fear, tied to the past to the last.
—O Citizens, let us frankly confess
We know our lives are lived by lies.
And, Citizens, let us not be estranged.

Surely the wars will end, there will be peace
                    (A mad world, my masters,
                    A world senseless and cruel),
Goodness will not seem strange as bearded ladies,
Riches will not be wasted by the fool,
And knowledge will not be shabby genteel.
Great works of art will not evoke the jeers
Of those whose ignorance is arrogant,
                    (A sad world, my masters,
                    Yet beautiful, withal).

Grotesque and awkward as the ironclad knights,
An arch-Shakespearean radical recites:
Duncan is dead, and Desdemona, innocent,
Is choked to death. The true, the good,
And the beautiful have been struck down
Because of what they are. No matter what you say,
This is not brushed away. No matter what you say,
This is the way it is, year by year and day by day.

The Past's Great Power Overpowers Every Hour

                    Dear Citizens,
We live upon the past and day by day
The past destroys us. Who can look back?
And who can see the back of his head?
And who can see the depths of his mind?
Who can so turn his head upon his neck
That as he runs he holds the past in view?
For who can look both north and south at once?

Come, let us play *cache-cache* or blind-man's bluff,
And pin the tail on the abundant goat
                    for all our guilt,
As if we did not know in blind-man's bluff
And all the arts and all the games each one

But seeks himself? As if you never knew at all
That everywhere you tour, you take yourself.

        When, Citizens,
I placed a seashell to my ear, I heard
My heart roar PANDEMONIUM,
                 which was to say
Every devil from hell yells in your heart,
Or shuffles coarsely as coal rides down a chute.

For is it not, in truth, an obscene play,
The past which senselessly recites in us,
Obsessive as the whippoorwill,
Like starlight on the pane, irrational,
—Inspired by what? inspired by the blaze
Of the true, the good, and the beautiful.

Awake, my dears, and be deceived no more:
What is our hope, except to tell the truth?

III

The Early Morning Light

In the real dark night of the soul, it is always
three o'clock in the morning.

—F. SCOTT FITZGERALD

The Winter Twilight, Glowing Black and Gold

That time of year you may in me behold
When Christmas trees are blazing on the walk,
Raging amid stale snow against the cold
And low sky's bundled wash, senseless as chalk.
Hissing and ravenous the brilliant plant,
Rising like eagerness, a rushing pyre
(As when the *tutti* bursts forth, and the chant
Soars up—hurrahing!—from the Easter choir).

But this is only true at four o'clock,
At noon the fifth year is once more abused,
I bring a distant girl apples and cake,
Pictures, secrets, lastly my swollen heart,
Now boxed and tied by what I know of art
—But as before accepted and refused.

She Was the Girl Within the Picture Frame

Sometimes the girl on boyhood's silver screen
—The surface makes me nervous as a cat—
Sometimes the girl Vermeer once marveled at,
For there is in her face the famous queen
Who makes all other ladies seem unseen
—Sometimes the Countess in the minuet
By Mozart, hopelessly her laureate,
—Darkling, I hardly know just what I mean.

The expensive suburb has begun to rot.
The latest boys and girls, fill of the ache
Of being, are knocking at the gate,
As if a deathless day began to dawn,
Old immortality their natural lot:

VAUDEVILLE FOR A PRINCESS

—This news is meaningless. For she was born,
Look, in some other world!—and you were not!

"My Love, My Love, My Love,
Why Have You Left Me Alone?"

Midmost my twenty-ninth eternity
When hope and expectation sank to ash,
I saw the girl superb in memory,
O far tree!—poplar!—in the lightning flash!
So that, being cowardly, I drank the fire
Which gave the coal-eyed Poe, in Baltimore,
The rocking enraptured sea of his desire,
The death he sang, black handsome nevermore.

Poor Poe! and curséd poets everywhere:
Taught by their strict art to reject the eas-
Y second-best, the well-known lesser good,
They cry exactly to the blank blue air
Love absolute, in the ancient wood
Conscious and scorned like curly Socrates.

"When You Said How You'd Give Me the Keys to My Heart"

Once waiting in that studied living room
Joy glittered and was very beautiful
As when a child you looked at vaudeville,
The song and dance man prancing like a groom,
The *savoir-faire* magician, quick as light,
—As if God said: You are again as pure
As numbers, innocence returns once more,
The past forgiven like bad dreams last night.

Your life begins once more, Eden anew!
—Real room, real life, anger and tiredness.
Hope and imagination like the blue
Which Cézanne saw, looking from loneliness:
Far off and cold the sky; and both of us
Accused and recognized by nothingness.

"One in a Thousand of Years of the Nights"

Serene, cool and composed, and easygoing
They think you are because your smiling face
Is still, and generous, and like a growing
Summer, big and rich and luminous.
The furies and the foibles do not show,
The sickness, sorrow, weakness, and the fall,
The heartbreak of the little pensive girl.
How beautiful you are you do not know,

Because you cannot see yourself at all
Because you have been beautiful so long,
—The law and lore of jewels as blind as snow.
It is so long since it was otherwise,
—And I will never be as once I was,
Furious at the crossroads, striking at what I do not know.

The Self-Betrayal Which Is Nothing New

> There are no second acts in American life.
> —F. SCOTT FITZGERALD

Look now, miraculous, *mirabilis*, and true!
The lightning flash or new America

Stumbled on foolishly! what can I do
To make myself most prosperous for her?
I asked myself, conjuring dignities:
Bestseller book or hit upon Broadway,
All of the limelight's bright banalities,
Hurried to Hollywood and a photoplay,

Or a high chair in the old academies?
Lucky or strong, I can get everything
But what I want the most! For having these,
I would be but a matinée's false king,
For in that glare and gilt, I would not be
The one who wants to know her endlessly.

I Wish I Had Great Knowledge or Great Art

I wish I had a pony or a trot
To read the obscure Latin of your heart,
Falsely I wish I were what I am not,
I would if but I could play any part
(After so many years to come to this!)
—And yet, I know, lost in this empty pass
The very shift and metamorphosis
Would merely bring me to the heart of loss.

For being what I am foists up the wish
—Once lifted from my being's element
I'd gasped with bulging eyes like a hooked fish,
Dumbfounded by my gratified intent:
Behold how in this trope, drawn from the sea,
Two worlds are separated endlessly.

"Don't Speak, Remember. Once It Happened, So It May Again."

To be with you is sudden happiness,
No matter what hours expectation rose.
It is exciting as early success
After the fears the adolescent knows,
The panicky conceit, the precious pose,
The stagefright at the footlights of the play.
But at your side joy grows as new as May
And like an orchestra the hour flows.

Or I am on a moving, modern boat
Victorious upon the seven seas
From Brooklyn to Hong-Kong. And every thought
Childhood and manhood could not appease
Forgiven in my mind. This is because
You have become my fear and my applause.

"There'll Be Others but Non So for Me"

Some *bon vivant* of the heart might have come for her,
If not for me, sick in all consciousness,
Someone as rich and gay as music is,
And not like me drawn by each straining cur
Ambition and desire loose to the game,
Some being unpossessed and generous.
She would have sung and been spontaneous,
And sauntered in the summer's foam and flame.

Yet from the sadness of what has not been,
Look how there is, above unhappiness,
A certain thing which is not meaningless;
Phoenix affection rises again and again,

Beyond the harm and loss wincing in us:
A bird still chants and is magnanimous.

"My Lips Went Livid for from the Joy of Fear"

Once by the false and rotten river, late
In the September light warm on the lawn,
We lounged all afternoon. But then came fate
As brutal as the day that I was born,
Disguised as two girls who became my luck,
Both Gibson beauties worshipped by a child.
My casual look was thoughtless as we smiled.
And then the image loomed serene and mild.

I wished that I was not my self and died,
Wishing to be the famous Southerner
Who seemed the fitting complement to her,
Is any imagination more infamous?
(After so many years to come to this!)
As if the famous past could be denied!

She Lives with the Furies of Hope and Despair

O Jan Vermeer of Delft, descend, come near
The Hudson and the West's last capital.
Here is the new Ophelia beautiful:
Only your lucid brush could make her clear
And vivid as the daughter of the Swan.
Vermeer, you too!—the early morning light
Only the sleepless see, gazing all night—
Return as faint and delicate as dawn.

THE COLLECTED POEMS OF DELMORE SCHWARTZ

Pretty and beautiful, romping and yet
Serene as statues of the classic age,
Her goodness generous in her luminous face,
Through cruel pride rack the world with rage,
Or power and vanity dance their minuet,
Her candor and her gaze are marvelous:
Marvelous shines her candor and her gaze.

Once in the Fire's Blaze I Touched the Seen

And if and when and should because I mean
To fall and dream and fall to seem because I hope
As when a fire's clear furs or fat tongues leap,
A flowing flawless flowering tulip scene:
Although I thought that only peasants sought
For happiness, strict happiness I touch
Because, though trivially, and in the bush
Of idiom's idiot (whom accident hath wrought),

I knew one scene. Let the Americas
Swallow me like a broken bird or toy,
Or come confusions of the Judgment Day,
Annulling that which was a perfect joy,
Because no matter what the cause, or long remorse,
I knew one scene of that romantic play.

The Heart Flies Up, Erratic as a Kite

Whistles like light in leaves, O light
And starlight on the heights, the reach of speech,
"I like you very much, but not tonight,"

And other true truths which no one can teach
Because emotion is a Christmas tree
Blazing and glaring after the holiday,
Quickly rushing to darkness, falling away,
Hissing like flakes, though sparkling brilliantly.

Evergreen, heart forever! The head afire
Flowing and flowering in a fountain's death
Declares all turns and burns and yet returns,
The breast arises from the falls of breath,
After the burst and lapsing of desire,
Light! Light like the deathless past remains.

Being Unused to Joyous Consciousness

Being suspicious of great happiness,
Let us a little while retreat and wait
To understand what freedom amid fate
Remains, for freedom is the sole access
To true desire. Time is most merciless
When generous. And we must hesitate;
Choose tremblingly before the deathless gate,
For this is life: nearby is nothingness.

But nonetheless, the more I think of it,
The more the promise grows, though difficult,
As in the hours when the headfirst child
Shudders amid his mother's mounting fit:
Small pain before the endless joy and guilt
With which the mind and heart will be beguiled.

He Does to Others What He Wants Them to Do to Him

To give too much and to expect too much
Is Timon's terror or tormenting track.
We of his kind but merely wish to touch,
Hold hands, joyous and generous. What lack
Makes for this drunkenness, spendthrift affection?
Like a scared horse, the heart rears up and neighs,
Running in panic from the least rejection,
And cannot play as a simple fountain plays,

Expecting nothing but to rise and fall,
Since it is false and true to hope at all
For gratitude and love. Yet who can cope
With hope, no matter what cynicism shows,
Precious and vain as adolescent prose.

Passing Beyond the Straits of Guilt and Doubt

Now I will have something to think about
Joyously for the rest of endless life.
Meanwhile, to pass the time and not to shout,
I'll think about the time cold as a knife,
And sometimes pause to laugh, or pause in awe,
Because each time I look at her again
Freshly I fall in love with her once more,
And seek new pseudonyms so that my pen

Will not reveal just who is beautiful,
Like a warm animal, yet like a queen,
Beyond my metaphor and parable,
—But this is vain, because, as she is seen,
A dunce will know exactly who I mean,
Lucky as Midas or as pitiful.

After the Passion Which Made Me a Fool

Not in this life, dark dear and pretty sister;
Not upon Eighth Street where the famous School
Of Paris echoes in colors which the painter
Drew from self-consciousness, a risky jewel;
Not in Vermont, in June, in the gay light,
Near the girl's school, used by the modern dancers;
—This is our junket to the end of the night
Mocked by true questions and by true, false answers.

—Some other life, dark pretty long hurt dear,
Some other world, perhaps, where all who marry
Live with their choice, however strong their fear,
Though like the hunch that hunchbacks carry
All of this life, it is no happiness,
Only the open wound of consciousness.

The Rumor and the Whir of Unborn Wings

Some girl serene, some girl whose being is
Affection, and in love with natural things,
In whom the summer like a choir sings,
Yet with a statue's white celebrities
Although the city falls. Golden and sleek,
Spontaneous and strong, quickened and one
To wake for joy, and to bring forth a son
Who climbs with conscious laughter every peak!

But well I know the party rush, the black
Rapids of feeling falling to a bride,
Trapped in the present or the body's lack,
Tall reason's new hat quickly thrown aside,
And soon a child rising and toiling like me
With the dark accidents of strange identity.

How Strange to Others, Natural to Me

Famous infatuation or disease
Has fixed in me until the end of life,
As if a monstrous sister or a wife
Made me a twin tied like the Siamese.
Hence must I wait in patience and in awe,
Knowing that every time I look at it,
No matter the pseudonym or counterfeit,
The same fate draws my passion like a law.

Though I conceal what is so powerful,
And fascinating as a naked queen,
And try all masks to hide from ridicule,
—It is in vain because I will be seen,
No one fools anyone except a fool:
Even the blind will know just what I mean.

"The Desperanto of Willynully"

Her father's early portrait shows
Her gaze turned inward and her hands
In a delicate diffident pose,
Tiger-lilies lightly clasped.
Who shall say he understands
What fingers on flowers signed and masked?

Ten years are used and cast aside.
This year is evil more than most.
Those lights were false. For she remains,
Rising from all that she denied,
Like great parks on this hurried coast,
And statues through the dirty rains.

Crude I Abide in This Society

Rude now with pride and with humility
I come upon a true, false argument
That every love must die because the sea
And waves of love fail like an accident.
All things must flash away; with them, love, too.
All flesh is trash and not like truth or rock
—Shall pass away! even the famous blue
Is clouded over quickly as tick-tock!

But longer, lasting longer, is the good
I found by fumbling fearful, mostly lost,
Seeking forgiveness, much misunderstood,
And all the knowledge which the sun distorts.
—But if my hope is false, these gifts will be
Like pictures to the blind a mockery,
Or Mozart to the deaf an irony,
Useless, senseless, gratuitous vanity.

Boy Wonders and Precocities Are Wrong

Who thrashed Goliath and whipped Caliban?
Let him appear and let his strength be known
In a new prodigy who snaps a stone,
Showing the dark horse underdog again
Winning against all odds and thrilling us
When bully braggart might is overthrown:
Samson and Cinderella set the tone,
They showed how virtue is victorious,

Their feats, as famous as the swaying waltz,
Make tyranny appear precarious.
—It is untrue. Such paradigms are false

In the early morning's waking consciousness:
We must be critics of success to see
What nothingness persists in victory.

Chaplin upon the Cliff, Dining Alone

Again I put away a gold rush hope:
It was my eye deluded me, my hopeful eye
Which looked at sunlight flashing like a whip.
Still in the untouched blue the sparkling sky
In the early morning light makes promises
—Too much, too little!—outstretched endlessly.
Perhaps true angels' unheard choruses?
Or maybe but a simple senseless sea?

With this uncertainty, rocked by two waves,
I paddle with my hands a middle sea
In a small boat alone; and if my gaze
Is full of anxious curiosity,
One more illusion will not fool my eye
Before I hope again as foolishly!

Twelfth Night, Next Year, a Weekend in Eternity

We who hang our hearts up, like Christmas stockings,
Find in them broken tiles fallen from the roof,
For Claus surely exists, but the thumbprint markings,
On every gift and windfall, seem to be the proof
That his hands are dirty, his fingers inkstained, and his arms weak,
So that he often pauses, carrying his heavy bag.
—Yet often in the morning, although it too can flag,
When I welcome what will come next, above the clock's tick-tick

The soul is a bird which has suddenly stopped singing:
And listening and silent, and silent and listening, and listening and silent,
It attempts to understand what its waiting has meant.
Then I think dear Claus, whose sleigh-bells are ringing,
A sad clown in polka gown whom my applause
Will once more invigorate, before the coming wars.

The Morning Light for One with Too Much Luck

Sick and used Cambridge in the suck-
Ing sound of slow rain at dead dawn
Amid the sizzle sound of car and truck
As if continually thin cloth were torn,

Blue light, plum light, fading violet light,
And then the oyster light of the wool sky:
Is this not, after all, appropriate
Light for a long used poet such as I?

The steady juices of the rain fulfill
November, ember, ashen ageing youth:
Here, my dear poet, with weather, wit, and will,
And a long look you learned to like the truth!

First Morning Is Untrue

First morning is untrue,
Then every hope is dead,
Faint light in the dark air,
When most I think of the blue,
Thinking the little I dare,
Abandoned to all care,

Capsized the heavy head,
Driven beyond old dread,
The morning faint or untrue,
A new world untrue, untrue!
Art, knowledge, and love betrayed
And the last hope lost in the blue.

Running Like Every Other Jill and Jack

O memory understood, in looking back!
This was my life amid the shocking guns
Of war far off and near. As one who runs
I was, as one, foot forward on the track,
Head turned, grotesque, loses like Orpheus
The girl gay, fey and frozen in the past,
Yet wins the smiles of beasts and knows, at last,
Touring the underworld brings happiness!

Moonlight upon the hat rack, picture, and clock,
Here have I come, here rule the modern powers.
—Forward with straining neck, darkness and lock
I open, doubled, transfixed looking back,
Glimpsing how valueless the flowing hours
Before this consciousness. Which stares and towers.

In the Blue Reign Under the Ancient Heights

He calls, enchained, forced in the darkened lights,
Giraffes of light like hanged men on the street,
Instructed by one hundred thousand nights
Entering and suffering sepia deceit.
October, December, remember summer, save

Him from the left wrong side of his face.
Guilt, like eczema, he must fear and crave,
Untutored by the mind's sufficient grace.

"Here is my heart," he chants, "here is my head,
"And here its secret parts," as he gave to all
Fruits, flowers, candy boxed, and easy to lift,
And not the rotten apple, brown with dread,
Ruined by remorse and gnawed on since the Fall,
—Surprise because they shun the fearful gift!

Demons and Angels Sing Ever in the West

The early morning always is untrue,
The self is nervous in a false distrust.
The mind knows once again how vague the blue,
And wades all memory because it must.
Leafshadows on the wall, carflights' flashed sleeves,
The city, sad and used, lies like a corpse
In the long silence as the first of leaves
Greenly, in August, to the brickwalk drops.

Now, midst the truths of silence, who believes
In noon, the city life, the thronging Square?
The present moment always is untrue!
Emotion and fantasy renew
The dreams the sleeper tries to criticize,
As light brings back old hope's ingenious lies.

How Each Bell Rings and Rings Forever More

This life is but fireworks at the fancy shore
Among the summer people, drinking gin,

Chilled by the vanity and senseless roar
Of breakers broken quicker than a pin,
By the moon broken, soaring and unheard,
—Thus we are tossed! by powers from afar,
By puns on rocks in Christ's most obscure word,
Or, when the moonlight glitters, by a star!

Look well and you will see there is no stay:
No one takes back a word, but once for all
What has been said can never be unsaid
No matter what trash and newness every day
The fresh years bring and break and take away:
This is the poet's power, this is his dread.

Cartoons of Coming Shows Unseen Before

I sat amid flickering shadows of the war,
Sad about being sad (in this capital
Where thought and art arose once, beautiful).
In the soft bland hypnotic dark I saw
Two motion pictures show how boy meets girl,
How poor young man may win the boss' daughter
Although he constantly gets in hot water;
Then came the newsreel's circumstantial whirl.

Churchill nudged Roosevelt. With handsome glee
Roosevelt winked! Upon life's peak they played
(Power is pleasure, though anxious. Power is free!)
Mah-jong or pat-a-cake with history:
They swayed like elephants in the gaiety
And the enormity of their success!

Dusk Shows Us What We Are and Hardly Mean

O evening like a frieze, late light serene,
The city fades beneath your passing poise,
The heavy huddled buildings look like toys,
The silence murmurs in the trees' thick green.
The Square—Georgian façade, or that late French
Baroque dear to the victors in the Civil War—
Thins to a postcard's picayune décor,
As the racked traffic lurches in a trench.

This transience shall instruct us like a gift.
Secret and strong beneath the city lights
(Scattered like rice in evening's growth and drift),
Our being's sources like a myth arise
From depths like mothers or the starlight's heights,
Whence we shall sing beyond the city's lies.

Hope Like the Phoenix Breast Rises Again

Who sang and sang beyond the war insane
And still must sing? by his own self betrayed
As by the city's grand and gross façade,
The skyline's emptiness and broken chain,
The empty heights, America's success,
Vain numbers infinite and meaningless,
Which bring the rich and poor boredom or pain,

Who love to go to parties, joke,
Drink and tell stories, kiss on New Year's Eve,
Having the habits of a country folk
Beneath the city's dress. Who can believe
All will arise and sing with us? Of love, love
Unknown and fabulous in old New York.

THE COLLECTED POEMS OF DELMORE SCHWARTZ

All Guilt and Innocence Turned Upside Down

He named each child Orestes, hunted down.
Two years are lived and now he sees more truth,
The furies turned to mercies and the brown
Baked ghosts kind friends, weeping with ruth
Because he turned and looked at them and fled
No more their staring faces, fearing the past
Risen renewed in him as if the dead
Sins of the parent throve in the son's breast.

This is the way, to halt, turn, and go back
To look long at the crime, to know it well,
To walk with care upon the rotten track
As agonized as all the fools in hell
—Then, then, dénouement done, like a May sun
Forgiveness frees and blesses everyone.

When Many Hopes Were Dead and Most Disguises

Nothing that he expected but surprises,
Seeking surprise like one at Luna Park
(All the grand ohs as genuine as a claque,
Cigars and dolls, exploded booby prizes);
Given each thing except the thing he wanted
(Like a rich girl who wants to be a boy)
Though what he wanted was the joy of joy
—If it was that—since each desire counted

For naught but the false hope that here, at last! . . .
—And now? While new illusion shines and rains
Like a bad Spring, what famous game remains?
To praise unmasking and unmaskers, do
With love what they did, trying to be true,
Before the shows and sketches have been passed.

VAUDEVILLE FOR A PRINCESS

The Self Unsatisfied Runs Everywhere

Sunday and sunlight ashen on the Square,
Hard wind, high blue, and clouded pennant sky,
Fifth Avenue empty in the autumn air,
As if a clear photograph of a dead day.
It was the Lord's day once, solemn and full
—Now I in an aftermath, desire spent,
Move with a will appeased and see a gull,
Then gulls drop from an arch—scythes of descent!—

Having, I think, no wish beyond the foam
Toppling to them at each fresh exercise,
Knowing success like fountains, perhaps more wise
Than one who hesitantly writes a poem
—But who, being human, wishes to be a gull,
Knows nothing much, though birds are beautiful.

Look, in the Labyrinth of Memory

Regard, O reader, how it is with me:
This year am I five thousand years of age,
Secure in Pharaoh's great society,
Like uncle Joseph, or a lesser mage.
This year will be the thirtieth eternity
The thirtieth time around the solar fire,
But if I count night watches, obviously
How I am aged in hope and dead desire!

For I am fifty years by sleepless toll:
And more than that! for every fresh event
Flashes upon the waiting wakeful soul
New light on what the past time might have meant:
And as we think of years, thinking like this,
Look, reader, how we stare at an abyss!

Today Is Armistice, a Holiday

Today is a holiday in the Western heart,
—Three cheers, my dears, we celebrate the peace!
If not a true peace, since we now take part
In a new death, this too, my peers, shall cease,
And once more some will study works of art,
And some will seek for Sunday in the Park
And some will search new dangers in the heart,
And some will find that knowledge is an ark.

But what? False ease I speak, false as the blue:
This life will be the same, precarious,
Kind, stupid, sullen, rich and marvelous
(New works are possible because of this)
—All false as feeling, for poor consciousness
Loses each day what never will return to us.

"I Am Very Exquisitely Pleased"

          Shhhhhhhhhhhh!
Suddenly certainly the music box begins
Tinkling as for the birthday of a child,
The dogs and fates awhile are reconciled
By motions soft aloft as Zeppelins.
And stops, continues, stops or mounts because
Of powers strange as stars. Or good or bad
Or both, but mostly much misunderstood,
True, false, and fabulous like Santa Claus.

             With incoherent braggadocio,
The storm flows overhead, beyond control,
—Yet who would play it like a radio
If but he could? These concerts to the soul
Have helpless strength like summer. One must go

Blindfolded and bewildered, groping and dumb,
Suspicious of the kingdom which has come.

Why Do You Write an Endless History?

"Why when you write do you most frequently
Look in your heart and stare at it both first
And last, half agonized by what you see
And half bemused, seeking what is accursed
Or blesséd in the past? And what demand
Is gratified?" I answered, hesitant
And slow: "I think I wish to understand
The causes of each great and small event

Chosen, or like thrown dice, an accident,
—My clumsiness each time I try to dance,
My mother's anger when I wore long pants:
For, as the light renews each incident,
My friends are free of guilt or I am free
Of self-accused responsibility."

from
Summer Knowledge:
New and Selected
Poems 1938–1958
(1959)

I

from
The Dream of
Knowledge

1.
The Dreams Which Begin
in Responsibilities

Out of the Watercolored Window, When You Look

When from the watercolored window idly you look
Each is but each and clear to see, not steep:
So does the neat print in an actual book
Marching as if to true conclusion, reap
The illimitable blue immensely overhead,
The night of the living and the day of the dead.

I drive in an auto all night long to reach
The apple which has sewed the sunlight up:
My simple self is nothing but the speech
Pleading for the overflow of that great cup,
The darkened body, the mind still as a frieze:
All else is merely means as complex as disease!

Someone Is Harshly Coughing as Before

Someone is harshly coughing on the next floor,
Sudden excitement catching the flesh of his throat:
Who is the sick one?
                    Who will knock at the door,
Ask what is wrong and sweetly pay attention,
The shy withdrawal of the sensitive face
Embarrassing both, but double shame is tender
—We will mind our ignorant business, keep our place.

But it is God, who has caught cold again,
Wandering helplessly in the world once more,
Now he is phthisic, and he is, poor Keats
(Pardon, O Father, unknowable Dear, this word,
Only the cartoon is lucid, only the curse is heard),
Longing for Eden, afraid of the coming war.

The past, a giant shadow like the twilight,
The moving street on which the autos slide,
The buildings' heights, like broken teeth,
Repeat necessity on every side,
The age requires death and is not denied,
He has come as a young man to be hanged once more!

Another mystery must be crucified,
Another exile bare his complex care,
Another spent head spill its wine, before
(When smoke in silence curves
                              from every fallen side)
Pity and Peace return, padding the broken floor
With heavy feet.
                    Their linen hands will hide
In the stupid opiate the exhausted war.

By Circumstances Fed

By circumstances fed
Which divide attention
Among the living and the dead,
Under the blooms of the blossoming sun,
The gaze which is a tower towers
Day and night, hour by hour,
Critical of all and of one,
Dissatisfied with every flower
With all that's been done or undone,
Converting every feature
Into its own and unknown nature;
So, once in the drugstore,
Amid all the poppy, salve and ointment,
I suddenly saw, estranged there,
Beyond all disappointment,
My own face in the mirror.

Cambridge, Spring 1937

At last the air fragrant, the bird's bubbling whistle
Succinct in the unknown unsettled trees:
O little Charles, beside the Georgian colleges
And milltown New England; at last the wind soft,
The sky unmoving, and the dead look
Of factory windows separate, at last,
From wind gray and wet:
                              for now the sunlight
Thrashes its wet shellac on brickwalk and gutter,
White splinters streak midmorning and doorstep,
Winter passes as the lighted streetcar
Moves at midnight, one scene of the past,
Droll and unreal, stiff, stilted and hooded.

II

from
Summer Knowledge

4.

The Fulfillment

At a Solemn Musick

Let the musicians begin,
Let every instrument awaken and instruct us
In love's willing river and love's dear discipline:
We wait, silent, in consent and in the penance
Of patience, awaiting the serene exaltation
Which is the liberation and conclusion of expiation.

Now may the chief musician say:
"Lust and emulation have dwelt among us
Like barbarous kings: have conquered us:
Have inhabited our hearts: devoured and ravished
—With the savage greed and avarice of fire—
The substance of pity and compassion."

Now may all the players play:
"The river of the morning, the morning of the river
Flow out of the splendor of the tenderness of surrender."

Now may the chief musician say:
"Nothing is more important than summer."

And now the entire choir shall chant:
"How often the astonished heart,
Beholding the laurel,
Remembers the dead,
And the enchanted absolute,
Snow's kingdom, sleep's dominion."

Then shall the chief musician declare:
"The phoenix is the meaning of the fruit,
Until the dream is knowledge and knowledge is a dream."

And then, once again, the entire choir shall cry, in passionate unity,
Singing and celebrating love and love's victory,
Ascending and descending the heights of assent, climbing and chanting
    triumphantly:

Before the morning was, you were:
Before the snow shone,
And the light sang, and the stone,
Abiding, rode the fullness or endured the emptiness,
You were: you were alone.

Darkling Summer, Ominous Dusk, Rumorous Rain

1

A tattering of rain and then the reign
Of pour and pouring-down and down,
Where in the westward gathered the filming gown
Of gray and clouding weakness, and, in the mane
Of the light's glory and the day's splendor, gold and vain,
Vivid, more and more vivid, scarlet, lucid and more luminous,
Then came a splatter, a prattle, a blowing rain!
And soon the hour was musical and rumorous:
A softness of a dripping lipped the isolated houses,
A gaunt gray somber softness licked the glass of hours.

2

Again, after a catbird squeaked in the special silence,
And clouding vagueness fogged the windowpane
And gathered blackness and overcast, the mane
Of light's story and light's glory surrendered and ended
—A pebble—a ring—a ringing on the pane,
A blowing and a blowing in: tides of the blue and cold
Moods of the great blue bay, and slates of gray
Came down upon the land's great sea, the body of this day
—Hardly an atom of silence amid the roar
Allowed the voice to form appeal—to call:
By kindled light we thought we saw the bronze of fall.

The Fulfillment

"Is it a dream?" I asked. To which my fellow
Answered with a hoarse voice and dulled insistence:
"Dream, is it a dream? What difference
Does it make or mean? If it is only a dream
It is the dream which we are. Dream or the last resort
Of reality, it is the truth of our minds:
We are condemned because this is our consciousness."

Where we were, if we were there, serene and shining
Each being sang and moved with the sleekness of rivers,
United in a choir, many and one, as the spires of flames in fire,
Flowing and perfected, flourishing and fulfilled forever,
Rising and falling as the carousel and palace of festival and victory.

"I was told often enough," my fellow said—
"You were told too—and you as little believed—
'Beware of all your desires. You are deceived.
(As they are deceived and deceptive, urgent and passing!)
They will be wholly fulfilled. You will be dead.
They will be gratified. And you will be dead!'"

In a fixed fascination, wonderstruck, we gazed,
Marveling at the fulfillment so long desired and praised.
There, effort was like dancing's its own pleasure.
There, all things existed purely in the action of joy—
Like light, like all kinds of light, all in the domination
        of celebration existed only as the structures of joy!

Then, as we gazed in an emotion more exhausting than mountains,
Then, when at last we knew where we had come,
It was then that we saw what was lost as we knew where we had been
(Or knew where we had been as we saw all that was lost!)
And knew for the first time the richness and poverty
Of what we had been before and were no more,
The striving, the suffering, the dear dark hooded mortality

Which we had been and never known, which we had resisted, detested,
       feared and denied, the rocks and the flowers and the faces
    of the needs and the hopes which had given us our reality!

The First Morning of the Second World

1
   Suddenly.
Suddenly and certainly, as I watched elsewhere, locked
And intent in that vigil in which the hunter is hunted
As the mind is, seeking itself, falconer, falcon and hawk, victor and
       victim,
Aware of the dry river beds, the droughts of the little deaths,
Sudden and overwhelming
Years rose and the damned waters of secret nature's underseas.
Where I had been before, tense and tired, was the edge of a winter wood.
The gun of the mind ached in my numb and narrowed gaze,
Trembled a little, aimed at the pathless wood, and the snow-clouded
       icewhite sky,
Hearing the rush not of the birds rising from bush and thicket thrashing
       and clacking,
But suddenly the pouring continuous sibilance of waterfalls,
Certainly and suddenly, for a moment's eternity, it was the
          ecstasy and stillness of the white
          wizard blizzard, the white god fallen, united,
          entirely whiteness
The color of forgiveness, beginning and hope.

Quickly then and certainly it was the river of summer, blue as the infinite
       curving blueness above us,
Little boats at anchor lolled or were lapped, and a yacht slowly glided.
It was wholly holiday, holiday absolute, a silk and saraband day, warm and
       gay and
Blue and white and vibrant as the pennants buoyant on the stadium
       near us,

White, a milk whiteness, and also all the colors flaring, melting, or flowing.
There hope was, and the hopes, and the years past,
The beings I had known and forgotten and half-remembered or
    remembered too often,
Some in rowboats sunned, as on a picnic, or waiting, as before a play,
    the picnic and *the* play of eternity as summer, siesta, and summit
—How could I have known that the years and the hopes were human
    beings hated or loved,
Or known that I knew less and more than I supposed I supposed?
(So I questioned myself, in a voice familiar and strange.)
There they were, all of them, and I was with them,
They were with me, and they were me, I was them, forever united
As we all moved forward in a consonance silent and moving
    Seated and gazing,
        Upon the beautiful river forever.

2

So we were as children on the painted wooden horses, rising and falling, of
    the carnival's carousel
Singing or smiling, at times, as the lyric of a small music tinkled above us
Saying: "The task is the round, the round is the task, the task and the round
    are a dance, and
There is nothing to think but drink of love and knowledge, and love's
    knowledge
When after and before are no more, and no more masks or unmasking,
    but only basking
(As the shining sea basks under the shining sun
In a radiance of swords and chandeliers dancing)
In the last love of knowledge, the first, when thought's abdication quickens
    thought's exaltation,
In the last blessing and sunlight of love's knowledge."

I hardly knew when my lips parted. Started to move slowly
As in the rehearsal of half-remembered memorized
    anthem, prayer, or spell
    of heartwelling gratitude and recognition.

My lips trembled, fumbled, and in the depths and death of thought
A murmur rose like the hidden humming of summer, when June sleeps
In the radiant entrancings of warm light and green security.
Fumbling, feeling for what I had long supposed I had grasped and
    cast aside as worthless,
        the sparks or glitters of pleasure, trivial and transient.

—The phrases like faces came, lucid and vivid, separate, united, sincere as
    pain
With the unity of meaning and emotion long lost, disbelieved or denied,
As I sought with the words I had known a candid translation.
So I said then, in a language intimate and half-understood:
"I did not know . . . and I knew . . . surely I once knew . . .
    I must have known . . .
Surely sometimes guessed at or suspected,
Knew and did not know what love is,
The measure of pleasure, heart of joy, the light and the heart of the light
Which makes all pleasure, joy and love come to be
As light alone gives all colors being, the measure and the treasure
Of the light which unites and distinguishes the bondage and freedom in
    unity and distinction
Which is love . . . Love? . . . Is love? What is love?"

Suddenly and certainly I saw how surely the measure and treasure of
    pleasure is being as being with, belonging
Figured and touched in the experience of voices in chorus.
        Withness is ripeness,
        Ripeness is withness,
        To be is to be in love,
            Love is the fullness of being.

3

For the gratification of action by those who enact it and at once
In the enacting behold it, actual and antiphonal, *as* antiphonal in
    another and others who are with them and look to them, toiling and
    smiling,

Know the act and their enaction and another's and others' who suffer the
    struggling,
The effort of effort, as in the toil and ecstasy of dancing and climbing,
When they know immediately within them what they see immediately
    without them, vivid in the faces, lucid in the voices,
Each creating and increasing the other, as fire in fire,
And as the lover knows *yes*, knows loving and being loved, *then*,
Kissing as he is kissed: then only effort is gratitude, then toil is ecstasy,
Suffering is satisfaction and both are neither but a third,
Beyond and containing the fear and the striving, the excitement and the
    rapture:
The self is another but with and wholly the self, loving and beloved;
Is neither no more and both, passing from both beyond to the being of
    being
Self-hooded selfhood seeks in the darkness and daylight blind and lost.

Suddenly, suddenly and certainly
Then it was as waking in the waters of morning, in winter,
Certainly it was the first morning again,
Waking in the first morning to a world outside of whiteness united,
Transfigured, possessed by the blessedness of whiteness and light,
A whiteness which was light and which was more than light,
And the inner morning and meaning of all light.

Suddenly it was the awe and moment when Adam first looked upon
    another self, a self like his own self, yet an absolute other and newness,
    being the beginning of being and love and loving and being loved
(Then all astonishment rippled to recognition, unbelievable,
Yet actual before him, growing with the certainty, serenity and majesty of
    morning).

Quickly and certainly it was the little moment when Lazarus
Thrusting aside the cold sweated linens,
Summoned by Jesus, snow and morning,
Thrust the stone to the side, the fell conclusion,
And knew all astonishment for the first time, wonderstruck
Not that he lived again, after the wood, the stone, the closing, nails, and
    black silence empty,

But that he had ever died. Knew the illusion of death confused with the
    reality of the agony of dying,
Knowing at last that death is inconceivable among the living
(Knowing the wish, the hope, the will, the luxury and ignorance of the
    thought that man can ever die)
Hearing the thunder of the news of waking from the false dream of life
    that life can ever end.

Summary Knowledge

Summer knowledge is not the winter's truth, the truth of fall,
        the autumn's fruition, vision, and recognition:
It is not May knowledge, little and leafing and growing green,
        blooming out and blossoming white,
It is not the knowing and the knowledge of the gold fall and
        the ripened darkening vineyard,
Nor the black tormented, drenched and rainy knowledge of birth,
        April, and travail,
The knowledge of the womb's convulsions, and the coiled cord's
        ravelled artery, severed and cut open,
        as the root forces its way up from the dark loam:
The agony of the first knowledge of pain is worse than death,
        or worse than the thought of death:
No poppy, no preparation, no initiation, no illusion, only
        the beginning, so distant from all knowledge
        and all conclusion, all indecision and all illusion.
Summer knowledge is green knowledge, country knowledge,
        the knowledge of growing and the supple recognition
        of the fullness and the fatness and the roundness of ripeness.
It is bird knowledge and the knowing that trees possess when
The sap ascends to the leaf and the flower and the fruit,
Which the root never sees and the root believes in the darkness
        and the ignorance of winter knowledge
—The knowledge of the fruit is not the knowledge possessed
        by the root in its indomitable darkness of ambition
Which is the condition of belief beyond conception of

experience or the gratification of fruition.
Summer knowledge is not picture knowledge, nor is it the
     knowledge of lore and learning.
It is not the knowledge known from the mountain's height, it
     is not the garden's view of the distant mountains of hidden fountains;
It is not the still vision in a gold frame, it is not the
     measured and treasured sentences of sentiments;
It is cat knowledge, deer knowledge, the knowledge of the
     full-grown foliage, of the snowy blossom and the rounding fruit.
It is the phoenix knowledge of the vine and the grape near
     summer's end, when the grape swells and the apple reddens:
It is the knowledge of the ripening apple when it moves to the
     fullness of the time of falling to rottenness and death.
For summer knowledge is the knowledge of death as birth,
Of death as the soil of all abounding flowering flaring rebirth.
It is the knowledge of the truth of love and the truth of growing:
     it is the knowledge before and after knowledge:
For, in a way, summer knowledge is not knowledge at all: it is
     second nature, first nature fulfilled, a new birth
     and a new death for rebirth, soaring and rising out
     of the flames of turning October, burning November,
     the towering and falling fires, growing more and
     more vivid and tall
In the consummation and the annihilation of the blaze of fall.

5.

Morning Bells

"I Am Cherry Alive," the Little Girl Sang

For Miss Kathleen Hanlon

"I am cherry alive," the little girl sang,
"Each morning I am something new:
I am apple, I am plum, I am just as excited
As the boys who made the Hallowe'en bang:
I am tree, I am cat, I am blossom too:
When I like, if I like, I can be someone new,
Someone very old, a witch in a zoo:
I can be someone else whenever I think who,
And I want to be everything sometimes too:
And the peach has a pit and I know that too,
And I put it in along with everything
To make the grown-ups laugh whenever I sing:
And I sing: *It is true; It is untrue;*
I know, I know, the true is untrue,
The peach has a pit, the pit has a peach:
And both may be wrong when I sing my song,
But I don't tell the grown-ups: because it is sad,
And I want them to laugh just like I do
Because they grew up and forgot what they knew
And they are sure I will forget it some day too.
They are wrong. They are wrong. When I sang my song, I knew, I knew!
I am red, I am gold, I am green, I am blue,
I will always be me, I will always be new!"

O Child, Do Not Fear the Dark and Sleep's Dark Possession

O child, when you go down to sleep and sleep's secession,
You become more and other than you are, you become
      the procession
Of bird and beast and tree: you are a chorus,
A pony among horses, a sapling in a dark forest,
Lifting your limbs and boughs to the sky, leafing.

And then you are one with the beaver, one
With the little animals warm in the sun
Resting and hidden when it is white winter:
   And in sleep's river you sleep
   Like the river's self and the marine
   Beings who mouth as they glide, nosing
    And sliding lithely and smoothly
     Gleaming serenely and sleekly.

The True-Blue American

Jeremiah Dickson was a true-blue American,
For he was a little boy who understood America, for he felt that he must
Think about *everything*; because that's *all* there is to think about,
Knowing immediately the intimacy of truth and comedy,
Knowing intuitively how a sense of humor was a necessity
For one and for all who live in America. Thus, natively, and
Naturally when on an April Sunday in an ice cream parlor Jeremiah
Was requested to choose between a chocolate sundae and a banana split
He answered unhesitatingly, having no need to think of it
Being a true-blue American, determined to continue as he began:
Rejecting the either-or of Kierkegaard, and many another European;
Refusing to accept alternatives, refusing to believe the choice of between;
Rejecting selection; denying dilemma; electing absolute affirmation:
 knowing
  in his breast
   The infinite and the gold
   Of the endless frontier, the deathless West.

"Both: I will have them both!" declared this true-blue American
In Cambridge, Massachusetts, on an April Sunday, instructed
  By the great department stores, by the Five-and-Ten,
Taught by Christmas, by the circus, by the vulgarity and grandeur of
  Niagara Falls and the Grand Canyon,
Tutored by the grandeur, vulgarity, and infinite appetite gratified and
  Shining in the darkness, of the light

On Saturdays at the double bills of the moon pictures,
The consummation of the advertisements of the imagination of the light
Which is as it was—the infinite belief in infinite hope—of Columbus,
      Barnum, Edison, and Jeremiah Dickson.

The Would-Be Hungarian

Come, let us meditate upon the fate of a little boy who wished to be
Hungarian! Having been moved with his family to a new suburb, having
    been sent to a new school, the only Catholic school in the new
    suburb,
Where all the other children were Hungarian,

He felt very sad and separate on the first day, he felt more and more
    separated and isolated
Because all the other boys and girls pitied and were sorry for him since he
    was not
Hungarian! Hence they pitied and were sorry for him so much they gave
    him handsome gifts,
Presents of comic books, marbles and foreign coins, peppermints and
    candy, a pistol, and also their devoted sympathy, pity and friendship

Making him sadder still since now he saw how all Hungarians were very
    kind and generous, and he was not

Hungarian! Hence he was an immigrant, an alien: he was and he would be,
Forever, no matter what, he could never become Hungarian!
Hungarian! Hence he went home on the first day, bearing his gifts and
    telling his parents how much he wished to be
Hungarian: in anguish, in anger,
Accusing them of depriving him, and misusing him: amusing them,
So that he rose to higher fury, shouting and accusing them

—Because of you I am a stranger, monster, orang-outang!
Because of you (his hot tears say) I am an orang-outang! and not
Hungarian! Worse than to have no bicycle, no shoes . . .

Behold how this poor boy, who wished so passionately to be
   Hungarian
Suffered and knew the fate of being American.
      Whether on Ellis Island, Plymouth Rock,
      Or in the secret places of the mind and heart
      This is America—as poetry and hope
      This is the fame, the game and the names of our fate:
      This we must suffer or must celebrate.

Is It the Morning? Is It the Little Morning?

Is it morning? Is it the little morning
Just before dawn? How big the sun is!
Are those the birds? Their voices begin
Everywhere, whistling, piercing, and joyous
All over and in the air, speaking the words
Which are more than words, with mounting consciousness:
And everything begins to rise to the brightening
Of the slow light that ascends to the blaze's lightning!

A Small Score

Meek, sang the crickets, wheat, meet, creek,
And the birds sang *tutti*, all of them:
      "Bubble, little,
      Whistle, pretty,
      Trickle, whittle,
      Lipping and dripping
      Sipping the well
      Where the fawn dipped
      Before dawn descended
      And darkness surrendered
      To the rising of the sovereign splendor,

The great bell and ball
Of supreme abundance and blazing radiance."
Thus, thus, the little birds sang in charming disorder and full chorus
To greet gravely, sweetly and most meetly
The blaze of majesty soaring in great oars,
And their twinkling and carolling grew more and more
sure as they saw the great roar of awe
arising surely all over the great blue
bay above them.

A Little Morning Music

The birds in the first light twitter and whistle,
Chirp and seek, sipping and chortling—weakly, meekly, they speak and
bubble
As cheerful as the cherry would, if it could speak when it is cherry ripe or
cherry ripening.
And all of them are melodious, erratic, and gratuitous,
Singing solely to heighten the sense of morning's beginning.
How soon the heart's cup overflows, how it is excited to delight and elation!

And in the first light, the cock's chant, roaring,
Bursts like rockets, rising and breaking into brief brilliance;
As the fields arise, cock after cock catches on fire,
And the pastures loom out of vague blue shadow,
The red barn and the red sheds rise and redden, blocks and boxes of slowly
blooming wet redness;
Then the great awe and splendor of the sun comes nearer,
Kindling all things, consuming the forest of blackness, lifting and
lighting up
All the darkling ones who slept and grew
Beneath the petals, the frost, the mystery and the mockery of the stars.
The darkened ones turn slightly in the faint light of the small morning,
Grow gray or glow green—
They are gray or green at once
In the pale cool of blue light;

They dream of that other life and that otherness
Which is the darkness, going over
Maple and oak, leafy and rooted in the ancient and famous light,
In the bondage of the soil of the past and the radiance of the future.
But now the morning is growing, the sun is soaring, all
That lights up shows, quickly or slowly, the showing plenitude of
    fountains,
And soon an overflowing radiance, actual and dazzling, will blaze and brim
    over all of us,
Discovering and uncovering all color and all kinds, all forms and all
    distances, rising and rising higher
        and higher, like a stupendous bonfire of consciousness,
Gazing and blazing, blessing and possessing all vividness and all darkness.

6.

The Kingdom of Poetry

Gold Morning, Sweet Prince

What the sad and passionate gay player of Avon avowed
With vivid exactness, eloquent variety is, as immense
As the sea is. The sea which neither the humble nor the proud
Can dam, control or master. No matter what our sense
Of existence, or whence we come or where we hope and seek
He knew us all before we were, he knew the strong, the weak,
The silly, the reticent, the pious, the powerful, the experience
Of fortune, sudden fame, extremes reversed, inevitable loss
Whether on land or sea. He knew mortality's immortality
And essential uncertainty, as he knew the land and sea.

He knew the reality of nobility.
He saw the cowering, towering power of treachery.
He hated the flakes and butterflies of lechery.
And he believed, at times, in truth, hope, loyalty and charity.

See: he saw what was and what is and what has yet to come to be:
A gentle monarch murdered in helpless sleep.
A girl by Regent Hypocrisy seduced.
A child by Archduke Ambition stabbed and killed.
A loving loyal wife by a husband loyal and brave,
Falsely suspected, by a handkerchief accused,
Stabbed by his love, his innocence, his trust
In the glib cleverness of a self-hating knave.

Look: Ophelia lolls and babbles in the river named Forever,
Never Never Never Never Never.
Cordelia is out of breath and Lear
Has learned at last that flattery is clever
That words are free, sentiments inexpensive, vows
And declarations worthless and priceless: at last he knows
How true love is sometimes speechless, always sincere.
He knows—and knows too late—that love was very near and dear.

Are all hearts and all girls always betrayed?
Is love never beyond lust, disgust, and distrust?

See: it is clear: Duncan is in his grave,
While Desdemona weeps beneath the willow tree,
Having been granted little time to weep, pray or rave:
Is this the truth, the truth which is one, eternal, and whole?
Surely the noble, the innocent, the gifted and the brave
Sometimes—surely, at times—prevail. Yet if one living soul
Is caught by cruelty and killed by trust
Whence is our consolation above or before the grave?

Ripeness is all: the rest is silence. Love
Is all; we are such stuff as love has made us
And our little life, green, ripe, or rotten, is what it is
Because of love accepted, rejected, refused and jilted, faded, raided,
    neglected or betrayed.
Some are defeated, some are mistreated, some are fulfilled, some come to
    flower and succeed
In knowing the patience of energy from the dark root to the rounding
    fruit.
And if this were not true, if love were not kind and cruel,
Generous and unjust, heartless and irresistible, painful to the savant and
    gentle to the fool,
Fecund and various, wasteful and precarious, lavish, savage, greedy and
    tender, begetting the lion and the lamb
The peacock, the spaniel, the tiger, the lizard, the chicken hawk and the dove,
All would be nothing much, all would be trivial, nothing would be enough,
    love would not be love.
For, as there is no game and no victory when no one loses
So there is no choice but the choice of love, unless one chooses
Never to love, seeking immunity, discovering nothingness.

This is the only sanctuary, this is the one asylum unless
We hide in a dark ark, and deny, refuse to believe in hope's consciousness,
Deny hope's reality, until hope descends, in the unknown, hidden and
    ultimate love,
Crying forever with all the others who are damned and hopeless that *love is
    not love.*

Gold morning, sweet prince, black night has always descended and has
    always ended,

Gold morning, prince of Avon, sovereign and king
Of reality, hope, and speech, may all the angels sing
With all the sweetness and all the truth with which you sang of anything
    and everything.

Vivaldi

e vo significando

Music consists of men in black and red climbing a broad staircase.
—GOETHE

Withness is all

In the dark church of music
    Which never is of land or sea alone

But blooms within the air inside the mind,
Patterns in motion and in action, successions
Of processionals, moving with the majesty of certainty
To part the unparted curtains, to bring the chandeliers
Into the saraband of courtiers who have bowed and curtsied,   *Allegro*
Turned somersaults in circuses, climbed masts and towers,   *con*
Or dived as from a glittering tower toward a glistening lake   *molto*
Diving daring and assured, fearless and precise
                to find in the darkness the dark church

Which music is: this is what music is
It has no meaning and is possessed by all meaning,
For music says:
        Remorse, here is the scar of healing,
        Here is a window, curiosity!
        And here, O sensuality, a sofa!
        Behold, for ambition's purposeless energy
        Mountains rising beyond the mountains
        More tense and steep than any known before

2

Devout
The processional (having a solemn majesty
Though childlike acrobats like flowers decorate   *Andante*
With flourishes and *entrechats* the passage to success
As queens serene crowned by poise, slowly
Are drawn in cars by dragons domesticated in the last of wars.)
Is uttered fully and yet freshly, newly and uniquely.
Uniquely and newly, freshly yet fully repeated then.

3

O clear soprano like the morning peal of the bluebells,
O the watercolors of the early morning,   *Scherzo*
con amore and *vivace!* dancing, prancing, galloping, rollicking!

This is the surrender to the splendor of being's becoming and being!
Here are all the flowers and the images of faces as flowers of fear   *Allegro*
 and hope, longing and despair,   *cantabile*
Here is the hour of the new blue flower
... Dissolved, consumed in this being which is the being of being,
So we are to be contained, so we are to be consumed
The iron flower of the flute possesses morning's intuition,
The cellist is as Gautama Buddha, curved like an almond,
Noah conducts the ark of all the dark beauty,
The first violinist is Assisi's Francis,
   blessing the trees, the cats, the birds,
    calling to them, his brothers and his
     sisters
The full orchestra responds to the virtuoso's cadenza:
"Love is the dark secret of everything
Love is the open secret of everything,
An open secret useless as the blue!"

Music is not water, but it moves like water,
It is not fire, but it soars as warm as the sun.
It is not rock, it is not fountain,

But rock and fountain, clock and mountain
Abide within it, bound together,
In radiance pulsing vibrating and reverberating,
Dominating the domination of the weather!

4

The music flowing as a river and a city
            and a city ringed about a river   *Adagio*
            and a river mastered by a city   *con*
Has destiny's look; the dictates of the heart   *molto*
And the heart's dictatorship must submit
To the score of the lyre gentled like all fire
To ashen falling failure. The music, although unseen,
Is hushed nor more nor less than snow's fall, slowly falling,
After being possessed by the dynasty of destiny
and then,
      and then,
Is suddenly more selfdelighting than a troop of birds in swinging   *Allegro*
      singing ringing curving flights   *vivace*
In curves and swerves, dipping and perching, perching and soaring, sailing.

The music declares:
"Is this what you want? Is this the goodness for which you have   *Coda*
      been here convened?
"To be, to become, and to participate in the sweet congress of serene
      attention?"
Silent, attentive, motionless, waiting,
      Save for the heart clutching itself and the hushed breathing
(A sudden cough!) sticks-in the enchantment's dancing,

The answered question is: Our being. Our presence. Our surrender.
Consciousness has consented, is consumed, has surrendered, to hear only
      the players playing:
Consciousness has become only and purely listening,
      The vivid world has been barred,
      The press of desire shut out
      All lights are dim save for this swan, unseen

The port and ark of Panurge, sailing the darkness
All desire consumed except the desire of this being,
The presence of this being, the being of this presence,
This present, this being: *this* is the being
The dream strives towards, and passion presses forward
   (Above the clouds and the shrouds,
   Rising like a plane forever)
   Far from the world of Caesar and Venus, calculation and sensuality,
     ratiocination and frustration,
This is the dark city of the hidden innermost wish,
   The motion beyond emotion,
     The power beyond and free of power,
       Beyond beyond within the withness of witness,
This is the immortality of mortality, this
Is supreme consciousness,
The self-forgetting in the self possessed and mastered
   In the elation of being open to all relation
No longer watchful, wakeful, guarded, wary, no longer striving and
   climbing:
This is the immortality of immortality
   Deathless and present in the presence of the deathless present.
This is the grasped reality of reality, moving forward
     Now and forever.

Sterne

To Gloria Macdonald

Held on bondage day and night
By dear my Lord Fauconberg. With whom I dined
At the Boar's Head. There the whole Pandemonium,
Assembled, supped. Have just been eating chicken, weeping,
Seated and weeping, the tears fall over it,
A bitter sauce.

I have doubled the Cape of Good Hope.
I have looked in Yorick's face.

I wish I were in Arno's vale,
Though here at Coxwold, days are princely
—A land of plenty, and I dine
On trout, on venison, and on wild fowl.

Yet as I eat my strawberries, for want of you
I am as melancholy as a cat. I have a cat now.
Sits beside me, quietly and gravely purrs
To my sorrows, gazes at me solemnly
As if he knew the reason of my pain!

—How soothable the heart is, dear Eliza!
Supported when it sinks pathetically
By a poor beast purring harmoniously!
When a poor cat purrs *pianissimo*
Me, me, poor Yorick harks to an anodyne
Dark and sweet as the poppy, fresh and rash as the cock's cocorico!

. . . Love, alas, has fled with thee
Whom all the night my wakeful eyes
(While all the day is blind to me!)
Imagine, summon, idolize
Standing before dim gates, or pitifully
(Such is my hope, my vanity!)
Waiting in the great green park most patiently!

Swift
_____

What shall Presto do for pretty prattle
To entertain his dears? Sunday: lightning fifty times!
This week to Flanders goes the Duke of Ormond!
Shall hope of him, although he loves me well!

All of my hopes now possible,
None certain. As, my lampoon
Talked up all over, cried up to the sky

—You are an impudent slut to be so positive
Though all has gone just as you said it would!
Sirrah! write constantly! don't I write every day
And sometimes twice? Stella writes like an emperor.

Sirrah, I am surprised forever—by myself!
Or by the others—dee dee: an angel child
Stupid in me, stupid or innocent
Astonished by the gush of vanity
The stone and eyes of pride—yet equally
By the least straw or glitter of nobility!
—Faith, Madame Dingley, what think you of the world to come?
Patience! Patience is a gay thing—O saucy rogues,
Patience is better than knowledge: be gay till I return.

Mr. Harley speaks every kind thing to me.
Truly, I do believe, would serve me if I stayed
—Called at the coffee house, stayed there a while,
Coldly conversed with Mr. Addison:

All our friendship and dearness now are off:
Is it not odd? I think he has used me ill:
I have as little pleasure as anyone
In all the world, although I am
In full favor with the entire ministry.
Nothing gives Presto any dream of happiness
But letters now and then from his deelest ones.

The pride of power, the pride and pleasure of place and power are Towers
And trivial toys which lure me grievously
Ravaging furiously in a lunation's infuriation . . .
Bursting the Rome in my head, my empire!
Gulliver? Gullible! The Caesars in my heart
Tell me how all infamy is possible,
And certain treacheries extremely probable!

I must take leave of deelest MD now. Prithee,
Be merry, patient girls and love your Presto.
I have read all the trash and I am weary:

Deelest lives, there is peace and quiet with thee
And thee alone. None have the leisure here for little things.
Farewell again, dear rogues; I am never happy
But when I think of thee MD. Sirrah,
I have had enough of courts and ministries.
I wish I were once more at Laracor:
Faith, do you know each syllable I write
I hold my lips exact for all the world
As if I talked the little language with MD.

Yesterday died the Duke of Ormond's daughter:
Poor dear, she was with child. She was
My favourite pet—save thee—I hardly knew
A being more valuable, more beautiful,
Of more nobility. I fear the certainty
That she was thrown away quite carelessly,
And merely lacked care. 'Tis clear, at any rate,
That she was very healthy naturally.
—Her Lord's a puppy. I'll no more of him,
Now that he's lost his only valuable . . .
—I hate life when I see it thus exposed
To accidents like these, so many thousands
Burthening the earth with their stupidity,
While such as she must die—abruptly—pointlessly.

Somebody is coming wants a little place.
My heart is set upon the cherry trees
By the river side. My saucy sluts
Farewell my deelest Nite poo dee MD . . .

Y'see a Sea that's ten miles wide, a town
On t'other side, ships sailing in the Sea
Discharging great Canons at MDs and mee,
I see a great Sky, Moon and Stars, and ALL:
                    I am a Fool.

Hölderlin

Now as before do you not hear their voices
Serene in the midst of their rejoicing
Chanting to those who have hopes and make choices
Clear as the birds in the thick summer foliage:
>   *It is! It is!*
>   *We are! We are!*
Clearly, as if they were us, and not us,
Hidden like the future, distant as the stars,
Having no more meaning than the fullness of music,
Chanting from the pure peaks where success,
Effort and desire are meaningless,
Surpassed at last in the joy of joy,
Chanting at last the blue's last view:
>   *It is! It is!*
>   *This is eternity! Eternity is now!*

Baudelaire

When I fall asleep, and even during sleep,
I hear, quite distinctly, voices speaking
Whole phrases, commonplace and trivial,
Having no relation to my affairs.

Dear Mother, is any time left to us
In which to be happy? My debts are immense.
My bank account is subject to the court's judgment.
I know nothing. I cannot know anything.
I have lost the ability to make an effort.
But now as before my love for you increases.
You are always armed to stone me, always:
It is true. It dates from childhood.

For the first time in my long life
I am almost happy. The book, almost finished,
Almost seems good. It will endure, a monument
To my obsessions, my hatred, my disgust.

Debts and inquietude persist and weaken me.
Satan glides before me, saying sweetly:
"Rest for a day! You can rest and play today.
Tonight you will work." When night comes,
My mind, terrified by the arrears,
Bored by sadness, paralyzed by impotence,
Promises: "Tomorrow: I will tomorrow."
Tomorrow the same comedy enacts itself
With the same resolution, the same weakness.

I am sick of this life of furnished rooms.
I am sick of having colds and headaches:
You know my strange life. Every day brings
Its quota of wrath. You little know
A poet's life, dear Mother: I must write poems,
The most fatiguing of occupations.

I am sad this morning. Do not reproach me.
I write from a café near the post office,
Amid the click of billiard balls, the clatter of dishes,
The pounding of my heart. I have been asked to write
"A History of Caricature." I have been asked to write
"A History of Sculpture." Shall I write a history
Of the caricatures of the sculptures of you in my heart?

Although it costs you countless agony,
Although you cannot believe it necessary,
And doubt that the sum is accurate,
. Please send me money enough for at least three weeks.

The Kingdom of Poetry

This is like light.

   This is light,
Useful as light, as charming and
   as enchanting . . .

. . . Poetry is certainly
More interesting, more valuable,
   and certainly more charming
Than Niagara Falls, the Grand Canyon, the Atlantic Ocean
And other much admired natural phenomena.
It is useful as light, and as beautiful.
   It is preposterous
Precisely, making it possible to say
One cannot carry a mountain, but a poem can be carried all over.
   It is monstrous
Pleasantly, for poetry can say, seriously or in play:

"Poetry is better than hope,
"For Poetry is the patience of hope, and all hope's vivid pictures,
"Poetry is better than excitement, it is far more delightful,
"Poetry is superior to success, and victory, it endures in serene blessedness
"Long after the most fabulous feat like fireworks has mounted and fallen.
"Poetry is a far more powerful and far more enchanting animal
"Than any wood, jungle, ark, circus or zoo possesses."

For Poetry magnifies and heightens reality:
Poetry says of reality that if it is magnificent, it is also stupid:
For poetry is, in a way, omnipotent;
For reality is various and rich, powerful and vivid, but it is not enough
Because it is disorderly and stupid or only at times, and erratically,
   intelligent:
For without poetry, reality is speechless or incoherent:
It is inchoate, like the pomp and bombast of thunder:
Its perorations verge upon the ceaseless oration of the ocean:
For reality's glow and glory, without poetry,
Fade, like the red operas of sunset,

The blue rivers and windows of morning.

The art of poetry makes it possible to say: *Pandemonium.*
 For poetry is gay and exact. It says:
 "The sunset resembles a bull-fight.
 "A sleeping arm feels like soda, fizzing."
Poetry resurrects the past from the sepulchre, like Lazarus.
It transforms a lion into a sphinx and a girl.
It gives to a girl the splendor of Latin.
It transforms the water into wine at each marriage in Cana of Galilee.
For it is true that poetry invented the unicorn, the centaur and the
 phoenix.
Hence it is true that poetry is an everlasting Ark,
An omnibus containing, bearing and begetting all the mind's animals.
Whence it is that poetry gave and gives tongue to forgiveness
Therefore a history of poetry would be a history of joy, and a history of
 the mystery of love
For poetry provides spontaneously, abundantly and freely
The petnames and the diminutives which love requires and without which
 the mystery of love cannot be mastered.

For poetry is like light, and it is light.
It shines over all, like the blue sky, with the same blue justice.
For poetry is the sunlight of consciousness:
It is also the soil of the fruits of knowledge
  In the orchards of being:
 It shows us the pleasures of the city.
 It lights up the structures of reality.
 It is a cause of knowledge and laughter:
 It sharpens the whistles of the witty:
 It is like morning and the flutes of morning, chanting and enchanted.
 It is the birth and rebirth of the first morning forever.
Poetry is quick as tigers, clever as cats, vivid as oranges,
Nevertheless, it is deathless: it is evergreen and in blossom; long after the
 Pharaohs and Caesars have fallen,
It shines and endures more than diamonds,
This is because poetry is the actuality of possibility. It is
 The reality of the imagination,
 The throat of exaltation,

The procession of possession,
The motion of meaning and
The meaning of morning and
The mastery of meaning.

The praise of poetry is like the clarity of the heights of the mountains.
The heights of poetry are like the exaltation of the mountains.
It is the consummation of consciousness in the country of the morning!

Seurat's Sunday Afternoon Along the Seine

To Meyer and Lillian Schapiro

What are they looking at? Is it the river?
The sunlight on the river, the summer, leisure,
Or the luxury and nothingness of consciousness?
A little girl skips, a ring-tailed monkey hops
Like a kangaroo, held by a lady's lead
(Does the husband tax the Congo for the monkey's keep?)
The hopping monkey cannot follow the poodle dashing ahead.

Everyone holds his heart within his hands:

A prayer, a pledge of grace or gratitude
A devout offering to the god of summer, Sunday and plenitude.

The Sunday people are looking at hope itself.

They are looking at hope itself, under the sun, free from the teething
    anxiety, the gnawing nervousness
Which wastes so many days and years of consciousness.

The one who beholds them, beholding the gold and green
Of summer's Sunday is himself unseen. This is because he is
Dedicated radiance, supreme concentration, fanatically threading
The beads, needles and eyes—at once!—of vividness and permanence.
He is a saint of Sunday in the open air, a fanatic disciplined

THE COLLECTED POEMS OF DELMORE SCHWARTZ

By passion, courage, passion, skill, compassion, love: the love of life and
    the love of light as one, under the sun, with the love of life.

Everywhere radiance glows like a garden in stillness blossoming.

Many are looking, many are holding something or someone
Little or big: some hold several kinds of parasols:
Each one who holds an umbrella holds it differently
One hunches under his red umbrella as if he hid
And looked forth at the river secretly, or sought to be
Free of all of the others' judgment and proximity.
Next to him sits a lady who has turned to stone, or become a boulder,
Although her bell-and-sash hat is red.
A little girl holds to her mother's arm
As if it were a permanent genuine certainty:
Her broad-brimmed hat is blue and white, blue like the river, like the
    sailboats white,
And her face and her look have all the bland innocence,
Open and far from fear as cherubims playing harpsichords.
An adolescent girl holds a bouquet of flowers
As if she gazed and sought her unknown, hoped-for, dreaded destiny.
No hold is as strong as the strength with which the trees,
Grip the ground, curve up to the light, abide in the warm kind air:
Rooted and rising with a perfected tenacity
Beyond the distracted erratic case of mankind there.
Every umbrella curves and becomes a tree,
And the trees curving, arise to become and be
Like the umbrella, the bells of Sunday, summer, and Sunday's luxury.
Assured as the trees is the strolling dignity
Of the bourgeois wife who holds her husband's arm
With the easy confidence and pride of one who is
—She is sure—a sovereign Victorian empress and queen.
Her husband's dignity is as solid as his *embonpoint*:
He holds a good cigar, and a dainty cane, quite carelessly.
He is held by his wife, they are each other's property,
Dressed quietly and impeccably, they are suave and grave
As if they were unaware or free of time, and the grave,
Master and mistress of Sunday's promenade—of everything!
—As they are absolute monarchs of the ring-tailed monkey.

If you look long enough at anything
It will become extremely interesting;
If you look very long at anything
It will become rich, manifold, fascinating:

If you can look at any thing for long enough,
You will rejoice in the miracle of love,
You will possess and be blessed by the marvelous blinding radiance of love,
    you will be radiance.
Selfhood will possess and be possessed, as in the consecration of marriage,
    the mastery of vocation, the mystery of gift's mastery, the deathless
    relation of parenthood and progeny.
All things are fixed in one direction:
    We move with the Sunday people from right to left.

The sun shines
In soft glory
Mankind finds
The famous story
Of peace and rest, released for a little while from the tides of weekday
    tiredness, the grinding anxiousness
Of daily weeklong lifelong fear and insecurity,
The profound nervousness which in the depths of consciousness
Gnaws at the roots of the teeth of being so continually, whether in sleep or
    wakefulness,
We are hardly aware that it is there or that we might ever be free
Of its ache and torment, free and open to all experience.

The Sunday summer sun shines equally and voluptuously
Upon the rich and the free, the comfortable, the *rentier*, the poor, and those
    who are paralyzed by poverty.
Seurat is at once painter, poet, architect, and alchemist:
The alchemist points his magical wand to describe and hold the Sunday's
    gold,
Mixing his small alloys for long and long
Because he wants to hold the warm leisure and pleasure of the holiday
Within the fiery blaze and passionate patience of his gaze and mind
Now and forever: O happy, happy throng,
It is forever Sunday, summer, free: you are forever warm

THE COLLECTED POEMS OF DELMORE SCHWARTZ

Within his little seeds, his small black grains,
He builds and holds the power and the luxury
With which the summer Sunday serenely reigns.

—Is it possible? It is possible!—
Although it requires the labors of Hercules, Sisyphus, Flaubert, Roebling:
The brilliance and spontaneity of Mozart, the patience of a pyramid,
And requires all these of the painter who at twenty-five
Hardly suspects that in six years he will no longer be alive!
—His marvelous little marbles, beads, or molecules
Begin as points which the alchemy's magic transforms
Into diamonds of blossoming radiance, possessing and blessing the visual:
For look how the sun shines anew and newly, transfixed
By his passionate obsession with serenity
As he transforms the sunlight into the substance of pewter, glittering,
    poised and grave, vivid as butter,
In glowing solidity, changeless, a gift, lifted to immortality.

The sunlight, the soaring trees and the Seine
Are as a great net in which Seurat seeks to seize and hold
All living being in a parade and promenade of mild, calm happiness:
The river, quivering, silver blue under the light's variety,
Is almost motionless. Most of the Sunday people
Are like flowers, walking, moving toward the river, the sun, and the river
    of the sun.
Each one holds some thing or some one, some instrument
Holds, grasps, grips, clutches or somehow touches
Some form of being as if the hand and fist of holding and possessing,
Alone and privately and intimately, were the only genuine lock or bond of
    blessing.

A young man blows his flute, curved by pleasure's musical activity,
His back turned upon the Seine, the sunlight, and the sunflower day.
A dapper dandy in a top hat gazes idly at the Seine:
The casual delicacy with which he holds his cane
Resembles his tailored elegance.
He sits with well-bred posture, sleek and pressed,
Fixed in his niche: he is his own mustache.
A working man slouches parallel to him, quite comfortable,

Lounging or lolling, leaning on his elbow, smoking a meerschaum,
Gazing in solitude, at ease and oblivious or contemptuous
Although he is very near the elegant young gentleman.
Behind him a black hound snuffles the green, blue ground.
Between them, a wife looks down upon
The knitting in her lap, as in profound
Scrutiny of a difficult book. For her constricted look
Is not in her almost hidden face, but in her holding hands
Which hold the knitted thing as no one holds
Umbrella, kite, sail, flute or parasol.

This is the nervous reality of time and time's fire which turns
Whatever is into another thing, continually altering and changing all
    identity, as time's great fire burns (aspiring, flying and dying),
So that all things arise and fall, living, leaping and fading, falling, like
    flames aspiring, flowering, flying and dying—
Within the uncontrollable blaze of time and of history:
Hence Seurat seeks within the cave of his gaze and mind to find
A permanent monument to Sunday's simple delight; seeks deathless joy
    through the eye's immortality;
Strives patiently and passionately to surpass the fickle erratic quality of
    living reality.

Within this Sunday afternoon upon the Seine
Many pictures exist inside the Sunday scene:
Each of them is a world itself, a world in itself (and as a living child links
    generations, reconciles the estranged and aged so that a grandchild is a
    second birth, and the rebirth of the irrational, of those who are forlorn,
    resigned or implacable),
Each little picture links the large and small, grouping the big
Objects, connecting them with each little dot, seed or black grain
Which are as patterns, a marvelous network and tapestry,
Yet have, as well, the random freshness and radiance
Of the rippling river's sparkle, the frost's astonishing systems,
As they appear to morning's waking, a pure, white delicate stillness and
    minuet,
In December, in the morning, white pennants streaked upon the
    windowpane.

He is fanatical: he is at once poet and architect,
Seeking complete evocation in forms as strong as the Eiffel Tower,
Subtle and delicate too as one who played a Mozart sonata, alone, under
    the spires of Notre-Dame.
Quick and utterly sensitive, purely real and practical,
Making a mosaic of the little dots into a mural of the splendor of
    order:
Each micro pattern is the dreamed of or imagined macrocosmos
In which all things, big and small, in willingness and love surrender
To the peace and elation of Sunday light and sunlight's pleasure, to the
    profound measure and order of proportion and relation.

He reaches beyond the glistening spontaneity
Of the dazzled Impressionists who follow
The changing light as it ranges, changing, moment by moment, arranging
    and charming and freely bestowing
All freshness and all renewal continually on all that shows and flows.

Although he is very careful, he is entirely candid.
Although he is wholly impersonal, he has youth's frankness and, such is his
    candor,
His gaze is unique and thus it is intensely personal:
It is never facile, glib, or mechanical,
His vision is simple: yet it is also ample, complex, vexed, and profound
In emulation of the fullness of Nature maturing and enduring and toiling
    with the chaos of actuality.

An infinite variety within a simple frame:
Countless variations upon a single theme!
Vibrant with what soft soft luster, what calm joy!
This is the celebration of contemplation,
This is the conversion of experience to pure attention,
Here is the holiness of all the little things
Offered to us, discovered for us, transformed into the vividest
    consciousness,
After the shallowness or blindness of experience,
After the blurring, dirtying sooted surfaces which, since Eden and since
    birth,

Make all the little things trivial or unseen,
Or tickets quickly torn and thrown away
En route by rail to an ever-receding holiday:
—Here we have stopped, here we have given our hearts
To the real city, the vivid city, the city in which we dwell
And which we ignore or disregard most of the luminous day!

. . . Time passes: nothing changes, everything stays the same. Nothing is
    new
Under the sun. It is also true
That time passes and everything changes, year by year, day by day,
Hour by hour. Seurat's *Sunday Afternoon along the Seine* has gone away,
Has gone to Chicago: near Lake Michigan,
All of his flowers shine in monumental stillness fulfilled.
And yet it abides elsewhere and everywhere where images
Delight the eye and heart, and become the desirable, the admirable, the
    willed
Icons of purified consciousness. Far and near, close and far away
Can we not hear, if we but listen to what Flaubert tried to say,
Beholding a husband, wife and child on just such a day:
Ils sont dans le vrai! They are with the truth, they have found the way
The kingdom of heaven on earth on Sunday summer day.
Is it not clear and clearer? Can we not also hear
The voice of Kafka, forever sad, in despair's sickness trying to say:
"Flaubert was right: *Ils sont dans le vrai!*
Without forbears, without marriage, without heirs,
Yet with a wild longing for forbears, marriage, and heirs:
They all stretch out their hands to me: but they are too far away!"

THE COLLECTED POEMS OF DELMORE SCHWARTZ

7.

The Deceptive Present, the Phoenix Year

The World Was Warm and White When I Was Born

The world was warm and white when I was born:
Beyond the windowpane the world was white,
A glaring whiteness in a leaded frame,
Yet warm as in the hearth and heart of light.
Although the whiteness was almond and was bone
In midnight's still paralysis, nevertheless
The world was warm and hope was infinite
All things would come, fulfilled, all things would be known
All things would be enjoyed, fulfilled, and come to be my own.

How like a summer the years of youth have passed!
—How like the summer of 1914, in all truth!—
Patience, my soul, the truth is never known
Until the future has become the past
And then, only, when the love of truth at last
Becomes the truth of love, when both are one,
Then, then, then, Eden becomes Utopia and is surpassed:
For then the dream of knowledge and knowledge knows
Motive and joy at once wherever it goes.

I Am a Book I Neither Wrote nor Read

I am a book I neither wrote nor read,
A comic, tragic play in which new masquerades
Astonishing as guns crackle like raids
Newly each time, whatever one is prepared
To come upon, suddenly dismayed and afraid,
As in the dreams which make the fear of sleep
The terror of love, the depth one cannot leap.

How the false truths of the years of youth have passed!
Have passed at full speed like trains which never stopped
There where I stood and waited, hardly aware,

How little I knew, or which of them was the one
To mount and ride to hope or where true hope arrives.

I no more wrote than read that book which is
The self I am, half-hidden as it is
From one and all who see within a kiss
The lounging formless blackness of an abyss.

How could I think the brief years were enough
To prove the reality of endless love?

The Conclusion

How slow time moves when torment stops the clock!
How dormant and delinquent, under the dawn,
The uproarious roaring of the bursting cock:
Now pain ticks on, now all and nothing must be borne,
And I remember: pain is the cost of being born.

2

For when the flowers of infatuation fade
The furs which love in all its warmth discloses
Become the fires of pride and are betrayed
By those whom love has terrified and pride has made afraid.

No matter what time prepares, no matter how time amazes
The images and hopes by which we love or die,
Pride is not love, and pride is merely pride,
Until it becomes a living death which denies
How it is treacherous, and faithless: how it betrays
Everyone, one by one, and every vow,
Seeking praise absolute, hides with other whores
Whom pride and time seduces and love ignores.

THE COLLECTED POEMS OF DELMORE SCHWARTZ

This will be true long after heart and heart
Have recognized and forgotten all that was ripening, ripe, rotten-ripe and
    rotten:
Have known too soon, too soon by far how much of love has been forgotten:
Have known the little deaths before death do us part:
Nothing will ever pass at last to nothingness beyond decay
Until the night is all, and night is known all day.

The Sequel

First love is first death. There is no other.
There is no death. But all men live forever
And die forever. If this were not true,
We would be more deceived, still more deceived
Than this belief deceives us, whether or not
We think that we believe or we think
Those who believe are deceived. But to believe
That death is the sweet asylum of nothingness:
Is the cruel sick dream of the criminal and the suicide:
Of those who deny reality, of those who steal from consciousness,
Of those who are often fugitive, of those who are afraid to live,
Of those who are terrified by love, and
      Those who try—before they
          Try to die—to disappear
            And hide.

The Dark and Falling Summer

The rain was full of the freshness
    and the fresh fragrance of darkening grapes,
The rain was as the dark falling of hidden

And fabulous grapes ripening, great blue thunderheads moving slowly,
    slowly blooming.
The dark air was possessed by the fragrance of freshness,
By a scattered and confused profusion until
After the tattering began, the pouring down came
And plenitude descended, multitudinous:
Everywhere was full of the pulsing of the loud and fallen dark.

The Winter Twilight, Glowing Black and Gold

That time of year you may in me behold
When Christmas trees are blazing on the walk,
Raging against stale snow and the cold
And low sky's bundled wash, deadwhite as chalk.

Hissing and ravenous the brilliant plant:
Rising like eagerness, a rushing pyre
(As when the *tutti* foams up and the chant
Soars up—hurrahing!—from the Easter choir).

But this is only true at four o'clock.

At noon the fifth year is again abused:
I bring a distant girl apples and cake,
Marbles, pictures, secrets, my swollen heart
Now boxed in the learning and music of art:

But once more, as before, accepted and refused.

All of the Fruits Had Fallen

All of the fruits had fallen,
The bears had fallen asleep,

And the pears were useless and soft
Like used hopes, under the starlight's
Small knowledge, scattered aloft
In a glittering senseless drift:
The jackals of remorse in a cage
Drugged beyond mirth and rage.

Then, then, the dark hour flowered!
Under the silence, immense
And empty as far-off seas,
I wished for the innocence
Of my stars and my stones and my trees
All the brutality and inner sense
A dog and a bird possess,
The dog who barked at the moon
As an enemy's white fang,
The bird that thrashed up the bush
And soared to soar as it sang,
A being all present as touch,
Free of the future and past
—Until, in the dim window glass,
The fog or cloud of my face
Showed me my fear at last!

The Foggy, Foggy Blue

When I was a young man, I loved to write poems
    And I called a spade a spade
And the only only thing that made me sing
    Was to lift the masks at the masquerade.
I took them off my own face,
    I took them off others too
And the only only wrong in all my song
    Was the view that I knew what was true.

Now I am older and tireder too
     And the tasks with the masks are quite trying.
I'll gladly gladly stop if I only only knew
     A better way to keep from lying,
And not get nervous and blue
     When I said something quite untrue:
I looked all around and all over
     To find something else to do:
I tried to be less romantic
     I tried to be less starry-eyed too:
But I only got mixed up and frantic
     Forgetting what was false and what was true.

But tonight I am going to the masked ball,
     Because it has occurred to me
That the masks are more true than the faces:
     —Perhaps this too is poetry?
I no longer yearn to be naïve and stern
     And masked balls fascinate me:
Now that I know that most falsehoods are true
     Perhaps I can join the charade?
That is, at any rate, my new and true view:
     Let live and believe, I say.
The only only thing is to believe in everything:
     It's more fun and safer that way!

I Did Not Know the Truth of Growing Trees

On the suburban street, guarded by patient trees
Two family houses huddled. As I passed the lamplight's teas,
In the mid-winter evening when the snow's light made
Of the glowing supper hour a blue lost shade:
A blond girl stood at the window and looked toward the snow:
Her glance hid hatred's hot-bed, which had sickened long ago,
And then our glances met: and I fell suddenly,
My eyes reached to touch the bark of the nearest tree,

My hands stretched to touch the rough and broken
Bark to feel, again and again, in instance and a token
Of reality's texture. The picture window showed
How often beauty conceals the heart's diseased death-ridden toad:
How often romance is a passing dance: but the tree is true:
And this is what I did not know, although I always thought I knew how a
    growing tree is true.

All of Them Have Gone Away, Although They Once Were Near

All of them are fixed, although each has gone away,
Eva and Sinbad, dead these seven years,
Betty and Mrs. Muller, heroines in a play,
Which has not been performed: the soul is in arrears
To all that touch it slightly or ring it like a bell,
For once they have departed, I stand as on a roof
And see them as they were then, troubled and unwell,
For all these things are still now and now I am aloof
Not anxious, nor impetuous, not nervous, but free,
Knowing the past unalterable, and that it must now be
Like the sun in the sky and the sun in the great unsettled forever drunken
    sea!

I Did Not Know the Spoils of Joy

When that I was and a little tiny boy,
    With a hey ho, the wind and the rain.
I did not know the truth of joy:
    I thought that life was passed in pain.

Then, when I came to thought and art,
    The flowers of hope began to wilt:

I glowed disgusted with my heart,
    As cynicism salved my guilt.

When youthful hopes proved true and false,
    As hard-earned riches fade and pall,
I thought the mind lied like a waltz
    Which chants love as a brilliant ball.

And when I followed where sleep fled
    I woke amid the mixing dream:
My self or others hurt my head,
    I heard the frigid Furies scream.

Yet, when I fled from this estate,
    I drove the quickest car to bliss:
With drunken fools I struck at fate,
    Charmed, by the falls of consciousness.

A great while ago the world began,
    With a ho ho, the fog and the mist,
The Pharaohs are in power again,
    The endless wind and rain persist.

Illusion and madness dim the years:
    Mere parodies of hope, at best,
And yet, through all these mounting fears,
    How I am glad that I exist!
        For now I know the spoils of joy:
        I only knew the spells of joy.

How strange the truth appears at last!
I feel as old as wornout shoes:
I know what I have lost or missed,
Or certainly will some day lose
I know the follies whom I kissed,
Whom self-deception will accuse——

And yet this knowledge, like the Jews,
Can make me glad that I exist!

Although I must my self accuse
Not when I win, but when I lose:
Although this knowledge comes and goes,
Although the wind and the rain persist:
How I am glad that I exist!
　　　With a hey ho, the stupid past,
　　　　　And a ho ho, a ha ha and a hurrah at last.

I Waken to a Calling

I waken to a calling,
A calling from somewhere down, from a great height,
Calling out of pleasure and happiness,
And out of darkness, like a new light,
A delicate ascending voice,
Which seems forever rising, never falling
Telling all of us to rejoice,
To delight in the darkness and the light,
Commanding all consciousness forever to rejoice!

The Deceptive Present, the Phoenix Year

As I looked the poplar rose in the shining air
Like a slender throat,
And there was an exaltation of flowers,
The surf of apple tree delicately foaming.

All winter, the trees had been
Silent soldiers, a vigil of woods,
Their hidden feelings
Scrawled and became
Scores of black vines,
Barbed wire sharp against the ice-white sky.

Who could believe then
In the green, glittering vividness of full-leafed summer?
Who will be able to believe, when winter again begins
After the autumn burns down again, and the day is ashen,
And all returns to winter and winter's ashes,
Wet, white, ice, wooden, dulled and dead, brittle or frozen,
Who will believe or feel in mind and heart
The reality of the spring and of birth,
In the green warm opulence of summer, and the inexhaustible vitality and
    immortality of the earth?

May's Truth and May's Falsehood

> "Outside the cicadas are singing fit to burst, a harsh screeching, ten times
> stronger than crickets, and the scorched grass takes on the lovely tones of
> old gold."
> —VAN GOGH, LETTER TO HIS BROTHER

All through the brilliant blue and gold afternoon
All space was blossoming: immense and stately against the blue heights
The sailing, summer-swollen milky and mounting clouds: colossal
    blossoms,
And the dark statues of the trees on the blue and green ground, flowing.
    And every solid thing
Moved as in bloom, leafing, opening wing upon wing to the sun's
    overwhelming lightning!
And every solid sight was a great green drum, throbbing and pulsing in the
    growing vividness of the greenness darkening
So that the litter and ripple of the river was excited by the advent and
    descent of light upon its slow flowing:
The river was opulence, radiance, sparkle, and shine, a rippling radiance
    dancing light's dances;
And the birds flew, soared, darted, perched, perched and whistled, dipped
    or ascended
Like a ballet of black flutes, an erratic and scattered metamorphosis of the
    villages of stillness into the variety of flying:

THE COLLECTED POEMS OF DELMORE SCHWARTZ

The birds were as a transformation of trunk and branch and twig into the
    elation which is the energy's celebration and consummation!

—It was difficult, then, to believe—how difficult it was and how painful it
    was to believe in the realty of winter,
Beholding so many supple somersaults of energy and deathless feats of
    superexuberant vitality, all self-delighting,
Arising, waving, flying, glittering, and glistening as if in irresistible
    eagerness,
Seeking with serene belief and undivided certainty, love's miracles, tender,
    or thrashing, or thrashing towards tenderness boldly.
        It was necessary to think of pine and fir,
        Of holly, ivy, barberry bush and icicle, of frozen ground,
            And of wooden tree, white or wet and drained,
        And of the blackened or stiffened arms of elm, oak and maple
        To remember, even a little, that existence was not forever
            May and the beginning of summer:
It was only possible to forget the presence of the present's green and gold
    and white flags of flowering May's victory, summer's ascendancy and
    sovereignty,
By thinking of how all arise and aspire to the nature of fire, to the flame-
    like climbing of vine and leaf and flower,
And calling to mind how all things must suffer and die in growth and birth,
To be reborn, again and again and again, to be transformed all over again.

The desire of the bud and the flower and the fruit the tree and the vine
    to be devoured and to be phoenix in nature, fulfilled in the phoenix
    sensuality of blood and of wine, or stilled in the mud near the root
    under the ground once more awaiting the sun's domination, the sun's
    great roar and fire.

How Strange Love Is, in Every State of Consciousness

How strange love is in every kind of consciousness:
How strange it is that only such gentleness
Begets the fury of joy and all its tenderness,

That lips and hands for all their littleness
Can move throughout the body's wilderness
Beyond the gaze of consciousness, however it towers
Possessed and blessed by the power which flowers as a fountain flowers!

The Mounting Summer, Brilliant and Ominous

A yellow-headed, gold-hammered, sunflower-lanterned
Summer afternoon: after the sun soared
All morning to the marble-shining heights of the marvelous blue
Like lions insurgent, bursting out of a great black zoo,
As if all radiance rode over and roved and dove
To the thick dark night where the fluted roots clutched and grasped
As if all vividness poured, out poured
Over, bursting and falling and breaking,
As when the whole ocean rises and rises, in irresistible, uncontrollable
    motion, shaking:
The roar of the heart in a shell and the roar of the sea beyond the
    concessions of possession and the successions of time's continual
    procession.

During December's Death

The afternoon turned dark early;
The light suddenly faded;
The dusk was black although, elsewhere, the first star in the cold sky
    suddenly whistled,
And I thought I heard the fresh scraping of the flying steel of boys on
    roller skates
Rollicking over the asphalt in 1926,
And I thought I heard the dusk and silence raided
By a calm voice commanding consciousness:

Wait: wait: wait as if you had always waited
And as if it had always been dark
And as if the world had been from the beginning
A lost and drunken ark in which the only light
Was the dread and white of the terrified animals' eyes.
And then, turning on the light, I took a book
That I might gaze upon another's vision of the abyss of consciousness—
The hope, and the pain of hope, and the patience of hope and its torment,
   its astonishment, its endlessness.

A Dream of Winter, Empty, Woolen, Ice-White and Brittle

The leaden sky of winter whitened, brightened a little
By what is hidden and beyond it now, became a luminous
Gray, as if the color of smoke curtained the fire
Which was open and offered freely all through the halcyon
Summer, blue and gold—when the great blond and yellow light blazed and
   imagined or implied
Infinite hope, endless love—as promise? as abyss?
      as the depth of absolute loss
      where every heart is lost at last?
The angel or the star which wakened the eye to consciousness
Whispered new intimations, and forgotten truth, concealed and
   ambiguous,
In the ultimate box-seat and balcony of the blue: "You
Were what you are not now, now you are what you were not, and you are
Open and ever-ripening and far less than you may become or be
Within the future's bewildering reality:
Then perhaps you will be a new and astonishing, undreamed actuality:
And then, surely, you will be far different and other
Than the half-believed, half-deceived, revery and lyric of your gazing,
   gaping, grasping, flickering, fumbling desperate and possessed
   memory!"

In the Green Morning, Now, Once More

In the green morning, before
Love was destiny,
The sun was king,
And God was famous.

The merry, the musical,
The jolly, the magical,
The feast, the feast of feasts, the festival
Suddenly ended
As the sky descended
But there was only the feeling,
In all the dark falling,
Of fragrance and of freshness, of birth and beginning.

8.

The Phoenix Choir

Once and for All

Once, when I was a boy,
Apollo summoned me
To be apprenticed to the endless summer of light and consciousness,
And thus to become and be what poets often have been,
A shepherd of being, a riding master of being, holding the sun-god's
    horses, leading his sheep, training his eagles,
Directing the constellations to their stations, and to each grace of place.
But the goat-god, piping and dancing, speaking an unknown tongue or the
    language of the magician,
Sang from the darkness or rose from the underground, whence arise
Love and love's drunkenness, love and birth, love and death, death and
    rebirth
Which are the beginning of the phoenix festivals, the tragic plays in
    celebration of Dionysus,
And in mourning for his drunken and fallen princes, the singers and
    sinners, fallen because they are, in the end,
Drunken with pride, blinded by joy.

And I followed Dionysus, forgetting Apollo. I followed him far too long
    until I was wrong and chanted:
"One cannot serve both gods. One must choose to win and lose."
But I was wrong and when I knew how I was wrong I knew
What, in a way, I had known all along:
This was the new world, here I belonged, here I was wrong because
Here every tragedy has a happy ending, and any error may be
A fabulous discovery of America, of the opulence hidden in the dark
    depths and glittering heights of reality.

Cupid's Chant

Cupid is
    The king of flutes.
Cupid's kiss

Wakes winter's roots.
Cupid touches
    A color's curve.
Cupid reaches
    Apples, peaches,
        Eye and nerve.

A tutor of Venus
      In the dark of the sun,
He knows and he teaches
      That the clever are stupid
      For the stupid discover
How sleep and love are warm and one.

2

Cupid is
A student of leaves,
A scholar of Eros,
A savant of consciousness,
And of sleep's wine-dark seas;
Of the heights of the birds
And the insides of words,
The seed within Adam,
The birth, the death, and the rebirth
Which breathes in Eve
—All that is seedy, loamy, rising, fickle, growing, seeking, flowing,
    flowering, and unknowable, all that we hope and hardly dare to believe.

Psyche Pleads with Cupid

O heart, O dearest heart, dusk again becomes black night
As quickly as the falling of a leave: and I am left
Fondling the formless faceless presence I love, quite lost:

THE COLLECTED POEMS OF DELMORE SCHWARTZ

—All that I am is seed, all that I am is morning, waiting to see,
All that I am is flower, forbidden the light and hidden
In sleep's purpose and sleep's patience, power and growth:
So I must ask again, knowing how it angers you
And knowing that you would be more angered if you knew
How much this mostly unasked question obsesses me:
Why is love dark?
Why must your face remain concealed from me?
My sisters taunt and torment me. They say
I have invented a religion, a superstition, a deity
To hide the love of a monster or monstrous usages
Nursed by love's absence, love's unquelled desire.
Must you be hidden from me forever?
My sisters sometimes say that I will never see
The strangeness or the strange face of the deity
To whom I am espoused in reality or in the dark forest of fantasy!

Does your face possess the glitter and radiance
Possessed by your voice? Your voice possesses
A bell clarity, a trumpet brilliance, a harpsichord delicacy.
It is blessed by the gentleness of the first morning, exquisitely!
Sometimes it has a sunset's roaring eloquence and turbulence
. . . Yet my sisters laugh at me. And think of me
As one who is very strange, as one possessed
By lunacy, or by a dream dispossessed, when in all blessedness
—By joy overcome, beside myself, outside myself, in ecstasy's aftermath—
I come and say to them that God has captured and kidnapped me!
Dearest, is all love dark? Must all love be
Hidden in night from the one who is nearest?
Or is the mystery of divinity an abyss of black?
How then can you come to me? why do you come back?
Why do you desire my love? Is it love, in truth, if I lack
The sight and vision which begins all intimacy?

Narcissus

THE MIND IS AN ANCIENT AND FAMOUS CAPITAL

The mind is a city like London,
Smoky and populous: it is a capital
Like Rome, ruined and eternal,
Marked by the monuments which no one
Now remembers. For the mind, like Rome, contains
Catacombs, aqueducts, amphitheatres, palaces,
Churches and equestrian statues, fallen, broken or soiled.
The mind possesses and is possessed by all the ruins
Of every haunted, hunted generation's celebration.

"Call us what you will: we are made such by love."
We are such studs as dreams are made on, and
Our little lives are ruled by the gods, by Pan,
Piping of all, seeking to grasp or grasping
All of the grapes; and by the bow-and-arrow god,
Cupid, piercing the heart through, suddenly and forever.

Dusk we are, to dusk returning, after the burbing,
After the gold fall, the fallen ash, the bronze,
Scattered and rotten, after the white null statues which
Are winter, sleep, and nothingness: when
Will the houselights of the universe
Light up and blaze?
                    For it is not the sea
Which murmurs in a shell,
And it is not only heart, at harp o'clock,
It is the dread terror of the uncontrollable
Horses of the apocalypse, running in wild dread
Toward Arcturus—and returning as suddenly . . .

THE FEAR AND DREAD OF THE MIND OF THE OTHERS

—The others were the despots of despair—

The river's freshness sailed from unknown sources—

. . . They snickered giggled, laughed aloud at last,
They mocked and marveled at the statue which was
A caricature, as strained and stiff, and yet
A statue of self-love!—since self-love was
To them, truly my true love, how, then, was I a stillness of nervousness
So nervous a caricature: did they suppose
Self-love was unrequited, or betrayed?
They thought I had fallen in love with my own face,
And this belief became the night-like obstacle
To understanding all my unbroken suffering,
My studious self-regard, the pain of hope,
The torment of possibility:
How then could I have expected them to see me
As I saw myself, within my gaze, or see
That being thus seemed as a toad, a frog, a wen, a mole.
Knowing their certainty that I was only
A monument, a monster who had fallen in love
With himself alone, how could I have
Told them what was in me, within my heart, trembling and passionate
Within the labyrinth and caves of my mind, which is
Like every mind partly or wholly hidden from itself?
The words for what is in my heart and in my mind
Do not exist. But I must seek and search to find
Amid the vines and orchards of the vivid world of day
Approximate images, imaginary parallels
For what is my heart and dark within my mind:
Comparisons and mere metaphors: for all
Of them are substitutes, both counterfeit and vague:
They are, at most, deceptive resemblances,
False in their very likeness, like the sons
Who are alike and kin and more unlike and false
Because they seem the father's very self: but each one is

—Although begotten by the same forbears—himself,
The unique self, each one is unique, like every other one,
And everything, older or younger, nevertheless
A passionate nonesuch who has before has been.
Do you hear, do you see? Do you understand me now, and how
The words for what is my heart do not exist?

THE RIVER WAS THE EMBLEM OF ALL BEAUTY: ALL

. . .
The river was the abundant belly of beauty itself
The river was the dream space where I walked,
The river was itself and yet it was—flowing and freshening—
A self anew, another self, or self renewed
At every tick of eternity, and by each glint of light
Mounting or sparkling, descending to shade and black
—Had I but told them my heart, told how it was
Taunted at noon and pacified at dusk, at starfall midnight
Strong in hope once more, ever in eagerness
Jumping like joy, would they have heard? How could they?
How, when what they knew was, like the grass,
Simple and certain, known through the truth of touch, another form and
     fountain of falsehood's fecundity——
Gazing upon their faces as they gazed
Could they have seen my faces as whores who are
Holy and deified as priestesses of hope
               —the sacred virgins of futurity—
Promising dear divinity precisely because
They were disfigured ducks who might become
And be, and ever beloved, white swans, noble and beautiful.
                    Could they have seen how my faces were
Bonfires of worship and vigil, blazes of adoration and hope
—Surely they would have laughed again, renewed their scorn,
Giggle and snickered, cruel. Surely have said
This is the puerile mania of the obsessed,
The living logic of the lunatic:
I was the statue of their merriment,
Dead and a death, Pharaoh and monster forsaken and lost.

. . .

My faces were my apes: my apes became
Performers in the Sundays of their parks,
Buffoons or clowns in the farce or comedy
When they took pleasure in knowing that they were not like me.

. . .

I waited like obsession in solitude:
The sun's white terror tore and roared at me,
The moonlight, almond white, at night,
Whether awake or sleeping, arrested me
And sang, softly, haunted, unlike the sun
But as the sun. Withheld from me or took away
Despair or peace, making me once more
With thought of what had never been before——

Abraham

To J. M. Kaplan

I was a mere boy in a stone-cutter's shop
When, early one evening, my raised hand
Was halted and the soundless voice said:
"Depart from your father and your country
And the things to which you are accustomed.
Go now into a country unknown and strange
I will make of your children a great nation,
Your generations will haunt every generation of all the nations,
They will be like the stars at midnight, like the sand of the sea."
Then I looked up at the infinite sky,
Star-pointing and silent, and it was then, on that evening, that I
Became a man: that evening of my manhood's birthday.

I went then to Egypt, the greatest of nations.
There I encountered the Pharaoh who built the tombs,
Great public buildings, many theatres, and seashore villas:
And my wife's beauty was such that, fearing his power and lust,

I called her my sister, a girl neither for him nor for me.
And soon was fugitive, a nomad again.
Living alone with my sister, becoming very rich
In all but children, in herds, in possessions, the herds continually
Increased my possessions through prodigies of progeny.

From time to time, in the afternoon's revery
In the late sunlight or the cool of the evening
I called to mind the protracted vanity of that promise
Which had called me forth from my father's house unwillingly
Into the last strangeness of Egypt and the childless desert.
Then Sarah gave me her handmaid, a young girl
That I might at least at last have children by another
And later, when a great deal else had occurred,
I put away Hagar, with the utmost remorse
Because the child was the cause of so much rivalry and jealousy.

At last when all this had passed or when
The promise seemed the parts of dream,
When we were worn out and patient in all things
The stranger came, suave and elegant,
A messenger who renewed the promise, making Sarah
Burst out laughing hysterically!

But the boy was born and grew and I saw
What I had known, I knew what I had seen, for he
Possessed his mother's beauty and his father's humility,
And was not marked and marred by her sour irony and my endless anxiety.

Then the angel returned, asking that I surrender
My son as a lamb to show that humility
Still lived in me, and was not altered by age and prosperity.

I said nothing, shocked and passive. Then I said but to myself alone:
"This was to be expected. These promises
Are never unequivocal or unambiguous, in this
As in all things which are desired the most:
I have had great riches and great beauty.

I cannot expect the perfection of every wish
And if I deny the command, who knows what will happen?"

But his life was forgiven and given back to me:
His children and their children are an endless nation:
Dispersed on every coast. And I am not gratified
Nor astonished. It has never been otherwise:
Exiled, wandering, dumbfounded by riches,
Estranged among strangers, dismayed by the infinite sky,
An alien to myself until at last the caste of the last alienation
The angel of death comes to make the alienated and indestructible one a
    part of his famous society.

Sarah

The angel said to me: "Why are you laughing?"
"Laughing! Not me! Who was laughing? I did not laugh. It was
A cough. I was coughing. Only hyenas laugh.
It was the cold I caught nine minutes after
Abraham married me: when I saw
How I was slender and beautiful, more and more
Slender and beautiful.
                        I was also
Clearing my throat; something inside of me
Is continually telling me something
I do not wish to hear: A joke: A big joke:
But the joke is always just on me.
He said: you will have more children than the sky's stars
And the seashore's sands, if you just wait patiently.
Wait: patiently: ninety years? You see
The joke's on me!"

Jacob

All was as it is, before the beginning began, before
We were bared to the cold air, before
Pride. Fullness of bread. Abundance of idleness.
No one has ever told me what now I know:
Love is unjust, justice is loveless.

So, as it was to become, it was, in the black womb's ignorance
Coiled and bound, under the mother's heart.
There in the womb we wrestled, and writhed, hurt
Each other long before each was other and apart,
Before we breathed: who then committed greed,
Impersonation, usurpation? So, in the coming forth,
In the noose and torment of birth, Esau went first,
He was red all over. I followed him, clutching his heel,
And we were named: Esau, the one of the vivid coat,
Jacob, the one who clutches the heel of the one
Who has a vivid coat. The names were true
As the deceptive reality into which we were thrown.
For I did not know what clutching was, nor had I known
Would I have known whose heel I clutched, my brother's or my own!

So, the world we entered then and thus was one
In which the second must be second that the first may be first.
The world of precedence, order, other, under and above,
The darkness, sweetness, confusion and unity of love!
How the truth of our names became, as we grew, more true,
Growing like truth. How could it be otherwise? For truth abides
Hidden in the future, in the ambush of the marvelous,
Unknown and monstrous, at the very heart of surprise.

The gift was mind. The gift was eminence. The gift
Like every gift, was guilt. The guilt began
In the darkness and dark mystery where all begins.
The mystery of the perpetual invisible fires whence flow

The very beasts and woods where—

> with what happiness!
> what innocence!—

Esau my brother hunted, cantering like the horses of summer,
And sleeping, when he returned, the sleep of winter farms,
Spontaneous and blessed, like energy itself, sleeping or awake.
Until the hour when the angel struck!

So it was: so:
O angel of the unspeakable,
Why must a gift be guilt and hurt the gifted one?
O angel of the unspeakable, power of powers,
Locking my reins, my arms, my heart all night
So that my body was burdened as with the load of all stones
Dost thou remember what, in the darkness, I cried,
During the desperation in which I died
The last death of hope and the little deaths of the heart
Wrestling and writhing between two rivers—on one bank,
Esau, awaiting me, like a river slept—beneath me once more.
"Hast thou not seen," I cried aloud, to the unspeakable,
"Esau my brother: his handsome hunting heart upon a horse?"
How should it seem so strange that I should win,
Since victory was my gift? Unjust, like every gift,
A something neither deserved, nor gained by toil . . .
How else could it be gift and given?
Favor: favored: favorite:
Gold hair: great strength: Esau was very tall,
Possessed by the supple grace of the sea's waves, breaking.

Now Joseph is, as I was: in Egypt's pit,
In that accustomed depth and isolated height
The solitude of eminence, the exiled intelligence,
Which separated me even as it created me:
Estranged and unloved, gifted and detested,
Denied the love of the servants and the dogs.
Joseph a stranger in Egypt may only know
What I have known: my gifts, my victory, my guilt.
For Egypt is a country like a gift.

The gift is loved but not the gifted one.
The coat of many colors is much admired
By everyone, but he who wears the coat
Is not made warm. Why should the gift be the cause of pain,
O thou unspeakable? Must the vivid coat
Of eminence elect the favored favorite
As scapegoat or turncoat, exile or fugitive,
The loved of mother and God, and by all others
Shunned in fear or contempt?
                                        I knew what it was,
When Joseph became my favorite: knew the sympathy
Of the long experience of the unasked-for gift:
Knew the nature of love: how many colors
Can a coat have? What should we wish, if
We could choose? What should I desire
—Not to have loved my son, the best of sons?
Rejected the choice of love? Should I have hidden
My love of him? Or should he have concealed the self
I loved, above all others, wearing the coat
Which is customary, the coats his brothers wore?
To how many coats can a color give vividness?
How can the heart know love, and not love one the more?
Love is unjust: justice is loveless.

Lincoln

Manic-depressive Lincoln, national hero!
How just and true that this great nation, being conceived
In liberty by fugitives should find
—Strange ways and plays of monstrous History—
This Hamlet-type to be the President—

This failure, this unwilling bridegroom,
This tricky lawyer full of black despair—

He grew a beard, becoming President,
And took a shawl as if he guessed his role,
Though with the beard he fled cartoonists' blacks,
And many laughed and were contemptuous,
And some for four years spoke of killing him—

He was a politician—of the heart!—
He lived from hand to mouth in moral things!
He understood quite well Grant's drunkenness!
It was for him, before Election Day,
That at Cold Harbor Grant threw lives away
In hopeless frontal attack against Lee's breastworks!

O how he was the Hamlet-man, and this,
After a life of failure made him right,
After he ran away on his wedding day,
Writing a coward's letter to his bride—
How with his very failure, he out-tricked
The florid Douglas and the abstract Davis,
And all the vain men who, surrounding him,
Smiled in their vanity and sought his place—

Later, they made him out a prairie Christ
To sate the need coarse in the national heart—

His wife went insane, Mary Todd too often
Bought herself dresses. And his child died.
And he would not condemn young men to death
For having slept, in weakness. And he spoke
More than he knew and all that he had felt
Between outrageous joy and black despair
Before and after Gettysburg's pure peak—

He studied law, but knew in his own soul
Despair's anarchy, terror and error,
—Instruments had to be taken from his office
And from his bedroom in such days of horror,
Because some saw that he might kill himself:

When he was young, when he was middle-aged,
How just and true was he, our national hero!

Sometimes he could not go home to face his wife,
Sometimes he wished to hurry or end his life!
But do not be deceived. He did not win,
And, it is plain, the South could never win
(Despite the gifted Northern generals!)
—Capitalismus is not mocked, O no!
This stupid deity decided the War—

In fact, the North and South were losers both:
—Capitalismus won the Civil War—

—Capitalismus won the Civil War,
Yet, in the War's cruel Colosseum,
Some characters fulfilled their natures' surds,
Grant the drunkard, Lee the noble soldier,
John Brown in whom the Bible soared and cried,
Booth the unsuccessful Shakespearean,
—Each in some freedom walked and knew himself,
Then most of all when all the deities
Mixed with their barbarous stupidity
To make the rock, root, and rot of the war—

"This is the way each only life becomes,
Tossed on History's ceaseless insane sums!"

Starlight Like Intuition Pierced the Twelve

The starlight's intuitions pierced the twelve,
The brittle night sky sparkled like a tune
Tinkled and tapped out on the xylophone.
Empty and vain, a glittering dune, the moon
Arose too big, and, in the mood which ruled,
Seemed like a useless beauty in a pit;

And then one said, after he carefully spat:
"No matter what we do, he looks at it!"

"I cannot see a child or find a girl
Beyond his smile which glows like that spring moon."
"—Nothing no more the same," the second said,
"Though all may be forgiven, never quite healed
The wound I bear as witness, standing by;
No ceremony surely appropriate,
Nor secret love, escape or sleep because
No matter what I do, he looks at it——"

"Now," said the third, "no thing will be the same:
I am as one who never shuts his eyes,
The sea and sky no more are marvelous,
And I no longer understand surprise!"
"Now," said the fourth, "nothing will be enough
—I heard his voice accomplishing all wit:
No word can be unsaid, no deed withdrawn
—No matter what is said, he measures it!"

"Vision, imagination, hope or dream,
Believed, denied, the scene we wished to see?
It does not matter in the least: for what
Is altered, if it is not true? That we
Saw goodness, as it is—*this* is the awe
And the abyss which we will not forget,
His story now the sky which holds all thought:
No matter what I think, think of it!"

"And I will never be what once I was,"
Said one for long as narrow as a knife,
"And we will never be what once we were;
We have died once; this is a second life."
"My mind is spilled in moral chaos," one
Righteous as Job exclaimed, "now infinite
Suspicion of my heart stems what I will
—No matter what I choose, he stares at it!"

"I am as one native in summer places
—Ten weeks' excitement paid for by the rich;
Debauched by that and then all winter bored,"
The sixth declared. "His peak left us a ditch!"
"He came to make this life more difficult,"
The seventh said, "No one will ever fit
His measure's heights, all is inadequate:
No matter what I do, what good is it?"

"He gave forgiveness to us: what a gift!"
The eighth chimed in. "But now we know how much
Must be forgiven. But if forgiven, what?
The crime which was will be; and the least touch
Revives the memory: what is forgiveness worth?"
The ninth spoke thus: "Who now will ever sit
At ease in Zion at the Easter feast?
No matter what the place, he touches it!"

"And I will always stammer, since he spoke,"
One, who had been most eloquent, said, stammering.
"I looked too long at the sun; like too much light,
So too much goodness is a boomerang,"
Laughed the eleventh of the troop. "I must
Try what he tried: I saw the infinite
Who walked the lake and raised the hopeless dead:
No matter what the feat, he first accomplished it!"

So spoke the twelfth; and then the twelve in chorus:
"Unspeakable unnatural goodness is
Risen and shines, and never will ignore us;
He glows forever in all consciousness;
Forgiveness, love, and hope possess the pit,
And bring our endless guilt, like shadow's bars:
No matter what we do, he stares at it!

What pity then deny? what debt defer?
We know he looks at us like all the stars,
And we shall never be as once we were,
This life will never be what once it was!

Uncollected Poems

Poems Published in Magazines and Anthologies, 1932–1962

E. A. P.—A Portrait

You do not see deep, deep, into a mirror
Or into faces, either, or into words.
You take us up with gentleness so quiet;
With unlearned tolerance you always listen.

You do not understand, you do not know;
But in that ignorance you breed a love
That makes us happy for a little while.

Open the windows some summer evening,
Go to the piano and brush away the jazz.
Play "Hearts and Flowers" softly, "Home, Sweet Home,"
And touch us all with you, and human music,
And hold us all within your heart of warmth.

The Saxophone

This sobbing fits the city—can't you see,
Listening to that croon, a sprawling drunkard
Under the leprous light of dimming lamp-posts
As day flows in between the tall, tall buildings?
A streetcar's hollowing of night's steep silence;
Old beggars, blind, scratching yellowish violins;
The subway's sound or any newsboy's call,
Or someone's weeping on a quiet street?
—I know the saxophone was born from this.
When people are asleep and darkness holds
The city with soft hands, I watch and listen.
Sometimes I think I see the city placing
Its mouth upon a saxophone and playing
—Almost as mothers kiss their little children.

Automobile

How can its clean and shiny stride be human,
Though human words and hands have formed its length?
A tiger, coiled inside a gear, responds
To prodding motions with a mobile strength.

Just tolerate our will, and cruise the streets,
O brutal plunge, stern prodigy of stuff
Too foreign to ourselves and separate . . .
Your lithe, steel-cradled force is not enough:

For we will place ourselves in you each day,
And we will speak and touch and love and know.
How much you'll be of us we cannot say,
But human blood in cylinders will flow

Until the tawny coldness of your gleam
Is moulted, melted, changed to animal heat,—
Transfigured, to a body, pulsing, warm,
A bright extension of our human feet.

Darkness

(In the Japanese manner)

What words should be said
When this eternal curtain
Slowly falls again?

Aubade

(*Qu'il vienne, qu'il vienne,*—Rimbaud)

Awaken, awaken
The doors of morning open.

It is time for pure attention's
White breakfast,
The sky deepens dimensions,
The sun, fat fist,
Punches the window
Nursing blue shadow.

Awaken, awaken
The doors of morning open.

As a glass magnifies,
May the eyes widen,
To seek the shy quiddities
Marinely hidden,
Attend the glisten
Of least thought, listen—

Awaken, awaken
The doors of morning open.

Washington Bridge, December 1929

Now in the darkness of the year
When afternoons, grown still, more chill and drifting,
Voyage unseen to dusk and blue loose night,
The wind is voiding our dream of spring.

But all day long the rivets pulse, and cables
Crescent a river newly, cradle a word. . . .
—Will the gray sky gather the world to death?
Over the hush and sleep an iron breath

Tremendously *is*. . . . No wind nor snow
Refutes this fleshed geometry, this birth,
Curving the strength of life over the earth.

Saturday's Child

I think of blue confetti, amusement parks
And lighted Christmas trees, while carnivals
Parade like Roman candles in my mind . . .
How should I dumb this rage? What should I say?

Within the pagan tent of holiday
Grow memories to brood upon and cherish
—And fling on Monday from the gargoyled church
Of consciousness into a weary heart

Whose large remorse requires expectation
Of every joy that Saturday donates
To taunt that synthesis of monotone
And toil and firecrackers which is life.

At This Moment of Time

Some who are uncertain compel me. They fear
The Ace of Spades. They fear
Love offered suddenly, turning from the mantelpiece,
Sweet with decision. And they distrust
The fireworks by the lakeside, first the spuft,

Then the colored lights, rising.
Tentative, hesitant, doubtful, they consume
Greedily Caesar at the prow returning
Locked in the stone of his act and office.
While the brass band brightly bursts over the water
They stand in the crowd lining the shore,
Aware of the water beneath Him. They know it. Their eyes
Are haunted by water.

Disturb me, compel me. If it is not true
"That no man is happy," that is not
The sense which guides you. If we are
Unfinished (we are, unless hope is a bad dream),
You are exact. What will come next
Has not yet come. You tug my sleeve
Before I speak, with a shadow's friendship,
And I remember that we who move
Are moved by clouds that darken midnight.

Metro-Goldwyn-Mayer

I looked toward the movie, the common dream,
The afi and she in close-ups, nearer than life,
And I accepted such things as they seem,

The easy poise, the absence of the knife,
The near summer happily ever after,
The understood question, the immediate strife,

Not dangerous, nor mortal, but the fadeout
Enormously kissing amid warm laughter,
As if such things were not always played out

By an ignorant arm, which crosses the dark
And lights up a thin sheet with a shadow's mark.

Poem

You, my photographer, you, most aware,
Who climbed to the bridge when the iceberg struck,
Climbed with your camera when the ship's hull broke,
And lighted your flashes and, standing passionate there,
Wound the camera in the sudden burst's flare,
Shot the screaming women, and turned and took
Pictures of the iceberg (as the ship's deck shook)
Dreaming like the moon in the night's black air!

You, tiptoe on the rail to film a child!
The nude old woman swimming in the sea
Looked up from the dark water to watch you there;
Below, near the ballroom where the band still toiled,
The frightened, in their lifebelts, watched you bitterly—
You hypocrite! My brother! We are a pair!

Poem

Old man in the crystal morning after snow,
Your throat swathed in a muffler, your bent
Figure building the snow man which is meant
For the grandchild's target,
                              do you know
This fat cartoon, his eyes pocked in with coal
Nears you each time your breath smokes the air,
Lewdly grinning out of a private nightmare?
He is the white cold shadow of your soul.

You build his comic head, you place his comic hat;
Old age is not so serious, and I
By the window sad and watchful as a cat,
Build to this poem of old age and of snow,

And weep: you are my snow man and I know
I near you, you near him, all of us must die.

Poem

The heart, a black grape gushing hidden streams,
Streams hidden as the cold farms under sidewalks,
Burdened with stones, such as the tallest buildings,
Bursts, pops like firecrackers, pops and bursts,
When a train chuffs from the station in full flowers,
—Or, smoke being the type of dream, great dreams.

The heart would also go away in thunder,
Admired by throngs, exploding rhetoric!

But when it comes, escape is small, the door
Creaks, the worms of fear spread veined, the furtive
Fugitive, looking backward, sees his
Ghost in the mirror, his shameful eyes, his mouth diseased.

The Silence in Emptiness Accused Him Thus
"A Privileged Character"

Am I indeed guilty in privilege?
And am I stained in the commonweal's guilt?
What did I do? and how did I assent?
What good and gold will I gain, which they defend?
When did I lie and say this age is good?
I am a twice-torn critic from way back!

America! Tarawa! in the Pacific seas—
I went to Tarawa with the seaborne boys

At the silver screen: how far I was,
Seated in the soft dark, nervous or sick,
(O to be 4F, now that war is here,
Sang the ground-glass cynics with a jocose jeer).
I saw the marked Marines gaze at the Petty girl
(Nude as a peeled banana, comely as pears),
(Lust never again will rise in some of them),
I saw them pray at sunset in the strength
Young manhood shows in sunburnt summer's health:
(Many of them were dead in the next dusk)
What can I say to down my privilege?
What but the roulette reason, like gold hair?
The grace, the luck, the accidents which tear
The heart and head, formless as fallen rags.
The spinning ball which stops at here, not there,
Made you serene as steeplejacks on high,
Full of the joy of life and the juice and the sleep,
Left me a twice-told critic, whipped by fear,
Shocked by the memory of every year.

—This is no answer to the hopeless dead,
I cannot justify myself or judge
My privilege, my lush largesse, my life.
Description is my only strength and grace,
Merely to love the truth and as I gaze
(Student and paid admission who
Wades forth to Tarawa at the silver screen)
Let John who was as much estranged as I
Now in the last estrangement judge the truth!

Sonnet

Others may fear this goddess, but none will
(Whether you brag or wail, how can you know?)
Fear her as you do, like a criminal!
Doubt, hope, and passion driven like the snow

THE COLLECTED POEMS OF DELMORE SCHWARTZ

Downward to nameless death in a dark month.
Until you talk too much and quite unclearly—
Yet when these fumbling ways have nearly
Reduced you to your knees, once more a myth

From a child's book comes shouting like good news,
The princess and the monster changed by her
To what he wished to be, fluent with poise,
As probable as in America
True games in which no one can lose,
Or perfect marriages of girls and boys.

Kilroy's Carnival

A Poetic Prologue for TV

And now, for relief, variety, a change of key, a shift in tone, I will recite a
poem or anthem by Canderon . . . :

We live while we see the sun
Where living and dreaming are one.
And life has taught me merely this:
Man dreams the life that he is
Until life's dream is undone.
The king dreams that he is king!
(—Stop! stop! what a thing to say:
Whether in earnest or in play—).

And all the praise he receives
Is written on the wind and the leaves,
Or in frost streaked upon the pane
Or in the dribbling of the rain;
It is dust and not laurel or bay
When death ends all in a breath:

Where, then, the pomp of a throne?
It perishes sooner than the bone

In the other dream which is death.
Man dreams whatever he may be
And no man knows his own dream:
As I, too, dream and behold
That I dream, dreaming that all pain
Is a blessing disguised, and untold.

What is life? A tale poorly told?
What is life? Images which seem
The reality at the end of a dream!
The greatest of all goods is small:
The belief that life is a dream,
And that is all that it is: all!

Now let us hear a lyric which may or may not be appropriate.

A POPULAR SCORE

O Nirvana
Don't you wait for me
I'm going with mañana
She's the only girl for me.

I don't want Miss America,
I don't want Miss Paree,
My girl is Miss Utopia,
We're going steadily.

I don't want the boss' daughter,
She might be a wife-in-law,
And say her father bought her
A fortune-hunting bore!

So get along Nirvana,
I've fallen for mañana,
She's my only marijuana
She's the only bride for me.

From here out to Montana
From here to Caroline
There's only one mañana,
Mañana shall be mine!

I'm all through with plurality,
I have a blind date with reality,
We're going steadily:
So get along Nirvana,
My girl is sweet Mañana,
She's the only hope for me.

Philology Recapitulates Ontology, Poetry Is Ontology

Faithful to your commandments, O consciousness, O

Holy bird of words soaring ever whether to nothingness or
                    to inconceivable fulfillment slowly:

And still I follow you, awkward as that dandy of ontology
                    and as awkward as his albatross and as

Another dandy of ontology before him, another shepherd
                    and watchdog of being, the one who

Talked forever of forever as if forever of having been
                    and being an ancient mariner,

Hesitant forever as if forever were the albatross

Hung round his neck by the seven seas of the seven Muses,

And with as little conclusion, since being never concludes,

Studying the sibilance and the splashing of the seas and of
                    seeing and of being's infinite seas,

Staring at the ever-blue and the far small stars and
the faint white endless curtain of the
twinkling play's endless seasons.

Poem

Faithful to your commands, O consciousness, O

Beating wings, I studied

The roses and the muses of reality,

The deceptions and the deceptive elation of the redness of
of the growing morning,

And all the greened and thorned variety of the vines of
error, which begin by promising

Everything and more than everything, and then suddenly,

At the height of noon seem to rise to the peak or dune-like
moon of no return

So that everything is or seems to have become nothing, or of no
genuine importance:

And it is not that the departure of hope or its sleep has
made it inconceivable

That anything should be or should have been important:

It is that the belief in hope itself was not, from the
beginning, before conscious believing, the
most important of all beliefs.

This is the worst illness, and the profoundest, most
detestable sacrilege,

To believe that hope was smoke only, the smoke of the
                flickering fires of the heart's desires,

And had no root in the soaring sun, summer, and the stars'
                infinitely distant fires.

Spiders

Is the spider a monster in miniature?
His web is a cruel stair, to be sure,
Designed artfully, cunningly placed,
A delicate trap, carefully spun
To bind the fly (innocent or unaware)
In a net as strong as a chain or a gun.

There are far more spiders than the man in the street supposes
And the philosopher-king imagines, let alone knows!
There are six hundred kinds of spiders and each one
Differs in kind and in unkindness.
In variety of behavior spiders are unrivalled:
The fat garden spider sits motionless, amidst or at the heart
Of the orb of its web: other kinds run,
Scuttling across the floor, falling into bathtubs,
Trapped in the path of its own wrath, by overconfidence drowned and
    undone.

Other kinds—more and more kinds under the stars and the sun—
Are carnivores: all are relentless, ruthless
Enemies of insects. Their methods of getting food
Are unconventional, numerous, various and sometimes hilarious:
Some spiders spin webs as beautiful
As Japanese drawings, intricate as clocks, strong as rocks:
Others construct traps which consist only
Of two sticky and tricky threads. Yet this ambush is enough
To bind and chain a crawling ant for long enough:
The famished spider feels the vibration
Which transforms patience into sensation and satiation.

The handsome wolf spider moves suddenly freely and relies
Upon lightning suddenness, stealth and surprise,
Possessing accurate eyes, pouncing upon his victim with the speed of surmise.

Courtship is dangerous: there are just as many elaborate and endless
    techniques and varieties
As characterize the wooing of more analytic, more introspective beings:
    Sometimes the male
Arrives with the gift of a freshly caught fly.
Sometimes he ties down the female, when she is frail,
With deft strokes and quick maneuvers and threads of silk:
But courtship and wooing, whatever their form, are informed
By extreme caution, prudence, and calculation,
For the female spider, lazier and fiercer, than the male suitor,
May make a meal of him if she does not feel in the same mood, or if her
    appetite
Consumes her far more than the revelation of love's consummation.
Here among spiders, as in the higher forms of nature,
The male runs a terrifying risk when he goes seeking for the bounty of
    beautiful Alma Magna Mater:
Yet clearly and truly he must seek and find his mate and match like every
    other living creature!

The Choir and Music of Solitude and Silence

Silence is a great blue bell
Swinging and ringing, tinkling and singing,
In measure's pleasure, and in the supple symmetry of the soaring of the
    immense intense wings glinting against
All the blue radiance above us and within us, hidden
Save for the stars sparking, distant and unheard in their singing.
And this is the first meaning of the famous saying,
The stars sang. They are the white birds of silence
And the meaning of the difficult famous saying that the sons and daughters
    of morning sang,

Meant and means that they were and they are the children of God and
    morning,
Delighting in the lights of becoming and the houses of being,
Taking pleasure in measure and excess, in listening as in seeing.

Love is the most difficult and dangerous form of courage.
Courage is the most desperate, admirable and noble kind of love.

So that when the great blue bell of silence is stilled and stopped, or broken
By the babel and chaos of desire unrequited, irritated and frustrated,
When the heart has opened and when the heart has spoken
Not of the purity and symmetry of gratification, but action of insatiable
    distraction's dissatisfaction,
Then the heart says, in all its blindness and faltering emptiness:
There is no God. Because I am hope. And hope must be fed.
And then the great blue bell of silence is deafened, dumbed, and has
    become the tomb of the living dead.

All Night, All Night

> I have been one acquainted with the night
> —ROBERT FROST

Rode in the train all night, in the sick light. A bird
Flew parallel with a singular will. In daydream's moods and attitudes
The other passengers slumped, dozed, slept, read,
Waiting, and waiting for place to be displaced
On the exact track of safety or the rack of accident.

Looked out at the night, unable to distinguish
Lights in the towns of passage from the yellow lights
Numb on the ceiling. And the bird flew parallel and still,
As the train shot forth the straight line of its whistle,
Forward on the taut tracks, piercing empty, familiar—

The bored center of this vision and condition looked and looked
Down through the slick pages of the magazine (seeking
The seen and the unseen) and his gaze fell down the well.
Of the great darkness under the slick glitter,
And he was only one among eight million riders and readers.

And all the while under his empty smile the shaking drum
Of the long determined passage passed through him
By his body mimicked and echoed. And then the train,
Like a suddenly storming rain began to rush and thresh
The silent or passive night, pressing and impressing
The patients' foreheads with a tightening-like image
Of the rushing engine proceeded by a shaft of light
Piercing the dark, changing and transforming the silence
Into a violence of foam, sound, smoke and succession.

A bored child went to get a cup of water,
And crushed the cup because the water too was
Boring and merely boredom's struggle.
The child, returning, looked over the shoulder
Of a man reading until he annoyed the shoulder.
A fat woman yawned and felt the liquid drops
Drip down the fleece of many dinners.

And the bird flew parallel and parallel flew
The black pencil lines of telephone posts, crucified,
At regular intervals, post after post
Of thrice crossed, blue-belled, anonymous trees.

And then the bird cried as if to all of us:

> O your life, your lonely life
> What have you ever done with it,
> And done with the great gift of consciousness?
> What will you ever do with your life before death's knife
> Provides the answer ultimate and appropriate?

As I for my part felt in my heart as one who falls,
Falls in a parachute, falls endlessly, and feel the vast

Draft of the abyss sucking him down and down,
An endlessly helplessly falling and appalled clown:

This is the way that night passes by, this
Is the overnight endless trip to the famous unfathomable abyss.

This Is a Poem I Wrote at Night, Before the Dawn

This is a poem I wrote before I died and was reborn:
—After the years of the apples ripening and the eagles soaring,
After the festival here the small flowers gleamed like the first stars,
And the horses cantered and romped away like the experience of skill;
    mastered and serene
Power, grasped and governed by reins, lightly held, by knowing hands.

The horses had cantered away, far enough away
So that I saw the horses' heads farther and farther away
And saw that they had reached the black horizon on the dusk of day
And were or seemed black thunderheads massy and ominous waves in the
    doomed sky:
And it was then, for the first time, then that I said as I must always say
All through living death of night:
It is always darkness before delight!
The long night is always the beginning of the vivid blossom of day.

Words for a Trumpet Chorale Celebrating the Autumn

"The trumpet is a brilliant instrument."
—DIETRICH BUXTEHUDE

Come and come forth and come up from the cup of
Your dumbness, stunned and numb, come with
The statues and believed in,
Thinking *this is nothing*, deceived.

Come to the summer and sun,
Come see upon that height, and that sum
In the seedtime of the winter's absolute,
How yearly the phoenix inhabits the fruit.
Behold, above all, how the tall ball
Called the body is but a drum, but a bell
Summoning the soul
To rise from the catacomb of sleep and fear
To the blaze and death of summer,

Rising from the lithe forms of the pure
Furs of the rising flames, slender and supple
Which are the consummation of the blaze of fall and of all.

To Helen

(After Valéry)

O Sea! . . .'Tis I, risen from death once more
To hear the waves' harmonious roar
And see the galleys, sharp, in dawn's great awe
Raised from the dark by the rising and gold oar.

My fickle hands sufficed to summon kings
Their salt beards amused my fingers, deft and pure.
I wept. They sang of triumphs now obscure:
And the first abyss flooded the hull as if with falling wings.

I hear the profound horns and trumpets of war
Matching the rhythm, swinging of the flying oars:
The galleys' chant enchains the foam of sound;
And the gods, exalted at the heroic prow,
E'en though the spit of spray insults each smiling brow,
Beckon to me with arms indulgent, frozen, sculptured, and dead long long
    ago.

The Journey of a Poem Compared to
All the Sad Variety of Travel

A poem moves forward,
>   Like the passages and percussions of trains in progress
>   A pattern of recurrence, a hammer of repetitive occurrence

>   a slow less and less heard
>   Low thunder under all passengers
Steel sounds tripping and tripled and
Grinding, revolving, gripping, turning, and returning
As the flung carpet of the wide countryside spreads out on
>   each side in billows

And in isolation, rolled out, white house, red barn, squat silo,
Pasture, hill, meadow and woodland pasture
And the stripped poles step fast past the train windows
Second after second takes snapshots, clicking,
Into the dangled boxes of glinting windows
Snapshots and selections, rejections, at angles, of shadows
A small town: a shop's sign—GARAGE; and then white gates
Where waiting cars wait with the unrest of trembling
Breathing hard and idling, until the slow descent
Of the red cones of sunset: a dead march: a slow tread and heavy

Of the slowed horses of Apollo
—Until the slowed horses of Apollo go over the horizon
And all things are parked, slowly or willingly
into the customary or at random places

Aria

(from Kilroy's Carnival)

"Kiss me there where pride is glistening,
Kiss me where I am round or ripened fruit,

Kiss me wherever however whenever
    I am supple and flare and bare,
Let the belle be rung as long as I am young,
    let ring and fly like a great bronze wing
Until I am shaken from blossom to root."

"—I'll kiss you wherever you think you are poor,
Wherever you shudder, feeling tiny or skinny, striped or barred,
Feeling you are bloodless, cheerless, chapless or marred
    Until, until
    Your gaze has been stilled
Until you are shamed again no more!
I'll kiss you until your body and soul
    —the mind in the body being fulfilled—
Suspend their dread and civil war.

Poem

    On that day of summer, blue and gold,
All space was blossoming, not only
The white blooms of the sailing summery clouds,
In the shadows of the trees' statues flowing down,
Under the glittering blue and the sky's lightning,
But every solid thing was opening,
Having put forth leaf and bud,
The first tendril of
    The trees were flowering,
The hills were as green drums throbbing and pulsing,
And the river was excited by the light which foamed upon it,
Flowing and sparkling excitement from the rippling folds
      the rippling radiance,
As the birds darted, perched, bubbled, dipped, and perched,
Like a ballet of dark flutes, like a transformation of twigs
    into starlings,
Like the arising of branches into troops of geese—

THE COLLECTED POEMS OF DELMORE SCHWARTZ

And as the sun of June burned all afternoon there was nothing
     but the elation and celebration of the motions
     of energy everywhere.

Poem

Remember midsummer: the fragrance of box, of white roses
And of phlox. And upon a honeysuckle branch
Three snails hanging with infinite delicacy
—Clinging like tendril, flake and thread, as self-tormented
And self-delighted as any ballerina,
     just as in the orchard,
Near the apple trees, in the over-grown grasses
Drunken wasps clung to over-ripe pears
Which had fallen: swollen and disfigured.
For now it is wholly autumn: in the late
Afternoon as I walked toward the ridge where the hills begin,
There is a whir, a thrashing in the bush, and a startled pheasant, flying out
    and up,
Suddenly astonished me, breaking the waking dream.

Last night
Snatches of sleep, streaked by dreams and half dreams
—So that, aloft in the dim sky, for almost an hour,
A sausage balloon—chalk-white and lifeless looking—floated motionless
Until, at midnight, I went to New Bedlam and saw what I feared
     the most—I heard nothing, but it
     had all happened several times elsewhere.

Now, in the cold glittering morning, shining at the window,
The pears hang, yellowed and over-ripe, sodden brown in
     erratic places, all bunched and dangling,
Like a small choir of bagpipes, silent and waiting. And I rise now,
Go to the window and gaze at the fallen or falling country
—And see!—the fields are pencilled light brown
     or are the dark brownness of the last autumn

—So much has shrunken to straight brown lines, thin as the
     bare thin trees,
Save where the cornstalks, white bones of the lost forever dead,
Shrivelled and fallen, but shrill-voiced when the wind whistles
Are scattered like the long abandoned hopes and ambitions
Of an adolescence which, for a very long time, has been merely
A recurrent target and taunt of the inescapable mockery of memory.

Apollo Musagete, Poetry, and the Leader of the Muses

Nothing is given which is not taken,

Little or nothing is taken which is not freely desired, freely, truly and fully.

"You would not seek me if you had not found me": this is true of all that is
     supremely desired and admired . . .

"An enigma is an animal," said the hurried, harried schoolboy;

And a horse divided against itself cannot stand;

And a moron is a man who believes in having too many wives: what harm
     is there in that?

O the endless fecundity of poetry is equaled
By its endless inexhaustible freshness, as in the discovery of America and
     of poetry.

Hence it is clear that the truth is not strait and narrow but infinite:
All roads lead to Rome and to poetry
               and to poem, sweet poem
               and from, away and towards are the same typography.

Hence the poet must be, in a way, stupid and naïve and a little child;

Unless ye be as a little child ye cannot enter the kingdom of poetry.

Hence the poet must be able to become a tiger like Blake, a carousel like
    Rilke.

Hence he must be all things to be free, for all impersonations
                    a doormat and a monument
                    to all situations possible or actual
The cuckold, the cuckoo, the conqueror, and the coxcomb.

It is to him in the zoo that the zoo cries out and the hyena:
"Hello, take off your hat, king of the beasts, and be seated, Mr. Bones."

And hence the poet must seek to be essentially anonymous,
        He must die a little death each morning,
            He must swallow his toad and study his vomit
                as Baudelaire studied *la charogne* of Jeanne Duval.

The poet must be or become both Keats and Renoir and Keats *as* Renoir,
Mozart as Figaro and Edgar Allan Poe as Ophelia, stoned out of her mind
            drowning in the river called forever river and ever . . .

Keats as Mimi, Camille, and an aging gourmet.
He must also refuse the favors of the unattainable lady
(As Baudelaire refused Mme. Sabatier when the fair blond summoned
    him,
For Jeanne Duval was enough and more than enough, although she
    cuckolded him
With errand boys, servants, waiters; reality was Jeanne Duval.
Had he permitted Madame Sabatier to teach the poet a greater whiteness,
His devotion and conception of the divinity of Beauty would have suffered
    an absolute diminution.)

The poet must be both Casanova and St. Anthony,

He must be Adonis, Nero, Hippolytus, Heathcliff, and Phaedre,
        Genghis Kahn, Genghis Cohen, and Gordon Martini
            Dandy Ghandi and St. Francis,

Professor Tenure, and Dizzy the dean and Disraeli of Death.

He would have worn the horns of existence upon his head,
He would have perceived them regarding the looking-glass,
He would have needed them the way a moose needs a hat rack;
Above his heavy head and in his loaded eyes, black and scorched,
He would have seen the meaning of the hat-rack, above the glass
Looking in the dark foyer.

For the poet must become nothing but poetry,
He must be nothing but a poem when he is writing
Until he is absent-minded as the dead are
    Forgetful as the nymphs of Lethe and a lobotomy . . .
       ("the fat weed that rots on Lethe wharf")

He must be Iago, Desdemona, and a willow tree;
He must be torn between church and state . . . like Antigone
          (father and life . . .)

He must be a nymphomaniacal whore yet preserve his virginity,
The virginity of the empty paper's whiteness, snow and liberty;
Unless he succeeds, how can he unite in a single thought
        Morning and death?
        (Desire and transcendence)

        How can he possess
    The dreams and extremes of hope and despair
           (which are named Death and morning)?

He must wish to dance at everyone's wedding,
He must wish to be everyone and everything,
He must be a Trappist, but eloquent as Trotzky,

        Chaste but a gigolo,
        The Czar yet Figaro.

Hence, how can he be anything but nothing or zero

If this dramatis personae is ever a necessity?

Poem

In the morning, when it was raining,
Then the birds were hectic and loudy:
Through all the reign is fall's entertaining
Their singing was erratic and full of disorder:
They did not remember the summer blue
Or the orange of June. They did not think at all
Of the great red and bursting ball
Of the kingly sun's terror and tempest, blazing,
Once the slanting rain threw over all
The colorless curtains off the ceaseless spontaneous fall.

The First Night of Fall and Falling Rain

The common rain had come again
Slanting and colorless, pale and anonymous,
Fainting falling in the first evening
Of the first perception of the actual fall.
The long and late light had slowly gathered up
A sooty wool of clouded sky, dim and distant more and more
Until, at dusk, the very sense of selfhood waned,
A weakening nothing halted, diminished or denied or set aside,
Neither tea, nor, after an hour whiskey,
Ice and then a pleasant glow, a burning,
And the first leaping wood fire
Since a cold night in May, too long ago to be more than
Merely a cold and vivid memory.
Staring, empty and without thought
Beyond the rising mists of the emotion of causeless sadness,
How suddenly all consciousness leaped in spontaneous gladness;
Knowing without thinking how the falling rain (outside, all over)
In slow sustained consistent vibration all over outside
Tapping window, streaking roof, running down runnel and drain

Waking a sense, once more, of all that lived outside of us,
Beyond emotion, for beyond the swollen distorted shadows and lights
Of the toy town and the vanity fair of waking consciousness!

Posthumously
Published Poems

America, America!

I am a poet of the Hudson River and the heights above it,
    the lights, the stars, and the bridges
I am also by self-appointment the laureate of the Atlantic
    —of the peoples' hearts, crossing it
        to new America.

I am burdened with the truck and chimera, hope,
    acquired in the sweating sick-excited passage
        in steerage, strange and estranged
Hence I must descry and describe the kingdom of emotion.

For I am a poet of the kindergarten (in the city)
    and the cemetery (in the city)
And rapture and ragtime and also the secret city in the heart and mind
This is the song of the natural city self in the 20th century.

It is true but only partly true that a city is a "tyranny of numbers"
(This is the chant of the urban metropolitan and metaphysical self
After the first two World Wars of the 20th century)

—This is the city self, looking from window to lighted window
When the squares and checks of faintly yellow light
Shine at night, upon a huge dim board and slab-like tombs,
Hiding many lives. It is the city consciousness
Which sees and says: more: more and more: always more.

Two Lyrics from *Kilroy's Carnival, A Masque*

I. ARIA

"—Kiss me there where pride is glittering
Kiss me where I am ripened and round fruit
Kiss me wherever, however, I am supple, bare and flare

(Let the bell be rung as long as I am young:
    let ring and fly like a great bronze wing!)

"—I'll kiss you wherever you think you are poor,
Wherever you shudder, feeling striped or barred,
Because you think you are bloodless, skinny or marred:
    Until, until
    your gaze has been stilled—
Until you are shamed again no more!
I'll kiss you until your body and soul
    the mind in the body being fulfilled—
Suspend their dread and civil war!"

II. SONG

Under the yellow sea
Who comes and looks with me
For the daughters of music, the fountains of poetry?
Both have soared forth from the unending waters
Where all things still are seeds and far from flowers
And since they remain chained to the sea's powers
May wilt to nonentity or loll and arise to comedy
Or thrown into mere accident through irrelevant incident
Dissipate all identity ceaselessly fragmented by the ocean's
    immense and intense, irresistible and insistent action,
Be scattered like the sand is, purposely and relentlessly,
Living in the summer resorts of the dead endlessly.

Phoenix Lyrics

I

If nature is life, nature is death:
It is winter as it is spring:
Confusion is variety, variety

And confusion in everything
Make experience the true conclusion
Of all desire and opulence,
All satisfaction and poverty.

II

When a hundred years had passed nature seemed to man
        a clock
Another century sank away and nature seemed a jungle
        in a rock
And now that nature has become a ticking and hidden
        bomb how we must mock
Newton, Democritus, the Deity
The heart's ingenuity and the mind's infinite uncontrollable
        insatiable curiosity.

III

Purple black cloud at sunset: it is late August
and the light begins to look cold, and as we look,
listen and look, we hear the first drums of autumn.

News of the Gold World of May

News of the Gold World of May in Holland Michigan:

"Wooden shoes will clatter again
    on freshly scrubbed streets—"

The tulip will arise and reign again from awnings and windows
        of all colors and forms
            its vine, verve and valentine curves

upon the city streets, the public grounds
    and private lawns
(wherever it is conceivable
that a bulb might take root
    and the two lips, softly curved, come up
possessed by the skilled love and will of a ballerina.)

The citizens will dance in folk dances.
    They will thump, they will pump,
    thudding and shoving
    elbow and thigh,
    bumping and laughing, like barrels and bells.

Vast fields of tulips in full bloom,
    the reproduction of a miniature Dutch village,
    part of a gigantic flower show.

Occasional Poems

I CHRISTMAS POEM FOR NANCY

Noël, Noël
We live and we die
Between heaven and hell
Between the earth and the sky
And all shall be well
And all shall be unwell
And once again! all shall once again!
    All shall be well
By the ringing and the swinging
    of the great beautiful holiday bell
Of Noël! Noël!

II SALUTE VALENTINE

I'll drink to thee only with my eyes
When two are three and four,
And guzzle reality's rise and cries
And praise the truth beyond surmise
When small shots shout: More! More! More! More!

III RABBI TO PREACH

Rabbi Robert Raaba will preach
        on "An Eye for an Eye"
            (an I for an I?)
(Two weeks from this week: "On the Sacred Would")
At Temple Sholem on Lake Shore Drive
—Pavel Slavensky will chant the liturgical responses
And William Leon, having now thirteen years
        will thank his parents that he exists
To celebrate his birthday of manhood, his chocolate
Bar Mitzvah, his yum-yum kippered herring, his Russian Corona.

The Greatest Thing in North America

This is the greatest thing in North America:
Europe is the greatest thing in North America!
High in the sky, dark in the heart, and always there
Among the natural powers of sunlight and of air,
Changing, second by second, shifting and changing the light,
Bring fresh rain to the stone of the library steps.

Under the famous names upon the pediment:
        Thales, Aristotle,
Cicero, Augustine, Scotus, Galileo,
Joseph, Odysseus, Hamlet, Columbus and Spinoza,
Anna Karenina, Alyosha Karamazov, Sherlock Holmes.

And the last three also live upon the silver screen
Three blocks away, in moonlight's artificial day,
A double bill in the darkened palace whirled,
And the veritable glittering light of the turning world's
Burning mind and blazing imagination, showing, day by day
And week after week the desires of the heart and mind
Of all the living souls yearning everywhere
From Canada to Panama, from Brooklyn to Paraguay,
From Cuba to Vancouver, every afternoon and every night.

Love and Marilyn Monroe

(After Spillane)

Let us be aware of the true dark gods
Acknowledging the cache of the crotch
The primitive pure and powerful pink and gray
        private sensitivities
Wincing, marvelous in their sweetness, whence rises
        the future.

Therefore let us praise Miss Marilyn Monroe.
She has a noble attitude marked by pride and candor
She takes a noble pride in the female nature and torso
She articulates her pride with directness and exuberance
She is honest in her delight in womanhood and manhood.
She is not a great lady, she is more than a lady,
She continues the tradition of Dolly Madison and Clara Bow
When she says, "Any woman who claims she does not like
        to be grabbed is a liar!"
Whether true or false, this colossal remark
        states a dazzling intention . . .

    It might be the birth of a new Venus among us
    It atones at the very least for such as Carrie Nation
    For Miss Monroe will never be a blue nose,
        and perhaps we may hope

That there will be fewer blue noses because
        she has flourished—
Long may she flourish in self-delight and the joy
        of womanhood.
A nation haunted by Puritanism owes her homage and
        gratitude.

Let us praise, to say it again, her spiritual pride
And admire one who delights in what she has and is
(Who says also: "A woman is like a motor car:
        She needs a good body."
And: "I sun bathe in the nude, because I want
        to be blond all over.")

    This is spiritual piety and physical ebullience
    This is the vivid glory, spiritual and physical,
    Of Miss Marilyn Monroe.

from The Graveyard by the Sea

(After Valéry)

This hushed surface where the doves parade
Amid the pines vibrates, amid the graves;
Here the noon's justice unites all fires when
The sea aspires forever to begin again and again.
O what a gratification comes after long meditation
O satisfaction, after long meditation or ratiocination
Upon the calm of the gods
Upon divine serenity, in luxurious contemplation!

What pure toil of perfect lightning enwombs, consumes,
Each various manifold jewel of imperceptible foam,
And how profound a peace appears to be begotten and begun
When upon the abyss the sunlight seems to pause,
The pure effects of an eternal cause:
Time itself sparkles, to dream and to know are one. . . .

UNCOLLECTED POEMS

The Spring

(After Rilke)

Spring has returned! Everything has returned!
The earth, just like a schoolgirl, memorizes
Poems, so many poems. . . . Look, she has learned
So many famous poems, she has earned so many prizes!

Teacher was strict. We delighted in the white
Of the old man's beard, bright like the snow's:
Now we may ask which names are wrong, or right
For "blue," for "apple," for "ripe." She knows, she knows!

Lucky earth, let out of school, now you must play
Hide-and-seek with all the children every day:
You must hide that we may seek you: we will! We will!

The happiest child will hold you. She knows all the things
You taught her: the word for "hope," and for "believe,"
Are still upon her tongue. She sings and sings and sings.

Late Autumn in Venice

(After Rilke)

The city floats no longer like a bait
To hook the nimble darting summer days.
The glazed and brittle palaces pulsate and radiate
And glitter. Summer's garden sways,
A heap of marionettes hanging down and dangled,
Leaves tired, torn, turned upside down and strangled:
Until from forest depths, from bony leafless trees
A will wakens: the admiral, lolling long at ease,
Has been commanded, overnight—suddenly—:

In the first dawn, all galleys put to sea!
Waking then in autumn chill, amid the harbor medley,
The fragrance of pitch, pennants aloft, the butt
Of oars, all sails unfurled, the fleet
Awaits the great wind, radiant and deadly.

Archaic Bust of Apollo

(After Rilke)

We cannot know the indescribable face
Where the eyes like apples ripened. Even so,
His torso has a candelabra's glow,
His gaze, contained as in a mirror's grace,

Shines within it. Otherwise his breast
Would not be dazzling. Nor would you recognize
The smile that moves along his curving thighs,
There where love's strength is caught within its nest.

This stone would not be broken, but intact
Beneath the shoulders' flowing cataract,
Nor would it glisten like a stallion's hide,

Brimming with radiance from every side
As a star sparkles. Now it is dawn once more.
All places scrutinize you. You must be reborn.

What Curious Dresses All Men Wear

What curious dresses all men wear!
The walker you met in a brown study,
The President smug in rotogravure,
The mannequin, the bathing beauty.

The bubble-dancer, the deep-sea diver,
The bureaucrat, the adulterer,
Hide private parts which I disclose
To those who know what a poem knows.

Sonnet Suggested by Homer, Chaucer, Shakespeare, Edgar Allan Poe, Paul Valéry, James Joyce, et al.

Let me not, ever, to the marriage in Cana
Of Galilee admit the slightest sentiment
Of doubt about the astonishing and sustaining manna
Of chance and choice to throw a shadow's element
Of disbelief in truth—Love is not love
Nor is the love of love its truth in consciousness
If it can be made hesitant by any crow or dove or
      seeming angel or demon from above or from below
Or made more than it is knows itself to be by the authority
      of any ministry of love.

O no—it is the choice of chances and the chancing of
      all choice—the wine
which was the water may be sickening, unsatisfying or
      sour
A new barbiturate drawn from the fattest flower
That prospers green on Lethe's shore. For every hour
Denies or once again affirms the vow and the ultimate
      tower
Of aspiration which made Ulysses toil so far away from
      home
And then, for years, strive against every wanton desire,
      sea and fire, to return across the
      ever-threatening seas
A journey forever far beyond all the vivid eloquence
      of every poet and all poetry.

Sonnet on Famous and Familiar Sonnets and Experiences

(With much help from Robert Good, William Shakespeare,
John Milton, and little Catherine Schwartz)

Shall I compare her to a summer play?
She is too clever, too devious, too subtle, too dark:
Her lies are rare, but then she paves the way
Beyond the summer's sway, within the jejune park
Where all souls' aspiration to true nobility
Obliges Statues in the Frieze of Death
And when this pantomime and Panama of Panorama Fails,
"I'll never speak to you agayne"—or waste her panting breath.

When I but think of how her years are spent
Deadening that one talent which—for woman is—
Death or paralysis, denied: nature's intent
That each girl be a mother—whether or not she is
Or has become a lawful wife or bride
—O Alma Magna Mater, deathless the living death of pride.

Yeats Died Saturday in France

Yeats died Saturday in France.
Freedom from his animal
Has come at last in alien Nice,
His heart beat separate from his will:
He knows at last the old abyss
Which always faced his staring face.

No ability, no dignity
Can fail him now who trained so long
For the outrage of eternity,
Teaching his heart to beat a song

In which man's strict humanity,
Erect as a soldier, became a tongue.

from A King of Kings, A King Among the Kings

Come, let us rejoice in James Joyce, in the greatness of this poet,
  king, and king of poets

For he is our poor dead king, he is the monarch and Caesar of English,
  he is the veritable King of the King's English

    The English of the life of the city,
    and the English of music;

Let them rejoice because he rejoiced and was joyous;

For his joy was superior, it was supreme, for it was accomplished

After the suffering of much evil, the evil of the torment of pride,

By the overcoming of disgust and despair by means of the confrontation
  of them

By the enduring of nausea, the supporting of exile, the drawing from
   the silence of exile, the pure arias of the
   hidden music of all things, all beings.

For the joy of Joyce was earned by the sweat of the bow of his mind
   by the tears of the agony of his heart;

    hence it was gained, mastered, and conquered,
     (hence it was not a gift and freely given,
     a mercy often granted to masters,
     as if they miraculous were natural—)

For he earned his joy and ours by the domination of evil by
        confrontation and the exorcism of language
        in all its powers of imitation and
        imagination and radiance and delight. . . .

Now He Knows All There Is to Know: Now He Is Acquainted with the Day and Night

(Robert Frost, 1874–1963)

Whose wood this is I think I know:
He made it sacred long ago:
He will expect me, far or near
To watch that wood immense with snow.

That famous horse must feel great fear
Now that his noble rider's no longer here:
He gives his harness bells to rhyme
—Perhaps he will be back, in time?

All woulds were promises he kept
Throughout the night when others slept:
Now that he knows all that he did not know,
His wood is holy, and full of snow,
and all the beauty he made holy long long ago
In Boston, London, Washington,
And once by the Pacific and once in Moscow:
      and now, and now
      upon the fabulous blue river ever
      or singing from a great white bough

And wherever America is, now as before,
      and now as long, long ago
He sleeps and wakes forever more!

      "O what a metaphysical victory
      The first day and night of death must be!"

A Dream of Whitman Paraphrased, Recognized and Made More Vivid by Renoir

Twenty-eight naked young women bathed by the shore
Or near the bank of a woodland lake
Twenty-eight girls and all of them comely
Worthy of Mack Sennett's camera and Florenz Ziegfeld's Foolish Follies.

They splashed and swam with the wondrous unconsciousness
Of their youth and beauty
In the full spontaneity and summer of the fleshes of awareness
Heightened, intensified and softened
By the soft and the silk of the waters
Blooded made ready by the energy set afire by the nakedness of the body,

Electrified: deified: undenied.

A young man of thirty years beholds them from a distance.
He lives in the dungeon of ten million dollars.
He is rich, handsome and empty standing behind the linen curtains
Beholding them.
Which girl does he think most desirable, most beautiful?
They are all equally beautiful and desirable from the gold distance.
For if poverty darkens discrimination and makes perception too vivid,
The gold of wealth is also a form of blindness.
For has not a Frenchman said, Although this is America . . .

What he has said is not entirely relevant,
That a naked woman is a proof of the existence of God.

Where is he going?
Is he going to be among them to splash and to laugh with them?
They did not see him although he saw them and was there among them.
He saw them as he would not have seen them had they been conscious
Of him or conscious of men in complete depravation:
This is his enchantment and impoverishment
As he possesses them in gaze only.

. . . He felt the wood secrecy, he knew the June softness
The warmth surrounding him crackled
        Held in by the mansard roof mansion
He glimpsed the shadowy light on last year's brittle leaves fallen,
        Looked over and overlooked, glimpsed by the fall of death,
Winter's mourning and the May's renewal.

Albert Einstein to Archibald MacLeish

I should have been a plumber fixing drains
And mending pure white bathtubs for the great Diogenes
(who scorned all lies, all liars, and all tyrannies),

And then, perhaps, he would bestow on me—majesty!
(O modesty aside, forgive my fallen pride, O hidden majesty,
The lamp, the lantern, the lucid light he sought for
        All too often—sick humanity!)

The Poet

The riches of the poet are equal to his poetry
His power is his left hand
        It is idle weak and precious
His poverty is his wealth, a wealth which may destroy him like Midas
Because it is that laziness which is a form of impatience
And this he may be destroyed by the gold of the light which never was
On land or sea.
He may be drunken to death, draining the casks of excess
That extreme form of success.
He may suffer Narcissus' destiny
Unable to live except with the image which is infatuation
Love, blind, adoring, overflowing

Unable to respond to anything which does not bring love quickly or
    immediately.

. . . The poet must be innocent and ignorant
But he cannot be innocent since stupidity is not his strong point
Therefore Cocteau said, "What would I not give
To have the poems of my youth withdrawn from existence?
I would give to Satan my immortal soul."
This metaphor is wrong, for it is his immortal soul which he wished to
    redeem,
Lifting it and sifting it, free and white, from the actuality of
        youth's banality, vulgarity,
        pomp and affectation of his early
        works of poetry.

So too in the same way a Famous American Poet
When fame at last had come to him sought out the fifty copies
of his first book of poems which had been privately printed
by himself at his own expense.
He succeeded in securing 48 of the 50 copies, burned them
And learned then how the last copies were extant,
As the law of the land required, stashed away in the national capital,
at the Library of Congress.
Therefore he went to Washington, therefore he took out the last two copies
Placed them in his pocket, planned to depart
Only to be halted and apprehended. Since he was the author,
Since they were his books and his property he was reproached
But forgiven. But the two copies were taken away from him
Thus setting a national precedent.

For neither amnesty nor forgiveness is bestowed upon poets, poetry and
    poems,
For William James, the lovable genius of Harvard
spoke the terrifying truth: *"Your friends may forget, God*
        may forgive you, But the brain cells record
        your acts for the rest of eternity."
What a terrifying thing to say!
This is the endless doom, without remedy, of poetry.
This is also the joy everlasting of poetry.

The Studies of Narcissus

The mind is a city like London,
Smoky and populous: it is a capital
Like Rome, ruined and eternal,
Marked by the monuments which no one
Now remembers. For the mind, like Rome, contains
Catacombs, aqueducts, amphitheatres, palaces,
Churches and equestrian statues, fallen, broken or soiled.
The mind possesses and is possessed by all the ruins
Of every haunted, hunted generation's celebration.

"Call us what you will: we are made such by love."
We are such studs as dreams are made on, and
Our little lives are ruled by the gods, by Pan,
Piping of all, seeking to grasp or grasping
All of the grapes; and by the bow-and-arrow god,
Cupid, piercing the heart through, suddenly and forever.

Dusk we are, to dusk returning, after the burning,
After the gold fall, the fallen ash, the bronze,
Scattered and rotten, after the white null statues which
Are winter, sleep, and nothingness: when
Will the houselights of the universe
Light up and blaze?
                          For it is not the sea
Which murmurs in a shell,
And it is not only heart, at harp o'clock,
It is the dread terror of the uncontrollable
Horses of the apocalypse, running in wild dread
toward Arcturus—and returning as suddenly. . . .

Alone, obsessed as the devout, I waited:
Under the mast of my head, my eyes sailed forth,
Fed by an abundance so multitudinous
I knew it must be infinite:

Between the sleek, rippling and glittering silks
Delight in the light mounted and mounted in me
        and doubt itself
        and doubt
Fathered the dolls of possibility
Until they shone as the progeny of hope,
The dazzling diamonds my demon denied and loved
—Distant or hidden sources nurtured the sorcery
And miracles of radiance, flowed out of depths
Or struck, like lightning, from heights I merely guessed.

How the sky shone: look how my leaves are curved
And black, how they possess and are possessed
By every brilliance, radiance, and vividness—
—How could they know I had discovered the self?
By studying the marvels of my hope
And all the variety and poverty of my face
Within the supple marble where the leaves
Of swirling waters were more numerous,
        as various
As falsehood, more fecund than fantasy,
And infinite as numbers . . . space was a colosseum,
And infinite as numbers . . .
The silence was the drum, and drums, of space,
Waiting and beating,
Throbbing, expectant, before all triumph, all miracles
       to come. . . .

Within the river's folds and folding fields
I gazed until I looked for the rippled dream

Of seeing myself at last a being I loved,
Loved by a being beautiful enough to love—

. . . The river holds the summer's pride, the sum
Of sun and summer, gold and golding glow:
Love is reality—as in the beginning it was—
And love is destiny. The reality of the ecstasy

Riding into the womb begot the city,
Planted or sowed the future's flowers and powers
      . . . again, again . . .
Inmost was utmost:
Under the mast of my head
My eyes sailed forth and searched
The sleek silks and curving softnesses:
The river was reality and various plurality
And made me other than I was at each
Ripple of its irresistible flowing:
I thought: God is in love, in love with possibility,
His love are his loves, his love is enough
To make the promiscuity of actuality . . .
—The river was full of bells as the sun rose,
Shuddering ripples grew to the radiance
Of chandeliers at noon, the blazing sun
Became a jewel of inexhaustible opulence. . . .

The blazing sunlight is the world itself:
The black heart of the ego shines and shines in vain,
Weak as the moonlight, like a kind of moonlight—

The river rose from sovereign sources, secret steeps,
Until, under the sun, it was a dream of diamonds

Or in the winter, frozen, within
The snow's hushed infinite,
It was a kind of moonlight,
A pathos of white silence, white
And silent, lighted by the moon's white silence—

How blond the light of summer is, how round
And how profound the blue contained and loved
Within the river's flowing glass, glinting and glittering—
Brightening and darkening, freshening, shadowing
In its irresistible going and going, holding
Glowing, and glowing being's immense plurality!

The game of the mystery of reality
Began when the first thought concealed itself,
When the speech of ripened lips
Hid what was already hidden, or not yet known.

For long as lore, desire was narrative,
Gratified in imagination's will,
And longer still I read the handsome story—
Venus as absolute in joy's full glory!

Eternity is the roar you hear
When you hold a sea shell close to your ear.

It is not the sound of the knock of the pounding heart,
It is not the roar of the insatiable sea, erupting upon the shore,

It is the eternal roar of eternity, the lightning and the thunder
Of each moment's subjection and rejection—the eternal
      roar of judgment and resurrection—

. . . After utter forgiveness, what knowledge
Can be possessed by consciousness?
Forgive: do not forget. Remember and live,
For life is rooted in memory's damnation and blessedness.
And life is hope, hope rooted in the past as it is
      known, remembered, and controlled
      by the future's hopes, the future's flowers.

Look: I looked at the dancers, swaying,
Under the lanterns, in the olive garden,
      the fat vineyard, the apple orchard,
Or bordering the river where the boats are anchored,
Bound to the shore and lolling, like the dancers:
They do not know the secret of summer,
They do not possess the natural knowledge of the river,
Yet they sigh and quicken, murmur to the music,
Delighted that they exist, for all love's agony
      and all love's ecstasy,
They are not ashamed they touch each other, nor afraid

THE COLLECTED POEMS OF DELMORE SCHWARTZ

They are beautiful enough to touch and love,
They wish to touch each other, touching and touched,
Before the cause becomes the truth, before the root
      Becomes the fruit, because. . . .

We are all—look!—the figments of the imagination's aspiration!
Are the follies or followers of intense and hot infatuation:
Each heart is liege to Venus, queen and empress of the
      seas and ports of consciousness;
And thus, as Venus from the sea arose and came to be,
The self I know, Narcissus as he is known, was born,
      within the river, arising shocked—
Gazing or gaping at the river's every-being, ever-becoming:
The river was my mother: it was my school
And was and is the only school because
Knowledge is only the knowledge of love,
And every story is the story of love,
And every storyteller is a lovelorn ghost!

The river was the abundant belly of beauty itself,
The river was the dream space where I walked,
The river was itself and yet it was—flowing and freshening—
A self anew, another self, or self renewed
At every tick of eternity, and by each glint of light
Mounting or sparkling, descending to shade and black
—Had I but told them my heart, told how it was
Taunted at noon and pacified at dusk, at starfall midnight
Strong in hope once more, ever in eagerness
Jumping like joy, would they have heard? How could they?
How, when what they knew was, like the grass,
Simple and certain, known through the truth of touch,
      another form and fountain of falsehood's fecundity—
Gazing upon their faces as they gazed
Could they have seen my faces as whores who are
Holy and deified as priestesses of hope
      —the sacred virgins of futurity—
Promising dear divinity precisely because
They were disfigured ducks who might become
And be, and ever beloved, white swans, noble and beautiful.

Could they have seen how my faces were
Bonfires of worship and vigil, blazes of adoration
            and hope
—Surely they would have laughed again, renewed their scorn,
Giggled and snickered, cruel. Surely have said
This is the puerile mania of the obsessed,
The living logic of the lunatic:
I was the statue of their merriment,
Dead and a death, Pharaoh and monster forsaken and lost.

My faces were my apes: my apes became
Performers in the Sunday of their parks,
Buffoons or clowns in the comedy or farce
When they took pleasure in knowing that they were not like me.

I waited like obsession in solitude:
The sun's white terror tore and roared at me,
The moonlight, almost white, at night,
Whether awake of sleeping, arrested me
And sang, softly, haunted, unlike the sun
But as the sun. Withheld from me or took away
Despair or peace, making me once more
With thought of what had never been before—
—The others were the despots of despair—

The river's freshness sailed from unknown sources—

. . . They snickered giggled, laughed aloud at last,
They mocked and marveled at the statue which was
A caricature, as strained and stiff, and yet
A statue of self-love!—since self-love was
To them, truly my true love, how, then, was I a stillness of nervousness
So nervous a caricature: did they suppose
Self-love was unrequited, or betrayed?
They thought I had fallen in love with my own face,
And this belief became the night-like obstacle
To understanding all my unbroken suffering,
My studious soft-regard, the pain of hope,
The torment of possibility:

How then could I have expected them to see me
As I saw myself, within my gaze, or see
That being thus seemed as a toad, a frog, a wen, a mole.
Knowing their certainty that I was only
A monument, a monster who had fallen in love
With himself alone, how could I have
Told them what was in me, within my heart, trembling, and passionate
Within the labyrinth and caves of my mind, which is
Like every mind partly or wholly hidden from itself?
The words for what is in my heart and in my mind
Do not exist: But I must seek and search to find
Amid the vines and orchards of the vivid world of day
Approximate images, imaginary parallels
For what is in my heart and dark within my mind:
Comparisons and mere metaphors: for all
Of them are substitutes, both counterfeit and vague:
They are, at most, deceptive resemblances,
False in their very likeness, like the sons
Who are alike and kin and more unlike and false
Because they seem the father's very self: but each one is
—Although begotten by the same forbears—himself,
The unique self, each one is unique, like every other one,
And everything, older or younger, nevertheless
A passionate nonesuch who before has been.
Do you hear, do you see? Do you understand me now, and how
The words for what is my heart do not exist?

Once, far from me in the distance, in a grove, concealed
Hidden, she thought, I heard a girl
Screaming with joy, joy absolute,
Joy unheard of before, and never known,
And given to me or given
By me to girls: I had never been. . . .
How many thoughts, like lightning strokes, occurred
And seemed more true than any truth I knew!

Came with no concentration, no
Concern or effort, toiling up the path,
Sparkled like the radiance or stood like the oars

Whence all the radiance arrives, the sunlight's swords:

Each thought an intuition, instant,
Spontaneous, coherent in the mind
Of words: and seemed and were and are
—As first I named them—endless sentences
Proven abundantly in all the instances
Experience unveiled, although it was
—In so many other ways—astonishing!

This was an endless sentence which I learned
Or recognized in the fluent river's school:
Everything is always somewhere else; or it is
Present—when undesired—in an embarrassment
Of riches, a profusion prolific and inexhaustible,
An oppression of luxury, like Midas's gold.

This is an endless sentence which I saw
As student at the river's universal school:
The cause of that boundless ecstasy in which
A man had plunged that screaming girl,
—A triumph so triumphant all is lost
Save for the sweetness at the source
Within, intense, of such an intensity
That blessed in the loss of consciousness
It seems, at first, a kind of death—so much
Like death that the fearful self, beholds beholding
Upon the brink, all of the terror of love,
Draws back and the first time never is endured!

I knew the parable of trying to see
The truth behind the face, the mind behind
The surface, the radiance within
The radiance, within the shining radiance
And thus I missed matchless magnificence
So many times! Since, at times,
Appearance is reality and not a mask—
        Is neither secret nor masked:

The apple is the apple which is red
And ripe upon the tree—but only then
During the time of ripening, before
The fall, long long after the flower
—The times of flowering and the flowers are
The scenes of falsehood most of all!
This too is a parable of reality,
It is as well a parable of love,
And love's reality, after the flowers,
After the green and growing fruit.

I was, for a long time, every kind
Of shining angel: kind of angle,
And kind of light: each point of view
Drew up something new, or some which
I never knew. Every picture possessed
Four sides, and four thousand sides and sights.
Each time I looked or read between the lines
I saw the mount of Venus suddenly.
I found myself upon the island named
Cytherea—the lake of summer capital.

I visited the house of Orpheus,
His house, his garden and his park,
The horses which he loved and which he lost . . .
Finding the beasts of hell, to whom he sang
Not to regain his lost Eurydice,
But to be free of the ice-like pain and stone of loss.
—The music which he made and sang to gain
That liberty was strange, a strangeness and a mockery.

The present is the future. We are there
—Or going where we wished to be—the past
Is but a version of the future which
Is likely to be false. The present is
The future twice: first it is the future of the hope
By which we live and die, direct or drive the will
Of toil, the mind of effort; second, it is

The comparison of the present as it is
And as it was conceived by hope, before,
When past was present still, not yet unmasked.

How many structures of reality
I saw within the river: light which was at once
Insight, the sweet access of being which
The radiance of knowledge gives and gives
With a purity and freedom which no other thing,
Consumed, confers, neither the bread nor wine
On which we fed on the dark god's holidays.

                                   Height:
                                    Light:
The river of all rivers, the motion of emotion
The feeling of the real and [*words missing*]
The feast of reality and
Your holy word
An infinite bliss, given as
Infinitely as
It is infinitely gifted:
Let it be, let your kingdom
Descend in all splendor
When we ring
The bells of morning and the bells of mortality
Swinging and singing
            as the ever freshness
Which flowers forever in the dark patience
Of the strength of hope and the truth
Of the heart which the heart itself
Seldom knows, and never wholly believes.

You would not have found
What is so precious to you, if you had not
Been seeking it. And: if you had sought it,
You would not have found it: Let it come! Let it come!

This is true too: if you find only
What you bring in your seeking,

THE COLLECTED POEMS OF DELMORE SCHWARTZ

—Yet: you would not have found it,
If you had not been able to recognize it!

—This is the dynasty of discovery:
It is ruled by a dialectic of poles apart:
                    The synthesis is thus:

It is true. It is not real:
You find what you possess: you seek
What you do not know you have
                    that you possess.

The river sang: there are many truths,
Look: how they glitter and ripple, radiant,
And the river chanted: many truths—did you know?
                    do you believe?
Are better than one truth. This is
The doctrine of the magician and musician:
But reality is magical and musical.
It comprehends the stones and the hearts of men.
And all the variety between these two
Extremes completes the comparison
Which makes all dreams poor and inadequate
Once set in contrast with reality's ingenuity.

Those who knew passion and compassion after me
Misunderstood my purity, my poverty,
The elation through privation, the motion of devotion.

Sisyphus, Oedipus, Theseus, Heracles,
Cupid and Psyche . . .

        They never knew—or knew for the first time,
        The [*word missing*] of the rain,
            nor for the first time
Knew the new flow of the heartbeats of love,
A thing—and experience—which, never having been
            known before
Did not possess the status of what exists,

                the dusk of doubt,
But merely the status of hope, the state of dusk
And doubt, and fear, rising and falling.

. . . It is not true: it never had been true.
The moon shines on the loved and the unloved
The music mounted to the minds
Of those who could and those who could not hear:
The music blooming, blossoming, flowering and flowing forth
For those who have fallen or are falling in love:
Behold it—behold that ghost of sentiment—
        that ghostly
                and sentimental ghost.

At first the river was a simple window
Empty, in shadow: immensity was a waste:
How wide the silence was, when I looked up
Beholding the sky's blue capital,
Thinking it empty, although beautiful
. . . I did not think it was the louver of the dead,
Nor think it was the palace of the stars' dancers—

—How could they understand my study and my hope
Or understand the study of hope itself
When all the knowledge came, at last, to this?
That all hope is at heart only then hope
That hope is true, or at least true enough,
That hope itself will still be possible
After each new illusion and conclusion,
And after each recognition of delusion!

Since love is reality, reality is love!
And the fear of the fading of feeling
Is the disease of the withering of hope, the hope
That the self will, at last, be born again anew, renewed
—Will wholly arise
When the living awaken
From the thickets of sleep and the mines of night
Withdrawing from the death of self-deception,

No longer master nor monster, no longer
Demon nor despot, strong, strong as illusion, stronger . . .

What blooms after the lisping, lipping dimnesses
When night in all its formless vagueness is over all
The beauty of the body of the river?
The roses are pink because of the weight of fragrance.
The leaves are green because green aspires to arise to radiance.
The river is the ripening or the ripened
Harvest of all the passing shows which move and shine
Between the soil, the sun, and the brilliant or dark sky.

The river is the hymn wherein
The ultimate vineyards of variety
Become the plums and grapes of dawn and dusk
In a plenitude so multitudinous
It must be infinite and infinitely generous:
It is the dance in which abundance falls and follows,
       forever moving
In all the moods and modes of fertility and fruitfulness.
—Branches, trees, brooded over the pool:
Salmon slipped lithely under the ripples, in grooves
And the salmon of the sunlight still gleamed until
All became [*manuscript breaks off*] . . .

O the brio, & presto, & allegro of the river when
              the sun
Blazed down on it, and it sang, mingling brights and
              blues:
What ghost a sovereign ruled the sources, distant,
              concealed,
Changing the depths under the merrying light, mica-glittering
              so furious: so joyous:
                   so spontaneous!

A suave bush.

I was in the presence of the mystery

Of the amplitude of abundance, dancing,
Multitudinous abundance, the majesty
Of ample infinitude, flowing and overflowing.

I was in the presence of the mystery
Of the plenitude and the majesty
Of the gifts and the giving and the grant
Of the ever-flowing process of reality:
Love is knowing in unknowing
Love is the majesty of the mystery
Of the abundance of surrender
When suddenly all the senses chant,
And the mind, caught in the anthem,
[*missing lines*]

Who but the fallen angel of consciousness
Sings with so much radiance of the clarity of reality?
The mastery of victory? The reality of hope?

I have supped and sucked and sickened in the valley
            of desperation.
I have been terrified—and in the darkness lost,
I have turned and sought despair as consolation
            or agony's cessation,
I surrendered or thought I surrendered forever,
            drawing the shades
Which shut out the blue rivers of morning, ending
            my vigil,
Telling myself that the self was nothing, and all was
            nothingness,
Nature was nothingness, and desire was nothing but
            passage,
The passage from darkness to nothingness to dark
            nothingness.

—*Then* I was almost glad that it was thus, thinking
            it must be thus,
Thinking that all my other thoughts had been (how else
            must it seem, might it seem, must it be

to most of us?)
Deceptions, illusions, delusions, satanic imaginations,
          hideous
          In the end, as the snake-like convolutions
          of the brain
          Which were the source and force of
          hallucination.
And I knew the rise and the return after the failure
          and the fall.
I knew and now I know the tone and the chant of rapture,
          supreme and surpassing all, of the lost,
          saved, the jubilee of those having
          awakened from the dream
          by the dream's conclusion.

Placidly at dusk—in hushed serenity
The hushed serene
Arose above the green
The waters were choirs wherein the sunlight chanted
The silence of space was a great blue balloon
Mounted aloft, waiting and attentive
The great blue bell, the dome which holds
          The daylight and the night
The noon of turquoise diamonds diamonding
          and gold golding
          and radiance entranced and ringing
     dancing in all the kinds of lances. . . .

. . . Thou art confessed!
The roots of riverhood
          are not in rain!

A brass of gleaming,
A pewter reticence,
A lucency, a transparency
The passing shows of
          plangent passions . . . starlings,
          star-winged
          starwings

Tapered.

. . . Were there lovers before me? How could there be since I
Discovered the self or—to insist again—
Invented it, by staring in a glass
And misconceiving the image of my face:
Of those who have fallen in love since then,
[*missing lines*]

The river possesses and continually blesses
Dreams of the sky in many disguises,
The sessions of its processions discover
All glittering radiance within the exaltation
Of the visual and visible imagination!

Under the meadows of the milk way
Under the marvels of the marble blue
The faint and bonewhite moonlight, faintly shining,
Seemed and sustained the mystery, or apparition
Glimpsed and guessed all day in the sun's glory,
And all the stories
Rippled and sparkled momentarily to me
—For first, I thought, the flowers existed only
In the contemplation of the stars. And then

The stars became the petals of the flowers
Of powers hidden, infinite and generous,
Flowing over, overflowing in boundless plenitude,
Possessing and possessed, blessing and blessed—
All luxury, fulfillment and largesse.
The river's coat—which half-concealed and half-revealed
The curves of sleekness, the slopes of suppleness
As the current rode and flowed, promised a tenderness
My face attracted, and an allure which promised me . . .

The river sang again of truth's variety,
Which is the light's plurality and ingenuity.
Lighting up, and misleading if too long believed.
        The light

Lolling upon the river's flow, descanted
On how all things are magnified and multiplied,
How emulation is an exaltation. The trees
Became a grove, a slowly curving orchard,
The river's tree became the harp, immense, of goddesses.
The river sang and said:
Death is not a spectacle or a catastrophe,
It is a distant eminence, far off, powerless, same as a point of view,
        Having nothing to do with love and victory
Nor with Dionysus, nor Apollo . . .
Phoenix fulfillment and fatherhood
Are other and otherwise to be understood.

—The poet is a shepherd of being,
The poet is the one who keeps the archives of the stones,
And makes immortal the lady among the rocks
And is the crying of the rocks, and draws in his flocks
To the fortitude of the acceptance of experience.

Another's face allure and desire, fixed on me,
And that was why I looked and looked,
Was why the others laughed until they shook,
Rollicking, looking into their own
Perfected self-deception, dark and sweet as the bone.

—Other than all the others and my self
        The river was
Sleekness and silk and supple,
        —The infinite blue above became, I saw,
Tender and infinite—
        An arch, contained yet magnified, within the flow,
Curving and curved, upon the river's face
The beauties of the stream supported my utmost dream!

A simple door opens upon an abyss . . .

Commanded reality, or uncommanded?
When I stare with much desire, my face becomes
A squint, a frown, and something falsified by hope,

UNCOLLECTED POEMS

Impatience, eagerness: and what I see
Is neither what I desire nor what is there:
My grasping gaze seizes what is a blur
And makes a hybrid of the blur and my desire,
A fiction and distortion of the uniqueness of reality.

Art thou not fortunate? Hast thou not seen
The foetus-like, the hideous, the obscene?
Yet equally, the admirable and the beautiful
In the leaves, darkened, but glittering and green
Within the river's glass fallen but supernatural—
. . . My faces were my apes: my apes became
Idolatrous . . .

. . . The sunlight became a jubilee of canaries:
Its genius engendered fury upon fury of blaze,
And then the beating of great wings began, the eagles rose
Above the orchards where the apples fattening and burned, burned.
From plump green to rounded red . . .
And I was lifted far above the hope and dread of love, above
The will and pounce of the chicken hawks, the willows of the dove.
Then love was but the door of mystery.
It was no more the terror beyond all mastery,
And ceased to be the midnight's leaping mystery.

I heard:
"The engine sighed softly,"
I listened to the machine's persistent drone, moan
"He commanded real fear,"
And felt the stage fright of guilt
The sweat of sympathy . . .

      : death to apes

The gods demanded, required, commanded
Instead of a cock, a pigeon,
a dog, a goat, or a pig,
The sacrifice of a culprit, a cupid.

"She ruffled the cards: she shuffled them
       She shuffled them agayne,
Those who deserve to die,
Die the death they deserve,"

Drums: white drums: the white round drums
Of the slowly swaying buttocks of drunken girls.

Poem to Johann Sebastian Bach

(For Julian)

Out of the watercolored windows, when you look,
Each is but each, and plain to see, not deep:
So does the neat print in an actual book,
Marching as if to true conclusion, keep
The illimitable blue immensely overhead
And the night, night of the living and the dead.

Brother and brother, of one Father,
Near and clear and far,
How indeed we mistake each other.
Despair, and fear, and care.

I drive in an auto all night long to reach
That place where all wheels grip no place and cease,
I never end the turning world, the breach
Where no spring is, nor winter is, but peace:
The only absolute stillness is the frieze
Of the escalator where the damned crowds rise.

Brother and brother, of one Father,
Near, and clear, and far,
How, afterward, we will know each other.
Beware, and share, and care.

Poem for Jacques Maritain and Leon Trotzky

The Gentile night and the white stars in congress
Still the traffic's racked energy;
And the hurdy-gurdy newsreel of memory
Flashes the past in its stilted sadness,

Standing on what brink then? By my room's window,
Thinking of the sources of situation
—Of the people's confrontation
When they see themselves dirty in another's shadow!

O Marxist drunk at the teats of Tiresias,
Is night still close to morning? Will the morning
Once more from rumorous darkness release us?

Tonight is more than night and more than meaning.
Stars are the buds of morning, do you know?
Look, in the West, at the white moon dreaming of snow.

The Maxims of Sisyphus

(SISYPHUS' SUCCESS)

Although I was tenacious, I never learned
    the wisdom and will of tenacity;
Although I was persistent, and praised for persistence,
At first faint falling off of inspiration's desire
    the black hood of despondency covered my face,
    fell over it
To till and toil and delve and dig, dumb in the darkness
    chinning and clutching, darkened and weakened
I never knew until . . . nor knew how the piddling puddling
    persistent will is the perpetual way,
    the royal real route to the richest fulfillment.

. . . Persistent, but faint of heart, passionate and
     yet apathetic,
     How often I turned my face away,
     How often avoided unpleasant imperfection,
     squeamish and absolute, and did not run up against
     the taboo abomination, but ran away and ran back.
     Running away instead of running running through
How could I perceive how often success was won after
     many repeated Sisyphean failures
     (When I often had been drunken with the romance
     and fortune of spontaneity, when often the more
     the effort, the worse the denial or outcome or . . .
     When all that I most wanted was near as my hands
     and feet, and had been, ever. . . .

How Can He Possess

     How can he possess
The dreams and extremes of hope and despair . . .
     (which are named Death and Morning)?

He must wish to dance at everyone's wedding.
He must wish to be everyone and everything.
He must be a Trappist, but eloquent as Trotzky,

     Chaste but a gigolo,
     the Czar yet Figaro.

Hence how can he be anything but nothing or zero
If this *dramatis personae* is ever a necessity?

Sonnet

I follow thought and what the world announces
I lean to hear, and leaning too far over,
Fall, and babied by confusion, cover
Myself in drowse, too tired by such bounces.
But in sleep are dreams across zigzagging snow
Descending quietly and slow, like minutes,
And on this peace the soul again begins its
Rhetoric of desire, older than Jericho,
And rails once more, like birds of early morning
Urchinous on branches and like newsboys,
"Extra, this is the meaning of life,
Here is the real good, beyond all turning,"
Till night goes home, astonished by such cries,
I wake up, and, to feel superior, I laugh.

The Power and Glory of Language

Lordly and mighty language—eagle of time and space,
Giving to the mind the possession and freedom of both,
Touring and traveling in the ancient whiteness and blueness,
Sailing in the winedark of Greece and olive green Mediterranean,
Seeking cinnamon and wisdom in the Orient's scriptures,
Harking to and holding the whistle of birds and lisping
Of infants and the joshing and jargon of boys, the squawk
And the yelp, the echo and the innuendo and belly-laugh,
Giggle, horse-laugh, titter, and snicker, containing
The midnight of meaning and the lightning of insight,
The small stars of the perception of white flowers
And falling flakes, the fingertip and the city, the continent
Of love, the first flush of Eros and the plunging delirium
(Which is a dying and a little death), her unbearable ecstasy
Began, the pulse and gong clamored and hammered,
She whimpered with pleasure, she sobbed in the procession

Of passion, she slid down the valley of the fury of joy
On skis which soared as she fell . . .

What have they called the little girl? Perdita, Judith, Marina?
The grace of language, which is the living ghost and holy spirit
Of joy (because it is unseen, it is gifted with wings,
and is small enough and powerful enough to be all things),
It is a bond and a meeting place
It is a currency which passes all borders
And proceeds through all nations,
It is given to all who take it
It is aristocratic as well as democratic.

The Sequel, the Conclusion, the Endlessness

For thus, since the body's death is quick, seems less,
Consoled or hidden by unconsciousness,
While every little death lies sprawling and awake
In the sleepless glade of consciousness,
Therefore the body's death seems the liberty
Of nothingness, the dream of every suicide,
Criminal, and tyrant, afraid of each little death,
Or sickened by the terror of new hope,
Or certain, again, that every death of any hope
Concludes all hope and makes the body's death
More desirable than the recurrent torment of the years
Of life with a dead heart and pathos instead of hope:
Or hope that hope may be reborn once more
Only to be disappointed as before:
This is the ignorant bigotry of all despair:
This is the Utopia of all suicide.

The final dream of liberty we believe
And suicides seek with certainty
Is also their first vision of reality:
If it is true, it is not because either fear

Or crime are key to profundity and aware,
Revealing the heart of reality and the heart's reality.
For if they were, how would it be possible to start
The games which begin the hope and end in the death of hope,
the body's death, and the death of the heart?

Poem: How Marvelous Man's Kind Is

When it is very dark, we see the stars clearly
—EMERSON

The universe is a machine for the making of gods
—BERGSON

How we marvel and must when most
Struggle to life and possess
That self or sense of the self
Which is either a hope or a myth
Shinnying the steeples of death
For the pigskin or fleece of pride!

If this passion did not exist
The captains and killers of wars
Surely would not persist
To their stone and pose;
And none would follow his dream
To the extremes of living and death:
Their soldiers, dreamstruck, enlist
Because they believe in a myth!

How we live! How we live by this!
Citizens of fantasy!
Pennants above an abyss
Limp, or blown stupidly.
As though the dream be true
Tomorrow in the country of the blue.

Now before we reach that shore
We are too sure or too unsure,
Fearing lunatic kings, or once more
Lunatics of intuitive doubt
—Caligula or Descartes!—
Till the truth of death do us part
From the stories and theatres of the heart.

When I Remember the Advent

When I remember the advent of the dazzling beauty
    As it descended, sudden and unknown,
I turn again to stiffened stone, alone
    With the poverty of having known the dazzling of beauty,
But only as a memory is known, only as a lake,
    A weekend or midnight
Know the glory streaming the great blue heights
    Riding in a storm of white disorder
    The cavalry of Aurora Borealis.

The Famous Resort in Late Autumn

The shouting of the sea and the storm storming
Was loud and louder, loud enough to waken the rocks
    & to shock
The stilt-borne salt-burnt spray-pocked creaking
    boardwalk
Which looking upon the ever-freshness of the unresting
foaming erupting ocean as an ancient crippled
    and exhausted old man
    gazing from the shore
As if the day and the summer and the carnival
    were no more

But only & forever the low and leaden night
Of the senseless sea struggling with the awakened rocks.

He Who Excuses Himself Also Accuses Himself

Listen, the dark lark chants once more
    Only the guilty are truly good!
A truth heartbreaking as war
    The penitent have understood.

Harken, how the demon once more sings
    As once, of love, to Socrates,
Or blesses the blankness of the snow,
    Since white is all colors, in disguise.

The dark bird whispers: *Have you understood
How only the guilty can be truly good?*

To a Fugitive

The night you got away, I dreamed you rose
Out of the earth to lean on a young tree.
Then they were there, hulking the moon away,
The great dogs rooting, snuffing up the grass.
You raise a hand, hungry to hold your lips
Out of the waiting air; but lights begin
Spidering the ground; O they come closing in,
The beam searches your face like fingertips.

Hurry, Maguire, hammer the body down,
Crouch to the wall again, shackle the cold
Machine guns and the sheriff and the cars:
Divide the bright bars of the cornered bone,

Strip, run for it, break the last law, unfold,
Dart down the alley, race between the stars.

Poem

      . . . window . . . winter . . .
The winter woods are wire and black
And by a vivid death possessed:
The orchard trees describe a rack
Upon the snow's blank vacant breast.
          . . . a shroud, a cloud, a lunar myth . . .
The trees' stripped lines writhe and arise
As in a Fury's passionate cry.
As if there were, beyond surprise,
A secret meaning in the sky!
           Is there? There is!
                Sure or perhaps?
                   Sure as perhaps.
The pulse of being is faint and low
As the gray cloth of the snow sky:
The scene is true as summer's show,
The woods of winter are a lie
             true as most truths.

Praise Is Traditional and Appropriate

I loved the wood because I found in it
Mushrooms, berries, beetles, birds and other words,
Hedgehogs, squirrels, memories, quarrels,
    and the damp smell
Of dead leaves, and former lives.
        I reached the first barn
—where wheat was stored—halfway up the slope

of the ravine
And saw her dancing, glancing twinkly eyes
Full of the hope and love which all thought mean,
And slate-green, slate-blue, blue or black like the sunrise
Skies, and in their variety and in their sheen
I thought that she was looking down at me
As if she understood past, present, and futurity.

The Dances and the Dancers

All of us delight in dancing and in beholding dances:
    Some of us desire a horse ballet
        Great and heavy horses,
Percherons with limbs like heavy but supple sandbags
    Dragging and lumbering in an *Alla Tedesca,*
        and then, at the horse show, the cavalry of Vienna,
        and then the sleek race horses of Saratoga:

All of us delight in the formal dancing of others
    Because we are bursting with the force of uncontrollable
        desire:
        Hence, where there are horses, as where there are rivers
and skaters—*Virtuoisi* of the body's ebullience and deftness,
    By the spirit captured
        and trained to rapture.

Then there is a party of the city, the theatre and the school,
Then there is a dancing of the heart and the heart's birthday.
And even at the numbed peak of intensest winter cold
The skaters below the hill on the frozen lake
    or white courts,
Turn like the stars in free constellations
Under the blue; a cold shining, and seem more radiant
    and serene,
Than statues of the white goddess, Juno, the classic
        and imagined queen.

Previously
Unpublished Poems

Dr. Levy

I sat on the curbstone, my face in my hands.
Dun buildings surrounded me. The glossy blue loft
Cold and star-pointing arena of desolation
Augmented my stage, whose rich experience begins
To unfold more strangers, events still more ambiguous.

Ah, how my clownish aspect soothed me then!
Crumpled up, knees akimbo, cheek upon one knee,
How fit this was to bring the sour-sweet tears
Again and again!
                    not that I failed
To tuck up my overcoat collar, for the dim wind
Grew into huffing sound and chilled.

Then, as I set there, I heard his footsteps' approach
And stop. But I did not look up,
But he touched my shoulder gently, and I turned and saw him
In evening clothes, as suave and foreign in seeming
As a magician or an undertaker
Or a master of ceremonies. Then he said,
"Perhaps I can help you," and tipped his top hat,
Which pleased me greatly, for such dignity
Touched my wound and matched my self-regard.

"Go away," I said, "Please go away," like the child
Unwilling to part with his sulk and its sweet attention,
And I dried my eyes with dainty and delicate dabs,
Snuffled, pouted, rested my chin on my knee.
"Can't you see that I want to be left alone?"
(For the druggist's anger still offended me),
"Nothing is wrong and I don't need anyone's help,"
"You would not be here, in tears, on the curbstone,
If all were well." (His diction impressed me
Very much.) "Are you a foreigner?" I asked,
Momently abstracted to this.
                        "I am a doctor,

And my name is Levy. But in more ways, perhaps,
I can help you, young boy." And he lifted me up
And he dried my tears with his handkerchief
Which gushed still more because he did this, touching
My plight with his pity, renewing my pity.
Yes, and the silk of his handkerchief increased
The kindness. We who are sensible animals
Laugh and cry over such materials.

He helped me up, he lifted me up. Self-conscious,
My motions jerked. He straightened my overcoat,
Tugged at its collar and dusted me off, each blow of his hand
Striking reverberated gratitude.
                                        "Come," he said,
"Whatever is wrong, there is nothing to be gained
By this sobbing. Let us go and let us get
Something to eat. That will be good for you."
"Dr. Levy," I said, enjoying his title,
"Will you too tell me that nothing is wrong,
Not crediting my word?"
                                "No, I know very well
That that would be worse. I know
How much can be wrong. But tell me what troubles you."
Then I told him, as we walked to the lunchroom,
And he shook his head and sighed and then he said:
"So young to be overtaken by the bad dream,
Your clouded head so soft and so willing
To accept the cinema of the heart and reject
The south of sleep and the forgetful games.
The necessitous meeting made more cruel
By the sad druggist who lost long ago."

This soothed me, though scarcely understood.
"What is your name?" I told him. "Joseph," he said,
"You must not be given to tears and you must not
Turn away your face from all that confronts you.
You must not, if you hope to find your brother."

"How can I help but cry? How can I help it,
Having to seek my brother among six million."
"I will help you to look for your brother," he said.
"I will go with you and show you what I know,
And what you do not know and what I do not know,
For all this may help you. But I do not say,
I know where he is, and I cannot be sure
That we will find him."
                              "Dr. Levy," I said,
And I burst into boiling tears, as I said this,
"You are very generous, unlike the sad druggist."

He took my arm, as if to reprove my tears,
And he had already taken my hope,
Dimmed my fear and comforted me,
With his sorrowing Jewish eyes, his handsome face,
And the urgent tenderness of his voice.

On backless stools, at the all-night lunchroom,
Amid the clattered dishes, our arms on the grease-stained counter,
Confronted by the nickel coffee urn, I ate and he on whom
I depended watched me, eating nothing himself,
Intent upon me. I ate great gobs
Of my sandwich, choking nascent sobs,
Embarrassed by his gaze as I chewed. The counter man
Was thumbing his tabloid.
                              "I will have to speak
At times as if in riddles or foreign languages,
For the actual is difficult as if Latinity
Billed the vivid street with advertising posters,
And the Father of lights were Roman."

"I do not understand what you have just said,"
And I quailed, knowing again the weakness
Which faltered and hurt and brought me to error.
I pushed away the fat coffee cup,
Unable to eat.
                    "That is what I mean to say,
That you will not always understand me

Immediately, but only after a time.
But finish your food now, now more than ever
You need to be well-fed." And he made me finish
And he paid, the bills in his wallet assuring me,
And we issued into the anonymous night once more,
Its chill and gloom unlessened.

"Dr. Levy," I said, as we walked on,
"How can I really thank you?" and I held him
By his coat sleeve, then suddenly, taken by feeling,
Knelt before him. "So, I thank you,
Knowing no other way, because you help me
To find my brother."
                              As he raised me up
And patted my shoulder, in deprecation,
Shaking wagons rapped far-off, hooves' waterfalls
Clapped through the stillness.

The Error

I lay near sleep, all that is left of Eden,
Amid six million souls, equally precious,
For all are ladies and gentlemen in looking glasses
And all, in this hotel or hospital,
New York's great co-existence, brushing silence,
Had turned away to sleep from their hearts' bondage.

The auspices of silence thus conferred,
The watching self chafed less and less,
I fell as one falls
In an elevator, floor after floor,
In soft and equal fall descending,
The pillow clouding and the bed a puddle
Of warmth and tiredness and no will requisite,
On this midnight of December nineteen thirty-one.

Where were you then, when suddenly I woke up,
Remotely anxious, weakly disturbed,
Where were you, Monitor, who finds the darkness
And the beginning in which long is hidden
All that we are and do not choose,
The unwilled faces of the unwilled self?

But I arose from bed, not knowing why,
And walked to the bedroom window. Looking down
Into the backyard, there I saw
Like an old photo, brown and smudged or dim,
Snow on the courtyard, violet and fairy,
The winter's dainty fête in New York City.

Then was I smitten by intrinsic pleasure,
Momently, by this delicate coming,
Blueshadowed snow upon the backyard's alley,
Amid the clotheslines, the ashcans, and the darkness
And the dun sky of December.
                              Then I saw,
His vacant face scored by the roof's black line,
The moon's fell ash, which has deceived me wholly,
And with my error I turned back to bed, my brother
Softly sighing his sleep in the bed beside mine.

My brother beside me, the moonlight five floors below,
Now the beginning of uncontrollable fear,
Fear that is formless, emotion without an object,
Like the loose film
Of the darkness about me, rising
Until I pressed my face in the pillow's softness,
Startling sparks in my runaway eyes.

Upon the blackboard of my pillowed eyes
I saw a circle drawn in thick white chalk,
And this was a hole and in this hole, deep down,
I saw my father lying in his coffin, and I
Felt nothing. Then I saw,

That this was no funeral chapel, but a morgue,
For floored there lay pale snow, or colder marble,
And then I saw that this was nothing. Then I knew
That I was in a hole, a coffin and a morgue
And nothing. And in my terror
I struck my head against the bedpost,
In the chaos of terror.
                              "If I turn on the light,"
I said to myself, "If I wake up my brother,
If I switch on the lamp and touch my brother,
If I do that which I can do as easy
As shaking my head" (I shook my head) "and touching
My mouth" (I touched my mouth) "I will see on his face
His daily look, his unconcern (as he gulps down
The wet in his mouth, as his eyes struggle
With the sudden light), his recognition.
And I will know (when he says, "What's the matter")
That nothing is wrong."
                              Ace-high, tip-top! I drank
My joy, released from pain, in convalescent peace,
In grateful weakness prone.
And I yawned in relief! and I thanked my brother!
I wished that he would be
Near as my hands and feet, near as my heart,
For fifty-six or for ten thousand years,
Until the least of fear lost every shade.

O adulterous night, obscure and obscene,
Known to the elevator boy and the prostitute,
Skated by the streetcar, dim as the subway,
O perpetual returning night, picture of death,
You are the blindness in each man's flickering eye,
The blindness I would touch when I tell this,
That then, turning in bed, too near to the edge,
I fell to the carpeted floor like a clown,
Stunned by this fault to broken shocking terror,
Afraid to move, afraid to turn, outstretched,
Afraid of the dim white of my pajamas.

I lifted a shoe from the floor and I slid
My hand over the leather, and then, as if to say,
"How much I know, and knowing, need not fear,"
Unlaced the shoe and laced the shoe again,
And all these contacts comforted so much
That I turned to the bed's leg, slid my hands
Down it, slid my bare feet on the carpet's
Felt, and each substance, touched, increased
My calm, my sense thus brushed,
                              but terror
Returned, terror choking me, and I reached
To the lamp, and I turned on the switch, but then
No light flashed on, and I waited,
And I ran to my brother's bed to wake him,
But the bed was empty, my brother was not there.

The Sad Druggist

Exhausted, yet hopeful, wan and yet longing
Loaded with self-distrust,
I dressed in the dark, knowing that I must go,
And find my brother before my mother woke,
(Responsibility less clear obsessed me).
Comforted only by the knowledge
Involved in dressing, each garment
As I donned it, swathed me like a bandage,
Wounded as if I had four faces,
(What a comfort clothes are! like love and sleep
They charge with poise and they hide the self
From its pitying interest and its darting glances),
Each button locked my heart which like a crab
Clutched on, squeezing itself alone,
Gasping, my dearest brother's absence its vacuum.

Then as I tiptoed from the apartment,
Tiptoed not to awaken my mother,
Down the stairs, into the hallway, grateful
To see the light again, then, then was begun
That Monitor's voice who watched me always,
Seated, an eye or miner's light,
Upon my head, directing the gushing plum
Beneath my breast to crash its fortissimo
Anguish, beating out time, heartbroken bleeding:
"You who, teetering adolescence, do not know
What you do, what is done—nor what you can do
Stop, do not go on! the memory,
Of all your father's forewarns: go back to sleep!"

Still utterly a child, yet I went on
(More fugitive because of this placeless voice)
Into the long street, guarded gravely
By apartment houses, whose pyramidal shadow
Increased by silent span my desolation
(For in such stillness all buildings stand and hold
Of such a silence the execution of dread),

But, suddenly abstracted, I tiptoed on the curbstone!
Perfectly interested, in pure pleasure, separate
From my aching fear,
I tiptoed on and teetered but took care,
Enacting precision!
               and turned the corner:
Frail moonlight, ghastly as whitewash,
Greeted me, bringing back the fear which crouched,
It seems, waiting on all sides,
                 so that
Seeing far-off a lighted drugstore, I went there,
Longing to speak to someone:
                   "Is it too late,"
I asked "to get an ice cream soda?"
Timid and longing.
                 "I will see," said the druggist,
Out of a tiredness which now I know,

THE COLLECTED POEMS OF DELMORE SCHWARTZ

For he, behind the counter, read a book,
"If any ice-cream is left."
                                    "There is," he said.
"There is!" I thought, grateful for the least good.

How far and how apart I sat there then,
Hunched on the backless stool.
                                    Thus, sipping, I
Communicated with my dying childhood,
Sliding away beneath me.
                                    "Why,"
Asked the druggist, mopping the marble counter
With a wet rag "is a young boy like you
Still up so late?"
                                    Rapt in immediate sweetness,
I took the straw from my mouth, hesitant,
Doubtful, afraid of ridicule.
                                    "Because
I could not sleep," I said, returning to my soda,
Absorbed in pleasure.
                                    "You ought to be in bed
Asleep," the druggist said.
                                    "My brother's gone,"
I blurted out. "I woke up and the bed
Next to mine was empty. Something is wrong
Or he would not go away. Now I don't know
Where to look for him. I don't know
Where to begin."
                                    I saw, suddenly, startled,
My face flat on the fountain's mirror.
"Listen," the druggist said, "Go home, go home
And go to bed. Nothing is wrong,
Except with you. Your brother has not left.
He is still there. I know. I know your dream,
It is incurable as love, and a settled cough."
I paled at this: "How can you tell from here
That he has not gone? How can you know?"
And I stiffened in fear.
                                    "I know, I know.

Go home and go to bed and go to sleep."
"Don't keep saying that. Can't you see that that's
Much worse? If I was wrong at first,
Then I am worse off now and wrong again!"
I said this, blushing hotly, self-betrayed.
"This is as I thought: like anyone,
Not care for your brother moves you,
No one, seeking his brother, drinks sweet soda,
No one, in such an absence, salves himself
With carbonated pleasure!"
                              "No, I care
For my brother very much. Never before,
Since he was born, have we been separated,
But sleeping side by side for fifteen years."

"You care for yourself and not him. You nurse
Yourself and tend yourself."
                              "Who else," I shouted,
"Will care for me? Who else? Who else is there?
Who will take care of me?"
I said this in a childish voice.
                              "Don't shout. Go home
And go to bed."
                  "Stop saying that. Who wants
Your advice? Who are you, anyway,
To tell the sick that they're well?"
"Stop shouting or get out. You can't shout here."
"What would you do if someone really
Were sick? What would you do, would you
Send them away like this? My brother's gone
And I must look for him."
                              "Stop shouting."
                                                "I
Won't listen to you. Something else troubles you
And you visit your pain upon me." "Get out!
Get out!" the druggist said, seizing my shoulders,
Dragging me to the door, putting me out
With one last thrust.
                        I burst into hot tears

But did not struggle. Then he shut the door,
Behind me, snapping it closed. The lights went out,
And I was alone, at night's great mercy, once more.

Sweden and Switzerland Are Hardly Far

Maybe in Sweden, stretched in snow, not near,
There, maybe, I might have a studied life,
Distant at last from hope, news, love and fear,
And know the warm depths of a simple wife.
Or Switzerland, amid a glittering white,
Days of all flash, under the sunlight's sparkle, amid the sunlight's flashes,
There I might find the other side of the night, a natural day and night,
And the spontaneity which a child splashes.

But I deceive myself with images:
Let all things pass away! This is my wish.
Snow is the world's death, the scrimmages
With which the fall begins and blows, unleash
Contempt in him, indifference, and disdain
And a brief freedom from incurable pain.

Stopping Dead from the Neck Up

Whose booze this is, I ought to think I know.
I bought it several weeks ago.
It stands there stolid on the shelf
Making me feel lower than low
Reminding me how I am low,
Making me think of Crane and Poe.

My fatlipped mouth must think it queer
To stop without a single beer,

To stop without a *single* beer
The deadest day I ever spent
In boredom and in self-contempt,
Sober, sour, discontent.

My fingers have begun to shake,
My nerves think there is some mistake.
The only other thought I think
Is how I failed to be a rake,
A story which should take the cake.

The booze stares at me like a brink.
But I must wait for five, I think.
Long hours must pass, before I drink;
Long hours and slow, before I drink.

In the Dirty Light of a Winter Day

(The rock and shock of deception and suspicion)

With cannonball and loaded eyes
He looked upon the city's life—
Now twenty years are passed. But he is there
Upon the window seat in his tenth year
Sad separate and desperate all afternoon,
Alone, with loaded eyes, as he looks down
Upon the silent empty winter afternoon
Silent the street and empty, Sunday's silence,
Shaded and silent the store fronts under the boxed apartment houses
Save when a car passes with the sound of the sighing
Of tires over the black top paving, or sudden
In eruption the fresh sounds of boys' roller-skating
The rapid racket, the crashing, whistling or scraping
Over the asphalt
                    Now twenty years are used

And known. Yet he is there. He is still there.
Or there is there, and then is now. The past
Is present. Or the present is the past,
He is locked in the windows of the walls of his tenth year,
His mind framed in the window, his heart exiled on the fifth floor
Looking with cannonball and loaded eyes
Down the city street, afraid of the other boys.

Song

Fog in stony December: it is well,
The season's character being clear,
That every shape of error veil
Building and transient streetcar. War
Fitly is made in summer, since it takes
The class of 1913 when they are
Immortal June. But still the buyer buys
His stocks, his sticks, his fur-coat, and such cakes
Still when the wind pursues its idiot fate,
Bearing the knife-edged cold and the radio's lies.

Beaded or smoky, much comfort is in fog,
Russia and Germany are near and far,
Dim in the subway, thunder and horror wait,
And all turn in their sleep to question where they are.

Lyrics of Atonement

1.

How slow time moves when pain looks at the clock,
How dormant and delinquent, under the dawn

The excited roaring of the uproarious cock:
Now torment ticks and everything is borne,
Until I think: pain is the cost of being born
But after all and nothing have been mourned
Rebirth begins as joy begins to mock
Death from the heights of morning's brilliant scorn.

2.

She flees from me that sometime did me seek
With naked foot statuesque in my houses.
Yet she was stony, angered, tearful and made sick
Because long illness made me less than quick
To play the role which puberty proposes
And yield to dark infatuation's slippery slick
Skyfall and chute, the avalanche and fall of all romances:
How I was wrong to hesitate before the gate, waiting
To be spontaneous with candid promises, bringing
                    her blond reality
The vividness of roses, the calm of hope sustained, and pain's
                sincerity.

"Gross goose, you are undone"

Gross goose, you are undone,
Night's mystery has begun,
The sources of your being
Are far beyond your seeing//
        fear
I feel some unknown good
Wearing a pitchblack hood
Comes to me now at nightfall,
And will not be delightful

Exercise

Pieces of myself distant from me
Exist in different places, well-dispersed . . .
Letters, I mean, which betray me gauche,
Shame and throw back, too convulsed by touch,
All over America and burning Europe
Illuminated in white stationery:

—Especially my lies: these must be justified,
Or in the end forgiven, by myself or him
Who is my hope or meaning, if I knew!
I must create an attitude for this case too!

Exercise

And wiped the tears forever from my eyes,
(Forever, that is, grave in memory!
Levy with his money, handkerchief,
And motorcar, showed me how long to look
And when I used the phone and spoke for miles,
He kept me to my place, not flown away,
From sympathy, interest, love, or fear
(Seeking the most complex of things, a brother dear!

The Body's Sweet Secret and Secret Sweet

A desperate story,
Dear Citizens:
The private parts take flashlight photographs
Of sensuous events and hang them up
Like portraits of the dead upon the wall.

Later, these images, blurring, become
Outmoded daguerreotypes. They fall through sleep
Like store signs struck by a hurricane.

And no one understands the nights which drain
Strength from the waking mind's most natural power
Because the mystery consumes with fear.

What do they mean, these feigning photographs?
They say, *You are in love with everyone.*
The guilt of love has made you deathly sick.

Alas! you only seek yourself in love:
Caught in that darkness, who can recognize
The true, the good, and the beautiful?

The Trip by Car

THE occasions come back to me. The trip by car
Was not a journey on the map
                              between two towns,
Albany and Saratoga. It was an exhilaration
At going away and going somewhere new—
Later, a tiredness (motion jiggling the kidneys)
At watching the road, handling the wheel,
                              toeing the gas-pedal.
We passed Socony, passed the last green light,
                              the end of Saratoga,
Speeded on the open highway, U.S. 9, past post
                    after post
Of the telephone company, the simple black lines on which
Voices are crucified. (Your images, said Hivnor,
Are these of the student, tourist, and vacationist,
And he was right. But the same, he said, is true
Of Shakespeare and myself!) We passed cows grazing,
                              a small stream,

A bridge across the Mohawk river, Gothic and bare,
And climbed a hill and the car lost power, striving,
Regained it as we went down once more,
                              (Brilliant! said Berryman,
The word he always uses when impressed):
A whitewashed line defined the road's two halves,
And I kept close to it, far from the right hand side,
                              conscious, half-conscious,
Active habits guiding me, guiding the car,
The image of the road ahead dwelling in my gaze,
                              but not my attention.

I tried to look, to feel, to see, green hill, small farm,
Auto-camp of small bungalows in a single file
                              like out-house, dog-house, or toy,
As aspects of our culture, our values, our divinities.

Images please me, but I look away,
So much more interested in "what it means,"
                    the generality
                    true for you and true for me:
Metaphor is, said Alexander's teacher,
The hallmark of genius. O it is, I see
The one actual formal thing no other art,
No painting, music, statue, or movie
                    can provide:
Let me look for it more often, since I enjoy it;
                    he is,
Let me say of some new author,
                    a tourist of the heart,
He sees what the guides show him, nothing more,
                    much less
Than the blind beggar, the playing child,
                    the cook
In the kitchen all day long, at night in bed
                    with the chauffeur or the butler,
He sees what he wants to see, dilettante, diletto,
Vistas, sunsets, old monuments, and fancy rugs,

Good restaurants and special dishes, quaintness, strangeness,
Never the psyche struggling to realize its values.

The road familiar after several trips, I start to look,
                              I start to ask myself
(Tired of driving, the freshness worn off already)
How far we have come, glance at the mileage,
—What was it at the start?—think of the trip in return,
A tedious thought
                              (psychologize, psychologize,
open the human heart and mind, and all will look,
As quickly as at scenes of sexual pleasure,
Two lovers taking off their clothes, touching each other,
                    the strangeness of naked human flesh,
                    the brown-pink of nipple and penis).

A JOURNEY to something new, a journey away
From habit and emptiness, a journey through the heart,
By means of the Chevrolet
                    between Saratoga and Albany,
As one has exercised to whip the dogged body,
                    and glow with repulsive
                              eddying blood.

Exercise in Preparation for a Pindaric Ode to Carl Hubbell

Long after Archibald Macbeth has chased
His last bandwagon,
                    long long after
Many a boy scout on the shores of Hamburg
Has learned at last what the Prince of Boy Scouts meant—

    "My wife Eleanor
    Hates war—
    I hate Eleanor,
    I Hate War!"

"I am a Pacifist: We are all Pacifists!"
(Macdeath has murdered Truth: out, out, brief Honor!
A poet's but a poor opportunist
Full of pastiche and echo!)
                              Long after, Carl,
You will be fabulous: may my song show how!

If but our culture were less disunited,
A poet such as I, "young and promising,"
Might hope to know so great an athlete

(Can I discuss these things with Philip Slav,
Or John ('There'll Always Be an England') Berryman?
Would Dwight MacNeice MacPherson care at all?
Or Harry (Holier-Than-Thou) Levin?)

Carl! I saw you once go into Loew's,
After you lost 1–0 to Paul Dean,
And wished to say, Tough luck, Carl Old Boy!
But the words choked in my throat—
                              How many times
From Coogan's Bluff as from the walls of Troy
Have I not gazed between the crevices
Of the upper and lower grandstand down below,
In desperate interest and open fear
That a short single would break up the game!

—Spring, immoral Spring, is now upon us,
And in my twenty years of tense devotion
To the great Giant cause, this is the worst
Spring I remember. Bill Jurges, racked
With headaches, on his way to Mayo Clinic,
Terry without a shortstop! But worst of all
The power of the Dodgers who so long
Competed with the comic strips,
                              Alas, Babe Herman,
Otototototoi! Otototototoi! you who once tried
To steal second with the bases loaded!
It is a wonder then that I am moved to taunt

Drite MacBride MacNeil MacDeath MacPherson?
Whose Id cries night and day, "My invective,
May it always be right! But my invective,
Right or wrong!" While nearby, Nancy,
Like Patience sitting on a monument,
Puts olives, the basis of Greek culture,
In the Martinis. . . . . . (inspiration fading)

Love the Dark Victor Whom No One Evades

As I stared down from my dark balcony,
Bertram Bravura, also excused from war,
Also a poet sick from infancy

Arrived to pass the time of day with me
—"Poet," I questioned him, "with what new poem
Do you seek to pay our eternal debt

To our vocation which to none permits
Certainty, satisfaction, or the least
Sense of conclusion such as carpenters

Behold in standing chairs?"
                              "Compeer," he said,
"Chiefly of love I sing, the druggist's power
(Is not his place the capital of modern life?)

What power more than his can make love pure?
He has the means to make love's meaning clear,
He, he alone makes love as such secure,

Love the dark victor whom no one outwits!"
"Poet," I said, "vowed so the world itself
(We who live by the word by the word die!),

Critics will say you smirk and lack good taste,
Yet I admit you touch love at the quick,
Love the dark victor whom no one escapes.

And what have we to sing but love and death
In praise and humble fear, when the god comes?"
The professional secret rippled in our smiles.

"Now love is love and nothing else but love,"
He shouted joyously as if he danced,
"I care not what the Pope in Rome may say,

Better than he I know the common weal.
Now love and sensuality at last may be
Cut from each other's self as by a knife,

Now children may be chosen beings who
Grow from the certainty of marriages.
I celebrate the stores which set love free

From dark hot-headed immediacy.
It is not good for man to be alone,
Said God in Eden Park, composing Eve,

A dictum which the Pope in Rome ignores,
Although of all true marriages the only cause.
It is not good for marriages to be

Aught but the free election of the mind,
And the whole being's suffrage, which as in sleep
When the whole being gives itself to the dark deep.

I celebrate the light on Eros' face
When boys and girls find out just what they are
By just experiment and at a depth

Don Juan and Casanova never knew!"
"You are of the Eden party," I exclaimed,
Intent upon the country of the blue,

Upon the beautiful, the good, and the true:
You know how difficult and far they are.
But what," I asked, "of promiscuity?

Does it not gain carte blanche through such a use?"
He answered me with joyous certainty,
"O no! I damn all promiscuity

I tell each boy to tell each learned girl
'Not he who knew you first possesses you,
But he who knows you last.' And to the girls

'What has he now who knew your body once?
He has not you, if he has any thing!
This is the way to come to love's true self,

This is the only way by which to bind
The act of darkness to the gazing mind,
Love the dark victor whom no one avoids.

Now if the critics wish to say I smirk,
They do not see my poignant and hot tears,
Nor how I care for boys and girls in love.

Tell this in Gath, in Brooklyn, on Broadway,
Teach all Giovannis ultimate dismay!"
So spoke this poet as he danced away.

Domine Deus

I looked up and the Awful Building
Leaned down, and I refused to cease to persist
In looking up at the building
                              leaning down
                                        so that

My God!
        that building fell down on me, and I
Shuddered but walked on, staring at the staring
Crowds which watched me, attracted by that
Accident, as they thought, of which you were
                                      I knew

The Reason, Father,
                and I smiled, I would surely
Have sung
        In Him I trust, singing surely,
Had I the voice for song;
               until I came home,
There by the apartment house, by the curb,
A white ambulance trembled, its bell ringing and ringing,
Like all the gongs of hell, and from that white
Ambulance, my God! was carried, O Father!
My only brother next to whom, sleeping
And waking, my heart beat nineteen years, and he
Was killed, his back broken, his face
Silly and loose,
          so that, in my despair,
I walked up the stairs quickly, not numb, no,
Fully aware, thinking quietly of your
Immediate thought immediately penetrating
The turning Americas and the falling world;
Walking up, I thought this, and on the third floor
Gertrude harshly shut the door, and on the fourth floor
I could not see anymore,
              and still I thought
Of Him whose thought made heaven and made earth.

I did not weep until I woke in unbelief.
God, I believe, help my unbelief.
Always in dreams belief is real as touch.
But was this not a perfect dream as such?

Immortality

In the long whitewalled room awaking,
A nurse wheeling a tray, a man moaning
From the next bedside, and then, suddenly,
Darkness once more, and with a Giant arguing
The softness of petals, the solidness of the building,
The tenderness of eyelids, the character of stone,
The better life, the warm good, in chorus or alone.

Awaking once more, thirsty. The nurse bringing
The softness of water, which, lapped, spilling,
On the scarf of the nightgown. The nurse angered,
Guilt once more. The man in the next bed crying,
"Eleanor, Eleanor, why did you do it? Don't say you
Didn't." And turning to the pillow and its softness
Gratefully.

Darkness once more. Buying and selling
Shoes and olives, forgiveness and company
With a dwarf urgent, jumping up and down, always
Excited. Awaking once more. Dry mouth and headache.
Gazing at the many beds, one patient reading,
One biting his nails, one sleeping, one speaking softly
With his sister, one saying: "Nurse, I am hungry!"

Dusk at the tall windows. And then desiring
In unrest on the softness of the pillow,
For something softer than the pillow, soft as
"Anna would give me, Nurse. If she were here, she would."
"I would like to be alone. Not with so many sick."
"Oh!" said the nurse, gravely shaking her head,
"Oh, no! not at all! Don't you know that you're dead?"

Notes

THIS EDITION

This edition of *The Collected Poems of Delmore Schwartz* reprints all five of the full-length books of poems that were printed in the poet's lifetime. *Summer Knowledge* reprinted the poems in *In Dreams Begin Responsibilities* with minor revisions, but I have used for my copy-text the text of 1938, which favored "I . . . Fucked Venus" over "I . . . Plucked Venus." The versions with later revisions have been available in print for decades. (Also included here are four poems from *Summer Knowledge* that originally appeared in earlier volumes, but that are enough revised to be considered distinct versions.) Delmore's "second" book of poetry is his translation of Rimbaud's *A Season in Hell*, which went out of print in 1940. In this edition it is categorized as original poetry, for it is for original poetry that we sometimes read translations, and it is as original poetry that this stimulating translation has its greatest value. Delmore's third book of poetry was actually the New Directions Poet of the Month chapbook *Shenandoah: A Verse Play*, released in November 1941. It is the only one of Delmore's five verse plays to be printed in single-volume form. Two others appeared in anthologies, and one, *Dr. Bergen's Belief*, appeared in *In Dreams Begin Responsibilities* in 1938. None of the five verse plays are included in this edition, for all five are readily available in *Shenandoah and Other Verse Plays*, edited by Robert Phillips (BOA Editions). Delmore's next book,

Genesis: Book One (New Directions, 1943) has become all but impossible to find. Beat-up ex-library copies without dust jackets, but tears and markings, go for $1,000 when they can be found. *Vaudeville for a Princess* (1950) is here restored to print for the first time in seventy years, another volume that is virtually unobtainable. Its prose "bagatelle" interludes are not given here as they can all be found in *The Ego Is Always at the Wheel*, edited by Robert Phillips (New Directions). Delmore's final book, *Summer Knowledge*, is given here without the text of the poems from *In Dreams Begin Responsibilities*, with the exception of one poem, constituting a distinct version. For each of the five books, the first printing is taken as the copy-text. The Notes give publication information for the poems. But there is a sixth book, a book-length poem, *Genesis: Book Two*, which has never been published before except in a few brief excerpts printed by James Atlas in a New Directions anthology. The original, numbered, fair-copy manuscript ran to about five hundred pages in length. The extant surviving pages of Delmore's typescript number about 350. A selection from what survives of the fair-copy typescript is here published for the first time. The late poems posthumously edited by Robert Phillips in *Last and Lost Poems* (New Directions) are given here as well; to those are added seventeen previously unpublished poems.

FROM IN DREAMS BEGIN RESPONSIBILITIES (1938)

Published by New Directions on December 12, 1938, in an edition of one thousand copies.

IX "The heavy bear who goes with me,"
Twentieth Century Verse, 12–13, October 1938 (as "Imitation of a Fugue").

XI "My heart beating, my blood running,"
Life and Letters To-day, Spring 1938, Vol. 18, No. II (as "Dedication in Time").

The Ballad of the Children of the Czar
Partisan Review, January 1938, Vol. IV, No. 2.

Socrates' Ghost Must Haunt Me Now
New Directions in Prose and Poetry 1938 (as "Poem").

For the One Who Would Not Take His Life in His Hands
The New Republic, July 13, 1938, Vol. XXXXV, No. 1232.

O Love, Sweet Animal
New Directions in Prose and Poetry 1937 (as "Song").

By Circumstances Fed
New Directions in Prose and Poetry 1938 (as "Poem"). *Summer Knowledge* prints this in a distinct version, which is given in this edition.

What Is to Be Given
See variant version in *Summer Knowledge*.

A Young Child and His Pregnant Mother
New Directions in Prose and Poetry 1938 (as "A Young Boy and His Pregnant Mother").

At This Moment of Time
New Directions in Prose and Poetry 1937 prints this in a distinct version, which is given in this edition.

The Sin of Hamlet
New Directions in Prose and Poetry 1938.

Tired and Unhappy, You Think of Houses
Reprinted in *Senior Scholastic*, November 26, 1945, Vol. 47.

Parlez-Vous Francais?
New Directions in Prose and Poetry 1938.

In the Naked Bed, in Plato's Cave
Poetry, January 1938, Vol. LI, No. IV.

Sonnet: The Beautiful American Word, Sure
Mosaic 1, November–December 1934 (where it is untitled).

Sonnet: The Ghosts of James and Peirce in Harvard Yard
Common Sense, April 1938, Vol. VII, No. 4 (as "Sonnet: The Philosophers").

A SEASON IN HELL (1939)

Published by New Directions in 1939, in an edition of 810 copies. A second edition, with revisions, was published as New Classics 2 in 1940.

GENESIS: BOOK ONE (1943)

Published by New Directions in 1943.

FROM GENESIS: BOOK TWO

Previously unpublished. Written in the 1930s and '40s. Delmore Schwartz Papers, Beinecke Library, Yale University.

The page numberings are Delmore's.

VAUDEVILLE FOR A PRINCESS AND OTHER POEMS (1950)

Published by New Directions on September 22, 1950, in an edition of 1600 copies.

I. Vaudeville for a Princess
On a Sentence by Pascal
Partisan Review, January 1950, Vol. XVII, No. 1.

"My Mind to Me a Kingdom Is"
Accent, Winter 1950, Vol. X, No. 2.

I Did Not Know the Spoils of Joy
Partisan Review, January 1950, Vol. XVII, No. 1. *Summer Knowledge* prints this in a distinct version, which is given in this edition.

True Recognition Often Is Refused
Poetry, April 1950, Vol. 76, No. 1 (as "True Recognition is Often Refused").

Starlight Like Intuition Pierced the Twelve
The Kenyon Review, Summer 1944, Vol. VI, No. 3 (as "The Starlight's Intuitions Pierced the Twelve"). *Summer Knowledge* prints this in a distinct version, which is given in this edition.

II. The True, the Good, and the Beautiful
He Heard the Newsboys Shouting "Europe! Europe!"
Partisan Review, March–April 1947, Vol. XIV, No. 2.

The Silence Answered Him Accusingly
Partisan Review, March–April 1947, Vol. XIV, No. 2.

Such Answers Are Cold Comfort to the Dead
Partisan Review, March–April 1947, Vol. XIV, No. 2.

Lunas Are Tempting to Old Consciousness
The Nation, September 16, 1950, Vol. 171, No. 12.

III. The Early Morning Light
The Winter Twilight, Glowing Black and Gold
Partisan Review, January 1950, Vol. XVII, No. 1. *Summer Knowledge* prints this in a distinct version, which is given in this edition.

She Was the Girl Within the Picture Frame
The Kenyon Review, Spring 1950, Vol. XII, No. 2 (as stanza IV of "The Early Morning Light").

"My Love, My Love, My Love, Why Have You Left Me Alone?"
Poetry, April 1950, Vol. 76, No. 1.

"When You Said How You'd Give Me the Keys to My Heart"
The Kenyon Review, Spring 1950, Vol. XII, No. 2 (as stanza II of "The Early Morning Light").

"One in a Thousand of Years of the Nights"
Commentary, March 1950, Vol. 9, No. 3.

"Don't Speak, Remember. Once It Happened, So It May Again."
Commentary, March 1950, Vol. 9, No. 3.

The Heart Flies Up, Erratic as a Kite
Poetry, April 1950, Vol. 76, No. 1.

The Rumor and the Whir of Unborn Wings
Poetry, April 1950, Vol. 76, No. 1.

"The Desperanto of Willynully"
Poetry, April 1950, Vol. 76, No. 1.

Chaplin upon the Cliff, Dining Alone
Poetry, April 1950, Vol. 76, No. 1.

Twelfth Night, Next Year, a Weekend in Eternity
Poetry, April 1950, Vol. 76, No. 1.

The Morning Light for One with Too Much Luck
Commentary, March 1950, Vol. 9, No. 3.

Cartoons of Coming Shows Unseen Before
Commentary, March 1950, Vol. 9, No. 3.

Dusk Shows Us What We Are and Hardly Mean
Partisan Review, January 1950, Vol. XVII, No. 1.

Hope Like the Phoenix Breast Rises Again
Poetry, April 1950, Vol. 76, No. 1.

All Guilt and Innocence Turned Upside Down
The Kenyon Review, Spring 1950, Vol. XII, No. 2 (as stanza V of "The Early Morning Light").

When Many Hopes Were Dead and Most Disguises
The Kenyon Review, Spring 1950, Vol. XII, No. 2 (as stanza III of "The Early Morning Light").

The Self Unsatisfied Runs Everywhere
Poetry, April 1950, Vol. 76, No. 1.

Look, in the Labyrinth of Memory
Commentary, March 1950, Vol. 9, No. 3.

Today Is Armistice, a Holiday
Commentary, March 1950, Vol. 9, No. 3.

Why Do You Write an Endless History?
Poetry, April 1950, Vol. 76, No. 1.

FROM SUMMER KNOWLEDGE:
NEW AND SELECTED POEMS
1938–1958 (1959)

Published by Doubleday & Company, Inc., in 1959. Winner of the 1959 Bollingen Prize.

The Dreams Which Begin in Responsibilities
Out of the Watercolored Window, When You Look
1930s.

Someone Is Harshly Coughing as Before
Partisan Review, February 1938, Vol. IV, No. 3 (as "Poem").

By Circumstances Fed
In Dreams Begin Responsibilities (1938).
This represents a distinct version.

Cambridge, Spring 1937
Ca. 1937.

The Fulfillment
At a Solemn Musick
The Kenyon Review, Summer 1958, Vol.
XX, No. 3.

Darkling Summer, Ominous Dusk,
Rumorous Rain
The New York Times, May 22, 1958
(second section only, as "Candlelight
and the Heart of Fall").

The Fulfillment
Art News Annual XXIV, 1955.

The First Morning of the Second
World
The Kenyon Review, Autumn 1955, Vol.
XVII, No. 4.

Summer Knowledge
Poetry, May 1959, Vol. 94, No. 2.

Morning Bells
"I Am Cherry Alive," the Little Girl
Sang
Partisan Review, Spring 1958, Vol. XXV,
No. 2 (as "Poem").

O Child, Do Not Fear the Dark and
Sleep's Dark Possession
The Kenyon Review, Summer 1958,
Vol. XX, No. 3 (as "Poem"), where
John Crowe Ransom prints the poem
twice, in versions identical to each
other with the exception of a phrase in
line 4.

The True-Blue American
The New Republic, January 3, 1955,
Volume 132, Number 2, Issue 2094
(as "The Innocence and Windows of
Children and Childhood").

The Would-Be Hungarian
The New Republic, January 10, 1955,
Volume 132, Number 1, Issue 2093
(as "The Children's Innocent and
Infinite Window").

A Small Score
Mutiny, Early Winter 1958, Vol. 2, No. 1
(as "A Little Morning Music").

A Little Morning Music
The New Yorker, April 18, 1959, Vol.
XXXV, No. 9.

The Kingdom of Poetry
Gold Morning, Sweet Prince
Vivaldi
The New Yorker, December 6, 1958, Vol.
XXXIV, No. 42.

Sterne
The New Republic, January 31, 1955,
Volume 132, Number 5, Issue 2097 (as
"Yorick").

Swift
Poetry, May 1959, Vol. 94,
No. 2.

Hölderlin
Partisan Review, March–April 1954, Vol.
XXI, No. 2.

Baudelaire
Partisan Review, March–April 1954, Vol.
XXI, No. 2.

Seurat's Sunday Afternoon Along the Seine
Announced as "coming" in the December 1958 issue of *Art News*. However, I was unable to locate the poem in any of the issues for 1959.

The Deceptive Present, the Phoenix Year
The World Was Warm and White When I Was Born
The Kenyon Review, Summer 1958, Vol. XX, No. 3 (as "Sonnet").

I Am a Book I Neither Wrote nor Read
Commentary, May 1958, Vol. 25, No. 5 (as "Sonnet").

The Conclusion
Partisan Review, Winter 1959, Vol. XXVI, No. 1, where it is dated September 1, 1957.

The Sequel
The Kenyon Review, Summer 1958, Vol. XX, No. 3.

The Dark and Falling Summer
The New Yorker, September 6, 1958, Vol. XXXIV, No. 29.

The Winter Twilight, Glowing Black and Gold
Vaudeville for a Princess (1950). A variant version.

The Foggy, Foggy Blue
The Kenyon Review, Summer 1958, Vol. XX, No. 3 (as "The Foggy, Foggy Playboy").

I Did Not Know the Spoils of Joy
Vaudeville for a Princess (1950). Variant version.

I Waken to a Calling
Commentary, May 1958, Vol. 25, No. 5 (as "Poem").

How Strange Love Is, in Every State of Consciousness
Mutiny, Early Winter 1958, Vol. 2, No. 1 (as "Poem").

The Mounting Summer, Brilliant and Ominous
Poetry, May 1959, Vol. 94, No. 2.

During December's Death
The New Yorker, December 20, 1958, Vol. XXXIV, No. 44.

In the Green Morning, Now, Once More
Partisan Review, Summer 1958, Vol. XXV, No. 3 (as "Poem").

The Phoenix Choir
Once and for All
The Kenyon Review, Summer 1958, Vol. XX, No. 3.

Narcissus
THE MIND IS AN ANCIENT AND FAMOUS CAPITAL
New Republic, December 15, 1958.

THE RIVER WAS THE EMBLEM OF ALL BEAUTY: ALL
Poetry, May 1959, Vol. 94, No. 2.

Abraham
Commentary, March 1959, Vol. 27, No. 3.

Sarah
Commentary, March 1959, Vol. 27, No. 3.

Jacob
Commentary, May 1958, Vol. 25, No. 5.

Lincoln
Genesis: Book One (1943).

Starlight Like Intuition Pierced the Twelve
Vaudeville for a Princess (1950). Variant version.

POEMS PUBLISHED
IN MAGAZINES AND
ANTHOLOGIES, 1932–1962

E. A. P.—A Portrait
The Poets' Pack of George Washington High School, Ed. Members of the Poetry Club and The Poetry Class 1927–1931. New York: William Rudge, 1932. Reprinted in *The Hollow Reed*, Ed. Mary J. J. Wrinn, New York: Harper & Brothers, 1935.

The Saxophone
The Poets' Pack of George Washington High School, Ed. Members of the Poetry Club and The Poetry Class 1927–1931. New York: William Rudge, 1932. Reprinted in *The Hollow Reed*, Ed. Mary J. J. Wrinn, New York: Harper & Brothers, 1935.

Automobile
The Poets' Pack of George Washington High School, Ed. Members of the Poetry Club and The Poetry Class 1927–1931. New York: William Rudge, 1932. Reprinted in *The Hollow Reed*, Ed. Mary J. J. Wrinn, New York: Harper & Brothers, 1935.

Darkness
The Poets' Pack of George Washington High School, Ed. Members of the Poetry Club and The Poetry Class 1927–1931. New York: William Rudge, 1932.

Aubade
Mosaic, November–December 1934, Vol. 1, No. 1.

Washington Bridge, December 1929
The Hollow Reed, Ed. Mary J. J. Wrinn, New York: Harper & Brothers, 1935.

Saturday's Child
The Hollow Reed, Ed. Mary J. J. Wrinn, New York: Harper & Brothers, 1935.

At This Moment of Time
New Directions in Prose and Poetry 1937. Variant version.

Metro-Goldwyn-Mayer
New Directions in Prose and Poetry 1937.

Poem: You, my photographer
Poetry, February 1937, Vol 49.

Poem: Old man in the crystal morning after snow
Poetry, February 1937, Vol 49.

Poem: The heart, a black grape gushing hidden streams
Poetry, January 1938, Vol. 51; Schwartz used the last quatrain as the closing quatrain of "The Sin of Hamlet" in *In Dreams Begin Responsibilities* (1938).

The Silence in Emptiness Accused Him Thus "A Privileged Character"
Partisan Review, March-April 1937.

Sonnet: Others may fear this goddess, but none will
The Kenyon Review, Spring 1950, where it is given as the first numbered stanza of "The Early Morning Light," every other separate, numbered stanza of which became a sonnet in *Vaudeville for a Princess* (1950).

Kilroy's Carnival: A Poetic Prologue for TV
The New Republic, December 1, 1958.

Philology Recapitulates Ontology, Poetry Is Ontology
Prairie Schooner, Summer 1959, Vol. 33.

Spiders
The New Republic, July 27, 1959.

The Choir and Music of Solitude and Silence
The New Republic, September 28, 1959.

All Night, All Night
The New Republic, March 21, 1960.

This Is a Poem I Wrote at Night, Before the Dawn
The New Republic, October 23, 1961.

Words for a Trumpet Chorale Celebrating the Autumn
The New Republic, November 13, 1961.

To Helen (After Valéry)
The New York Times, February 6, 1962.

The Journey of a Poem Compared to All the Sad Variety of Travel
The Kenyon Review, Spring 1962, Vol. 24.

Aria (from *Kilroy's Carnival*)
The New Republic, April 23, 1962.

Poem: On that day of summer, blue and gold
The New Republic, October 19, 1959.

Poem: Remember midsummer: the fragrance of box
The New Republic, July 16, 1962.

Apollo Musagete, Poetry, and the Leader of the Muses
Poetry, October 1962.

Poem: In the morning, when it was raining
The New York Times, October 27, 1962.

POSTHUMOUSLY PUBLISHED POEMS

America, America!
Last and Lost Poems (1979). Robert Phillips assigns this a composition date of 1954.

Two Lyrics from *Kilroy's Carnival, A Masque*
Last and Lost Poems (1979). Robert Phillips assigns this a composition date of 1962.

Phoenix Lyrics
Last and Lost Poems (1979). Robert Phillips assigns the first of these a composition date of 1957, the second and third composition dates of 1958.

News of the Gold World of May
Last and Lost Poems (1979). Robert Phillips assigns this a composition date of 1954.

Occasional Poems
Last and Lost Poems (1979). Robert Phillips assigns the first of these a composition date of 1958, the second a composition date of 1961, and the third a date of 1959.

The Greatest Thing in North America
Last and Lost Poems (1979).

Love and Marilyn Monroe (After Spillane)
Last and Lost Poems (1979). Robert Phillips assigns this a composition date of 1955.

***from* The Graveyard by the Sea (After Valéry)**
Last and Lost Poems (1979). Robert Phillips assigns this a composition date of 1961.

The Spring (After Rilke)
Last and Lost Poems (1979). Robert Phillips assigns this a composition date of 1965.

Late Autumn in Venice (After Rilke)
Last and Lost Poems (1979). Robert Phillips assigns this a composition date of 1965.

Archaic Bust of Apollo (After Rilke)
Last and Lost Poems (1979). Robert Phillips assigns this a composition date of 1965.

What Curious Dresses All Men Wear
Last and Lost Poems (1979). Robert Phillips assigns this a composition date of 1938.

Sonnet Suggested by Homer, Chaucer, Shakespeare, Edgar Allan Poe, Paul Valéry, James Joyce, et al.
Last and Lost Poems (1979). Robert Phillips assigns this a composition date of 1964.

Sonnet on Famous and Familiar Sonnets and Experiences
Last and Lost Poems (1979). Robert Phillips assigns this a composition date of 1961.

Yeats Died Saturday in France
Last and Lost Poems (1979). Robert Phillips assigns this a composition date of 1939.

***from* A King of Kings, A King Among the Kings**
Last and Lost Poems (1979).

Now He Knows All There Is to Know: Now He Is Acquainted with the Day and Night
Last and Lost Poems (1979). Robert Phillips assigns this a composition date of 1963.

A Dream of Whitman Paraphrased, Recognized and Made More Vivid by Renoir
Last and Lost Poems (1979). Robert Phillips assigns this a composition date of 1962.

Albert Einstein to Archibald MacLeish
Last and Lost Poems (1979). Robert Phillips assigns this a composition date of 1961.

The Poet
Last and Lost Poems (1979). Robert Phillips assigns this a composition date of 1954.

The Studies of Narcissus
Last and Lost Poems (1979). Robert Phillips assigns this a composition date of 1958.

Poem to Johann Sebastian Bach
Last and Lost Poems (Second edition, 1989). Robert Phillips assigns this a composition date of 1934.

Poem for Jacques Maritain and Leon Trotzky
Last and Lost Poems (Second edition, 1989).

The Maxims of Sisyphus
Last and Lost Poems (Second edition, 1989). Robert Phillips assigns this a composition date of 1954.

How Can He Possess
Last and Lost Poems (Second edition, 1989).

Sonnet
Last and Lost Poems (Second edition, 1989). Robert Phillips assigns this a composition date of 1938.

The Power and Glory of Language
Last and Lost Poems (Second edition, 1989).

The Sequel, the Conclusion, the Endlessness
Last and Lost Poems (Second edition, 1989). Robert Phillips assigns this a composition date of 1958.

Poem: How Marvelous Man's Kind Is
Last and Lost Poems (Second edition, 1989).

When I Remember the Advent
Last and Lost Poems (Second edition, 1989).

The Famous Resort in Late Autumn
Last and Lost Poems (Second edition, 1989). Robert Phillips assigns this a composition date of 1956.

He Who Excuses Himself Also Accuses Himself
Last and Lost Poems (Second edition, 1989).

To a Fugitive
Last and Lost Poems (Second edition, 1989).

Poem
Last and Lost Poems (Second edition, 1989).

Praise Is Traditional and Appropriate
Last and Lost Poems (Second edition, 1989).

The Dances and the Dancers
Last and Lost Poems (Second edition, 1989).

PREVIOUSLY UNPUBLISHED POEMS

Dr. Levy
Delmore Schwartz Papers, Beinecke Library, Yale. 1930s. Early draft of *Genesis*.

The Error
Delmore Schwartz Papers, Beinecke Library, Yale. 1930s. Early draft of *Genesis*.

The Sad Druggist
Delmore Schwartz Papers, Beinecke Library, Yale. 1930s. Early draft of *Genesis*.

Sweden and Switzerland Are Hardly Far
Delmore Schwartz Papers, Beinecke Library, Yale.

Stopping Dead from the Neck Up
Delmore Schwartz Papers, Beinecke Library, Yale.

In the Dirty Light of a Winter Day
Delmore Schwartz Papers, Beinecke
Library, Yale.

Song: Fog in stony December: it is
well,
Delmore Schwartz Papers, Beinecke
Library, Yale.

Lyrics of Atonement
Delmore Schwartz Papers, Beinecke
Library, Yale.

"Gross goose, you are
undone"
Delmore Schwartz Papers, Beinecke
Library, Yale.

Exercise: Pieces of myself distant
from me
Delmore Schwartz Papers, Beinecke
Library, Yale.

Exercise: And wiped the tears forever
from my eyes
Delmore Schwartz Papers, Beinecke
Library, Yale.

The Body's Sweet Secret and Secret
Sweet
Delmore Schwartz Papers, Beinecke
Library, Yale.

The Trip by Car
Delmore Schwartz Papers, Beinecke
Library, Yale.

Exercise in Preparation for a Pindaric
Ode to Carl Hubbell
Delmore Schwartz Papers, Beinecke
Library, Yale.

Love the Dark Victor Whom No One
Evades
Delmore Schwartz Papers, Beinecke
Library, Yale.

Domine Deus
Delmore Schwartz Papers, Beinecke
Library, Yale.

Immortality
Delmore Schwartz Papers, Beinecke
Library, Yale.

Acknowledgments

It took four years to make this book. A lot of people were responsible for bringing it about, and I have many individuals to thank. I owe my first thanks to the late Robert Phillips, Delmore Schwartz's former editor and literary executor, for suggesting that I take on this project and for encouraging me throughout. I owe my next thanks to Joshua Schwartz, Delmore Schwartz's literary executor, and to Declan Spring and Barbara Epler at New Directions for their cooperation in preparing this virtually complete edition of Delmore Schwartz's poetry. I owe special thanks to Jonathan Galassi at Farrar, Straus and Giroux for enthusiastically pouncing on the opportunity to publish this book, as I hoped he would.

Next, I am indebted to the scholars who devoted their time and knowledge without pay to assisting in preparing this edition for publication. My hugest debt is to a lady of Lebanon who wished for anonymity. She went through scans of all of Delmore Schwartz's papers at Yale and wrote a descriptive catalogue of what she found. She identified the location of all the pages of the unpublished *Genesis: Book Two*, and she identified and transcribed all the unpublished poems. While her country was preparing for war, she was preparing *The Collected Poems of Delmore Schwartz* for publication. She asked for no thanks or credit. Graham Christian, Ho Chien Lee, and Cassandra Allen made the initial transcriptions of all the published poems. Graham Christian and Michael Londra transcribed *Genesis: Book Two*. I am also indebted to the staffs at the Beinecke Rare Book and Manuscript Library, Yale University, and the Cambridge Public Library, and to these institutions.

Thanks also to those who helped make it possible for me to do this work: Harvey Mazer; Deena Mazer; Michael Londra; Tonya Lifshits; Jessica Monk; Rob Chalfen; Ruth Lepson; Marc Vincenz; Charlie Huisken; Angela Manley; Philip Nikolayev; Stephen Sturgeon; Karen Cruscoe; Michael Prince; Christopher Ricks; Geoffrey O'Brien, William Galbraith; Michael Slipp; Ben Sudarsky; Kevin Gallagher; Jim Dunn; Jay Howard; and Ryan Alvanos. I must stop for at a certain point the list becomes countless. My apologies to anyone I've forgotten. It's been a long four years.

BEN MAZER
Cambridge, Massachusetts

Index of Titles and First Lines

INDEX OF TITLES AND FIRST LINES

INDEX OF TITLES AND FIRST LINES

INDEX OF TITLES AND FIRST LINES